Spatial Economics Volume I

Stefano Colombo
Editor

Spatial Economics Volume I

Theory

palgrave
macmillan

Editor
Stefano Colombo
Department of Economics & Finance
Università Cáttolica del Sacro Cuore
Milano, Italy

ISBN 978-3-030-40097-2 ISBN 978-3-030-40098-9 (eBook)
https://doi.org/10.1007/978-3-030-40098-9

This Palgrave Macmillan imprint is published by the registered company Springer Nature Switzerland AG.
The registered company address is: Gewerbestrasse 11, 6330 Cham, Switzerland

Contents

Notes on Contributors

Juan Carlos Bárcena-Ruiz is Associate Professor of Economics at the Universidad del País Vasco-Euskal Herriko Unibertsitatea (UPV-EHU), Spain, where he now teaches microeconomics and he has taught industrial organization.

Ricardo Biscaia is a researcher at the Centre for Research in Higher Education Policies (CIPES), Porto, Portugal. His research interests include higher education studies, bibliometrics, and location theory. His work has been published in journals such as *Public Administration Review*, *Papers in Regional Science*, and *Cambridge Journal of Economics*.

Kurt R. Brekke is a full professor in the Department of Economics at the Norwegian School of Economics, Norway, and a chief economist at the Norwegian Competition Authority. He is also a research fellow at Center of Economic Studies Information und Forschung (CESifo), research associate at Bergen Center for Competition Law and Economics (BECCLE), and research associate at the Institute for Research in Economics and Business Administration (SNF).

F. Javier Casado-Izaga is Associate Professor of Economics at the Universidad del País Vasco-Euskal Herriko Unibertsitatea (UPV-EHU), Spain, where he now teaches macroeconomics and he has taught spatial economics, microeconomics, game theory, and industrial organization, among others.

Stefano Colombo is Associate Professor of Economics at the Università Cattolica del Sacro Cuore, Milano, Italy. He has written numerous articles on spatial economics, industrial organization, and regional science. He was ranked among the Top 100 by a number of 10 core regional science publications. He is an advisory editor of *Journal of Industrial and Business Economics*.

José M. Gaspar is a researcher at the Research Centre in Management and Economics (CEGE), Católica Porto Business School of the Universidade Católica Portuguesa, Portugal. He is also an external researcher at Center for Economics and Finance at University of Porto (CEF.UP), and a former member of the Regional Studies Association.

John S. Heywood is Distinguished Professor of Economics at the University of Wisconsin-Milwaukee, Milwaukee, USA. The author of more than 150 academic articles, he studies the theory of optimal licensing, mergers, and mixed oligopolies. This research is often set in spatial models and has appeared in the *Journal of Political Economy*, *Journal of Public Economics*, and *the International Journal of Industrial Organization*, among other outlets. He also does research in labor economics and serves as the chief editor of the *British Journal of Industrial Relations*.

Zemin Hou is a postdoctoral researcher at Northeastern University, China.

Fu-Chuan Lai is a research fellow at Academia Sinica and teaches Regional Economics at the National Taipei University and National Chengchi University, Taiwan. He is the President of the Chinese Regional Science Association, Taiwan.

Luca Lambertini is Full Professor of Economics at the University of Bologna, Italy. He is a member of the Technical Committee 2.4 of the International Federation of Automatic Control (IFAC) and the associate editor of Dynamic Games and Applications.

Simon Loertscher is Professor of Economics in the Department of Economics and Director of the Centre for Market Design at the University of Melbourne, Australia. His research focus is at the intersection of industrial organization with market and mechanism design. He has recently published articles in the *Journal of Political Economy*, *Theoretical Economics*, *Journal of Economic Theory*, *Games and Economic Behavior*, *AEJ: Microeconomics*, *The RAND Journal of Economics*, and *Journal of Economic Literature*.

Isabel Mota is an assistant professor at the Faculty of Economics, University of Porto, Portugal, where she teaches game theory, regional economics, and microeconomics. She is also a full researcher at the Center for Economics and Finance at University of Porto (CEF.UP). Her published work includes articles in *Papers in Regional Science* and *Computational Economics*, among others.

Yong Qi is Full Professor of Industrial Economics at Northeastern University, China. He is a member of the China Academy of Northeast Revitalization (CANR) and of the council of Association of Quantitative Economics of Liaoning.

Carlo Reggiani is Lecturer in Microeconomics at the University of Manchester, UK. He also taught at the University of Bologna, University of York, and Singapore Institute of Management. He is an editor of *The Manchester School.*

Marcella Scrimitore is Associate Professor of Economics at the University of Salento, Italy, and a research fellow of Rimini Centre for Economic Analysis (RCEA), Waterloo, CA. She is a member of the editorial board of *Theoretical Economics Letters* and author of articles published in the *Oxford Economic Papers*, *Journal of Economic Behavior and Organization*, and *Theory and Decision*, among others.

Luigi Siciliani is a full professor in the Department of Economics and Related Studies at the University of York, USA, where he directs the M.Sc. in Health Economics. He is an editor of the *Journal of Health Economics* and the chair of the Kenneth Arrow Award Committee. He is a member of the European Commission Expert Panel on Effective Ways of Investing in Health since 2017.

Odd Rune Straume is a full professor in the Department of Economics at the University of Minho, Portugal, where he is an integrated member of the Centre for Research in Economics and Management (NIPE). He is also a research fellow at CESifo and research associate at Bergen Center for Competition Law and Economics (BECCLE), and he is an associate editor of the *Journal of Health Economics* and the *Bulletin of Economic Research.*

Shiqiang Wang is Assistant Professor of Economics at the Institute of Economics, Chinese Academy of Social Sciences, China. He mainly studies the theory of vertical relations and restraints, optimal licensing, and mixed oligopoly. This research is often set in spatial models and has appeared in the *International Journal of Industrial Organization.*

Guangliang Ye is Professor of Economics and Vice President at Hainan University, China. His recent research focuses on antitrust and regulation, with particular emphasis on oligopoly with mixed ownership structure. He has written numerous scholarly articles, which have appeared in many publications including the *Organization Science*, *Journal of Comparative Economics*, *Journal of Economic Behavior and Organization*, *International Journal of Industrial Organization*, and *Regional Science and Urban Economics.*

List of Figures

List of Tables

Part I

Classic Models

1

Classic Spatial Models

Stefano Colombo

1.1 Introduction

In this chapter, we illustrate some classic spatial models. Starting from the seminal paper of Hotelling (1929), space has become a crucial variable in the economic analysis of oligopolistic models.[1] The aim of this chapter is mainly pedagogical: we aim to provide a useful collection of the principal classic spatial models, by illustrating their characteristics and the main results. Indeed, classic spatial models are a flexible tool which adopts the

[1]Obviously, the importance of the spatial dimension has been well recognized even before Hotelling. For example, Thunen (1826), Launhardt (1885), Marshall (1890), and Weber (1909) developed relevant frameworks to understand the implications of space for consumers and firms' behavior. However, none of these models has been used for plenty of applications as the Hotelling one and its epigones.

S. Colombo (✉)
Department of Economics & Finance, Università Cattolica del Sacro Cuore, Milano, Italy
e-mail: stefano.colombo@unicatt.it

S. Colombo (ed.), *Spatial Economics Volume I*,
https://doi.org/10.1007/978-3-030-40098-9_1

space dimension to model a wide array of economic questions, including industrial organization, regional science, and marketing. This is not an exhaustive review of spatial models. Indeed, hundreds and hundreds of spatial models have been developed by scholars; we have selectively chosen those contributions we believe represent the cornerstone of modern spatial economy, in order to provide a toolkit for those who are approaching this field for the first time.

Before starting, we briefly put forward the common characteristic of classic spatial models: classic spatial models do not want to represent "stylized facts", but, rather, to highlight and describe the forces that determine the choices of the firms or the consumers. Indeed, classic spatial models are often too simple to provide a good description for what happens in the real word, but they are sufficiently simple to capture which incentives are at work when the firms or the consumers take their decision. This is the main purpose of classic spatial models.

The rest of the chapter proceeds as follows. In Sect. 1.2 we introduce and describe the linear model. In Sect. 1.3, we consider the circular model. In Sect. 1.4 we describe some spatial models adopting price discrimination, whereas in Sect. 1.5 we introduce elastic demand. In Sect. 1.6 we discuss the "barbell" model. In Sect. 1.7 we consider a spatial model of vertical differentiation. Section 1.8 concludes.

1.2 The Linear Model

In this section, we describe the linear model, which is based on the work of Hotelling (1929). The aim of the model consists in providing a simple framework to describe product differentiation, that is, a situation where a slight decrease of the price of one firm does not determine an abrupt increase of the demand of that firm, but rather a gradual shift of demand. In fact, Hotelling was rather skeptical about Bertrand's (1883) criticism of Cournot (1838) equilibrium. Indeed, "in all [Bertrand's] illustrations of competition one merchant can take away his rival's entire business by undercutting his price ever so slightly. This discontinuities appear, though a discontinuity, like a vacuum, is abhorred by nature. More typical of real situations is the case in which the quantity sold by each merchant is a continuous function of two variables. His own price and his competitor's. Quite commonly a tiny increase in price by one seller will send only a few customers to the other" (Hotelling 1929, p. 44). Therefore, the linear model originates in order to show that price competition does not necessarily lead to the perfect competition outcome (the so-called Bertrand paradox). Intuitively, this happens because, once space is introduced, product differentiation arises, and this allows avoiding the Bertrand paradox. Nowadays, the linear (Hotelling) model is the most widely used model to describe oligopolistic competition between firms selling non-homogenous products.

Suppose there is a continuum of consumers located along a segment of length 1, from 0 to 1. The segment might have a "spatial" interpretation or a "product differentiation" interpretation. In the first case, the location of a consumer or a firm in the segment refers to the location in a strict physical sense (i.e., the consumer or the firm is really located at a certain point). In the second case, the segment is a metaphor of the product characteristic space. In this case, the location of a consumer represents the product's variety which is preferred by that consumer, whereas the location of a firm represents the product variety produced by that firm.

Consumers are uniformly distributed along the segment. Let $x \in [0, 1]$ indicate the location of each consumer on the segment. Each consumer buys just one or zero unit of good. That is, there is unit demand function. Suppose there are two firms, Firm A and Firm B, whose location is a and b, respectively. It is assumed, without loss of generality, that $0 \leq a \leq b \leq 1$ (in other words, Firm A is the firm which is located at the left). Furthermore, the firms cannot be located outside the segment. There are no production costs.

For the moment, we suppose that the locations of the firms are exogenous. In particular, we assume that $a = 0$ and $b = 1$.[2] The utility function of a consumer which is located at x and buys from Firms A and B is the following, respectively, $U_A = v - p_A - tx$ and $U_B = v - p_B - t(1 - x)$, where v is the reservation price of consumers,[3] p_A and p_B is the price set by Firms A and B, respectively, and $t > 0$

[2]It should be observed that the main purpose of spatial models is to derive *endogenously* the "locations" of firms. However, it might be useful to start with the case of exogenous locations.

[3]v is assumed to be sufficiently high so that the market is always covered in equilibrium.

is the unit transport cost sustained by the consumer when he goes to the firm's location to pick up the good (note that in the case of the product differentiation interpretation, this can be interpreted as a "disutility cost" deriving from purchasing a less-than-preferred product variety). It is important to note that the transport costs are linear in the distance. In what follows we derive the equilibrium prices. Suppose that the firms set simultaneously the price. First, observe that for any possible couple of prices (p_A, p_B), it is possible to determine a consumer whose location, say $\hat{x}$, is such that $U_A(p_A, p_B, \hat{x}) = U_B(p_A, p_B, \hat{x})$. Therefore, consumer $\hat{x}$ is indifferent between buying from Firm A and from Firm B. In addition, all consumers located at the left of $\hat{x}$ buy from Firm A, and all consumers located at the right of $\hat{x}$ buy from Firm B (formally, if $x < (>)\ \hat{x}$, then $U_A(p_A, p_B, \hat{x}) > (<)\ U_B(p_A, p_B, \hat{x})$). Therefore, the demand of Firm A is $\hat{x}$, and the demand of Firm B is $1 - \hat{x}$. By solving $U_A(p_A, p_B, \hat{x}) = U_B(p_A, p_B, \hat{x})$, we get $\hat{x} = \frac{p_B - p_A}{2t} + \frac{1}{2}$. The profit functions are therefore $\pi_A = p_A\hat{x}$ and $\pi_B = p_B(1 - \hat{x})$. By maximizing the profit functions, we have the following best-reply functions, $p_i(p_j) = \frac{p_j + t}{2}$, with $i, j = A, B$. By solving the system of best-reply functions, the equilibrium prices and profits follow: $p_i{}^* = t$ and $\pi_i * = \frac{t}{2}$. Therefore, when products are differentiated, the firms avoid the Bertrand paradox, that is, the prices do not fall to the marginal cost level, and profits are positive. Intuitively, space introduces product differentiation. Indeed, consumers do not perceive the products as homogenous: even if the two products are identical, each consumer, all else being equal, prefers the closer firm to save on transport costs. In this sense, t is a measure of product differentiation, and the higher is t, the higher are the equilibrium prices and profits.

In what follows, we discuss what happens when firms decide where to locate before setting prices. That is, we look for the locations emerging endogenously in the model. We assume the following two-stage game[4]:

1. Stage 1. The firms choose simultaneously where to locate.
2. Stage 2. The firms choose simultaneously the price.

[4]This is not the only possible timing. For example, one might consider a simultaneous choice of location and price. However, the sequential timing is more reasonable when one considers that it is often more difficult to modify the location/product characteristic rather than the price.

Due to the dynamic structure of the game, the appropriate solution concept is the Subgame Perfect Nash Equilibrium (Selten 1975). Therefore, we solve the model by proceeding by backward induction. In other words, first we find the equilibrium prices for *any* possible pair of locations. Then, by anticipating the second-stage equilibrium prices, we find the first-stage equilibrium locations. Unfortunately, when Hotelling wrote his contribution, game theory has not appeared yet. Therefore, it is not surprising that the main conclusion in terms of expected locations is not correct. In particular, Hotelling (1929) claims that the two firms are expected to engage in a fierce competition in order to obtain greater demand, so that they will end up choosing the same central location (1/2) ("they crowd together as closely as possible", p. 53). This conclusion, even if not correct (see later), is well known as the Minimum Differentiation Principle.

As mentioned above, the Minimum Differentiation Principle does not hold in the original framework of Hotelling (1929), as shown in the famous contribution of D'Aspremont et al. (1979), whose model is based on a simple variation of the Hotelling model (quadratic transportation costs rather than linear transportation costs). In particular, D'Aspremont et al. (1979) show that the Minimum Differentiation principle is invalid at the Hotelling conditions. The main intuition is based on the following argument: in the Hotelling model there are no Subgame Perfect Nash Equilibria; therefore it cannot be said that firms decide to locate in the middle of the segment.

To understand this non-existence result, consider Fig. 1.1, where the total cost of purchase (i.e., price plus the transport costs) of each consumer is represented, given the locations a and b. Note that the demand might be discontinuous. Indeed, suppose that p_A reduces so much that $p_A = p_B - t(b - a)$, that is, the consumer located at b is indifferent between the two firms (i.e., $\hat{x} = b$). Note that also all consumers such that $x > b$ are indifferent between the two firms. Therefore, if p_A reduces a bit further, there is a jump in the demand of Firm A, because now Firm A serves all consumers. As a consequence, the profits of Firm A are illustrated in Fig. 1.2. They are continuous in p_A until $p_A = p_B - t(b - a)$,

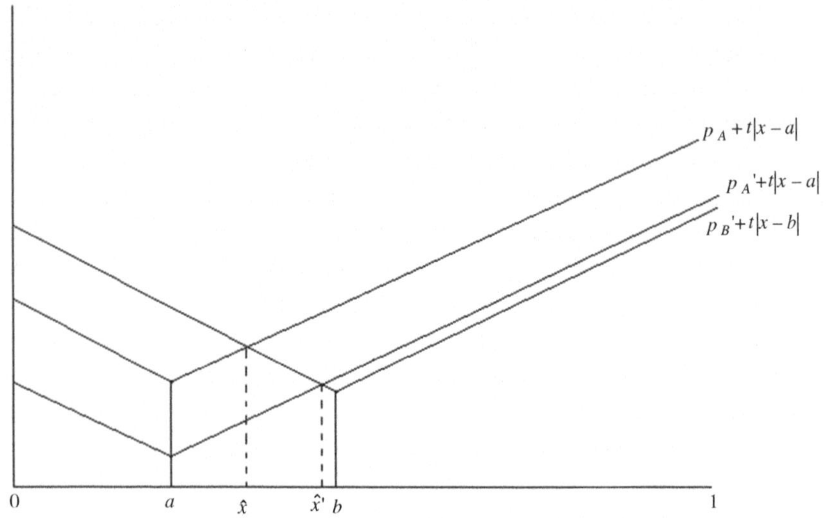

Fig. 1.1 Total cost of purchase

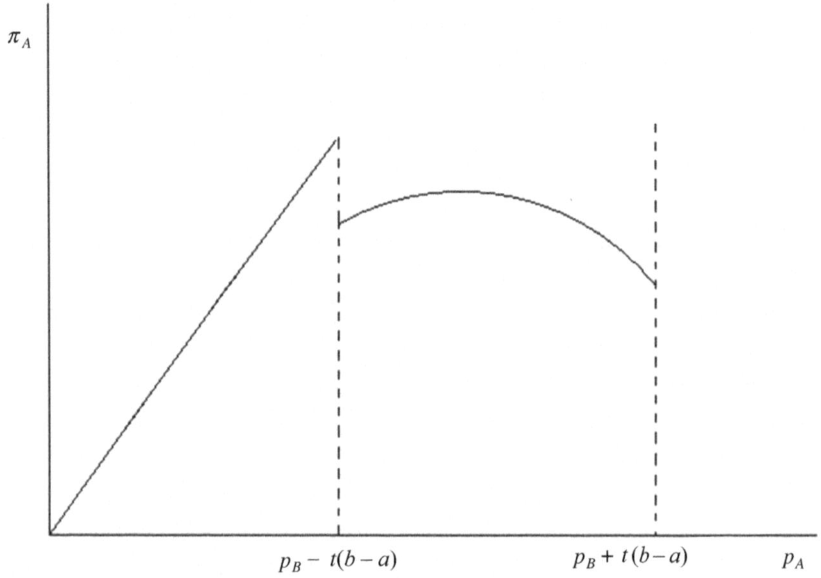

Fig. 1.2 The profits of Firm A

they are concave in p_A until $p_A = p_B + t(b - a)$, and then they are zero. Therefore, Firm A's profits are not *everywhere* continuous.

D'Aspremont et al. (1979) show that it is possible to find second-stage equilibrium prices only when the locations of firms satisfy certain conditions. In particular, the firms must be sufficiently distant from each other (alternatively, they must be located in the same point): if the firms are rather near to each other (but not located in the same point), there is no equilibrium in the second stage of the game. Intuitively, this happens for the following reason. If the two firms are quite near, each firm has a strong incentive to undercut the rival's price. Indeed, from Fig. 1.2 it can be observed that there are two local maxima, the first at $\tilde{p}_A = p_B - t(b - a) - \varepsilon$ and the second, say $\hat{p}_A(p_B)$, where the profit function is concave. In the first maximum, Firm A serves the whole market, and Firm B has no demand. So here there is no equilibrium, because Firm B would decrease the price to get a positive demand. Therefore, an equilibrium is possible if and only if $p_A* = \hat{p}_A(p_B*)$ and $p_B* = \hat{p}_B(p_A*)$. But this implies that $\hat{p}_i\left(p_j\right)$ must be a global maximum, and not just a local maximum, which in turn requires that the two firms are not too close to each other (intuitively, if the two firms are sufficiently distant, a focal firm should significantly reduce the price to serve the whole market, and thus this strategy is not profitable, that is, $\hat{p}_i\left(p_j\right)$ is a global maximum). On the other side, case $a = b$ is obvious: the two firms are undifferentiated, so the standard Bertrand argument applies and the prices are equal to the marginal costs.

Even more importantly, D'Aspremont et al. (1979) show that there are no Subgame Perfect Nash Equilibria in the original Hotelling framework. Indeed, if a and b satisfy the conditions for the existence of the price equilibrium in the second stage, the profits of Firm A (B) are increasing (decreasing) in a (b). Therefore, the two firms would like to move toward the center, but in this way, the locations end up not satisfying the conditions for the existence of the equilibrium prices in the second stage. At the same time, the pair $a = b$ cannot be an equilibrium, because each firm has the incentive to separate from the rival in order to get positive profits.

Therefore, the Minimum Differentiation Principle is invalid under the assumptions in Hotelling (1929). In order to explore the properties of the location-than-price equilibrium, D'Aspremont et al. (1979) propose to modify the original Hotelling model by adopting quadratic transportation costs rather than unit transportation costs. Therefore, the relevant utility functions become $U_A = v - p_A - t(a - x)^2$ and $U_B = v - p_B - t(b - x)^2$. By equating U_A and U_B, we get the indifferent consumer, $\hat{x}\,(a, b, p_A, p_B) = a + \frac{b-a}{2} + \frac{p_B - p_A}{2t(b-a)}$. To interpret this equation, note that, at equal prices, Firm A controls its own turf (the first term in the equation) and receives half of the consumers located between the two firms (the second term in the equation). The last term in the equation expresses the sensitivity of the demand to the price differential. It can be shown that the second-stage price equilibrium always exists, and it is given by $p_A\,(a, b) = \frac{t(b-a)(2+a+b)}{3}$ and $p_B\,(a, b) = \frac{t(b-a)(4-a-b)}{3}$. Now we consider the first-period choice of locations. Firm A maximizes (similarly for Firm B): $\pi_A\,(a, b) = p_A\,(a, b)\,\hat{x}\,(a, b, p_A\,(a, b)\,, p_B\,(a, b))$. The profits of Firm A are strictly decreasing in *a* (symmetrically, the profits of Firm B are strictly increasing in *b*). Therefore, the two firms separate as much as possible: this result is known as the Maximum Differentiation Principle. The maximum differentiation principle is the result of two contrasting forces (Tirole 1988). On the one hand, there is a *demand effect*, which captures the incentive of each firm to move toward to the center of the segment in order to increase the demand. On the other hand, there is also a *strategic effect* that describes the fact that, when A moves closer to B, the two firms are more similar and then competition is fiercer (indeed, the equilibrium price is lower when the two firms are located closer). Therefore, the strategic effect induces each firm to move toward the endpoints. Under the assumptions of D'Aspremont et al. (1979) model, the strategic effect always dominates, and therefore the unique equilibrium is characterized by maximum differentiation of the firms.

The linear model with quadratic transportation costs (D'Aspremont et al. 1979) has been proven to be particularly useful, as it allows a full characterization of the location-price equilibrium. For example, it can be used to discuss welfare implications. Suppose that a social planner wants to maximize the overall welfare. Clearly, due to the unit demand function, prices are simply a transfer from consumers to firms, and they do not affect welfare. Welfare depends (negatively) only on transportation costs. Therefore, welfare is maximized when the overall transportation costs are minimized, which occurs when the two firms are located at 1/4 and 3/4, respectively. Given that in equilibrium the two firms maximally differentiate, we can conclude that there is too differentiation in equilibrium. Intuitively, when choosing the location, each firm does not take into account the increase in the consumers' transportation costs, but just aims to avoid disruptive competition with the rival.

The linear model has been extended in many directions. Here we focus on some extensions which are particularly relevant. Economides (1986) considers a more general class of transportation costs. In particular, the transportation costs are assumed to be equal to $t|a - x|^{\alpha}$ and $t|b - x|^{\alpha}$ when buying from Firm A and Firm B, respectively, and with $\alpha \in [1, 2]$. Therefore, α measures the convexity of the transportation costs. Economides (1986) shows that when the transportation costs are sufficiently convex (i.e., $\alpha \in [5/3, 2]$), the Maximum Differentiation Principle holds, as the two firms choose to locate at the endpoints of the segment. However, when the degree of the convexity of the transportation costs is intermediate (i.e., $\alpha \in [63/50, 5/3]$), the location equilibrium is characterized by interior solutions, ranging from 0 to 0.3 for Firm A and from 1 to 0.7 for Firm B. Finally, when the transportation costs are almost linear (i.e., $\alpha \in [1, 63/50]$), there is no equilibrium. Therefore, on the one hand, Economides (1986) confirms that the Minimum Differentiation Principle does not hold even for more general transportation costs. On the other hand, he shows that the Maximum Differentiation Principle is valid only when the transportation costs are sufficiently convex. Another relevant extension concerns the assumption of the uniform distribution of consumers over the linear market. This assumption is mainly motivated by the need to find closed-form solutions. However, it is reasonable to imagine that in many situations consumers are not uniformly distributed. For example, suppose that the distribution of the consumers is symmetric around 1/2, but there is increasing density of consumers toward the center. In such a framework, Neven (1986) considers a location-price game. He shows that when the consumers are rather dispersed, the unique equilibrium consists in maximal differentiation of firms. However, if consumers are quite concentered around the center, partial differentiation of firms emerges in equilibrium. Indeed, when there are more consumers in the center of the market, the *demand effect* is rather strong, thus inducing the firms to move inner. Finally, both the Hotelling model (1929) and the D'Aspremont et al. (1979) model assume that firms are constrained to locate between the endpoints. However, in many situations, firms are free to locate outside the "city boundaries", that is, the firms can locate in points of the space where there are no consumers. Lambertini (1994) considers the D'Aspremont et al. (1979) model and explores the characteristics of the location-price equilibrium by removing the assumption $0 \leq a \leq b \leq 1$ and just assuming $a \leq b$. It is found that there is a unique equilibrium, where Firm A and Firm B locates at $-1/4$ and $5/4$, respectively, that is, the two firms locate outside the endpoints of the segment. Therefore, the firms maximally differentiate only if they are constrained to locate between 0 and 1; otherwise, the equilibrium differentiation is finite. Intuitively, the larger is the distance between the firms, the stronger is the demand effect and the weaker is the strategic effect: at the equilibrium locations $-1/4$ and $5/4$, the two effects compensate. Finally, it is worth mentioning the two-dimensional extension of the Hotelling linear market, which has been introduced by Tabuchi (1994). In particular, it is shown that, in a location-price game, in equilibrium the two firms maximize their distance in one dimension, but minimize their distance in the other dimension.

1.3 The Circular Model

The linear model (Hotelling 1929) has received relevant attention by economists. However, the existence of the boundaries often makes the model intractable when the firms are more than two. For example, Brenner (2005) finds analytically the location-price equilibrium in the case of three firms under quadratic transportation costs, and he also numerically characterizes the equilibrium up to nine firms. However, when the number of firms is larger than nine, a solution is hard to find, both analytically and numerically. The main problem with the linear market is that firms are intrinsically asymmetric. Indeed, the most-to-the-left and the most-to-the-right firms compete with just another firm; at the opposite, any other firm competes with two rivals.

The “classic” model that solves this kind of “asymmetry” in the Hotelling line is the circular model, which has been introduced by Vickrey (1964) and Salop (1979). The basic idea is very simple: instead of assuming that the consumers are distributed along a segment, they are distributed along a circle (of length 1). Now, no point is better than another. In what follows, we illustrate the main characteristics of the circular model.

As before, let $x \in [0, 1]$ indicate the location of consumers. Instead of considering just two firms, we consider a large number of identical potential firms. Firms are also located in the circle, and they can locate in just one position. Consumers wish to buy one unit of the good, and sustain linear transportation costs to move to the firm. The only cost sustained by a firm is the fixed cost f in the case of entry. Suppose the following two-stage entry-price game. In the first stage of the game, potential entrants simultaneously decide whether or not to enter. Let us indicate by n the number of firms that enter in the market. We assume that firms do not choose their locations: in particular, the firms are assumed to be automatically located equidistant from one another in the circle. In other words, maximal differentiation is assumed. It follows that the circle can be divided in n segments: the length of each of them is $1/n$. In the second stage of the game, the firms that are entered set simultaneously the price.

Since there are many identical firms, the number of firms in equilibrium is determined by the zero-profit condition (up to the integer problem).[5] We solve the game by backward induction. Consider the second stage. Assume that the number of firms that entered in the market is sufficiently high, so that there is competition between the existing firms (in other words, there are no local monopolies in the circle): intuitively, this amounts requiring that f is not too large. Let us focus on the focal firm, say Firm i. Since the firms are identical, we can assume that all

[5] That is, the number of firms must be an integer.

the other firms are setting the same price, say p. Note that Firm i has just two real competitors, that is, the two firms that surround it. For example, suppose Firm i is located at point 0 (or 1): its two competitors are the firms located at $1/n$ and $-1/n$. Consider a consumer located at $x \in [0, 1/n]$. This consumer is indifferent between buying from Firm i and its closest (to the right) competitor, if the following condition is verified: $v - p_i - tx = v - p - t\left(\frac{1}{n} - x\right)$, that is, $\hat{x} = \frac{p+t/n-p_i}{t}$. It follows that the demand of Firm i is $2\hat{x}$. The profit function is $2p_i\hat{x}$. By maximizing the profit function with respect to p_i, and then setting $p_i = p$, we get the equilibrium price: $p* = \frac{t}{n}$. Not surprisingly, the price increases with the level of product differentiation (t) and decreases with the number of competing firms (n). Due to symmetry, the demand of each firm in equilibrium is $1/n$. Let us consider now the first period. Since there is free-entry net of the entry costs, the equilibrium number of firms is determined by the zero-profit condition, which yields $n* = \sqrt{\frac{t}{f}}$. It is interesting to note that, in equilibrium, the price is higher than the marginal costs. However, the profits are zero, due to the free-entry conditions. This result is similar to the monopolistic competition of Chamberlin (1933) (Fig. 1.3).

The Salop model is useful also to derive implications on welfare. More specifically, is the equilibrium number of firms too high or too low from the point of view of welfare? Suppose that a social planner wants to maximize the overall welfare. Welfare is only determined by the equilibrium transportation costs. Note that, in equilibrium, the consumer's average transportation cost is $2n\int_0^{\frac{1}{2n*}} tx dx = \frac{\sqrt{tf}}{4}$. The social planner chooses n in such a way to minimize the sum of the average transportation costs and the overall cost of entry. Therefore, the optimal number of firms, n^o, is given by $n^o \in \arg\min\left[2n\int_0^{\frac{1}{2n}} tx dx + nf\right]$, that is, $n^o = \frac{n*}{2}$. We can conclude that the market generates too many firms in equilibrium. Excess of entry is due to fixed costs of entry. In particular, the private and the social incentives of entrance do not coincide: entrance is socially justified only if the savings in the transportation costs compensate for the entry costs, whereas the private incentive to entry is linked to stealing the business of other firms. However, it should be noted that

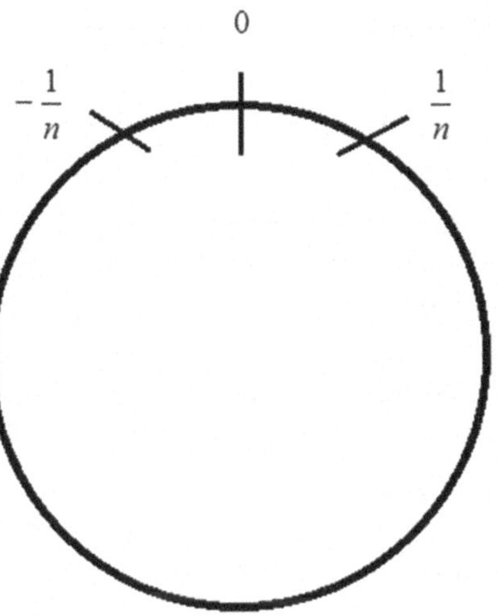

Fig. 1.3 The Salop model

this "excess of entry" result is not general. For example, Gu and Wenzel (2009) remove the assumption of unit demand function and introduce a demand function with constant elasticity. They show that the number of firms entering into the market in equilibrium decreases with the demand elasticity: when the demand elasticity is sufficiently large, there is insufficient entry from the welfare's point of view.

In general, the linear and the circular markets yield different outcomes, due to the asymmetric nature of the former and symmetric nature of the latter. Interestingly, the literature has developed a more general model aiming to encompass the basic models and limit cases. This model is known as the "quasi-linear" city and it has been introduced first by Takahashi and de Palma (1993). We briefly describe it. There is a unit length circular city with a caveat at point 0. When passing through this point, there is an additional cost equal to β (e.g., this cost can be interpreted as a barrier such as a congested bridge, a mountain, or a river). When this cost is nil, we have the standard circular model; when it is extremely high, no consumer passes through this point, and therefore we are back to the standard linear model. When β is intermediate, we have a mixture of the linear and the circular model.

1.4 Spatial Price Discrimination

One crucial assumption in Hotelling and Salop models is that the firms set the same price for all consumers. This kind of pricing technique is also known as FOB (free-on-board) or mill or uniform pricing. However, it is also possible that a firm sets a price which depends on the location of the consumer which is served. This pricing technique is known as "delivered" pricing. Therefore, delivered pricing is a peculiar form of price discrimination, where discrimination is based on location (Greenhut and Greenhut 1975). Alternatively, if we assume a "product differentiation" interpretation of the spatial models, delivered pricing can be interpreted as follows. The firm might produce a single standardized variety and sets a price for it: this is equivalent to FOB pricing. In contrast, the firm might decide to offer a basic product with a series of options with different prices: this is equivalent to delivered pricing.

Thisse and Vives (1988) introduce the analysis of price discrimination into the basic Hotelling linear model. They consider the following situation. There are two firms which are exogenously located at the endpoints of the Hotelling line (i.e., $a = 0$ and $b = 1$). The consumers sustain linear transportation costs. Before setting the price, each firm has to decide its own pricing policy, which might be uniform or discriminatory. If the firm chooses uniform price, it is constrained to set the same price for all consumers; if the firm chooses price discrimination, it is free to set a different price for each consumers. Note that spatial price discrimination is assumed to be "perfect", that is, there is a price for each possible location. The game is two-stage: in the first stage of the game, each firm commits to a pricing policy (U and D) which will be followed in the second stage. In the second stage of the game, the two firms set the price or the price schedule, depending on the first-period choice. The game is solved by backward induction, by starting from the last stage of the game and discussing each subgame in turn (indeed, there are four possible subgames).

Subgame UU: both firms have chosen uniform pricing in the first stage. The analysis is the same as in the case of the standard Hotelling model with linear transportation costs and maximum differentiation.

Subgame DD: both firms have chosen discriminatory pricing in the first stage. Consider a consumer located in x. Define with $p_i(x)$ the price charged by Firm $i = A, B$ to consumer x. The utility of that consumer when he buys from Firm A (B) is $u_A(x) = v - p_A(x) - tx$ ($u_B(x) = v - p_B(x) - t(1-x)$). The consumer buys from the firm which gives the higher utility; if the utility is the same, it is assumed that he buys from the nearer firm. Suppose that consumer x is nearer to Firm i. Given the price set by Firm $j \neq i$, the best thing Firm i can do is to set a price that gives the consumer the same utility he receives from Firm j: this is the highest possible price that guarantees that consumer x buys from i. Given that the price is never lower than the marginal costs, the equilibrium price schedules are $p_A(x)* = \begin{cases} t(1-x) - tx & if\ x \leq 1/2 \\ 0 & if\ x \geq 1/2 \end{cases}$ and $p_B(x)* = \begin{cases} 0 & if\ x \leq 1/2 \\ tx - t(1-x) & if\ x \geq 1/2 \end{cases}$. The firms' profits are $\pi_A^{DD}* = \int_0^{\frac{1}{2}} p_A(x) * dx = \frac{t}{4}$ and $\pi_B^{DD}* = \int_{\frac{1}{2}}^1 p_B(x) * dx = \frac{t}{4}$.

Subgame UD: only Firm B has chosen discriminatory pricing in the first stage. If the utility of the consumer is the same, he buys from the discriminating firm. The firm setting a uniform price moves first. Consider a generic consumer x. The best-reply function of Firm B consists in setting $p_B(x) = p_A + tx - t(1-x)$. If Firm A sets $p_A > t(1-x) - tx$, Firm B can always serve consumer x by undercutting the uniform price set by Firm A: therefore consumer x will always buy from Firm B. In order to have a positive demand, Firm A must set a uniform price such that $p_A \leq t(1-x) - tx$, which cannot be undercut by Firm B. Therefore, the highest uniform price is $p_A = t(1-x) - tx$. Solving for x, we obtain the most at the right consumer served by Firm A: $x_*' = (t - p_A)/2t$. Therefore, the demand of Firm A is x_*'. Maximizing the profits of Firm A with respect to p_A, we get $p_A{}^* = t/2$. Substituting p_A into the best-reply function of Firm B, we get the equilibrium price schedule: $p_B(x)* = \begin{cases} 2tx - t/2 & if\ x \geq 1/4 \\ 0 & if\ x \leq 1/4 \end{cases}$. The profits are $\pi_A^{UD}* = p_A * x*' = \frac{t}{8}$ and $\pi_B^{UD}* = \int_{x*'}^1 p_B(x) * dx = \frac{9t}{16}$.

Subgame DU: symmetric to subgame UD.

Table 1.1 Equilibrium profits in the Thisse and Vives model

π^A	π^B	
	U	D
U	$t/2$; $t/2$	$t/8$; $9t/16$
D	$9t/16$; $t/8$	$t/4$; $t/4$

We consider now the first stage of the game. In Stage 1, the two firms decide simultaneously whether to price discriminate (D) or not (U), by anticipating the equilibrium profits in Stage 2. Consider Table 1.1.

We observe that there is a unique pricing policy equilibrium, DD, and that the profits in DD are lower than in UU (Prisoner Dilemma). The intuition is the following. For any given pricing policy strategy of the rival, each firm would like to be as flexible as possible in setting prices. Therefore, each firm chooses D, which is the dominant strategy. However, when both firms price discriminate, competition is very fierce, as each firm can reduce the price in one location without fearing to reduce the price elsewhere. Therefore, the firms would be better off in UU, but they fail to coordinate on that equilibrium. The crucial difference between uniform pricing and discriminatory pricing has been well described by Hoover (1948): "The difference between market competition under FOB pricing [. . .] and discriminatory delivered pricing is something like the difference between trench warfare and guerrilla warfare. In the former case all the fighting takes place along a definite battle line; in the second case the opposing forces are intermingled over a broad area" (p.57).

Lederer and Hurter (1986) also consider spatial price discrimination. However, they are not interested in the resulting pricing policy equilibrium. In contrast, they consider a location-price game in a highly general spatial model and find an important relation between equilibrium locations and optimal locations. Consider a two-dimensional compact market region denoted as S (i.e., there is no specific assumption about the shape of the space). Let the locations of Firm A and Firm B be indicated by $z_A = (x_A, y_A)$ and $z_B = (x_B, y_B)$, respectively. The marginal costs of production of Firm A and Firm B are c_A and c_B, respectively. Therefore, the two firms are not restricted to be symmetric. Let the location of a consumer in the space be indicated by $z \in \Re^2$. The consumers' distribution over S is a generic distribution $\rho(z)$. Let the cost of transporting the good from the plant to the consumer be given by $f_A(z_A, z)$ for Firm A and by $f_B(z_B, z)$ for Firm B (therefore, the transportation costs are sustained by the firms). The consumer buys from the cheapest source. If the two sources are equal, we assume that the consumer is served by the firm with the least total marginal costs (production plus transport costs). The firms are assumed to perfectly price discriminate. That is, they can set a delivered price schedule where the price depends on the location of the consumer which is served. The game is two-stage: in the first stage of the game, the firms choose simultaneously the locations, and, in the second stage, they choose simultaneously the price schedule. In the second stage, the equilibrium price schedule is the following: $p_*(z_A, z_B, z) = \max [f_A(z_A, z) + c_A, f_B(z_B, z) + c_B]$. Intuitively, the proof is the following. If the low-cost firm does not serve the demand, it could undercut the low-price firm. The current low-price firm must be pricing above or at its marginal cost: thus by cutting its price, the low-cost firm can raise its profits. Furthermore, in equilibrium the low-cost firm must price at the marginal cost of the next efficient firm at each market point and that firm must price at its marginal cost. If the next most efficient firm priced above this amount, the low-cost firm would price at this price and would serve the demand. This would induce the next most efficient firm to cut its price.[6]

Now, we consider the first stage of the game, where the firms choose the locations by anticipating the equilibrium prices in the second stage of the game. Denote the social cost as the total cost incurred by the firms to supply demand to customers in S in a cost-minimizing manner. Therefore, it is $K(z_A, z_B) = \int \int_S \min [f_A(z_A, z) + c_A, f_B(z_B, z) + c_B]\rho(z)dz$. Note that the profits of Firm $i = A, B$ under the equilibrium prices can be written as follows: $\pi_i(z_A, z_B, p_*) = \int \int_S [f_j(z_j, z) + c_j]\rho(z)dz - K(z_A, z_B)$ with

[6]Note that there is no contradiction with the equilibrium prices in Thisse and Vives (1988) in the DD subgame. In that case the transportation costs were sustained by the consumers. Here the transportation costs are sustained by the firm. Therefore, the profit margin is the same.

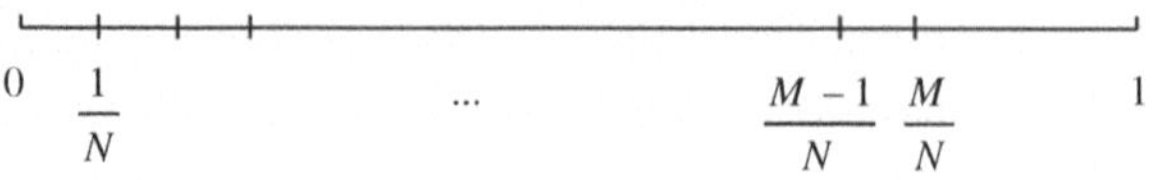

Fig. 1.4 Liu and Serfes model

$j \neq i$.[7] Therefore, the location equilibrium (z_{A*}, z_{B*}) minimizes the social costs, that is,[8] $K(z_{A*}, z_{B*}) \leq K(z_A, z_{B*})$ and $K(z_{A*}, z_{B*}) \leq K(z_{A*}, z_B)$.

The spatial models considered until now represent quite extreme situations. In Hotelling (1929), D'Aspremont et al. (1979) and Salop (1979) models assume that the firms set a uniform price for all consumers; in Lederer and Hurter (1986) and Thisse and Vives (1988), the firms set a different price for any possible location, thus implying "perfect" price discrimination. However, in many real-world situations, the firms are able to "imperfectly" discriminate, that is, they are able to set different prices for different "groups" of consumers, but they are able not to distinguish within each group.

The analysis of imperfect spatial price discrimination has been developed first by Liu and Serfes (2004). As in Hotelling (1929), the consumers are uniformly distributed on a linear segment of length 1 and sustain linear transportation costs. There is an information technology which allows the firms to partition the consumers into different groups: the linear market is partitioned into n sub-segments indexed by m, with $m = 1, \ldots, n$. Each sub-segment is of equal length, $1/n$. It follows that sub-segment m can be expressed as the interval $\left[\frac{m-1}{n}; \frac{m}{n}\right]$ (Fig. 1.4). A firm can price discriminate between consumers belonging to different sub-segments, but not between the consumers belonging to the same sub-segment. The cost of using the technology is zero. Denote with p_i^m the price set by Firm $i = A,B$ on consumers belonging to sub-segment m. Assume that $n = 2^k$, with

[7]Indeed,

$$\begin{aligned} \pi_i(z_A, z_B, p*) &= \int\int_S \left[f_j(z_j, z) + c_j - f_i(z_i, z) - c_i\right]\rho(z)dz \\ &= \int\int_S \left[f_j(z_j, z) + c_j\right]\rho(z)dz - \int\int_S \min\left[f_j(z_j, z) + c_j, f_i(z_i, z) + c_i\right]\rho(z)dz. \\ &= \int\int_S \left[f_j(z_j, z) + c_j\right]\rho(z)dz - K(z_A, z_B) \end{aligned}$$

[8]The continuity of function K on S also guarantees that the location equilibrium exists.

$k = 1, 2, 3, 4 \ldots$. Therefore, the higher is n, the higher is the information precision. When $n \to \infty$, we have the perfect price discrimination model of Thisse and Vives (1988); at the opposite, when $n \to 2$ the model is close as possible to the uniform pricing case of Hotelling (1929).

Liu and Serfes (2004) consider the case of firms which are exogenously located at the endpoints of the segment (i.e., $a = 0$ and $b = 1$).[9] As in Thisse and Vives (1988) in the first stage of the game, the firms simultaneously decide between D and U and in the second stage set the prices.

Subgame UU: both firms have chosen uniform pricing in the first stage.

The analysis is the same as in the case of the standard Hotelling model with linear transportation costs and maximum differentiation.

Subgame DD: both firms have chosen discriminatory pricing in the first stage. Consider segment m. Define x^{m*} as the consumer on segment m which is indifferent between buying from Firm A and from Firm B for a given couple of discriminatory prices, p_A^m and p_B^m. Equating the utility in the two cases and solving for x, we get $x^m* = \frac{1}{2} + \frac{p_B^m - p_A^m}{2t}$. Therefore, the demand of Firm A and Firm B on segment m is, respectively, $d_A^m = \frac{1}{2} + \frac{p_B^m - p_A^m}{2t} - \frac{m-1}{n}$ and $d_B^m = \frac{m}{n} - \frac{1}{2} - \frac{p_B^m - p_A^m}{2t}$. Therefore, the profits of Firm i on segment m are $\pi_i^m = p_i^m d_i^m$. Define $m_A \equiv \frac{n}{2} - 1$ and $m_B \equiv \frac{n}{2} + 2$, with $m_B > m_A$. The equilibrium price schedules in DD are as follows: if $m_A < m < m_B$, then $p_A^m* = \frac{t(4-2m+n)}{3n}$ and $p_B^m* = \frac{t(2+2m-n)}{3n}$; if $m \leq m_A$, then $p_A^m* = t\left(1 - \frac{2m}{n}\right)$ and $p_B^m* = 0$; and if $m \geq m_B$, then $p_A^m* = 0$ and $p_B^m* = t\left(\frac{2m-2-n}{n}\right)$. Intuitively, Firm A is a constrained monopolist in all segments $m \leq m_A$, whereas Firm B is a constrained monopolist in all segments $m \geq m_B$; the two firms compete in the remaining segments. Therefore, in each segment where a firm is a constrained monopolist,

[9] Colombo (2011) extends to the case of endogenous locations.

the firm sets the highest price that allows serving the whole sub-segment without being undercut by the rival. The firms' profits are therefore

$$\Pi_A^{DD}* = \sum_{m=1}^{m_A} \frac{t}{n}\left(1-\frac{2m}{n}\right) + \sum_{m=m_A+1}^{m_B-1} \frac{t(4-2m+n)}{3n}\left(\frac{2-m}{3n}+\frac{1}{6}\right)$$
$$= \frac{t\left(9n^2-18n+40\right)}{36n^2}$$

$$\Pi_B^{DD}* = \sum_{m=m_A+1}^{m_B-1} \frac{t(2+2m-n)}{3n}\left(\frac{m+1}{3n}-\frac{1}{6}\right) + \sum_{m=m_B}^{n} \frac{t}{n}\left(\frac{2m-2-n}{n}\right)$$
$$= \frac{t\left(9n^2-18n+40\right)}{36n^2}.$$

By comparing the profits in the case UU and the profits in the case DD, it can be observed that the profits in the case of imperfect price discrimination are always lower than the profits in the case of uniform pricing. However, the profits in DD are U-shaped in the precision of segmentation, *n*. Indeed, there are two contrasting forces at work, the *intensified competition* effect and the *surplus extraction* effect. The first refers to the fact that, when both firms sell positive quantities in a given segment of consumers, an information refinement intensifies competition. The second refers to the fact that some segments are monopolized by a firm, and on these segments, the firm extracts the consumer surplus. When *n* is low and it increases, the number of competitive segments increases: the intensified competition effect dominates, so the profits decrease. For further increases of *n*, the number of competitive segments is constant, but the number of monopolized segments increases: the surplus extraction effect dominates, so the profits increase.

Subgame UD: only Firm B has chosen discriminatory pricing in the first stage. Denote $m\hat{} = \frac{n+7}{4}$. The equilibrium prices are $p_A* = \frac{t(n+1)}{2n}$ and $p_B^m* = \begin{cases} \frac{t}{n} & if\ m = m\hat{} - 1 \\ \frac{t(4m-3-n)}{2n} & if\ m \geq m\hat{} \end{cases}$. The firms' profits are therefore $\Pi_A^{UD}* = \frac{t\left(n^2+2n+1\right)}{8n^2}$ and $\Pi_B^{UD}* = \frac{t\left(9n^2-6n+5\right)}{16n^2}$.

Subgame DU: only Firm A has chosen discriminatory pricing in the first stage. This case is symmetric to case UD.

Consider now the first stage of the game. By comparing the profits, it can be shown that if n is low, the dominant strategy is U and there is no Prisoner Dilemma, whereas if n is high, the dominant strategy is D and there is a Prisoner Dilemma. Therefore, we can conclude that the adoption of spatial price discrimination (and, consequently, the existence of a Prisoner Dilemma) emerges if and only if the information about the consumers' location is precise enough.

1.5 Spatial Models with Elastic Demand Functions

Classic models typically assume that consumers have unit demand functions (i.e., each consumer buys one or zero unit of good). However, it might be reasonable to assume that consumers might have elastic rather than unit demand functions. Introducing elastic demand function within a spatial model with uniform pricing is difficult. Indeed, as shown by Rath and Zhao (2001), equilibrium prices and equilibrium locations can only be defined implicitly (when transportation costs are quadratic). In general, introducing elastic demand functions into a spatial model with uniform pricing does not allow getting easily interpretable solutions (Peitz, 2002).

On the other hand, introducing elastic demand in a spatial model with (spatial) price discrimination is more fruitful, as shown by Hamilton et al. (1989). The Hamilton et al. (1989) model maintains the same assumptions of Hotelling (1929) with the only difference that each consumer has a linear demand function of this type: $p_x = 1 - (q_{A,x} + q_{B,x})$, where $q_{A,x}$ $(q_{B,x})$ is the quantity produced by Firm A (B) at location x. Therefore, as in Thisse and Vives (1988), the firms can spatially price discriminate, as they can deliver different quantities at different locations in the space, thus making the price different at any location. The firms pay linear transportation costs to ship the good from the plant to consumers. Therefore, the profits of

Firm A (B) at point x are $\pi_{A,x} = (1 - q_{A,x} - q_{B,x} - t|x - a|)q_{A,x}$ ($\pi_{B,x} = (1 - q_{A,x} - q_{B,x} - t|x - b|)q_{B,x}$). Overall profits of Firm A (B) are $\Pi_A = \int_0^1 \pi_{A,x} dx$ ($\Pi_B = \int_0^1 \pi_{B,x} dx$). Provided that the transportation costs are not too high, no point in the space is monopolized by one firm. The game is a two-stage location-than-quantity game. Consider the second stage. Each location x can be treated as a separated market. Indeed, due to spatial price discrimination, a firm's quantity decision at a particular location has no effect on other locations. As a result, at each location, the Cournot equilibrium is $q_{A,x}(a, b) = (1 - 2t|a - x| + t|b - x|)/3$ and $q_{B,x}(a, b) = (1 - 2t|b - x| + t|a - x|)/3$. By anticipating the second-stage equilibrium quantity schedules, in the first stage, each firm chooses the location that maximizes its own profits. There is a unique equilibrium, that is, $a* = b* = \frac{1}{2}$. Therefore, with spatial discrimination and quantity competition, agglomeration occurs. It should be mentioned that agglomeration in the case of spatial Cournot competition is a quite general result. For example, agglomeration arises in the case of different production costs throughout the city (Mayer 2000), in the case of product differentiation (Shimizu 2002), and in the case of different transportation costs (Colombo 2013).[10] Furthermore, since each firm's sales are distributed symmetrically around the market center, each firm is located so as to minimize the transportation costs associated with its sales pattern.

Hamilton et al. (1989) also consider the case where the firms set price rather than quantity in the second stage (Bertrand competition). The relevant demand function is now $q_x = 1 - p_x$: the consumer located at x buys from the firm charging the lower delivered price. When the delivered prices are equal, the firm with lower transport costs provides the good to the consumers. As under quantity competition, the price problem can be solved at each location separately. Following a standard Bertrand argument, the equilibrium price at location x is $p_{A,x}(a, b) = p_{B,x}(a, b) = \max\,[t|a - x|, t|b - x|]$. Note that, differently from the Cournot case, each location x is served by only one firm. Let

---

[10] However, it does not emerge in the case of hyperbolic demand function (Colombo 2016).

us consider now the first stage of the game. The equilibrium locations are $a* = 1 - b* = \frac{10t-8+\sqrt{(10t-8)^2+24t(4-3t)}}{24t}$. Therefore, with spatial price discrimination and price competition, agglomeration never occurs. Indeed, the firms do not locate in the same point to avoid zero profits. The equilibrium locations are such that the two firms locate between the first and third quartiles and very close to them.

The intuition can be summarized as follow. Under both Cournot and Bertrand, the firms select the locations that minimize the transportation costs, given the expected second-stage quantity/price schedules. Since under Cournot there is complete overlapping, the transport costs are minimized when each firm locates in the middle of the segment. In contrast, in Bertrand the market areas are completely disjointed: therefore, the two firms locate "close" to the first and the third quartiles in order to minimize the transport costs. Note that they do not locate at the first and third quartiles: as the price decreases uniformly from the boundary to the center, the firms sell more in the in-the-between region than in the hinterlands. Therefore, in order to reduce the transportation costs, the firms locate closer to the center (i.e., between the first and third quartiles). As the optimal locations are at the first and third quartiles, we can conclude that the unit demand assumption is a necessary condition for the equilibrium locations to be transport cost minimizing (Lederer and Hurter 1986). Furthermore, the dispersed locations in Bertrand make the total transport costs lower under Bertrand than under Cournot. Since the equilibrium prices are lower in Bertrand than in Cournot, we can conclude that welfare is higher under Bertrand.

1.6 The "Barbell" Model

The Hotelling model assumes uniform distribution of consumers. Non-uniform distribution of consumers makes it difficult to obtain closed-form solutions (see Sect. 1.2). However, one particular case of non-uniform distribution of consumers has received considerable attention due to its tractability. It is the case of consumers located at endpoints of the linear segment. This is the "barbell" model introduced by Hwang and

Mai (1990). This model is particularly appealing in a geographical/spatial perspective.

Suppose a segment from 0 to 1. Consumers are located at the two endpoints, the "cities". Denote by 1 (2) the city located at the left (right) endpoint. A monopolist has to decide the location and the price. Denote by $a \in [0, 1]$ the location of the monopolist. First, we consider the case where the monopolist cannot price discriminate, and then we will consider the case of price discrimination. The demand function in City 1 (2) is $q_1 = 1 - cp$ ($q_2 = 1 - dp$). Therefore, the higher is c and d, the flatter is the corresponding demand curve (so, c and d are positively related to demand elasticity). The monopolist sustains linear transportation costs to carry the good to the cities. The profits of the monopolist are $\pi = (1 - cp)(p - ta) + (1 - dp)(p - t(1 - a))$. By maximizing with respect to price, we get $p = \frac{2+tca+td(1-a)}{2(c+d)}$. Note that $\frac{\partial^2 \pi}{\partial a^2} = \frac{t^2(c-d)^2}{2(c+d)} \geq 0$. Therefore, the profits are convex in the location, a. It follows that the optimal location is either $a = 0$ or $a = 1$. By comparing $\pi(a = 0)$ with $\pi(a = 1)$, we get $a* = \begin{cases} 0 \\ 1 \end{cases} a* = \begin{cases} 0 & \text{if } c \geq d \\ 1 & \text{if } c \leq d \end{cases}$. That is, the firm locates where the demand curve is flatter. Indeed, at equal prices, the demand is larger when the demand curve is flatter. Therefore, in order to minimize the transportation costs, the monopolist locates where the demand curve is flatter (as here the quantity sold is larger). We consider now the case of spatial price discrimination. The profit function now is $\pi = (1 - cp_1)(p_1 - ta) + (1 - dp_2)(p_2 - t(1 - a))$. By maximizing, we get $p_1 = \frac{1+tca}{2c}$ and $p_2 = \frac{1+td(1-a)}{2d}$. Note that $\frac{\partial^2 \pi}{\partial a^2} = \frac{t^2(c+d)}{2} \geq 0$. Therefore, the profits are convex in a. By comparing $\pi(a = 0)$ with $\pi(a = 1)$, we get $a* = \begin{cases} 0 & \text{if } c \leq d \\ 1 & \text{if } c \geq d \end{cases}$. That is, the firm locates where the demand curve is steeper. Note that this result is the opposite with respect to uniform pricing. Indeed, under price discrimination, all else being equal, even if the firm sets a lower price where the elasticity is higher, in equilibrium the demand is lower in the market characterized by a flatter demand curve.[11] Therefore, the firm locates where the demand curve is steeper in order to minimize the transportation costs.

1.7 Vertical Differentiation

All the models we have considered until now assume that, at equal prices, some consumers prefer the product of Firm A, whereas others prefer the product of Firm B. That is, these models describe horizontal product differentiation. However, there are many situations where, at equal prices, all consumers prefer the product of, say, Firm A to the product of Firm B (e.g., because the quality of Firm A is higher). In this case, we refer to vertical product differentiation. Spatial models are also useful to analyze vertical product differentiation. In this case their correct interpretation is the product characteristic one.

In what follows, we discuss one of the most famous spatial models of vertical differentiation, which dates back to Shaked and Sutton (1982). Suppose that each consumer buys one or zero unit of the good. The preferences of the consumer, if he buys the good, are expressed by the following utility function, $U = \vartheta s - p$, where s is a quality index of the good. If the consumer does not buy the good, the utility is zero. Parameter ϑ is a taste parameter: all consumers prefer high quality to low quality, for a given price; however, a consumer with a high ϑ is more willing to pay to obtain a higher quality.[12] Suppose the following (uniform) distribution of tastes across the population: $\vartheta \in \left[\underline{\vartheta}, \overline{\vartheta}\right]$, where $\underline{\vartheta} > 0$. Furthermore, we assume for the moment that $\overline{\vartheta} \geq 2\underline{\vartheta}$ (i.e., there is "sufficient" heterogeneity). Suppose there are two firms, Firm A and Firm B. Firm A (B) produces a good of quality s_A (s_B), with $s_A \geq s_B$: that is, Firm A (B) produces the high (low)-quality good.

---

[11] In other words, the lower price is not sufficient to compensate for the higher sensitivity to the price of consumers.

[12] It can be shown that ϑ is the inverse of the marginal rate of substitution between income and quality. That is, consumers have different incomes, and wealthier consumers have a lower marginal utility of income and a higher ϑ.

Denote $\Delta \equiv s_A - s_B$. Consider a two-stage game. In the first stage, the two firms choose simultaneously the quality; in the second they choose simultaneously the price. Consider the second stage. Suppose the market is covered.[13] Denote by $\hat{\vartheta}$ the consumer which is indifferent between buying from Firm A and from Firm B. Solving $\vartheta s_A - p_A = \vartheta s_B - p_B$, we get $\hat{\vartheta} = \frac{p_A - p_B}{\Delta}$. Clearly, high-$\vartheta$ consumers buy the high-quality good, whereas low-ϑ consumers buy the low-quality good. Therefore, the demand functions are $D_A = \overline{\vartheta} - \hat{\vartheta}$ and $D_B = \hat{\vartheta} - \underline{\vartheta}$, and the profits are $\pi_A = p_A D_A$ and $\pi_B = p_B D_B$. By maximizing with respect to price, we get $p_A* = \frac{\Delta(2\overline{\vartheta} - \underline{\vartheta})}{3}$ and $p_B* = \frac{\Delta(\overline{\vartheta} - 2\underline{\vartheta})}{3}$. The equilibrium profits (for given qualities) are $\pi_A(p_A*, p_B*) = \frac{\Delta(2\overline{\vartheta} - \underline{\vartheta})^2}{9}$ and $\pi_B(p_A*, p_B*) = \frac{\Delta(\overline{\vartheta} - 2\underline{\vartheta})^2}{9}$. Therefore, the high-quality firm sets a higher price and gets higher profits. Furthermore, note that the prices increase with consumers' heterogeneity.

Consider now the first stage. Suppose that the quality choice is without cost. From the profit functions above, it is immediate to see that the two firms will maximally differentiate. In particular, suppose that s must belong to $\left[\underline{s}, \overline{s}\right]$. If we assume that $s_A \geq s_B$, then the equilibrium qualities would be $s_A* = \overline{s}$ and $s_B* = \underline{s}$ (maximal differentiation). The intuition is the same as for spatial models of horizontal differentiation: the firms differentiate in order to reduce price competition. In particular, the strategic effect dominates, so that, even if producing a high-quality good is costless, the low-quality firm reduces the quality of its good as much as possible, in order to soften price competition.[14] Clearly, if the two firms enter sequentially, the firm that enters first chooses $\overline{s}$, whereas the other chooses $\underline{s}$.

Suppose now that $\overline{\vartheta} < 2\underline{\vartheta}$ (low consumer heterogeneity). In this case, in the price equilibrium, Firm B has no demand. Therefore, it sets a price equal to zero, whereas Firm A sets a price equal to $\overline{\vartheta}\Delta/2$

[13] Under some appropriate restrictions on the parameters, this conjecture is correct in equilibrium.

[14] However, this conclusion is not always true: if the lowest level of quality is particularly low so that the market is uncovered, the low-quality firm would end up with zero demand. In this case, there is less than maximal differentiation in equilibrium.

and gets positive profits. Therefore, even if there are constant return to scale and no entrance costs, there is only one firm in the market. This is in contrast with the locational models under horizontal product differentiation, where there is an infinite number of firms when there are no entrance costs (see the Salop model when f tends to zero). In the case of vertical differentiation, when consumer heterogeneity is low, more intense price competition drives the low-quality firm out of the market. Indeed, if the lower quality is very "low", the low-quality firm cannot resist to the competition of the high-quality firm. More generally, the following "finiteness result" can be stated: provided that the marginal cost of quality does not increase too quickly with quality, there can be at most a finite number of firms with a positive market share in the industry regardless of entry costs.

Before concluding, it is worth stressing the existence of spatial models combining the "horizontal" and the "vertical" dimension: Gabszewicz and Thisse (1986) introduce vertical differentiation by allowing firms to be asymmetrically located outside the linear market, Dos Santos Ferreira and Thisse (1996) use asymmetric transport costs to generate vertical differentiation in the Hotelling set-up, and Gabszewicz and Wauthy (2012) nest horizontal and vertical differentiation by means of a measure of the "natural market" of each firm (i.e., when the "natural market" of a firm is the whole market, there is pure vertical differentiation; when the "natural market" of both firms is of equal size, there is pure horizontal differentiation).

1.8 Conclusions

This chapter illustrates some prominent classic spatial models. In particular, we consider some cornerstones of classic spatial economics, including the linear model, the circular model, and the vertical differentiation model, and some extensions to them. The aim of the chapter is mainly pedagogical: we want to discuss the main spatial models and their implications. Of course, many other relevant models are not discussed, even if they contribute to our comprehension of the role of space in shaping economic phenomena.

References

Bertrand, J. (1883). Revue de la theorie mathematique de la richesse sociale et des recherches sur les principles mathematiques de la theorie des richesses. *Journal des Savants*, 499–508.

Brenner, S. (2005). Hotelling Games with Three, Four, and More Players. *Journal of Regional Science, 45*, 851–864.

Chamberlin, E. (1933). *The Theory of Monopolistic Competition*. Cambridge: Harvard University Press.

Colombo, S. (2011). Discriminatory Prices and the Prisoner Dilemma Problem. *Annals of Regional Science, 46*, 397–416.

Colombo, S. (2013). Spatial Cournot Competition with Non-extreme Directional Constraints. *Annals of Regional Science, 102*, 157–169.

Colombo, S. (2016). Location Choices with Non-linear Demand Function. *Papers in Regional Science, 95*, S215–S226.

Cournot, A. (1838). *Researches into the Mathematical Principles of the Theory of Wealth*. English edition of Cournot (N. T. Bacon, Trans.). New York: Kelley, 1960.

D'Aspremont, C., Gabszewicz, J. J., & Thisse, J.-F. (1979). On Hotelling's Stability in Competition. *Econometrica, 47*, 1145–1150.

Dos Santos Ferreira, R., & Thisse, J.-F. (1996). Horizontal and Vertical Differentiation: The Launhardt Model. *International Journal of Industrial Organization, 14*, 485–506.

Economides, N. (1986). Minimal and Maximal Produce Differentiation in Hotelling's Duopoly. *Economics Letters, 21*, 67–71.

Gabszewicz, J. J., & Thisse, J.-F. (1986). On the Nature of Competition with Differentiated Products. *The Economic Journal, 96*, 160–172.

Gabszewicz, J. J., & Wauthy, X. J. (2012). Nesting Horizontal and Vertical Differentiation. *Regional Science and Urban Economics, 42*, 998–1002.

Greenhut, J. G., & Greenhut, M. L. (1975). Spatial Price Discrimination, Competition and Locational Effects. *Economica, 42*, 401–419.

Gu, Y., & Wenzel, T. (2009). A Note on the Excess Entry Theorem in Spatial Models with Elastic Demand. *International Journal of Industrial Organization, 27*, 567–571.

Hamilton, J., Thisse, J.-F., & Weskamp, A. (1989). Spatial Discrimination: Bertrand vs Cournot in a Model of Location Choice. *Regional Science and Urban Economics, 19*, 87–102.

Hoover, E. M. (1948). *The Location of Economic Activity*. New York: McGraw Hill.
Hotelling, H. (1929). Stability in Competition. *Economic Journal, 39*, 41–57.
Hwang, H., & Mai, C.-C. (1990). Effects of Spatial Price Discrimination on Output, Welfare, and Location. *American Economic Review, 80*, 567–575.
Lambertini, L. (1994). Equilibrium Location in the Unconstrained Hotelling Game. *Economic Notes, 23*, 438–446.
Launhardt, W. (1885). *Mathematische Begründung Der Volkswirtschaftslehre*. Leipzig: B.G. Teubner. Translated from German B.G. Teubner (1993) *Mathematical Principles of Economics*, Aldershot: Edward Elgar.
Lederer, P. J., & Hurter, A. P. (1986). Competition of Firms: Discriminatory Pricing and Location. *Econometrica, 54*, 623–640.
Liu, Q., & Serfes, K. (2004). Quality of Information and Oligopolistic Price Discrimination. *Journal of Economics & Management Strategy, 13*, 671–702.
Marshall, A. (1890). *Principles of Economics*. London: Macmillan.
Mayer, T. (2000). Spatial Cournot competition and heterogeneous production costs across locations. *Regional Science and Urban Economics, 30*, 325–352.
Neven, D. J. (1986). On Hotelling's Competition with Non-uniform Customer Distribution. *Economics Letters, 21*, 121–126.
Peitz, M. (2002). Price Competition in Address Models of Product Differentiation: Unit-Elastic Demand. *Economic Theory, 20*, 849–860.
Rath, K., & Zhao, G. (2001). Two Stage Equilibrium and Product Choice with Elastic Demand. *International Journal of Industrial Organization, 19*, 1441–1455.
Salop, S. C. (1979). Monopolistic Competition with Outside Goods. *BELL Journal of Economics, 10*, 141–156.
Selten, R. (1975). Re-examination of the Perfectness Concept for Equilibrium Points in Extensive Games. *International Journal of Game Theory, 4*, 25–55.
Shaked, A., & Sutton, J. (1982). Relaxing Price Competition Through Product Differentiation. *Review of Economic Studies, 49*, 3–13.
Shimizu, D. (2002). Product differentiation in spatial Cournot markets. *Economics Letters, 76*, 317–322.
Tabuchi, T. (1994). Two-Stage Two-Dimensional Spatial Competition Between Two Firms. *Regional Science and Urban Economics, 24*, 207–227.
Takahashi, T., & de Palma, A. (1993). A Unified Treatment of the Segment and the Circular Market Models. In H. Ohta & J.-F. Thisse (Eds.), *Does Economic Space Matter?* London: St Martin's Press.

Thisse, J. F., & Vives, X. (1988). On the Strategic Choice of Spatial Price Policy. *American Economic Review, 78*, 122–137.
Thunen, J. H. (1826). *Der Isolierte Staat in Beziehung Auf Landwirtschaft Und Nationalökonomie*. Hamburg: Perthes. Translated from German by C. M. Wartenberg (1966) *Von Thunen's Isolated State*, Oxford: Pergamon Press.
Tirole, J. (1988). *The Theory of Industrial Organization*. Cambridge: MIT Press.
Vickrey, W. S. (1964). *Microstatics*. New York: Harcourt, Brace and World.
Weber, A. (1909). *Uber Den Standort Der Industrien*. Tubingen: J.C.B. Mohr. Translated from German by C.J. Friedrich (1961) *The Theory of the Location of Industries*. Chicago: Chicago University Press.

2

Spatial Cournot Competition

Fu-Chuan Lai

2.1 Introduction

Competitive location theory started with Hotelling (1929),[1] who assumed that there are two identical firms selling homogenous goods to consumers living along a linear market with unit length (the "main street"). These consumers are uniformly distributed along this main street, and each buys exactly one unit of the product from the firm with the lowest full price (mill price plus linear transport cost). Firms pursue maximization of their own profits. They decide their locations simultaneously in the first stage

[1]Early spatial models such as Ricardo (1817), Von Thünen (1826), Weber (1909), and Christaller (1933) are focused on land use and simple location theory.

F.-C. Lai (✉)
Research Center for Humanities and Social Sciences, Academia Sinica, Nankang, Taipei, Taiwan

Department of Public Finance, National Chengchi University, Taipei, Taiwan
e-mail: uiuclai@gate.sinica.edu.tw

S. Colombo (ed.), *Spatial Economics Volume I*,
https://doi.org/10.1007/978-3-030-40098-9_2

of the game. In the second stage, they simultaneously determine the prices of their products. Hotelling (1929) "showed" that in equilibrium, these two firms will locate at the center of the linear market and share the market equally.

At first glance, Hotelling's model seems correct, so his model was later heavily cited, and there were many extended studies, such as Lerner and Singer (1937), Smithies (1941), and Downs (1957). However, 50 years later, D'Aspremont et al. (1979) proved that Hotelling's equilibrium result is invalid. The reason is that when the two firms locate close to one another, the price equilibrium provided by Hotelling (1929) cannot be sustained, because one of them will undercut the other and monopolize the entire market. In this situation, the profit of the undercutting firm is higher than what it would earn under co-existence, so the equilibrium of the Hotelling (1929) model is invalid; in fact, it is wrong.[2] D'Aspremont et al. (1979) proposed to use quadratic transport cost functions instead of linear transport cost functions, in order to make the game structure be correct, such that a price equilibrium exists for any location pair. However, their modification needs to pay a price, that is, the equilibrium locations will be at the two ends of the linear market, which is very different from Hotelling's observation about the reality.[3]

Since the Hotelling (1929) model had already been misused for 50 years at the time of d'Aspremont et al.'s work in 1979, once the model was proved to be wrong, its impact on the academic world was foreseeable. Many scholars have tried to save the Hotelling (1929) model with slight modifications or directly switch to using quadratic transport cost functions to avoid the game structure problem. Several attempts will be briefly introduced in the following, where spatial Cournot competition will be highlighted.

---

[2]Modern game theory had not yet appeared in 1929. For example, John Nash was born in 1928, and thus Harold Hotelling did not yet know of the so-called Nash equilibrium, not to mention the "subgame perfect Nash equilibrium" when he published his paper in 1929.

[3]Hotelling (1929) thought that cities are too concentrated in reality; the taste of apple ciders is too similar, and the churches of different denominations are too similar.

2.2 Attempts to Save the Hotelling (1929) Model

2.2.1 Non-Cournot Models

First, Graitson (1980) employed the max-min strategy for the two firms and thus changed the game structure. In his model, even though the opponent's price is reduced to zero, one firm can keep some parts of the market (and have a positive profit) by pricing just below the rival's price at its own position, or it can relocate to a point far enough away from the opponent's location that its rival will not undercut its price, and both firms can co-exist in the market. As a result, he found that the co-existence scenario dominates the max-min scenario and the final equilibrium locations fall at a quantile from both ends of the market.

Osborne and Pitchik (1987) allowed the firms in the Hotelling (1929) model to take mixed strategies in the price subgame. By way of their complex calculation process (solving a number of highly non-linear equations and some inequalities), they found approximate price equilibrium solutions for any combination of locations, although they couldn't really prove these price equilibria. This is because under mixed strategies, the strategy space of any price is a continuous interval, which made them unable to completely describe these mixed strategy equilibria. Even though they did not provide an analytical proof for the price equilibria that they proposed, the rigor of their arguments prevented the academic community from questioning the correctness of these price equilibria. Returning to the first stage (the location stage), if the location behavior is limited to pure strategies, they confirmed that there is (in a symmetrical sense) a unique subgame perfect equilibrium, where the firms' locations fall at about 0.27 from the two endpoints, respectively. Finally, they also calculated that if these firms are allowed to use mixed strategies in the location stage, then there is only one equilibrium in the symmetric case. Their greatest contribution was "confirming" (although they were unable to prove) that the Hotelling (1929) model has a unique location-price equilibrium as long as the firms are allowed to adopt mixed strategies.

Vogel (2008) concluded that because the profit functions of the Hotelling (1929) model are not globally quasi-concave, there is no pure-strategy equilibrium in some of the price subgames, so the Hotelling (1929) model does not have a pure-strategy subgame perfect Nash equilibrium (SPNE). Vogel (2008) constructed a model with several heterogeneous firms located on a unit circle and introduced an auxiliary game to redefine the indifferent consumers. He showed that when the difference of marginal production costs between any two adjacent firms is sufficiently small, there always exists an indifferent consumer between them, so a pure-strategy price equilibrium in each subgame exists.

Vogel (2008) also proved that as long as the marginal cost between firms is small enough, the auxiliary game's profit is an upper bound on the real game and any unilateral deviation strategy is unprofitable. In short, Vogel (2008) did not directly calculate the equilibrium solution of the Hotelling (1929) model (in fact, it does not exist), but indirectly obtained the equilibrium of the model by redefining the indifferent consumers, which is quite clever.

Anderson (1988) used the linear-quadratic transport cost function and found that unless the two firms are at the same point (and thus the equilibrium price is zero), undercutting always exists. Therefore, the linear-quadratic transport cost functions still cannot solve the problem of undercutting.

In a larger sense, all the above attempts either failed in the agglomerate result (say Graitson 1980; Anderson 1988) or used abstract mathematical methodology (say Osborne and Pitchik 1987; Vogel 2008), and thus none are fully satisfactory.

2.2.2 Spatial Cournot Models

2.2.2.1 Linear Models

It was not until Anderson and Neven (1991)[4] adopted the spatial Cournot competition model that the problem of inconsistency between the observation of reality and the mathematical problem of the Hotelling (1929) model was properly solved.[5] Anderson and Neven (1991) assumed that the demand at every point $x \in [0, 1]^6$ of the market is elastic:

$$p(x) = a - b\left(q_1(x) + q_2(q)\right),$$

where p is the market price, $a > 0$, $b > 0$ are parameters; and $q_i(x)$, $i = 1, 2$ are the quantity at x supplied by firm i, where their locations are $x_1 \in [0, 1]$ and $x_2 \in [0, 1]$, respectively. Shipping costs are also linear in distance. They proved that the two firms (even in the case of n firms) will choose the same location at the center of the market (i.e., $x_1 = x_2 = 1/2$). The critical contribution of Anderson and Neven (1991) is that the agglomeration regularity in the real world was supported from a theoretical aspect while keeping the linear transport rate the same as that in Hotelling (1929), but without any game structure problem.[7]

---

[4]Hamilton et al. (1989) assumed linear demand in each point of the Hotelling (1929) market, where firms engage in Cournot (Bertrand) competition in the second stage and they simultaneously choose their locations in the first stage and the transport costs are linear in volume and distance. They showed that firms will agglomerate at the market center when they engage in Cournot competition. Anderson and Neven (1991) is different from Hamilton et al. (1989) in that Anderson and Neven (1991) discussed the scenarios with a general transport cost function and multiple firms. The central agglomeration result was obtained in both Hamilton et al. (1989) and Anderson and Neven (1991).

[5]Earlier spatial Cournot models include Greenhut and Greenhut (1975), Greenhut and Ohta (1975), Norman (1981), Greenhut et al. (1987), and Ohta (1988), whose models assumed exogenous locations for firms.

[6]In fact, they assumed the length of the market is L. For simplicity, we here normalize the length of the market to be one.

[7]However, they abandoned the inelastic demand, price competition, and consumer-paid transport costs that were employed in Hotelling (1929).

For $x \in [0,1]$, the profit functions are $\pi_i(x) = [a - bQ(x) - t(x - x_i)] \cdot q_i(x)$, $i = 1, 2$, where $Q(\cdot) = q_1(\cdot) + q_2(\cdot)$. Then we can solve for

$$q_i(x) = \frac{a + t\left(|x_j - x|\right) - 2t\left(|x_i - x|\right)}{3b}, \tag{2.1}$$

$$p(x) = \frac{a + t\left(|x_i - x|\right) + t\left(|x_j - x|\right)}{3}, \tag{2.2}$$

$$Q(x) = \frac{2a - t\left(|x_i - x|\right) - t\left(|x_j - x|\right)}{3b}, \tag{2.3}$$

$$\pi_i(x) = \frac{\left[a + t\left(|x_j - x|\right) - 2t\left(|x_i - x|\right)\right]^2}{9b}, \quad i = 1, 2, \quad j = 1, 2, \quad i \neq j. \tag{2.4}$$

The total profit for firm i is

$$\begin{aligned} \Pi_i(x) &= \int_0^{x_1} \pi_i\left(x; x_1, x_2\right) dx + \int_{x_1}^{x_2} \pi_i\left(x; x_1, x_2\right) \\ &\quad + \int_{x_2}^{1} \pi_i\left(x; x_1, x_2\right) dx, \quad i = 1, 2. \end{aligned} \tag{2.5}$$

When the transport cost function is linear in distance, we can solve $\partial \Pi_1 / \partial x_1 = 0$ and $\partial \Pi_2 / \partial x_2 = 0$ simultaneously, yielding $x_1^* = x_2^* = 1/2$. This agglomeration result is also valid when there are n firms.

Ever since Anderson and Neven (1991) obtained an agglomeration equilibrium, many scholars have tried to obtain dispersed location equilibria under the spatial Cournot setting. The first attempt was by Chamorro-Rivas (2000a), who proved that if the reservation price in Anderson and Neven (1991) model is low enough, there is a dispersed location equilibrium in addition to the equilibrium in which firms agglomerate at the center of the market.

In Anderson and Neven (1991), the reservation price for each consumer (a) is assumed to be large ($a > 2t$) to ensure all market areas are served by the two firms. Chamorro-Rivas (2000a) discussed the scenarios of $t \leq \alpha \leq 2t$, such that some areas are only served by one of the firms.[8] In other words, the whole market can be divided into monopoly areas and duopoly areas, and the percentage of the former will increase as α decreases. After some calculations, he concluded that there exists a unique equilibrium location pair: $\left(x_1^*, x_2^*\right) = (1/2, 1/2)$, when $\frac{3}{2}t \leq \alpha \leq 2$; there exist two equilibrium location pairs, $\left(x_1^*, x_2^*\right) = (1/2, 1/2)$ and $\left(x_1^*, x_2^*\right) = \left(\frac{2\alpha-t}{4t}, 1 - \frac{2\alpha-t}{4t}\right)$, when $\frac{11}{10}t \leq \alpha \leq \frac{3t}{2}$; and when $t \leq \alpha \leq \frac{11}{10}t$, there exist two equilibrium location pairs: $\left(x_1^*, x_2^*\right) = (1/2, 1/2)$, and $x_1^* = \frac{1}{434t}\left(208t - 46\alpha - 4\sqrt{-117t^2 + 540\alpha t - 356\alpha^2}\right), x_2^* = 1 - x_1^*$.

Chen and Lai (2008) further extended Chamorro-Rivas (2000a) to include zoning policy, where the government can prohibit firms from locating in the area $(z, 1 - z)$ in order to preserve the amenities in this area. They showed that firms will locate at the boundary of the zoning area, that is, $\left(x_1^*, x_2^*\right) = [z, 1 - z]$. They also calculated the optimal zoning policy under different reservation prices. After some calculations, their results can be summarized as in Fig. 2.1, where $\beta \equiv \frac{\alpha}{t}$ and $\beta \geq 1$. The results obtained in Chamorro-Rivas (2000a) (i.e., no zoning) are plotted by dashed lines, and the optimal zoning varies with β. From Fig. 2.1, it is noticed that the government can enact a proper zoning policy to improve social welfare.

Pal and Sarkar (2002) extended Anderson and Neven (1991) to allow each firm to choose multiple stores. They showed that every store will locate at its quantity-median point, where the total transport costs to its right-hand-side market equal those of its left-hand-side market. If m is the number of stores for firm 1 and n is the number of stores for firm 2, then their numerical analysis showed that $x_1^* = 1/2$, $y_1^* = 1/2$ when $m = n = 1$; $x_1^* = 1/4 = y_1^*$, $x_2^* = 3/4 = y_2^*$ when $m = 2$, $n = 2$, and when $m = 1$, $n = 2$, $x_1^* = 1/2$ and $y_1^* = a - \sqrt{a^2 - \frac{a}{2} + \frac{1}{8}}$, $y_2^* = 1 - y_2^*$.

[8]The reservation price "a" in Anderson and Neven (1991) is replaced by "α" in Chamorro-Rivas (2000a). When $\alpha < t$, there exist some areas where no service is provided. This scenario, to the best of my knowledge, has not been analyzed in detail.

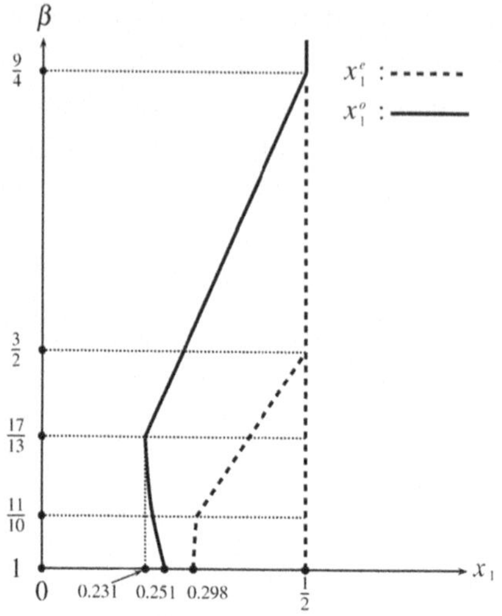

Fig. 2.1 The results in Chen and Lai (2008)

Note that their model obtained agglomeration location equilibrium and separation location equilibrium, depending on the number of plants.

Matsumura and Shimizu (2005) explored the welfare effects of the spatial Cournot model. They calculated the consumer surplus at each point of the market, and the profit of two (or more) firms, and found that the socially optimal locations are farther away than the equilibrium locations. However, the equilibrium locations will be farther away than the locations where the consumer surplus is maximized.

Mayer (2000) showed that firms agglomerate at the center when the production costs are identical at every point of the linear market or when the production costs are minimized at the center. Firms do not agglomerate at the center when the production costs have a globally concave distribution with the highest production costs at the center.

Gupta et al. (1997) examined the location equilibrium in Anderson and Neven (1991) with non-uniform population density functions. They showed that the agglomeration equilibrium is robust in most scenarios.

2.2.2.2 Circular Markets

Another breakthrough path for spatial Cournot competition started when Pal (1998) modified the Anderson and Neven (1991) model into a unit-length circular market and proved that the firms' locations are maximally separated, that is, the firms will locate at both ends of a diameter. Pal (1998) assumed a unit-length circular market, and assumed $x_2 = 1/2$, while $0 \leq x_1 \leq 1/2$. For $x \in (0, 1)$, the profit of firm 1 is

$$\pi_1 (x; x_1, x_2) = \frac{(\alpha - 2t|x_1 - x| + t|x_2 - x|)^2}{9b}. \tag{2.6}$$

In the first stage, firm 1's objective is

$$\max_{x_1} \Pi_1 (x_1, x_2) = \int_0^1 \pi_1 (x; x_1, x_2)\, dx. \tag{2.7}$$

Given $x_2 = 1/2$ and $0 \leq x_1 \leq 1/2$, we have

$$\begin{aligned} \Pi_1 \left(x_1, \tfrac{1}{2}\right) &= \int_0^{x_1} \frac{\left[\alpha-2t(x_1-x)+t\left(\frac{1}{2}-x\right)\right]^2}{9b}\, dx \\ &+ \int_{x_1}^{\frac{1}{2}} \frac{\left[\alpha-2t(x-x_1)+t\left(\frac{1}{2}-x\right)\right]^2}{9b}\, dx \\ &+ \int_{x_1}^{\frac{1}{2}} \frac{\left[\alpha-2t(x-x_1)+t\left(\frac{1}{2}-x\right)\right]^2}{9b}\, dx \\ &+ \int_{\frac{1}{2}+x_1}^{1} \frac{\left[\alpha-2t(1-x+x_1)+t\left(x-\frac{1}{2}\right)\right]^2}{9b}\, dx. \end{aligned} \tag{2.8}$$

The first-order condition and the second-order condition are solved as follows:

$$\frac{d\Pi_1 \left(x_1, \frac{1}{2}\right)}{dx_1} = \frac{4t^2 x_1 (2x_1 - 1)}{9b}, \tag{2.9}$$

$$\frac{d\Pi_1^2\left(x_1,\frac{1}{2}\right)}{dx_1^2}=\frac{4t^2\left(4x_1-1\right)}{9b}. \tag{2.10}$$

Only $x_1 = 0$ satisfies both the first-order condition (f.o.c.) and second-order condition (s.o.c.). Therefore, the unique locational solution is $\left(x_1^*, x_2^*\right) = (0, 1/2)$. The result of Pal (1998) seems to hint that in spatial Cournot competition, the shape of the market plays a decisive role. That is, in a linear market, all firms will agglomerate at the center of the market, but in a circular market, they will stay away from each other.[9] This conjecture was quickly broken by Matsushima (2001), who proved when there are n firms (and n is even) locating in a circular market, $\frac{n}{2}$ firms locating at point 0 and the other $\frac{n}{2}$ firms locating at point $\frac{1}{2}$ is an equilibrium. His result means that the shape of the market is not necessarily a key factor to determine the location of the firms. This finding has led many scholars to devote efforts to find the decisive factors in the location game with two or more firms. With endeavors by many scholars, this academic competition was soon ended.

Gupta et al. (2004) basically solved the problem of n firms' location selections (n can be either odd or even). They found that the firms' location choices should satisfy the "aggregate cost median condition" (see Eq. (2.20) later). Therefore, the equilibrium locations may be separated, aggregated, or partially dispersed and partially aggregated.[10]

Gupta et al. (2004) did not solve the equilibrium locations directly. Obviously, as the number of firms increases, the number of the market segments also increases exponentially, making the solution process more tedious and more difficult.

Following the same settings as Pal (1998), assume that the consumer is homogeneously distributed on a circle with a circumference of one.

[9] In addition, Shimizu (2002) found that in Pal's (1998) model, if the products are complementary (instead of substitutes), then the duopoly firms agglomerate at one point of the market. Yu and Lai (2003a) obtained results similar to that in Shimizu (2002) and extended their model to the situation in which each firm has two plants.

[10] In fact, Gupta et al. (2004) was composed of two separate articles, Gupta et al. (2003) and Yu and Lai (2003b), because they independently solved the same problem and submitted their papers to the *International Journal of Industrial Organization* at the same time; after the first reviewing process, the Editor asked for the two articles to be merged.

Considering that n manufacturers engage in Cournot competition, where $n \geq 2$, q_i and x_i indicate the number of products and the location of firm i, $i \in \{1, \ldots, n\}$. The quantities and locations of these n firms are represented by $(q_i)_{i=1}^n$ and $(x_i)_{i=1}^n$, respectively. They assumed a unit transport rate; therefore the profit function for firm i at x is

$$\pi_i(x_1, x_2, \ldots, x_n, x) = (p_i(x) - |x - x_i|)\, q_i(x), \quad i = 1, \ldots, n, \tag{2.11}$$

After some calculations, they obtained the equilibrium quantities and profits in the second stage

$$q_i(x_1, x_2, \ldots, x_n, x) = \frac{1}{n+1}\left(\alpha + \sum_{j=1}^{n} |x - x_j| - (n+1)\,|x - x_i|\right), \tag{2.12}$$

and

$$\pi_i(x_1, x_2, \ldots, x_n, x) = q_i(x_1, x_2, \ldots, x_n, x)^2, \quad i = 1, \ldots, n. \tag{2.13}$$

Back to the first stage, given the position of other vendors, the objective of firm i is

$$\begin{aligned} \max\ \Pi_i(x_1, x_2, \ldots, x_n) &= \int_0^1 \pi_i(x_1, x_2, \ldots, x_n, x)\, dx, \\ \text{s.t.} \qquad x_i &\in [0, 1), \quad i = 1, \ldots, n. \end{aligned} \tag{2.14}$$

In Firm i's profit function, Eq. (2.5) can be expanded to

$$\Pi_i(x_1, \ldots, x_n) = \int_0^{x_i} \pi_i(x_1, \ldots, x_n, x)\, dx + \int_{x_i}^{x_i+\frac{1}{2}} \pi_i(x_1, \ldots, x_n, x)\, dx + \int_{x_i+\frac{1}{2}}^{1} \pi_i(x_1, \ldots, x_n, x)\, dx.$$

Divide $\pi_i(x_1, \ldots, x_n)$ to x_i

$$\frac{\partial \pi_i (x_1, \ldots, x_n, x)}{\partial x_i} = 2q_i (x_1, \ldots, x_n, x) \frac{\partial q_i (x_1, \ldots, x_n, x)}{\partial x_i}, \quad (2.15)$$

where

$$\frac{\partial q_i (x_1,\ldots,x_n,x)}{\partial x_i} = -\frac{n}{n+1}\left(\frac{\partial |x-x_i|}{\partial x_i}\right)$$
$$= \begin{cases} -\frac{n}{n+1}\cdot\frac{\partial (x_i-x)}{\partial x_i} = \frac{-n}{n+1}, & \forall x \in [0, x_i) \cup \left[x_i + \frac{1}{2}, 1\right), \\ -\frac{n}{n+1}\cdot\frac{\partial (x-x_i)}{\partial x_i} = \frac{n}{n+1}, & \forall x \in \left[x_i, x_i + \frac{1}{2}\right). \end{cases} \quad (2.16)$$

Therefore, the first-order condition of $\Pi_i(x_1, \ldots, x_n)$ for x_i is

$$\frac{\partial \Pi_i (x_1,\ldots,x_n)}{\partial x_i} = \int\limits_0^{x_i} \frac{\partial \pi_i (x_1,\ldots,x_n,x)}{\partial x_i} dx + \int\limits_{x_i}^{x_i+\frac{1}{2}} \frac{\partial \pi_i (x_1,\ldots,x_n,x)}{\partial x_i} dx + \int\limits_{x_i+\frac{1}{2}}^{1} \frac{\partial \pi_i (x_1,\ldots,x_n,x)}{\partial x_i} dx$$
$$= \frac{2n}{n+1}\left\{ -\int\limits_0^{x_i} q_i (x_1, \ldots, x_n, x)\, dx + \int\limits_{x_i}^{x_i+\frac{1}{2}} q_i (x_1, \ldots, x_n, x)\, dx - \int\limits_{x_i+\frac{1}{2}}^{1} q_i (x_1, \ldots, x_n, x)\, dx \right\}. \quad (2.17)$$

Therefore, the first-order condition for the total profit is satisfied if and only if the following equation is valid:

$$\int_{x_i}^{x_i+\frac{1}{2}} q_i (x1, \ldots, x_n, x)\, dx = \int_0^{x_i} q_i (x_1, \ldots, x_n, x)\, dx + \int_{x_i+\frac{1}{2}}^{1} q_i (x_1, \ldots, x_n, x)\, dx. \quad (2.18)$$

Equation (2.18) implies that the optimal location for any firm must be consistent with the quantity-median of its products. In a circular market, the number of the median conditions can be further simplified. Notice that in a circular market, for any $x_i \in \left[0, \frac{1}{2}\right]$, we have

$$\int_{x_i}^{x_i+\frac{1}{2}} \alpha - n\,(|x - x_i|)\, dx = \int_0^{x_i} \alpha - n\,(|x - x_i|)\, dx + \int_{x_i+\frac{1}{2}}^{1} \alpha - n\,(|x - x_i|)\, dx, \quad (2.19)$$

because the term of $\alpha - n(|x - x_i|)$ in Eq. (2.19) is the same for each half circle. From the above Eqs. (2.12), (2.18), and (2.19), the first-order condition can be simplified to

$$\int_{x_i}^{x_i+\frac{1}{2}} \sum_{j \neq i}^{n} | x - x_j | \, dx = \int_{0}^{x_i} \sum_{j \neq i}^{n} | x - x_j | \, dx + \int_{x_i+\frac{1}{2}}^{1} \sum_{j \neq i}^{n} | x - x_j | \, dx. \tag{2.20}$$

Defining Eq. (2.20) as the aggregate cost median condition, it is a necessary condition for the optimal location for each firm.

Let LHS and RHS represent the left-hand side and the right-hand side of the aggregate cost median condition, respectively. That is, for any $x_i \in [0, 1/2]$,

$$\text{LHS} \equiv \int_{x_i}^{x_i+\frac{1}{2}} \sum_{j \neq i}^{n} | x - x_j | \, dx,$$

$$\text{RHS} \equiv \int_{0}^{x_i} \sum_{j \neq i}^{n} | x - x_j | \, dx + \int_{x_i+\frac{1}{2}}^{1} \sum_{j \neq i}^{n} | x - x_j | \, dx.$$

Given $(x_1, x_2, \ldots, x_{i-1}, x_{i+1}, x_n)$ and $x_i \in \left[0, \frac{1}{2}\right]$, the sign of $\frac{\partial^2 \Pi_i}{\partial x_i^2}$ is the same as the sign of the first derivative of *LHS* with respect to x_i. That is,

$$\begin{aligned} &\frac{\partial^2 \Pi_i(x_1,\ldots,x_n)}{\partial x_i^2} \\ &= \frac{2n}{n+1}\left\{\frac{n}{n+1} + \left(2q_i\,(x_1, \ldots, x_n, x)\Big|_{x=x_i+\frac{1}{2}} - 2q_i\,(x_1, \ldots, x_n, x)\Big|_{x=x_i}\right)\right\} \\ &= \frac{4n^2}{(n+1)^2}\left(\sum_{j \neq i}^{n} \left|x_i + \tfrac{1}{2} - x_j\right| - \sum_{j \neq i}^{n} \left|x_i - x_j\right|\right) \gtreqless 0 \\ &\Longleftrightarrow \quad h \overset{def}{=} \frac{\partial LHS}{\partial x_i} = \sum_{j \neq i}^{n} \left| x_i + \tfrac{1}{2} - x_j\right| - \sum_{j \neq i}^{n} \left|x_i - x_j\right| \gtreqless 0, \end{aligned}$$

Table 2.1 Partial numerical solution of Cournot competition in circular market

Number of firms	Location Equilibrium
$N=2$	$\left(0, \frac{1}{2}\right)$
$N=3$	$\left(0, \frac{1}{3}, \frac{2}{3}\right)$, and $\left(0, \frac{1}{2}, 0\right)$
$N=4$	$\left\{\left(0, \frac{1}{2}, x_1^2, x_1^2+\frac{1}{2}\right) \vert x_1^2 \in \left[0, \frac{1}{2}\right]\right\}$
$N=5$	$\left(0, \frac{1}{5}, \frac{2}{5}, \frac{3}{5}, \frac{4}{5}\right)$, $\left(0, 0, 0, \frac{1}{2}, \frac{1}{2}\right)$, and $\left(0, \frac{1}{3}, \frac{2}{3}, 0, \frac{1}{2}\right)$
$N=6$	$\left\{\left(0, \frac{1}{2}, x_1^2, x_1^2+\frac{1}{2}, x_1^3, x_1^3+\frac{1}{2}\right) \vert x_1^2, x_1^3 \in \left[0, \frac{1}{2}\right]\right\}$, and $\left(0, \frac{1}{3}, \frac{2}{3}, 0, \frac{1}{3}, \frac{2}{3}\right)$
$N=7$	$\left(0, \frac{1}{7}, \frac{2}{7}, \frac{3}{7}, \frac{4}{7}, \frac{5}{7}, \frac{6}{7}\right)$, $\left(0, 0, 0, 0, \frac{1}{2}, \frac{1}{2}, \frac{1}{2}\right)$, $\left(0, \frac{1}{5}, \frac{2}{5}, \frac{3}{5}, \frac{4}{5}, 0, \frac{1}{2}\right)$, $\left(0, \frac{1}{3}, \frac{2}{3}, 0, \frac{1}{2}, 0, \frac{1}{2}\right)$, and $\left(0, \frac{1}{3}, \frac{2}{3}, 0, \frac{1}{2}, \frac{1}{3}, \frac{5}{6}\right)$
$N=8$	$\left\{\left(0, \frac{1}{2}, x_1^2, x_1^2+\frac{1}{2}, x_1^3, x_1^3+\frac{1}{2}, x_1^4, x_1^4+\frac{1}{2}\right) \vert x_1^2, x_1^3, x_1^4 \in \left[0, \frac{1}{2}\right]\right\}$, and $\left(0, \frac{1}{2}, 0, \frac{1}{3}, \frac{2}{3}, 0, \frac{1}{3}, \frac{2}{3}\right)$
$N=9$	$\left(0, \frac{1}{9}, \frac{2}{9}, \frac{3}{9}, \frac{4}{9}, \frac{5}{9}, \frac{6}{9}, \frac{7}{9}, \frac{8}{9}\right)$, $\left(0, 0, 0, 0, 0, \frac{1}{2}, \frac{1}{2}, \frac{1}{2}, \frac{1}{2}\right)$, $\left(0, \frac{1}{7}, \frac{2}{7}, \frac{3}{7}, \frac{4}{7}, \frac{5}{7}, \frac{6}{7}, 0, \frac{1}{2}\right)$, $\left(0, \frac{1}{5}, \frac{2}{5}, \frac{3}{5}, \frac{4}{5}, 0, \frac{1}{2}, 0, \frac{1}{2}\right)$, $\left(0, \frac{1}{3}, \frac{2}{3}, 0, \frac{1}{3}, \frac{2}{3}, 0, \frac{1}{3}, \frac{2}{3}\right)$, $\left(0, \frac{1}{2}, \frac{1}{3}, \frac{5}{6}, \frac{2}{3}, \frac{1}{6}, 0, \frac{1}{3}, \frac{2}{3}\right)$, and $\left(0, \frac{1}{5}, \frac{2}{5}, \frac{3}{5}, \frac{4}{5}, 0, \frac{1}{2}, \frac{1}{5}, \frac{7}{10}\right)$

Note: Without loss of generality, assuming that at least one firm locates at point 0

which implies that *LHS* must be a negative slope at the optimal position x_i^*. In fact, instead of calculating the complicated f.o.c. and s.o.c., *LHS* and *RHS* are sufficient to imply whether any combination of locations is an equilibrium. After some calculations, they obtained the following Table 2.1. The contribution of Gupta et al. (2004) is significant, because it demonstrated various types of equilibrium location patterns and also triggered many subsequent studies and further discussion.

Matsumura and Matsushima (2012) introduced discontinuous transportation costs to re-examine the various equilibriums of Gupta et al. (2004). They use the linear-quadratic transport cost function

$T(x, x_i) \equiv t \cdot d(x, x_i) + \tau \cdot d(x, x_i)^2$, $t > 0$, $\tau > -t$, where x is a point in the market, x_i is the location of firm i, d is the distance, and t and τ are the unit transport rates. When $\tau = 0$, then this model degenerates to Gupta et al. (2004). If $t \neq 0$, $\tau > (<)0$, then the transportation rate is convex (concave). They finally proved that for the various equilibrium location patterns in Gupta et al. (2004), as long as $\tau \neq 0$ (i.e., the transport cost function is non-linear), only symmetric equilibrium patterns will be sustained, and asymmetric equilibria will no longer be valid.

Matsumura et al. (2005) explored firms' locations in terms of the type of transport costs (convex, linear, and concave) and found that the Pal-type equilibrium always exists, while the Matsushima-type equilibrium can only be established under certain conditions.

Matsumura and Shimizu (2006) showed that the Pal (1998)-type equilibrium (maximal differentiation) always appears in equilibrium if the transport rate is non-decreasing with distance.

Chamorro-Rivas (2000b) assumed that each of the duopolists can choose to open up, at most, two plants and the location patterns can be either neighboring ((A,2) next to (A,1) and (B,2) next to (B,1)) or intertwined ((A,1) locates between (B,1) and (B,2)). They showed that for the equilibrium locations, all plants are equally spaced and paired in the market (Fig. 2.2).

Pal and Sarkar (2006) generalized the Chamorro-Rivas (2000b) model to a multiple (m) plants and multiple firms (n) and showed that all plants (and plants of each firm) being located equidistantly is a unique SPNE when $n = 2$ and $m = 1$ and it is very likely results in multiple SPNE locations for other cases. Moreover, the SPNE may not be unique, because firms may choose different numbers of plants.

Sun (2010) employed the directional constraint in a circular market with Cournot competition,[11] where firms can only choose one direction (clockwise or counter-clockwise) to serve the whole market. This assumption is justified in reality, because each shipping journey involves some fixed costs, which is double when the shipping job is done by two trucks

[11]The directional constraint can be found in earlier studies in Cancian et al. (1995) and Lai (2001), where firms only engage in location competition.

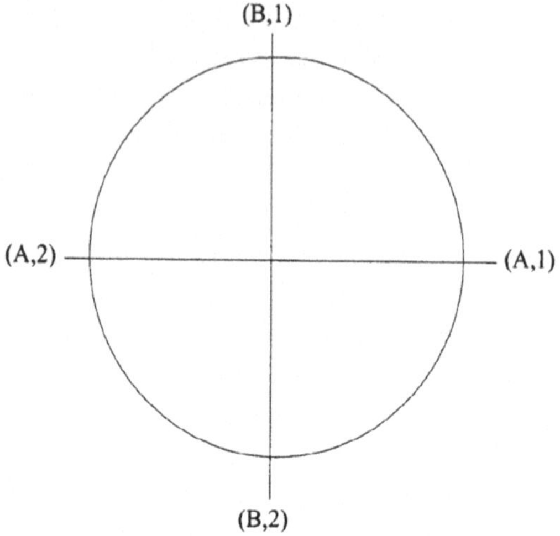

Fig. 2.2 The equilibrium location pattern in Chamorro-Rivas (2000b)

with different directions. Moreover, when two trucks deliver the products starting from the location of a firm with two opposite directions, the two trucks will meet at the point opposite to the firm's location, and they should return to the initial point with an empty load, which is a wasteful travel. He showed that when firms choose different directions, their locations will be at one point, while if they choose the same direction, then their locations will be the two endpoints of a diameter.

Cheng and Lai (2018) obtain the same location-direction equilibria with a different assumption from Sun (2010), instead of assuming a "first-entrant-takes-all" rule to capture the "one-house-one-outlet" phenomenon in water, electricity, natural gas, telephone, Internet, cable TV, and other service industries. Interestingly, their model is suitable for explaining the Treaty of Tordesillas in 1494 between Spain and Portugal, where both sides agreed to divide the newly discovered lands outside Europe along a meridian about 1770 km west of Cape Verde Island.

Yu (2007) showed that in a circular market with discrimination, the location equilibria in price competition are the same as those in quantity. That is, all the location equilibria in price competition, given the same number of firms, are identical to the equilibria in quantity competition.

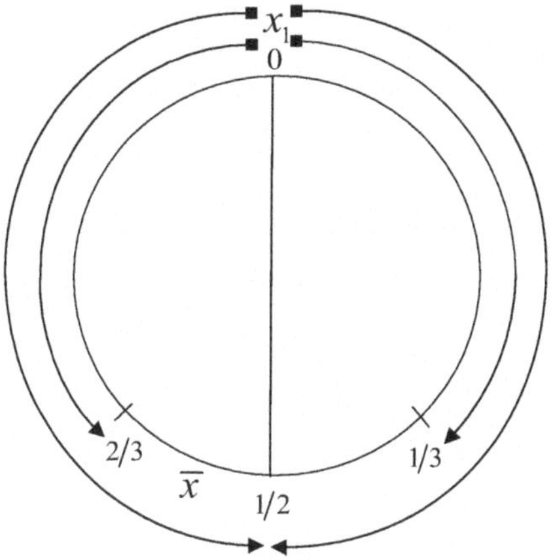

Fig. 2.3 Four dispatches with maximal service range $r = 1/3$ in Sun et al. (2017)

Matsushima and Matsumura (2003) proved that when there are n private firms and a public firm, the public firm locating at one endpoint of a diameter, while all the private firms agglomerate at the other end of this diameter, is a location equilibrium.

Sun et al. (2017) considered scenarios of Cournot competition in which the maximal service range of a truck is less than half of the perimeter of a circular market, and thus each of the duopoly firms should initiate more than two dispatches to serve the whole market. For example, supposing the maximal service range (r) is 1/3, a firm may either initiate four dispatches (Fig. 2.3) or three dispatches (Fig. 2.4) to serve the whole market. They found that when the fixed cost of a transportation vehicle is sufficiently low, there exists a unique outcome with the same location pattern as that in Pal (1998), and each firm delivers its products with four dispatches. When the fixed cost is sufficiently high, there exists a unique outcome such that firms' locations are less than the maximal difference, and each firm initiates three dispatches.

Guo and Lai (2019) analyzed the fully symmetric location equilibrium in two intersecting circular markets (see Fig. 2.5). Both circular markets are served by two homogenous firms which engage in Cournot competition at each point of these two circular markets. They showed that

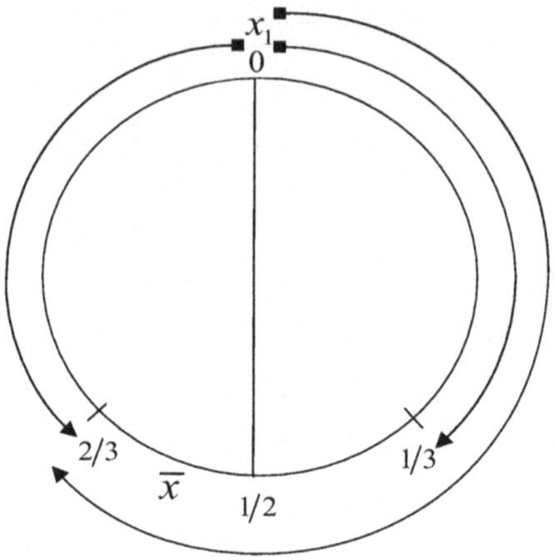

Fig. 2.4 Three dispatches with maximal service range $r = 1/3$ in Sun et al. (2017)

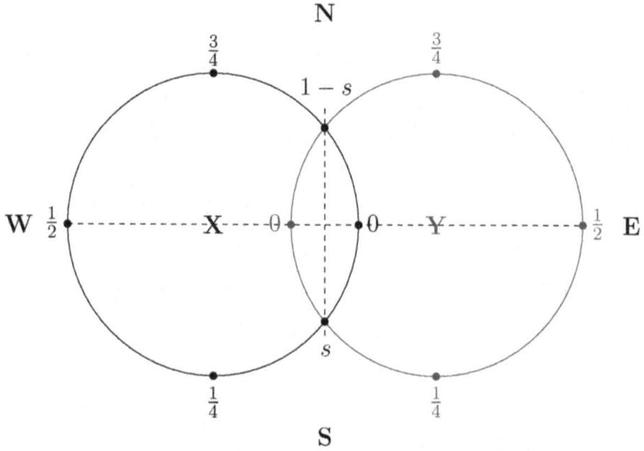

Fig. 2.5 Two intersecting circular markets in Guo and Lai (2019)

each firm locating at each of the intersecting points is the unique fully symmetric location equilibrium. The intuition of their result is clear: If a firm does not locate at an intersecting point, say $x_1 = 0$ for firm 1, then it should deliver its product to the ***Y*** market through the section $[0, s]$ in the ***X*** market, which produces no revenue and thus is a wasteful trip. Their model highlights the importance of traffic hubs, which can attract firms.

2.2.3 Linear Plus Circular Markets

Since the equilibrium location pattern in a linear market is quite different from that in a circular market, what is the location pattern if these two types of markets are combined? Ebina et al. (2011) developed a very smart method to integrate circular and linear markets. They assumed that there is a circular market with a unit length the same as Pal (1998). When products are shipped through the "0" point, an additional cost of $\beta \in [0, 1]$ is generated. This cost can be seen as a tariff; when $\beta = 0$, the model degenerates to Pal (1998). When β is large enough, the vendor will never pass through the "0" point, which is equivalent to degenerating to a linear model like Anderson and Neven (1991). They proved that when β is small or large, the equilibrium location patterns are unique, but when β is in the middle range, there exist multiple location patterns, and in a large part of the range of β, the location equilibrium is concentrated at the market center, while the dispersed location pattern is valid only when $\beta = 0$. Therefore, they believed that some asymmetric location patterns in a circular market are balanced on a knife's edge (i.e., unlikely to appear or not easily sustained).

In addition, Guo and Lai (2015) combined a linear market and a circular market such that a linear main street connects to an outer belt road. In particular, they allowed the main street to have a higher demand density than that of the outer belt road. When the demand in all markets is identical, the firms will locate at the two ends of the main street, which is the same as the result of Pal (1998), but as the demand density of the main street increases, the equilibrium locations gradually move toward the center of the main street to form results close (or equivalent) to Anderson and Neven (1991) (Fig. 2.6).

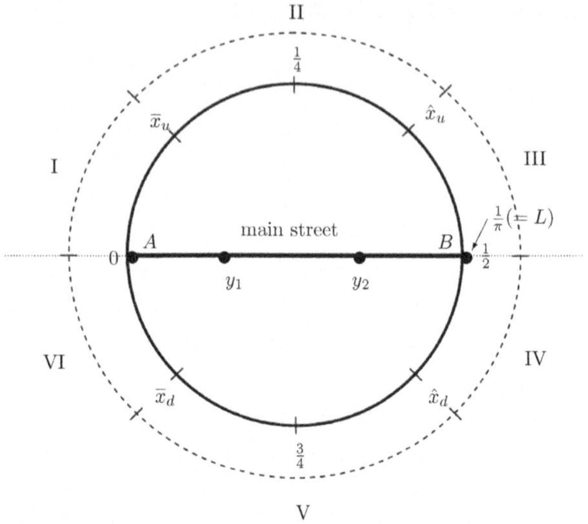

Fig. 2.6 A linear-circular market in Guo and Lai (2015)

2.3 Conclusions

Spatial Cournot competition with endogenous firms' locations of Hamilton et al. (1989) and Anderson and Neven (1991) is one of the literature streams avoiding the undercutting trap in Hotelling (1929). This stream is more successful than other attempts in that most equilibrium patterns in spatial Cournot models are very intuitive and fit the real-world phenomenon, namely, that all firms will agglomerate at the market center in most linear market, a fact observed by Harold Hotelling. In this chapter, the development of spatial Cournot competition in the past 30 years was analyzed along the two major axes of the linear market and the circular market (see Fig. 2.7). We believe that spatial Cournot competition will continue to develop and match the reality in the future.

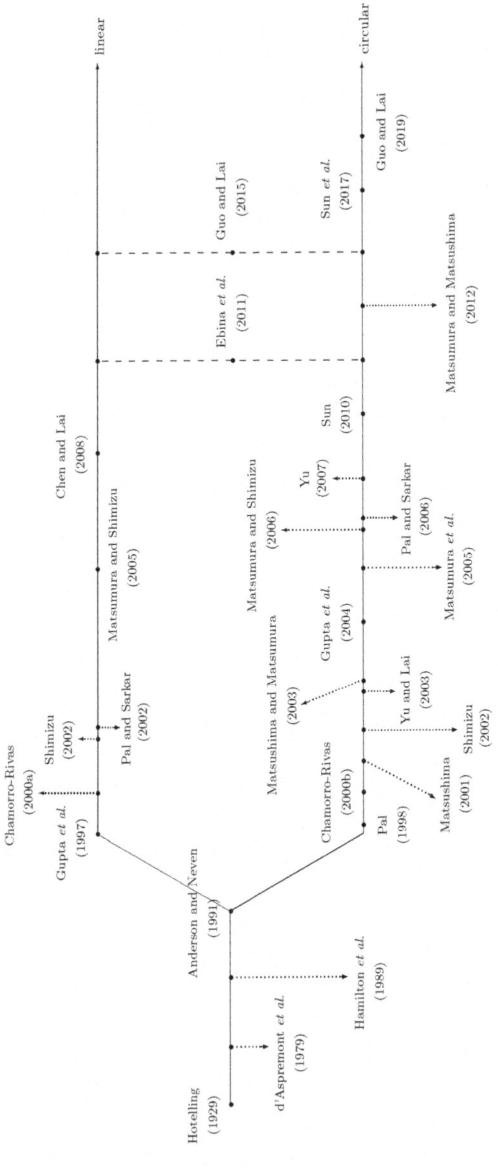

Fig. 2.7 Map of the spatial Cournot competition literature

References

Anderson, S. P. (1988). Equilibrium Existence in the Linear Model of Spatial Competition. *Economica, 55*, 479–491.

Anderson, S. P., & Neven, D. (1991). Cournot Competition Yields Spatial Agglomeration. *International Economic Review, 32*, 793–808.

Cancian, M., Bills, A., & Bergstrom, T. (1995). Hotelling Location Problems with Directional Constraints: An Application to Television News Scheduling. *Journal of Industrial Economics, 43*, 121–124.

Chamorro-Rivas, J.-M. (2000a). Spatial Dispersion in Cournot Competition. *Spanish Economic Review, 2*, 145–152.

Chamorro-Rivas, J.-M. (2000b). Plant Proliferation in a Spatial Model of Cournot Competition. *Regional Science and Urban Economics, 30*, 507–518.

Chen, C. S., & Lai, F.-C. (2008). Location Choice and Optimal Zoning under Cournot Competition. *Regional Science and Urban Economics, 38*, 119–126.

Cheng, Y. C., & Lai, F.-C. (2018). Spatial Competition in a Circular Market with Delivery Direction Choice. *Revista Portuguesa de Estudos Regionais (Portuguese Review of Regional Studies), 49*, 7–21.

Christaller, W. (1933). *Die zentralen Orte in Süddeutschland.* Translated from German by C.W. Baskin, 1966, *The Central Places of Southern Germany.* Englewood Cliffs, NJ: Prentice-Hall.

D'Aspremont, C., Gabszwicz, J., & Thisse, J.-F. (1979). On Hotelling's Stability in Competition. *Econometrica, 47*, 1145–1150.

Downs, A. (1957). *An Economic Theory of Democracy.* New York: Harper and Row.

Ebina, T., Matsumura, T., & Shimizu, D. (2011). Spatial Cournot Equilibria in a Quasi-Linear City. *Papers in Regional Science, 90*, 613–628.

Graitson, D. (1980). On Hotelling's Stability in Competition Again. *Economics Letters, 6*, 1–6.

Greenhut, J., & Greenhut, M. L. (1975). Spatial Price Discrimination, Competition and Locational Effects. *Economica, 42*, 401–419.

Greenhut, M. L., & Ohta, H. (1975). *Theory of Spatial Pricing and Market Areas.* Durham: Duke University Press.

Greenhut, M. L., Norman, G., & Hung, C. S. (1987). *The Economics of Imperfect Competition: A Spatial Approach.* Cambridge: Cambridge University Press.

Guo, W.-C., & Lai, F.-C. (2015). Spatial Cournot Competition in a Linear-Circular Market. *The Annals of Regional Science, 54*, 819–834.

Guo, W.-C., & Lai, F.-C. 2019. Spatial *Cournot Competition in Two Intersecting Circular Markets*. Working Paper.

Gupta, B., Pal, D., & Sarkar, J. (1997). Spatial Cournot Competition and Agglomeration in a Model of Location Choice. *Regional Science and Urban Economics, 27*, 261–282.

Gupta, B., Pal, D., & Heywood, J. (2003). *Where to Locate in a Circular City?* Working Paper. University of Cincinnati, Cincinnati, OH, USA.

Gupta, B., Lai, F.-C., Pal, D., Sarkar, J., & Yu, C.-M. (2004). Where to Locate in a Circular City? *International Journal of Industry Organization, 22*, 759–782.

Hamilton, J. H., Thisse, J.-F., & Weskamp, A. (1989). Spatial Discrimination: Bertrand vs. Cournot in a Model of Location Choice. *Regional Science and Urban Economics, 19*, 87–102.

Hotelling, H. (1929). Stability in Competition. *Economic Journal, 39*, 41–57.

Lai, F.-C. (2001). Sequential Locations in Directional Markets. *Regional Science and Urban Economics, 31*, 535–546.

Lerner, A., & Singer, H. (1937). Some Notes on Duopoly and Spatial Competition. *Journal of Political Economy, 45*, 145–186.

Matsumura, T., & Matsushima, N. (2012). Spatial Cournot Competition and Transportation Costs in a Circular City. *Annals of Regional Science, 48*, 33–44.

Matsumura, T., & Shimizu, D. (2005). Spatial Cournot Competition and Economic Welfare: A Note. *Regional Science and Urban Economics, 35*, 658–670.

Matsumura, T., & Shimizu, D. (2006). Cournot and Bertrand in Shipping Models with Circular Markets. *Papers in Regional Science, 85*, 585–598.

Matsumura, T., Ohkawa, T., & Shimizu, D. (2005). Partial Agglomeration or Dispersion in Spatial Cournot Competition. *Southern Economic Journal, 72*, 224–235.

Matsushima, N. (2001). Cournot Competition and Spatial Agglomeration Revisited. *Economics Letters, 73*, 175–177.

Matsushima, N., & Matsumura, T. (2003). Mixed Oligopoly and Spatial Agglomeration. *Canadian Journal of Economics/Revue canadienne d'Economique, 36*, 62–87.

Mayer, T. (2000). Spatial Cournot Competition and Heterogenous Production Costs Across Locations. *Regional Science and Urban Economics, 30*, 325–352.

Norman, G. (1981). Spatial Competition and Spatial Price Discrimination. *Review of Economic Studies, 48*, 97–111.

Ohta, H. (1988). *Spatial Price Theory of Imperfect Competition*. Austin, TX: Texas A&M University Press.

Osborne, M. J., & Pitchik, C. (1987). Equilibrium in Hotelling's Model of Spatial Competition. *Econometrica, 55*, 911–922.

Pal, D. (1998). Does Cournot Competition Yield Spatial Agglomeration? *Economics Letters, 60*, 49–53.

Pal, D., & Sarkar, J. (2002). Spatial Competition among Multi-Store Firms. *International Journal of Industrial Organization, 20*, 163–190.

Pal, D., & Sarkar, J. (2006). Spatial Cournot Competition Among Multi-Plant Firms in a Circular City. *Southern Economic Association, 73*, 246–258.

Ricardo, D. (1817). *On the Principles of Political Economy and Taxation*. London: John Murray, Albemarle-Street.

Shimizu, D. (2002). Product Differentiation in Spatial Cournot Markets. *Economics Letters, 76*, 317–322.

Smithies, A. (1941). Optimum Location in Spatial Competition. *Journal of Political Economy, 49*, 423–439.

Sun, C.-H. (2010). Spatial Cournot Competition in a Circular City with Directional Delivery Constraints. *Annals of Regional Science, 45*, 273–289.

Sun, C.-H., Tsai, J.-F., & Lai, F.-C. (2017). Spatial Cournot Competition in a Circular City with More Than Two Dispatches. *Japanese Economic Review, 68*, 413–442.

Vogel, J. (2008). Spatial Competition with Heterogeneous Firms. *Journal of Political Economy, 116*, 423–466.

Von Thünen, J. H. (1826). *Der Isolierte Staat in Beziehung auf Landtschaft under Nationalökonomie*, Jena, G. Fischer: Hamburg. English translation by C. M. Wartenberg, *Von Thunen's Isolated State*. Oxford: Pergamon Press, 1966.

Weber, A. (1909). *Über den Standort der Industrie*, translated by Friedrich. C.J, 1929, *Theory of the Location of Industries*. Chicago: The University of Chicago Press.

Yu, C.-M. (2007). Price and Quantity Competition Yield the Same Location Equilibria in a Circular Market. *Papers in Regional Science, 86*, 643–655.

Yu, C.-M., & Lai, F.-C. (2003a). Cournot Competition in Spatial Markets: Some Further Results. *Papers in Regional Science, 82*, 569–580.

Yu, C.-M., & Lai, F.-C. (2003b). *Cournot Competition Yields Spatial Avoiding Competition in Groups*. Working Paper. National Taipei University, Taipei 104, Taiwan.

3

Models of Spatial Competition: A Critical 2012–2018 Update

Ricardo Biscaia and Isabel Mota

3.1 Introduction

Spatial competition studies the locational interdependence among economic agents. One of the most prominent models on the topic is Hotelling (1929), and the model that was proposed in the paper led to a significant number of papers, whose roots are clearly in that seminal paper. In a previous paper (Biscaia and Mota 2013), the authors analyze the research in the field, focusing on the type of strategy (price vs.

R. Biscaia
CIPES – Centre for Research in Higher Education Policies, Rua Primeiro de Dezembro, Matosinhos, Portugal

I. Mota (✉)
Faculdade de Economia, Universidade do Porto, Rua Dr. Roberto Frias, Porto, Portugal

CEF.UP – Centre for Economics and Finance at University of Porto, Rua Dr. Roberto Frias, Porto, Portugal
e-mail: imota@fep.up.pt

S. Colombo (ed.), *Spatial Economics Volume I*,
https://doi.org/10.1007/978-3-030-40098-9_3

quantity competition), market (linear vs. circular), costs (production or transportation), and information (complete vs. incomplete) and its effects over the location equilibria. The authors concluded, among other things, that (1) there is a growing number of papers in the field; (2) papers on spatial competition were published in relevant journals, both in more specific outlets (industrial organization and regional economics) as well as in more general economics journals; and (3) the future of the field would depend on the capacity of researchers to find more interesting and innovative ways of studying spatial competition.

This paper extends the previous bibliometric study, including the articles from 2012 to 2018. A comparative analysis follows, focusing, firstly, on the type of journals that have been accepting papers from the field, to check whether there has been a change in terms of quality (measured by impact factor) or journal area (industrial organization, regional economics, or general economics) in these years, and, secondly, on a discussion on whether the topic is expanding, declining, or changing based on the results.

Afterward, the article proceeds by providing a classification of the identified papers according to the sub-topic of Hotelling that these articles are exploring. With that information, the reader can identify easily how the ideas in the field are evolving. We propose to separate the papers according to groups of assumptions, namely, whether the linear city is used in a Bertrand or Cournot setting, whether there is mill of delivered pricing, the number of firms in the market, whether there is perfect information, and whether there is an interesting novelty within the field. Then, and in order to study network structures between researchers in spatial competition, the paper analyzes the co-authorships by using social network analysis. The SNA allows the identification of cohesive subgroups of agents that interact with each other. First, a graph is built, considering the authors as nodes and the ties as co-authorships. Then, cohesive subgroups of authors are identified.

We conclude with a summary of results and expressing the belief that the paper will provide a very useful tool for those more and less experienced in the topic to conduct their research on Hotelling.

3.2 The Critical Update 2012–2018—A Bibliometric Exercise

The bibliometric exercise we designed has the goal of providing a simple analysis on the evolution of the field, without being too exhaustive. We aim at identifying whether the number of articles has increased, whether the publications in the field are being published in journal with high impact and in which type of journals, and which authors seem to be more relevant recently. Any reader will identify immediately if the field of spatial competition *à la* Hotelling is expanding or declining, to which journals they might submit articles on the field, and which are the most relevant authors on its recent history.

Our bibliometric analysis is based in SCOPUS. We conducted the search as similar as possible to Biscaia and Mota (2013) in order to make the results a natural continuation of that paper. Therefore, we sought the database for the words "Hotelling" or "spatial competition" on the article titles, abstracts, and keywords. This means that only one of the expressions is necessary for the paper to be included in the list. We believe these expressions will naturally encompass all papers of spatial competition based on Hotelling. Out of the results, we only considered those labeled by SCOPUS as "article" or "review," and we also considered only those with a year of publication of 2012 and so forth. We excluded those of 2019, in order to obtain a stable list of publications.

This first search provided us with 1329 publications. However, as in Biscaia and Mota (2013), we inspected every title and abstract in order to see if the paper qualified as a linear-city Hotelling related. This problem arises because Harold Hotelling is responsible for various important discoveries: There is a statistical test named after Hotelling, the Hotelling T-squared; in the literature of exhaustible resources, there is the "Hotelling rule"; and in microeconomics, there is the "Hotelling's lemma"; therefore, many articles were completely unrelated with spatial competition. After our inspection, we identified 330 articles on the topic. This is the final list of articles that we consider throughout all the analysis.

We start by providing an evolution on the number of papers per year in our list. Figure 3.1 shows these numbers, adding with information from

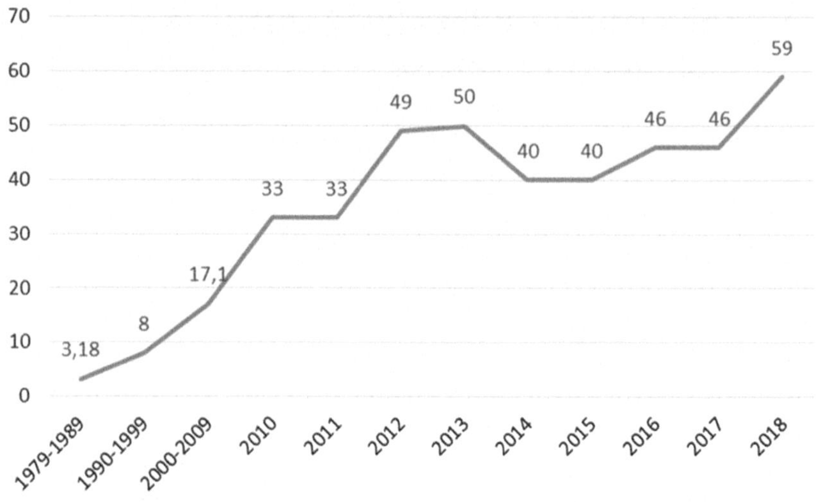

Fig. 3.1 Average number of articles per year in the field

Biscaia and Mota (2013). From the figure, the main conclusion is that the number of articles is increasing and keeps the trend that was observed between 1979 and 2011. In 2012–2013, there seems to be an abnormal increase in the number of papers, as well as in 2018. Still, the 00s decade will apparently have 1.5 times more papers than the previous decade.

While the suggested increase in the 80s and 90s might have come from groundbreaking papers at the time, such as d'Aspremont et al. (1979) and Anderson and Neven (1991), this increase in the most recent years cannot be dissociated with the increasing pressure for researchers to obtain publications, as well as the increase in the number of journals included in these databases. Furthermore, spatial competition models *à la* Hotelling are not used solely to understand location decisions of agents, but these models are also used as a building block for product differentiation in industrial economics, as location itself in regional studies, or to represent voters' preferences in the context of elections in political science.

In terms of the authors that have been publishing more on the topic during these years, we present Tables 3.1 and 3.2. Authors on Table 3.1 account for 10% of the publications in the topic during the 2012–2018 period; therefore, and naturally, all the articles are spread between a

Table 3.1 Most frequent authors on the 2012–2018 period

Author	Number of articles	Citations per paper
Dimitrios **Xefteris**	9	4.88
Fu-Chuan **Lai**	7	1
Noriaki **Matsushima**	6	6.5
Juan Carlos **Bárcena-Ruiz**	4	3.25
F. Javier **Casado-Izaga**	4	3.25
Wen-Chung **Guo**	4	1
Hamid **Hamoudi**	4	4.75
Toshihiro **Matsumura**	4	7.25
Luigi **Siciliani**	4	6.75
Odd Rune **Straume**	4	6.75

Citations as of 7 August 2019

Table 3.2 Most frequent authors on the 1979–2018 period

Author	Number of articles	Citations per paper
Noriaki **Matsushima**	13	20
Stefano **Colombo**	12	4.42
Fu-Chuan **Lai**	11	9.63
Ralph M. **Braid**	10	5.70
Toshihiro **Matsumura**	9	20.56
Jacques-François **Thisse**	9	57
Dimitrios **Xefteris**	9	4.9
Hamid **Hamoudi**	8	7.5
Odd Rune **Straume**	8	17
Luca **Lambertini**	7	11.57
Debashis **Pal**	7	38

Citations as of 7 August 2019

significant number of authors. The articles on the list have 707 mentions, so the average number of authors per article is 2.14. Of the 707 mentions referenced in the articles, 559 correspond to unique authors.

Out of the most recent articles, the authors with the most papers on the topic are Dimitrios Xefteris, Fu-Chuan Lai, and Noriaki Matsushima. In terms of citations per paper, and given that these papers have at most 7 years, there are no authors (out of this top) with more than 10 citations per paper, being Toshihiro Matsumura, Luigi Siciliani, and Odd Rune Straume those with most citations per article. When comparing the subsample of 2012–2018 with the combined lists forming 1979–2018, we

Table 3.3 Distribution of papers according to the continent of the authors

Continent	1979–2011 (Biscaia and Mota 2013)	2012–2018
Europe	46.86%	42.50%
Asia	14.98%	33.86%
North America	34.30%	18.18%
Other	3.86%	5.45%

can see that five authors (Stefano Colombo, Ralph Braid, Jacques Thisse, Luca Lambertini, and Debashis Pal) are the authors that seem to have published more in the past, but do not make it to the last 7 years' list, indicating that some of the references in the past are naturally being replaced by authors that are publishing more recently.

Table 3.3 presents the geographical distribution of the countries that are associated with the authors for each paper. The results present an important change compared to the results in Biscaia and Mota (2013), as the Asian continent gained prominence, apparently at the expense of the North American continent. Still, 42.5% of the papers had a European author, with Europe being the continent with most papers on the field.

In terms of the journals in which these articles are published, as expected, we see a significant variety of journals accepting articles on spatial competition *à la* Hotelling. Table 3.4 reveals the most frequent journals, as well as their 5-year impact factor for 2018.

As expected, we can see that most journals belong to the economics field. However, the most dominant types of journal are the ones belonging to economics in general and to regional and urban economics. With lower frequency, we find journals of industrial economics, game theory, and mathematics. It is very interesting to note that such a specific topic is still penetrating on general journals in economics. Additionally, one can see that journals with the short Paper format, such as *Economics Letters, Economics Bulletin, Bulletin of Economic Research*, and *Letters in Spatial and Resource Sciences*, are still very relevant for the field.

When comparing the results with the ones obtained in Biscaia and Mota (2013), there is a striking difference. In the 352 papers for 1979–2011, the top three journals (*Regional Science and Urban Economics, Economics Letters, International Journal of Industrial Organization* (IJIO)) had 109 articles, accounting for nearly a third of the field. Now, the

Table 3.4 Top journals in spatial competition—2012–2018

Journal	Number of articles	% of articles	5-year impact factor
Economics Letters	16	4.85	1.082
Annals of Regional Science	10	3.03	1.372
Journal of Economics –Zeitschrift Fur Nationalokonomie	10	3.03	1.24
Papers in Regional Science	10	3.03	1.992
Regional Science and Urban Economics	10	3.03	2.36
Games and Economic Behavior	9	2.73	1.285
Xitong Gongcheng Lilun Yu Shijian—System Engineering Theory and Practice	9	2.73	N.A.
Economics Bulletin	7	2.12	N.A.
Journal of Economics and Management Strategy	7	2.12	1.719
Economic Modelling	6	1.82	2.188
Information Economics and Policy	5	1.52	1.626
International Journal of Industrial Organization	5	1.52	1.452
B. E. Journal of Economic Analysis and Policy	4	1.21	0.556
European Journal of Operational Research	4	1.21	4.283
International Journal of Production Economics	4	1.21	5.631
Journal of Economic Behavior and Organization	4	1.21	2.261
Journal of Interdisciplinary Mathematics	4	1.21	N.A.
Management Science	4	1.21	5.555
Bulletin of Economic Research	3	0.91	0.523
International Journal of Game Theory	3	0.91	0.759
Journal of Applied Mathematics	3	0.91	N.A.
Journal of Economic Theory	3	0.91	1.458
Journal of Industrial Economics	3	0.91	1.514
Journal of Industry Competition and Trade	3	0.91	N.A.
Journal of Urban Economics	3	0.91	3.288
Letters in Spatial and Resource Sciences	3	0.91	N.A.
Managerial and Decision Economics	3	0.91	N.C.
Studies in Microeconomics	3	0.91	N.A.

N.A. Not available. The journal is not indexed in Thomson Reuters

N.C. Not calculated. The journal has not been indexed in Thomson Reuters for more than 5 years

articles are way more dispersed into different journals. We believe that this is related to three reasons: firstly, the increasing pressure to publish and the appearance of more journals in databases, such as SCOPUS, leading the researchers to invest in more diverse journals; secondly, a probable shift of orientation in journals and in scientific domains, which now are specializing less in a given subfield, in this case, of industrial economics and regional and urban economics; and, thirdly, the increase of publications coming from Asian authors (and subsequent decrease in publications from North Americans) might have dictated a different publication pattern for the field.

Regarding the impact factors of the journals where the articles were published, most journals have an impact factor higher than one, indicating that the articles in the field are still being published regularly in important outlets in the scientific community.

To conclude on this section, it can be seen that the contribution of Hotelling and its successors has withstood the test of time. The publications on the work of Hotelling have been increasing, span along different types of subareas of knowledge, and are published on outlets with impact in the scientific community. As citations are never decreasing as time passes, it is unfair to compare the relevance of the articles on the topic for 2012–2019 with the predecessors from 1979 to 2011. However, analyzing the journals in which these articles are published, we see that they are important journals in the field of economics, and therefore we can expect a similar relevance for these outlets. We can also see an important shift in terms of the nationality of authorships for these articles, with the emergence of China (with 76 articles with at least one Chinese author out of the 330, compared to 7 articles in 1979–2011) and the decline of the USA and Canada (with 80 articles in 2012–2018, compared to 147 articles in 1979–2011) changing significantly the mapping for the field.

3.3 Classification of the Papers

In this section, we propose to provide a simple classification of the articles based on an adaptation of the theoretical framework proposed in Biscaia and Mota (2013). This classification has a goal of indicating the reader what are the current trends in the field in terms of the theoretical approaches of the articles.

The roadmap was the following. Firstly, we identified whether the article attempted on explaining firms' location in a linear city, or studied the circular city of Salop (1979). In both of these cases, we labeled the papers as "Hotelling," meaning that the paper is in line with pure Hotelling-Salop approaches. If the paper did not attempt to explain location, but used the linear city for other purposes—generally as a building block for the understanding of other phenomena—we identified those purposes, by "distance" when geographical distance was implied, according to regional and urban economics or international economics; "product choice" when a preference continuum was implied, as in industrial organization; and "political spectrum" when the linear city was used as left-right spectrum in the line of Downs (1957).

Secondly, if the article follows a classical Hotelling approach as defined in the previous step, it is classified according to the assumptions that are used in its theoretical approach. The classifications relate to (1) price or quantity competition, (2) mill or uniform delivered pricing or pricing discrimination, (3) homogeneous or heterogeneous (other than location) product, (4) linear or quadratic transportation costs, (5) pure or mixed strategies, (6) two or more than two firms, and (7) linear, circular, or "more complex" market.

Thirdly, irrespectively of the paper, we classified according to what we thought was the main theme or main assumption of the paper. For each paper, we allowed a maximum of two expressions related to its main theme. For instance, such an expression could be "mixed duopolies" or "two-sided markets." As setting up new expressions is far from consensual and a very subjective task, we believe that this procedure unfolded into a natural and very far from random classification as the work progressed. This classification will help us signal any new tendencies that can be verified in the topic and could help clarifying the diversity of journals result that we obtained while analyzing Table 3.4.

Our first important barrier was the access to the papers in the list. Out of 330, we were unable to access 48 papers, meaning we only analyzed 282 papers. There is a clear pattern in the missings, as the years of 2018 and 2017 have double the missings per year compared to the period of 2012–2016. This is surely related with the authorship of the articles and their outlets, as most of the missings come from Chinese authors, whose publications rose more recently in the field.

Then, out of the 282 papers that were analyzed, we concluded that 22 of those—while falling into our bibliometric review and most of them citing the original paper of Hotelling—did not use the framework of Hotelling by any means. We classified those as "Does not use Hotelling". We decided not to remove them from the analysis in Sect. 3.2 for two reasons: firstly, to maintain comparability between this analysis and the one from Biscaia and Mota (2013), which did not have a full paper inspection like in this article; and, secondly, since we could not have access to all of the full papers that were analyzed in this article, removing these 22 non-Hotelling without having the chance of analyzing the entire list could have manipulated the results in Sect. 3.2, under- or over-representing some journals, countries, and authors. However, given that more than 90% of the analyzed papers in our list related to Hotelling, at the same time we obtained the confirmation that our bibliometric choice in SCOPUS was correct, even for the procedure that was used 7 years ago.

Table 3.5 provides the results per building block. As it can be calculated, 42% of the total of the articles analyzed were classified as "Hotelling," meaning that the nature of the paper was to find the location/product choice of firms within the linear city—or were studies on the circular city of Salop. This indicates that location is still an important motivation to address the legacy of Hotelling, as it was the same motivation Hotelling had when the 90-year-old article was written. Most interestingly, we can see that this motivation seems to be fading recently. In 2012 and 2013, a higher number of papers were concerned with location, while from 2014 onward, the relative importance of those "Hotelling" articles compared to the building blocks for distance, product choice, and political spectrum gained importance. This is probably a trend that can be expected in the future. As the legacy of Hotelling is being used in more fields, it can be expected that the linear city is more used as a building block for a number of issues, rather than being used to explain location itself.

Table 3.5 Distribution of papers per year and per building block—2012–2018

	Hotelling	Distance	Product choice	Political spectrum
Total	110	47	75	27
2018	16	9	16	6
2017	13	8	10	4
2016	13	8	13	1
2015	11	6	10	3
2014	10	8	9	6
2013	27	4	9	3
2012	20	4	8	4

Table 3.6 Distribution of papers according to their basic assumptions—2012–2018

Variable of competition		**Firms**		**Transportation costs**	
Price	Quantity	Homogeneous	Heterogeneous	Linear	Quadratic
96	6	85	21	54	55
Strategic profiles		**Timing**		**Number of firms**	
Pure	Mixed	Simultaneous	Sequential	Two	More than 2
103	2	96	15	88	21
Pricing			**Market**		
Mill	Uniform delivery	Discrimination	Linear	Circular	More complex
94	7	8	80	17	9
Pattern 1			**Pattern 2**		
16			28		

Pattern 1—price competition, homogeneous firms, linear transportation costs, pure strategies, simultaneous game, two firms, mill pricing, linear market; pattern 2—same as pattern 1, with quadratic transportation costs instead of linear

Table 3.6 refers to the distribution of articles according to the main assumptions that were used in constructing the location game. Remember that only the articles that were classified as Hotelling as in Table 3.5 were the ones subject to this classification. Additionally, some articles might have been classified in more than one category—say, it is relatively typical that articles addressing the location issue of "more than two firms" dedicate subsections to the two-firm case. There were also a few articles that were not classified because these were reviews, addendums, or very small notes.

According to our classification, a great number of articles are dealing with price competition, with pure strategy profiles, with simultaneous timing in all of the variables (which are sequentially treated in the typical location-price game), and with two firms and using homogeneous firms and mill pricing in a linear market setting. The results are unsurprising, since these assumptions constitute the base setting for a Hotelling (1929) or d'Aspremont et al. (1979) location and price model. In terms of changing the original assumptions of these models, the assumptions that seem to be broken more often are the firm homogeneity, the number of firms, and the linear nature of the market. Of course, our work is limited in the sense that some novelties that were introduced by the scientists might not have been captured by our proposal of classification. Some other assumptions have certainly been broken (e.g., imperfect information, payoff function of firms, R&D investments), and this should be taken into account.

In order to assess if researchers still use the exact same main assumptions as in Hotelling (1929) and d'Aspremont et al. (1979), we computed the number of articles that used exactly the assumptions as in these models and labeled them pattern 1 and pattern 2. 16 articles used the configuration in pattern 1; and 28 articles used pattern 2. This reveals that while most of the articles use these main assumptions, there are not many articles that use their entire set, meaning that, as expected, most articles at least change one of these assumptions. This result also means that these 16 plus 28 articles are certainly changing something else other than the assumptions we proposed for our classifications. Perhaps we can weakly conclude that more drastic changes are done in pattern 2 setting rather than in pattern 1 setting. That is, the quadratic transportation cost functions seem to be more prone to generate articles with significant novelties than the articles using linear transportation costs.

We have not mentioned the linear versus quadratic transportation cost issue yet. The articles are divided almost equally between these two sets of assumptions. This shows that the path-breaking discovery of d'Aspremont et al. (1979) stood the test of time and really changed the paradigm regarding the modeling strategies on the Hotelling's original linear transportation costs proposal.

Finally, we present the count of "main themes" that we identified in the papers. Since we ended up choosing 88 unique main themes, we only address those that were chosen more than seven times. These are presented in Table 3.7. The most frequent themes we identified were

Table 3.7 Division of articles according to their proposed main theme—2012–2018

Theme	Number of articles	Average year
Hotelling-Downs model	26	2015.15
Heterogeneous firms	18	2014.89
Network effects	17	2015.24
Mixed duopoly	16	2015.75
Product quality	15	2014.67
Imperfect information	15	2014.8
Graphs	10	2015.4
Variable transportation costs	10	2013.7
Repeated purchase	9	2016.67
Game theory	9	2015.89
Entry	8	2013.88
Innovation	8	2014.5
Multiple markets	8	2014.5
Price discrimination	7	2015.86
International economics	7	2013.57
E-commerce	7	2014.71
Heterogeneous consumers	7	2014.57
Advertising	7	2014.29
Dynamic markets	7	2013.86
Outside goods	7	2014.57
Vertical markets	7	2014

the adaptations of the Hotelling line toward the political spectrum: the Hotelling-Downs model. Eighteen articles focused mainly on attributing different characteristics to firms, either by providing advantages in costs or by allowing some firms to provide different types of products. A relatively recent wave is on network effects: purchasers might get extra utility if many other purchasers bought the same good. In 16 articles, some firms would be concerned with maximizing social welfare (public firms), while others would compete trying to maximize their profit (private firms), with this being a very recent approach, on average.

Out of these many themes, the one used in older years seems to be international economics (when the line is used to represent countries and one firm competing in each country, with the goal of understanding whether free trade is better than autarchy), while the most recent topic seems to be game theory (articles on Hotelling that were overly concerned with general equilibrium properties instead of analyzing the location/price/quantity results).

3.4 Co-authorship Patterns: A Social Network Analysis

In order to identify communication and network structures between researchers on spatial competition since 2012, this study analyzes the co-authorship patterns by using social network analysis. Social network analysis (SNA) can be simply described as a set of methods such as sociometrics and graphs for the analysis of social structures (de Nooy et al. 2011).

We start by excluding papers with only one author, as they do not allow analyzing co-authorships. With a total number of 234 papers, we then begin matching nodes to researchers and ties to co-authorships, thus forming a graph (using the Pajek 5.08 software). Based on the database, our network has 503 nodes (authors) and 565 ties (co-authorships) (Fig.3.2).

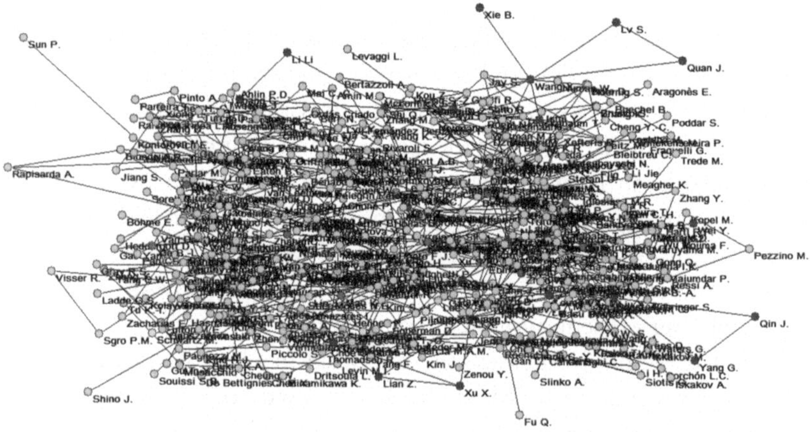

Fig. 3.2 Co-authorship networks in spatial competition, 2012–2018

Our network comprises mainly papers with 2 authors (124) and 3 authors (83), and for that reason, it has a low average degree, that is, the number of ties compared to the number of nodes is 2.24. We then use Pajek tools to identify the subnetworks that are denser, that is, with at least eight nodes. The four subnetworks are represented in Fig. 3.3:

We also calculate some statistical measures for each subnetwork, described in Table 3.8. The degree centralization measures the number of each node's adjacent edges (Csardi 2014). So, the nodes with higher degree are more central. Conversely, the betweenness centralization quantifies the number of times a node acts as a bridge along the shortest path between two other nodes (Csardi 2014).

Subnetworks A and C are similar, with nine authors each and an average degree of 3.33 and 3.11, respectively. In subnetwork A, Hua Zhao plays a crucial role: it is the author with more direct links (degree centralization), as well as the one with the most intermediation capacity (betweenness centralization) in this network. In subnetwork B, Noriaki Matsushima is the most central node, with the highest degree, closeness, and betweenness centralization measures. Non-surprisingly, this is one of the leading authors previously identified. However, this is the subnetwork with the lowest average degree. In subnetwork C, the scenario is not exactly the same: Zheng Wang is the author with higher degree centralization, but the one with higher betweenness is Changxin Liu. Finally, in subnetwork D, the author with more direct links is Feng Li. However, the one with higher intermediation capacity is Li Wang. In this subnetwork, the number of co-authorships is quite significant, with several papers with three and more authors.

The main result stemming from the social network analysis is, however, the low degree of connectedness between the authors of the 330 papers in the 2012–2018 list and among those authors who have published a high number of articles. Whenever a paper is done between two authors, very rarely these two authors end up collaborating with any other author, and that is why we found a very low number of subnetworks having more than eight nodes. Of course, this result also comes from the fact that a significant number of authors have only one publication in the field, therefore not having a sufficient number of papers to establish networks from the point of view of the SNA procedure.

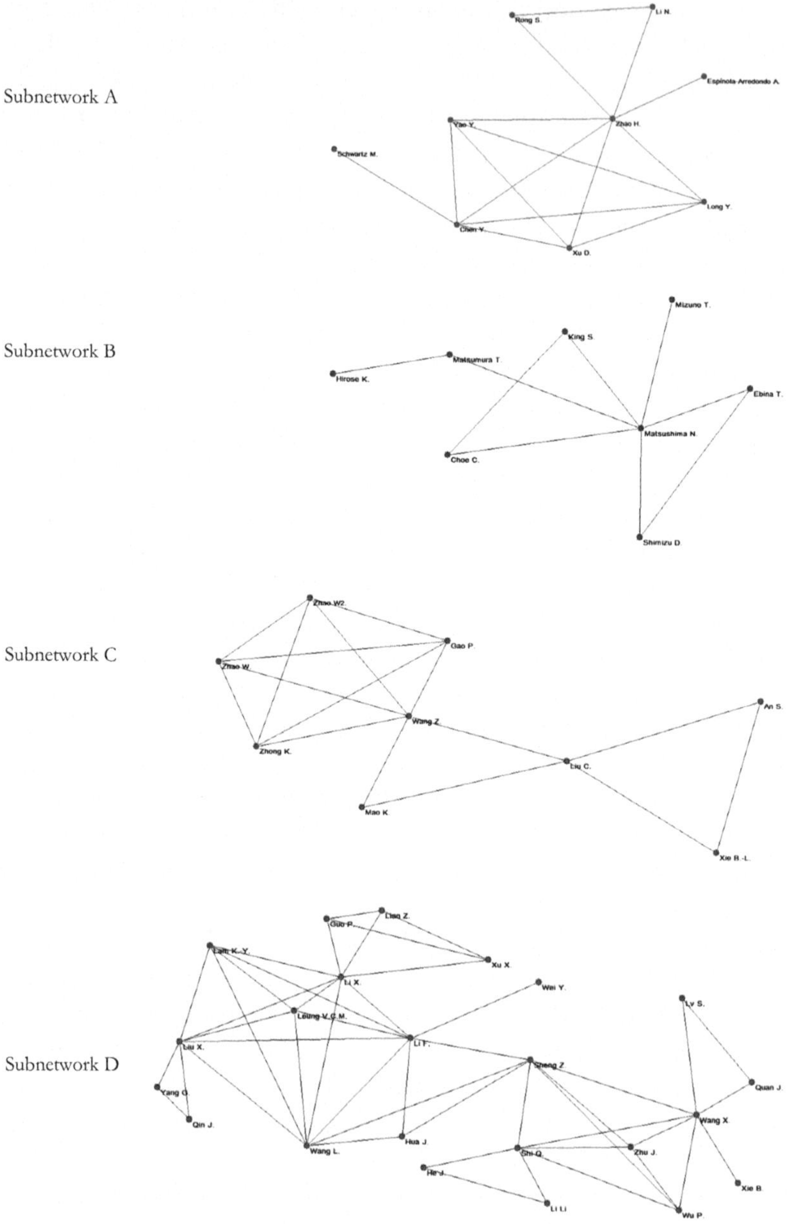

Fig. 3.3 Co-authorship subnetworks in spatial competition, 2012–2018

Table 3.8 Subnetworks with at least eight authors

	A	B	C	D
Nodes	9	8	9	23
Ties	15	11	14	47
Average degree	3.33	2.75	3.11	4.09
Betweenness centralization	0.167	0.204	0.035	0.186
Degree centralization	0.273	0.449	0.220	0.140

In fact, the resulting 4 subnetworks come only from a subset of 24 papers in our sample, suggesting that these are not very representative of the field. These results call for more collaboration between authors who work on Hotelling, as it could be a path for an increasing number of papers and more diversification in terms of the exploitation of different assumptions to the basic Hotelling and d'Aspremont et al. settings.

3.5 Conclusion

This paper had a very important departure point on the bibliometric and literature analysis of Biscaia and Mota (2013) and subsequently extended its bibliometric analysis for the period of 2012–2018. We sought the papers that were related with the seminal contribution of Hotelling and its linear city and attempted to characterize the field in the last 7 years.

We started on characterizing the field according to the authors and the journals in which Hotelling's articles were published. Firstly, we discover that on the authorship of the articles, while European authors seem to produce more articles on the field, an important part of the authorships shifted from North America to Asia, when comparing to the earlier period starting on 1979. This result can be naturally attributed to the increasing relevance of Asian countries on science, but the decline in North American authorships indicates that the Hotelling field might have lost popularity in North America, while retaining its importance and tradition in Europe.

Regarding publications in journals, we found that the articles are much more dispersed between different outlets than in previous years, where publications were more concentrated in few journals. In our opinion, this can be attributed due to four reasons: (1) an increase in the number of outlets, which allows for a (naturally) bigger dispersion; (2) a Hotelling framework more "stabilized" in terms of method for modeling horizontal differentiation or geographical distance; (3) an analysis on a shorter period of time, which does not give enough time for journals such as *Regional Science and Urban Economics* to accept a big number of Hotelling articles; and (4) an increase in Asian publications, which are most likely related with the increase in the number of Asian authors.

Next, and in order to provide some qualitative information on the content of the papers in the list, we analyzed the articles and classified them according to various criteria encompassing the way Hotelling line was used, the main themes behind the papers, and the assumptions that were used. We conclude that roughly 40% of the articles used the Hotelling setup to justify firms' location, while the other articles used it as a building block while studying other subjects. Among those articles using the Hotelling setup, we conclude that the articles are equally divided between using linear or transportation costs, revealing the relevance that the change proposed by d'Aspremont et al. (1979) still has in the literature. Inspecting the remaining changes in assumptions, we suspect that the articles following quadratic transportation costs are more innovative, since in these the main assumptions are kept, and therefore for these articles the sources of novelty should be outside the usual slight change in the assumptions.

Regarding the themes used in those papers, we identify a great heterogeneity between the papers in the list. In spite of the heterogeneity, the most frequent theme we identified were the Hotelling-Downs model and studies with heterogeneous firms and with network effects. The exercise of attributing themes to papers allowed us to conclude that the variety of approaches with the Hotelling framework is huge, therefore proving the importance of the contribution of such seminal paper in the literature.

Next, we attempted to analyze the relationships between the authors of those papers by analyzing co-authorship network using a social network analysis procedure. Our most important conclusion is that the networks in this field are very closed—that is, when working with other authors, usually these authors keep their partnerships, and therefore there are not many interactions among authors in this field. Of course, this can be attributed due to the great heterogeneity in the publications, in terms of both the approaches used and the geographical dispersion of authors—but perhaps it calls for a higher collaboration of the researchers on the topic.

This paper provides an adequate mapping of the Hotelling field in the past years, and therefore we believe it could very useful for researchers in the field to identify the most used approaches, the journals in which these articles are published, as well as the relevant authors in the field. It does not replace a "classical" literature review on the articles though, in the sense that the scientific contribution of the articles in the list is only superficially approached, but hopefully it should provide important insights and inspiration for the readers.[1]

References

Anderson, S., & Neven, D. (1991). CournotCompetition Yield Spatial Agglomeration. *International Economic Review, 32*, 793–808.

Biscaia, R., & Mota, I. (2013). Models of Spatial Competition: A Critical Review. *Papers in Regional Science, 9*(4), 851–871.

Csardi, G. (2014). Network Analysis and Visualization.Package 'igraph', http://igraph.org.

D'Aspremont, C., Gabzewicz, J. J., & Thisse, J. F. (1979). On Hotelling'sStability in Competition. *Econometrica, 47*, 1045–1050.

Downs, A. (1957). *An Economic Theory of Democracy*. New York: Harper and Row, New York.

de Nooy, W., Mrvar, A., & Batagel, V. (2011). *Exploratory Social Network Analysis with Pajek*. Cambridge: Cambridge University Press.

Hotelling, H. (1929). Stability in Competition. *Economic Journal, 39*, 41–57.

Salop, S. (1979). Monopolistic Competition with Outside Goods. *The Bell Journal of Economics, 10*, 141–156.

[1]Readers can e-mail Ricardo_Biscaia@hotmail.com to obtain the list of analyzed publications, as well as all the information we used throughout the chapter.

Part II

Reviews of Literature

4

New Economic Geography: Economic Integration and Spatial Imbalances

José M. Gaspar

4.1 Introduction

This chapter provides a comprehensive view as well as a conceptual discussion of the field of *New Economic Geography* (NEG). It starts by describing the background in adjacent fields of economics which made the surge of NEG possible. It then lays out the necessary ingredients of fundamental forces at work that define any NEG framework, assesses the state of the art in NEG and tracks the evolution of the field.

J. M. Gaspar (✉)
CEGE and Católica Porto Business School, Universidade Católica Portuguesa, Porto, Portugal

CEF.UP, University of Porto, Porto, Portugal
e-mail: jgaspar@porto.ucp.pt

S. Colombo (ed.), *Spatial Economics Volume I*,
https://doi.org/10.1007/978-3-030-40098-9_4

Krugman's seminal Core-Periphery (CP) model (Krugman 1991a) is perhaps the most well-known general equilibrium model that explains the riddle of uneven spatial development and, in particular, the forces that lead to spatial agglomeration of industry and the explanation on why spatial imbalances in the distribution of economic activities arise in an increasingly globalized economy. While the CP model is widely regarded as the precursor microfounded model in NEG, it is the combination of the seminal works by Paul Krugman, Masahisa Fujita, and Anthony Venables that marked the birth and clearly defined New Economic Geography as a field in its own right. However, economic agglomeration should not be held in a too general way, as its interpretation depends on the spatial and historical scale. In that sense, NEG cannot be held entirely as brand new, as there have been other equally high-quality papers in other fields of spatial economics, such as economic geography, urban economics, international trade and regional economics (Fujita 2010; Gaspar 2020a). As such, to provide an overall assessment of the subject requires one to identify both the early and the recent theoretical contributions in economics that serve as background to, or are intertwined with, NEG. Ever since, many researchers have devoted their attention towards providing more theoretical foundations and empirical research that add to the study of the geographical distribution of economic activities.

Several works building on Krugman's seminal CP model have emerged and extended its original framework in order to provide new insights on NEG and on the study of economic integration and its impact on the rise of spatial imbalances. Some have come to incorporate and endogenize the role of cities and urban systems (e.g. Fujita and Krugman 1995; Fujita and Ogawa 1982). Others explain the forces that contribute to, or drive away from, agglomeration outcomes, through the interaction of input-output linkages (e.g. Krugman and Venables 1995; Venables 1996). Another wave of NEG models have been dedicated to the study of the bilateral relations between agglomeration and regional growth (e.g. Baldwin and Martin 2004).

From within the economics community, it has been frequently argued that NEG needs to overcome several technical limitations that keep thwarting its development (Behrens and Robert-Nicoud 2011; Fujita and

Mori 2005; Gaigné and Thisse 2014). Outside economics, NEG was subject, ever since its dawn, with stark criticism stemming from the geographers' community devoted to economic geography (e.g. Martin 1999).

The rest of this chapter is organized as follows. Section 4.2 briefly describes the history of spatial economics prior to the emergence of NEG and discusses its main limitations in accounting for uneven spatial development in a fully integrated general equilibrium model that departed from the paradigm of constant returns to scale. Section 4.3 analyses the theoretical background—namely, the increasing returns revolution and the rise of New Trade Theory (NTT)—that paved the way for the emergence of the New Economic Geography. Section 4.4 provides a comprehensive discussion as well as a description of a simplified and analytically solvable version of the CP model that is meant to be pedagogical at illustrating the main forces that drive the Core-Periphery model and NEG at its heart. Section 4.5 briefly surveys the state of the art of NEG, including early developments, contributions from (and to) other fields and more recent contributions. In what follows, Sections 4.2, 4.3 and 4.5 closely follow Gaspar (2020a,b) in the account of an historical overview of NEG. Finally, Sect. 4.6 is left for some concluding remarks including some future avenues of research along which NEG could further improve and develop.

4.2 Spatial Economics Before NEG

In a broad sense, spatial economics includes all branches of economics that study economic processes and developments in geographical space, such as urban economics, location theory and regional economics. According to Fujita (2010), NEG falls into the class of a *general location theory*, that is, a theory of spatial economics that aims to explain the geographical distribution of agents in the space economy, together with its spatial price system and trade patterns. Thus, understanding the theoretical underpinnings of NEG requires one to cover the historical background of closely related subfields of spatial economics, mainly urban economics and location theory.

4.2.1 Urban Economics and Location Theory

Prior to NEG, there were many works in spatial economics that addressed the agglomeration of industry within a city or a system of cities, dating back to as far as von Thünen's model of land use and rent in *The Isolated State* in 1826. In fact, von Thünen (1826) was the first attempt to develop a general location theory which included ideas that were elaborated upon separately by theorists such as Launhardt (1885), Marshall (1890), Weber (1909), Hotelling (1929), Hoover (1937), Ohlin (1933), Christaller (1933), Lösch (1940) or Isard (1949). Notwithstanding, spatial economics remained at the periphery of economics until the 1990s. This was due to the lack of a unified framework, or of a comprehensive general location theory, that embraced both increasing returns and imperfect competition, the two basic ingredients comprising the formation of the actual space economy.

Urban economics, dating back to the works of Alonso (1964) and Mills (1967) provided microfoundations of urban agglomeration economies and explained the impact of neighbourhood effects and spatial externalities on the stratification of cities. Regarding the formation of city systems, Henderson (1974, 1991) is widely remarked as pioneering in a large flow of research that describes how cities with different sizes may emerge.

Location theory studies the spatial distribution of industry and variations in firms' costs and markups over prices. Rooted in Hotelling's spatial competition theory (Hotelling 1929), its spatial dimension abstracts itself from the usual geographical space, often dealing with differentiation across various domains, such as consumer heterogeneity in preferences for products. Since it spans across a wide array of different domains in economics, it is often perceived as not having well-enough-defined objective (Gaspar 2018).

Though relevant fields in their own right, neither urban economics nor location theory achieved the interest reached by NEG (Fujita and Thisse 2009). One of the reasons might be that NEG has a more well-defined and broad objective within economics. This was already evident in Walter Isard's (1956) complaint, whereby classical location theory, for instance, confined itself to a disintegrated framework of partial equilibrium theory, exogenous variables, linear transport costs and ad hoc demands (Blaug 1997).

4.2.2 The Spatial Impossibility Theorem

It took several decades to come up with an explanation on how economic spatial imbalances arise that departed from the dominant paradigm of constant returns to scale. The reason why it took so long hinged on the impossibilities imposed by this paradigm. The results regarding the shape of the space economy that are consistent with the neoclassical theory were discussed by authors such as Duranton and Puga (2004) and Fujita and Thisse (2009, 2013). Starrett's (1978) "Spatial Impossibility Theorem" provides a good account of the limitations inherent to the assumption of constant returns. The theorem states that in an Arrow-Debreu economy under constant returns to scale, with a finite number of agents and locations, homogeneous space and costly transportation, there is no competitive equilibrium in which actual transportation takes place. Therefore, if economic activities are perfectly divisible, there is a competitive equilibrium such that each location is autarkic and hence there is no reason for economic activities to cluster.

In order to explain spatial inequalities and regional specialization, one must thus relax at least one of the assumptions stated in the Theorem. Since transport costs are ubiquitous, explaining spatial imbalances requires one to assume heterogeneous space and/or non-convexity of production sets to allow for scale economies (Duranton 2008).

4.2.3 Comparative Advantages, Externalities and Imperfect Competition

Ever since, economic theory has witnessed the emergence of models of comparative advantages, models of agglomeration externalities and models of imperfect competition.

The first type of models focuses on exogenous regional asymmetries, such as the presence of a natural harbour or a particular climate, which confer geographical natural advantages that lead to specialization. In spite of their importance, these comparative advantages cannot account for the existence of full-fledged agglomerations and very high spatial imbalances (Fujita and Thisse 2009). The second type of models works under the framework of constant returns and perfect competition but allows for some sort of increasing returns that are external to firms. Ogawa and Fujita (1980) and Fujita and Ogawa (1982) were among the first attempts to explain the endogenous formation of multiple business districts within a city in terms of Marshallian externalities in the guise of positive spillovers among firms. However, the spatial distribution and rise of multiple cities with different sizes are implied by the counteraction between economies and diseconomies of agglomeration. This requires a step further in accounting for the microfoundations that generate these opposing forces. Thus, models of agglomeration externalities fail to give an account of the microeconomic interactions that lead to those spatial externalities.

The last class of models pertains to imperfect competition, under which pricing decisions by firms depend on the spatial distribution of the agents in the economy. In this class, we can find models of oligopolistic competition and monopolistic competition. The former assumes the existence of a reduced number of large firms who interact with each other strategically. Conversely, models of monopolistic competition are often chosen in detriment of the former, because the atomistic firm space precludes any strategic interaction, alleviating common problems such as existence and determinacy of equilibria which occurs frequently in oligopolistic competition. Since the monopolistically competitive framework implies increasing returns to scale at the firm level, transportation costs between regions imply that location decisions are not trivial (Gaspar 2018). Thus, both these factors help explain the geographical distribution of economic activities across different regions. A particularly useful monopolistic competition model is the Dixit-Stiglitz model (Dixit and Stiglitz 1977), where consumers exhibit taste for a horizontally differentiated bundle of varieties and there is a continuum of firms, each producing a single variety under increasing returns to scale.

Inasmuch as spatial distributions are a result of agglomeration forces operating against dispersion forces, I briefly advance the main principles that would come to lie at the core of NEG.

Price competition is known to be a strong dispersion force, as firms tend to relocate farther away from each other in order to avoid fiercer competition. On the other hand, product differentiation alleviates price competition and hence allows firms to locate where they have access to a bigger market and higher demand, and where transportation costs are lower, acting as an agglomeration force. The other principle at work generating agglomeration is dubbed the *home market effect* (Krugman 1980), with its roots in the New Trade Theory, whereby larger markets attract a share of firms that exceeds the relative size of its corresponding region.

4.3 Scale Economies: From Trade to Geography

In the field of economic geography, whose main concern is the study of migration flows of individuals and firms across the geographic landscape, it has long been recognized that economies of scale were decisive for the location of economic activity, namely, by theorists within regional economics such as François Perroux, Nigel Harris, Gunnar Myrdal or Albert Hirschman. Nonetheless, these insights were not supported by parsimonious models, especially models integrated in a general equilibrium framework. This would have to wait until the seminal contributions by Krugman (1991a,b) which marked the surge of the New Economic Geography. However, the seeds of NEG could already be found in Krugman (1979) which, in its final section, argued that patterns of migration can be analysed within the same framework as the New Trade Theory (NTT).

International trade has a long history in economics, and for the bulk of the field's history, patterns of trade have been explained by factor endowments and comparative advantages. These theories provided good explanations for trade patterns in the first half of the twentieth century. But after the Second World War, most trade started to take place between countries with similar technologies and similar factor endowments. Indeed, most new trade patterns consisted of "exchanges of similar products between similar countries, exemplified by the massive two-way trade in automotive products between the United States and China" (Krugman 2009). But while it was recognized by some economists that some countries only produced a small fraction of their potential intra-industry products because specialization in narrower ranges of intermediate products allowed for exploitation of economies of scale, this kind of reasoning was not envisaged by trade models up until the 1980s. The reason was that increasing returns at the firm level in trade theory required a general equilibrium model of imperfect competition.

4.3.1 Preferences and Increasing Returns

Increasing returns and economies of scale had long posed awkward problems for theorists. If larger firms face lower costs, then in principle one firm should supply the entire market. However, in the Dixit-Stiglitz model, this "monopolistic" logic is offset by a countervailing force: consumers' love for variety. People gain higher utility from having more products of different varieties than more of the same variety. This creates the incentive for firms to produce a large variety of products. However, the production of a new variety has setup costs, which leads to declining average costs as a larger quantity of the variety is produced and places a limit on the number of varieties the market can profitably supply. The market is therefore carved up among competing firms, each offering a differentiated product. The Dixit-Stiglitz model, with its subtly differentiated firms competing for variety-loving consumers, lent itself to explaining why, for example, Germany would import French cars and France would import German cars.

Krugman (1979) showed that when trade barriers fall, firms gain access to bigger markets, allowing them to expand production and obtain economies of scale. However, openness also exposes them to competition from rival foreign firms, paring their margins. Some firms may exit the markets due to losses, but between the domestic survivors and the foreign entrants, consumers still have more goods to choose from. Thus the gains from trade arise not from specialization, but from scale economies, fiercer competition and the ability to obtain a greater variety of products. Thus, the combination of love for variety, or "Dixit-Stiglitz preferences", with increasing returns at the plant level, allowed to generate trade patterns consistent with real-world data. Krugman (1979) also discussed the implications of impediments to trade between two countries when labour is inter-regionally mobile. Such considerations would be the precursors to the Core-Periphery model (Krugman 1991a).

4.3.2 Transport Costs and the Home Market Effect

The decrease in transportation costs has also been an important cause for the growth of trade. Krugman (1980) extended his 1979 model by incorporating transportation costs, allowing him to identify the home market effect, whereby large markets are relatively more attractive to firms and consequently tend to have a more than proportional share of firms due to increasing returns. The intuition is that, by concentrating production in the largest market, scale economies can be realized due to increasing returns and costly transportation is minimized. Moreover, lower transportation costs magnify the home market effect because they decrease the export hurdles to the smaller region.

But this view assumed that the market size is exogenous, that is, that consumers are not allowed to migrate between regions. The magnification of the home market effect through migration giving rise to endogenous regional asymmetries would be addressed by the Core-Periphery (CP) model (Krugman 1991a), which, together with the work by Fujita (1988), marked the birth of the New Economic Geography (NEG). Indeed, Fujita (1988) had already provided microfoundations for pecuniary externalities by considering product differentiation and firm-level scale economies to explain the endogenous formation of internal city structures. However, these contributions allowed to account for inequalities within a single city or region, but not for imbalances across different cities of regions.

4.4 The Core-Periphery Model

The Core-Periphery model begins with the same basic elements as NTT: monopolistic competition, increasing returns and love for variety. To these elements, the CP model adds free migration of (skilled) workers across space and industries and emphasizes on the role of transportation costs (of the iceberg type). Firms and workers are pulled towards the same location to reduce transportation costs of shipping goods (centripetal force). Conversely, populations are pulled apart by the desire to be close to natural inputs (centrifugal force), like farming land. Next, I shall provide a more detailed description of the mechanics of the CP model at work.

The starting point of the CP model is that the migration of some workers affects the global welfare and thus changes the relative attractiveness of both origin and destination regions. These effects can be seen as externalities because workers are *myopic* and do not take them into account in their decisions. The basic layout of the CP model comprises two regions and two sectors, one operating under monopolistic competition *à la* Dixit-Stiglitz and the other operating under perfect competition, and two factors of production. One factor is regionally immobile and is used as an input in the agricultural sector. The other is regionally mobile and is used as input in the industrial sector. There is a cumulative process whereby a larger market size and a lower "cost of living" work in a way that promotes agglomeration of industry in one region. As this region becomes bigger, so does the market, thus attracting more industry (the home market effect at work). This circular causation of forward linkages and backward linkages, noted by Krugman (1991a), generates a centripetal force. On the other hand, a more concentrated market enhances price competition, thus working as a dispersion force: the *market-crowding effect*. This is also called a centrifugal force.

All things considered, the key factor for determining the spatial distribution of industry is the level of transportation costs. As transport costs decrease, thus capturing the global tendency for higher economic integration (as intended by Krugman), both the agglomeration forces and dispersion forces increase; however, the net agglomeration forces overall increase because firms will be able to better exploit economies of scale in a single region and the export hurdles towards the other region decrease. Thus, the CP model is able to explain how large-scale agglomerations arise in an increasingly globalized economy. On the other hand, contrary to the neoclassical model that predicts only convergence, the CP model can account for both convergence and divergence.[1]

4.4.1 A Simple CP Model

In this section, I provide a "bare bones" version of the Footloose Entrepreneur (FE) model by Forslid and Ottaviano (2003), which is a slightly modified version of Krugman's CP (or alternatively, the FKV model; see Fujita et al. 1999b, Chap. 5) model that is more pedagogical because it is analytically solvable and displays all key features of the original CP model (as desired by its creators). It resembles the CP model in that the spatial concentration of activity requires labour migration and this migration is driven by real wage differences (Baldwin et al. 2003). The FE model displays both demand-linked circular causality and cost-linked circular causality. Since they are the factors responsible for the main features of the CP model, it remains so in the FE model. In fact, the FE model and the CP model are isomorphic in an economically meaningful state space (Robert-Nicoud 2005).

4.4.1.1 The Model and Short-Run Equilibrium

There are two regions $i = \{1, 2\}$, two kinds of labour and two productive sectors. Labour is divided between a unit mass of skilled workers that are inter-regionally mobile and unskilled workers of mass l that are inter-

[1]It should be noted that, prior to Krugman's CP model, von Thünen's seminal *The Isolated State* dating back to 1826 developed the first general equilibrium model to combine comparative advantages, theories of rents, factors-and-goods pricing, and a system of input-output to explain agricultural land use and rent. However, the CP model is pioneering in the sense that it was the first to unify the reasoning behind the monocentric spatial economy with a theory on agglomeration economies based on increasing returns to scale at the firm level (Fujita 2012), while also providing an explicit account of the circular causality between agglomeration of firms and agglomeration of inter-regionally mobile workers through demand linkages.

regionally immobile and equally distributed across regions, that is, $l_1 = l_2 = l/2$. The amount of skilled workers in region 1 is given by $x_1 \equiv x \in [0, 1]$ and fully describes the spatial distribution of agents in the economy.[2]

One sector produces an homogeneous good A under perfect competition that is freely tradable across regions and is produced one for one using unskilled labour. We take this good as the numéraire, such that both its price and the wage paid to unskilled workers are normalized to unity in both regions.

The other sector operates under Dixit-Stiglitz monopolistic competition and increasing returns to scale and produces horizontally differentiated varieties of manufactured goods. Manufactures are produced using one unit of immobile workers per unit of output and requires one unit of skilled workers to start production (i.e. production is footloose). Trade of the manufactured good is subject to transport costs of the iceberg type. That is, for each unit of good that is traded between region i and region j, the amount $\tau \in (1, +\infty)$ needs to be shipped.[3] Hence, we have $\tau_{ij} = \tau$, if $i \neq j$, and $\tau_{ij} = 1$ otherwise.

Agents in region i draw the following utility from consumption goods:

$$U_i = A_i^{1-\mu} M_i^{\mu}, \quad M_i = \left[\int_{s \in S} c_i(s)^{\frac{\sigma-1}{\sigma}} ds \right]^{\frac{\sigma}{\sigma-1}}, \tag{4.1}$$

where A_i is the amount of homogeneous goods consumed in region i, M_i is the constant elasticity of substitution (CES) composite of manufactured goods,[4] $\mu \in (0, 1)$ is the fraction of income spent on manufactured goods, $c_i(s)$ is the consumption of variety s that is produced by a manufacturing firm in region i and $\sigma > 1$ is the (constant) elasticity of substitution between varieties. Agents maximize utility in (4.1) subject to the budget constraint $P_i M_i + A_i = y_i$, where P_i is the regional price index and y_i corresponds to an agent's regional income. Utility

[2]The amount of skilled workers in region 2 is residually given by $1 - x$.

[3]In other words, the remainder $\tau - 1$ "melts in transit".

[4]Under these Dixit-Stiglitz preferences, agents exhibit "love for variety", in that they prefer to consume a bundle of diversified goods.

maximization yields the following demands:

$$M_i = \mu \frac{y_i}{P_i}, \quad A_i = (1-\mu)\, y_i, \quad c_{ij} = \frac{p_{ij}^{-\sigma}}{P_i^{1-\sigma}} y_i, \tag{4.2}$$

where c_{ij} is the demand for each manufactured variety produced in region j and consumed in region i, with:

$$P_i = \left[\int_{s \in S} p_i(s)^{1-\sigma} ds \right]^{\frac{\sigma}{\sigma-1}}. \tag{4.3}$$

Using (4.1) and (4.2), indirect utility is given by:

$$v_i(x) = \frac{y_i(x)}{P_i^{\mu}(x)}. \tag{4.4}$$

Given the assumption in fixed costs, market clearing for mobile labour implies that the number of varieties manufactured in a region equals its amount of skilled workers, that is, $S_i = x_i$. Profits and final output of a manufacturing firm are given, respectively, by:

$$\pi_i = \sum_{j=1}^{2} p_{ij} c_{ij} (x_j + l_j) - q_i - w_i, \quad q_i = \sum_{j=1}^{2} \tau_{ij} c_{ij} (x_j + l_j), \tag{4.5}$$

where w_i is the nominal wage paid to a skilled worker. Firm space is atomistic, such that each firm does not take into account the prices set by other firms. The profit maximizing of a firm who produces in region i and sells in region j is thus the usual markup over marginal cost:

$$p_{ij} = \frac{\sigma \tau_{ij}}{\sigma - 1}. \tag{4.6}$$

Given (4.6), the CES price index in (4.3) becomes:

$$P_i = \frac{\sigma}{\sigma - 1} [\phi + (1 - \phi)x_i]^{\frac{1}{1-\sigma}} , \qquad (4.7)$$

where $\phi \equiv \tau^{1-\sigma} \in (0, 1)$ is the trade freeness between regions 1 and 2.[5] It is readily observable that the price index is decreasing in x_i (since $\sigma > 1$). Intuitively, a production shift towards more local varieties in region i (since each firm produces a single variety s and the number of firms equals the number of skilled workers) alleviates the burden of transport costs, thus lowering the cost of living in region i. This is called the *cost-of-living effect.*

Given free entry, manufacturing firms earn zero profits at equilibrium, which using (4.5) and (4.6) translates into the following:

$$w_i = \frac{q_i}{\sigma - 1}.$$

Combining this with (4.2), (4.6), (4.7) and (4.5), we get the following expression for the nominal skilled wage in region i:

$$w_i = \frac{\mu}{\sigma} \sum_{j=1}^{2} \frac{\phi_{ij} Y_j}{\phi + (1 - \phi)x_j}, \qquad (4.8)$$

where $Y_i = \left(\frac{l}{2} + w_j x_j\right)$ corresponds to region i's total nominal income. The nominal wages w_1 and w_2 are thus readily obtainable as an explicit function of the spatial distribution $x \in [0, 1]$ by solving the corresponding system of two linear equations given by (4.8).[6]

[5] It is a converse measure of transport costs.

[6] Herein lies the main difference between the FE model and the CP model; in the latter, skilled workers enter both the fixed and the variable input requirements. By contrast, since marginal costs in the FE model do not depend on the wage paid to skilled workers, it is possible to obtain a closed-form expression of the nominal wage paid to skilled workers as a function of its spatial distribution. In other words, the FE model is solvable because the optimal prices in (4.6) are equalized across regions and independent from the location of firms and workers (Forslid and Ottaviano 2003).

It is possible to show that, for a high enough trade freeness ϕ, nominal skilled wages are higher in the region with more skilled workers.[7] Intuitively, this happens when the market-crowding effect is offset by the counteracting *market-access effect*. For a given level of expenditure, the former is the result of a decrease in the local price index and local demand per firm due to fiercer competition in larger markets. The latter is expressed by the fact that more skilled workers (and hence firms) imply more local expenditure and more operating profits, thus boosting nominal wages.

In the long run, the possibility of migration between regions generates demand-linked and cost-linked circular causality, whereby migration leads to relatively higher real wages in a region, which in turn fosters more migration towards that region. The resulting spatial distribution is a result of two counteracting forces: agglomeration forces (market-access and cost-of-living effects) and dispersion forces (market-crowding effect). It is the level of the trade freeness that determines which force(s) is (are) offset by the other(s).

4.4.1.2 Long-Run Equilibria and Qualitative Results

In the long run, skilled workers are allowed to choose the region that offers them the highest indirect utility. Migration of skilled workers in region 1 is assumed to be governed by the following *ad hoc* dynamics (as in Baldwin et al. 2003; Fujita et al. 1999b):

$$\dot{x} \equiv f(x) = x(1-x)\left[\ln v_1(x) - \ln v_2(x)\right]. \tag{4.9}$$

Long-run equilibria $x^* \equiv x \in [0, 1]$ satisfy $\dot{x} = 0$ and include the corner solutions $x = 1$ and $x = 0$, that is, full agglomeration in region 1 or in region 2, respectively. In what follows, we have taken the log of the indirect utility $v_i(x)$ in (4.4) in order to get rid of the exponent from

[7] For more detailed proofs on this point, I refer the reader to Forslid and Ottaviano (2003) or Baldwin et al. (2003).

the price index in (4.7), which bears no qualitative implications,[8] and would only make the analysis more cumbersome without allowing for any further insights.

The short-run indirect utility differential $\Delta v \equiv \ln v_1(x) - \ln v_2(x)$, using (4.2) and after solving (4.8) to get w_1 and w_2 as explicit functions of x, is given by:

$$\Delta v(x) = \ln\left[\frac{x\phi + (1-x)\psi}{(1-x)\phi + x\psi}\right] + \frac{\mu}{\sigma - 1}\ln\left[\frac{(1-x)\phi + x}{x\phi + (1-x)}\right], \quad (4.10)$$

where:

$$\psi = \frac{1}{2}\left[1 + \phi^2 - \frac{\mu}{\sigma}(1-\phi)^2\right].$$

Clearly, the symmetric distribution of skilled workers $x^* = \frac{1}{2}$ satisfies $\Delta v(x) = 0$ and is thus an invariant interior solution to $\dot{x} = 0$.[9] For the existence and determinacy of interior equilibria, it suffices to show that $\Delta v(x)$ has at most two turning points, that is, either $\Delta v(x)$ has a unique zero at $x^* = \frac{1}{2}$ or two more zeros $x^* \in (0, 1)$ that are symmetric around $x = \frac{1}{2}$.[10]

Next, we uncover the qualitative behaviour of the dynamics posited by (4.9) as the freeness of trade smoothly increases by studying the local stability of long-run equilibria. An equilibrium is stable if, after an exogenous migration that shifts skilled workers between regions, the dynamics will restore the initial spatial distribution.

First, we analyse the stability of the symmetric equilibrium. It is stable if $\frac{df}{dx}\left(\frac{1}{2}\right) < 0$. Differentiating (4.9) using (4.10) and evaluating at $x = \frac{1}{2}$, we get that the symmetric equilibrium is stable if:

$$\phi < \phi_b \equiv \frac{(\sigma - \mu)(\sigma - \mu - 1)}{(\mu + \sigma - 1)(\mu + \sigma)}, \quad (4.11)$$

---

[8]Nor quantitative in the determination of long-run equilibria x^*.

[9]A solution is said to be invariant if it exists in the entire range of parameter space.

[10]We refer the interested reader to Ottaviano (2001) for a detailed proof on this.

where $\phi_b \in (0, 1)$ is called the break point. In other words, the symmetric equilibrium is stable if the freeness of trade is low enough (below the break point) and unstable if it is high enough (above the break point). In order to ensure that $\phi_b > 0$, so that the symmetric equilibrium is not always stable, we assume that $\sigma > 1 + \mu$ (the "no black hole" condition, after Fujita et al. 1999b).

Second, we check the stability of corner solutions, that is, agglomeration. Without loss of generality, let us look at agglomeration in region 1. It is stable if the utility in region 1 is higher than the utility in region 2, that is, if $\Delta \upsilon(1) > 0$; it is unstable otherwise. Formally, using (4.10) and evaluating at $x = 1$, agglomeration is stable if:

$$\ln\left[\frac{2\phi\sigma}{\sigma\left(1+\phi^2\right)-\mu(1-\phi^2)}\right]-\frac{\mu}{\sigma-1}\ln(\phi)>0. \tag{4.12}$$

The derivative of (4.12) with respect to ϕ is positive, meaning that agglomeration is stable if $\phi > \phi_s$, where $\phi_s \in (0, 1)$, called the sustain point, is implicitly defined by equating (4.12) to zero. Agglomeration is unstable for a low enough trade freeness (if $\phi < \phi_s$).

Further than the local stability of invariant patterns studied above, we can get the whole picture of the dynamic properties of the model by studying the type of local bifurcation that the symmetric equilibrium undergoes, at the value of the trade freeness where the equilibrium interchanges stability, that is, for $\phi = \phi_b$. After some tedious calculations, it is possible to show the following:

$$\frac{\partial f}{\partial x}\left(\frac{1}{2};\phi_b\right)=0;\ \frac{\partial^2 f}{\partial x^2}\left(\frac{1}{2};\phi_b\right)=0;\ \frac{\partial f}{\partial \phi}\left(\frac{1}{2};\phi_b\right)=0$$
$$\frac{\partial^2 f}{\partial \phi\partial x}\left(\frac{1}{2};\phi_b\right)>0;\ \frac{\partial^3 f}{\partial x^3}\left(\frac{1}{2};\phi_b\right)>0.$$

According to Guckenheimer and Holmes (2002, p. 150), the conditions above ensure that symmetric dispersion undergoes a subcritical pitchfork

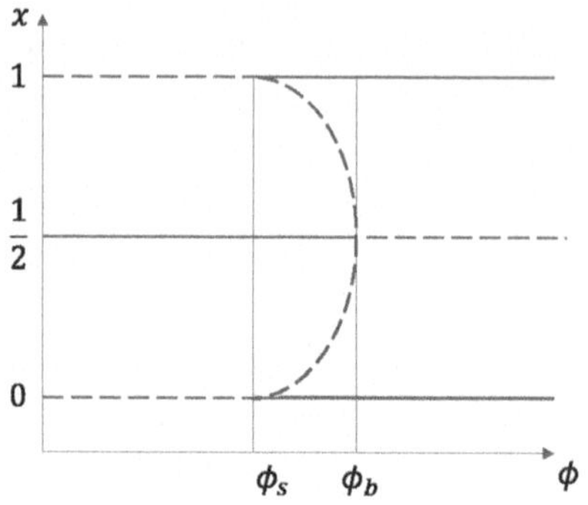

Fig. 4.1 Bifurcation diagram for the FE model. Solid lines denote stable equilibria. Dashed lines denote unstable equilibria

bifurcation at $\phi = \phi_b$, just as in the CP model (Fujita et al. 1999b). Figure 4.1 illustrates the bifurcation diagram for the FE model.

The additional insights conveyed by the existence of a supercritical pitchfork bifurcation are as follows. We have that $\phi_s < \phi_b$, that is, there is range for the trade freeness where both agglomeration and the symmetric equilibrium are simultaneously stable. If, for some $\phi \in (\phi_s, \phi_b)$, the economy is initially symmetrically dispersed, a temporary decrease in transport costs (increase in the trade freeness above ϕ_b) implies agglomeration in one region that is permanent, that is, there is *locational hysteresis*. Moreover, in that range of trade freeness, two additional interior long-run equilibria exist, symmetric around $x^* = \frac{1}{2}$, which are locally unstable. Also, once the trade freeness rises above the break point, there is catastrophic agglomeration as the transition is sudden and massive.

The whole picture depicted above illustrates how the level of transport costs affects the resulting spatial distribution and thus tells a compelling story on how the historical increase in economic integration explains large-scale industrial agglomeration. In a nutshell, when transport costs are very high (trade freeness is very low), industry is evenly dispersed across regions because agglomeration forces are outweighed by dispersion forces. As transport costs fall (trade freeness increases), so do both agglomeration and dispersion forces. However, the latter's fall is steeper because firms become able to better exploit scale economies in a larger region and avoid costly transportation. Eventually, for a low enough level of transport costs, agglomeration forces offset the dispersion forces, thus triggering the agglomeration of industry in a single region.

4.5 Developments in New Economic Geography

Ever since the seminal contribution by Krugman (1991a), several developments in NEG have come to build upon the framework of the CP model or similar versions (such as the FE model described in the previous section). Whether with just slight or with considerable modifications, many such contributions share at their foundation (at least some of) the basic ingredients that characterize NEG, namely, increasing returns, imperfect competition and transport costs. Upon this backbone, such extensions have allowed for a myriad of contributions. Some show results that are very close to the original CP, either attesting for its robustness or evidencing limitations grounded on persistent features that thwart further insights. Other contributions allowed to shed light on several aspects of the space economy such as the regional growth, the spatial sorting of heterogeneous agents or the hierarchical formation of city systems, among other developments. This section aims to provide a brief account of some of these developments.

4.5.1 Early NEG Models

In many early versions of the CP model (e.g. Fujita et al. 1999b; Krugman 1991a), Footloose Capital models (e.g. Martin and Rogers 1995) or FE models (e.g. Forslid and Ottaviano 2003; Ottaviano 2001; Ottaviano et al. 2002; Pflüger 2004), an inter-regionally immobile workforce was needed as "the pull of a dispersed rural market" (Krugman and Elizondo 1996) in order to generate the dispersive market- crowding effect. Without this mathematical device, there would be no place for dispersion of economic activities, as the incentive for firms to relocate in other regions in order to capture regional immobile demand would vanish.

In this case, if firms and mobile workers agglomerate in a single region, they are able to avoid transport costs altogether (Baldwin et al. 2003). This motivated Krugman and Elizondo (1996) to substitute immobile labour for commuting costs/land, that is, it is the use of congestible non-tradable resources that generate the single centrifugal force in the economy. Similarly, Helpman (1998) modified the CP model, eliminating immobile labour and considering a housing sector instead, to find that, when all the workers in the economy are inter-regionally mobile, more integration fosters dispersion rather than the agglomeration of economic activities. Murata (2003) also considered a CP model with only mobile workers that are heterogeneous regarding their preferences for residential location. In this case, it is heterogeneity that acts as the sole dispersion force in the model.

When we consider areas where factor mobility is more reduced than in the United States, such as the Euro Area, regional imbalances are much harder to explain through the intrinsic mechanisms of the CP model. Krugman and Venables (1995) and Venables (1996) introduced sources of agglomeration and dispersion forces in the guise of input-output linkages between firms. The main idea is that agglomeration in a region occurs because a more industrialized region offers a larger demand for intermediate goods, and vice-versa, generating a self-reinforcing process. There is also a market expansion effect, but in this case it is due to higher wages that leads to higher consumer demand. However, if wages are too high, some firms will want to relocate their production to the periphery, so there is also a dispersion force. The advantage of this framework is that a self-perpetuating agglomeration process may not be perpetual. Instead, economic integration yields a bell-shaped curve of spatial development. As such, this model accounts for the possibility of reindustrialization of the periphery after a period of gradual desertification.

A bell-shaped relationship between economic integration and spatial inequality was also uncovered by Fujita et al. (1999b) in a modified version of the CP model, whereby transportation in the agricultural sector is costly and in models where inter-regionally mobile agents are heterogeneous regarding their preferences towards residential location (e.g. Murata 2003; Tabuchi and Thisse 2002). Heterogeneity in location preferences implies that agents in the same region have different utility levels, which means that some agents are less willing to migrate than others. As a result, a higher dispersion of consumer preferences strengthens its role as a centrifugal force (Gaspar 2018). Whether stemming from heterogeneity or from transport costs in agriculture, there is an additional dispersion force which counteracts the net agglomeration forces from the manufacturing sector. Since the latter tend to vanish for a sufficiently high level of economic integration, industry will tend to re-disperse after an initial phase of agglomeration.

Core-Periphery analysis was deepened by Krugman (1993, 1996) and Fujita et al. (1999b) through the inclusion of more regions by extending the original CP model to a "racetrack economy". In Krugman (1993), 12 regions are uniformly distributed around a circumference (i.e. distances between adjacent regions are the same). Starting from a slight deviation from the uniform (symmetric) distribution around the circle, several simulations indicated convergence towards a spatial distribution, whereby industry is evenly dispersed across two regions that are placed at exact opposite sides of the circle.[11] This paved the way towards several future contributions that analyse the spatial distribution of economic activities in a multi-regional setup.

4.5.2 NEG and the Internal Structure of Regions and City Formation

Earlier and more recent developments in urban economics and their incorporation into NEG have allowed researchers to take account of inter-regional spatial structures and the emergence and formation of urban systems.

[11] This conjecture was later partially confirmed by Akamatsu et al. (2012), who showed the general existence of several bifurcation points for decreasing transport costs. At each bifurcation, the number of evenly industrialized regions halved, and the spacing between each adjacent region with industry doubled. Eventually, the economy would reach the state of two evenly industrialized regions at exact opposite sides of the circumference. Further decreases in transport costs, however, would lead to a final bifurcation with agglomeration in a single region.

The seminal paper by Fujita and Krugman (1995) was a precursor in explaining on how urban and agricultural land use patterns emerge endogenously. Their framework closely relates to that of the original CP model, except that all workers are inter-regionally mobile and the space economy is continuous and one-dimensional. As in Krugman and Elizondo (1996), the only centrifugal force here stems from the availability of land in the agricultural sector. The setting allows for a summary of the classic von Thünen model and of the Dixit-Stiglitz-Samuelson model used in NEG. It sets out from von Thünen's city centre, where industry is concentrated, surrounded by an agricultural hinterland displayed in concentric rings around the city centre. Its main prediction is that, provided that population does not exceed a certain threshold, a monocentric economy is a spatial equilibrium. However, as population expands further, the borders of the agriculture hinterland locate sufficiently far from the city centre so that firms find it attractive to locate out of the city centre, thus giving rise to a new city. This process is self-perpetuating as more cities arise to form an urban system.

In spite of the contribution by Fujita and Krugman (1995), economic geography still fell short of accounting for the distribution and different sizes of cities. Back in 1974, Vernon Henderson developed an approach that allowed him to describe the emergence of a hierarchy of cities. Fujita et al. (1999a) further extended this approach by considering several differentiated industrial goods in a model with NEG features. This was the first step in NEG towards reaching a theory of central places. Much later, Tabuchi and Thisse (2011) studied the rise of a hierarchical system of central places under the racetrack economy. Insights on the distribution and size of cities have also been uncovered in works such as Krugman (1996), Duranton and Puga (2001) or Murata and Thisse (2005), to name a few.

The cross-fertilization between NEG and urban economics has also allowed to shed light on other aspects such as selection and spatial sorting (e.g. Venables 2010) or the social interaction between agents across and within regions (e.g. Mossay and Picard 2011).[12]

---

[12]For an involved discussion of contributions on these topics, consult Gaspar (2018, Sec. 4.5.2).

4.5.3 Regional Growth

The CP model has also been extended to tackle issues in regional growth in works such as Fujita and Thisse (2003) and Baldwin and Martin (2004), who have attempted to take advantage of the common monopolistically competitive setup shared by both NEG and "new growth" theories. In Baldwin and Martin (2004), the focus is on the mobility of physical capital. Fujita and Thisse (2003) develop a framework that combines the original CP model with an endogenous growth model with horizontal innovation and inter-regionally mobile workers. They show that the growth rate of the global economy depends on the spatial distribution of an innovation sector across regions. As the economy agglomerates in a region, the innovation rate increases, benefiting all workers (including those in the periphery). However, workers in the core region enjoy a higher welfare compared with equally skilled workers in the peripheral region. As a result, there is a trade-off between spatial equity and economic growth.

Fujita and Thisse (2013) proposed a similar endogenous growth model, whereby skilled workers create blueprints that are necessary for the production of new varieties. The fixed cost of a manufacturing firm is equal to the cost of acquiring a patent, whereas the marginal cost uses only inter-regionally immobile labour (i.e. production is footloose). As in Fujita and Thisse (2003), growth is driven by horizontal innovation in expanding varieties and depends on the spatial distribution of innovation activities across the regions. Further, they introduce regional asymmetries in the transfer of knowledge across regions, reflecting the idea that there are frictions in the spatial diffusion of knowledge.

4.5.4 Beyond the CP Model

Krugman's CP model was so influential that many subsequent models (or their identical twins, as Robert-Nicoud (2005) put it) were deemed incremental, in the sense that their framework did not stray too much from the path followed by the original CP model. Of course, many such models were designed to improve tractability in order to derive analytical results that were otherwise unattainable in the CP model. Changes in these models were marginal so that their qualitative properties would be similar to the CP model, as often desired by their creators, but still amenable to algebraic manipulation. Such is the example of the so-called class of Footloose Entrepreneur models or the input-output linkages (or vertical linkages) models. That is, many models retained the framework with two-region, two-sector, Cobb-Douglas-CES preferences, along with the assumption of iceberg transport costs. As argued by Behrens and Robert-Nicoud (2011), such a stringent baseline framework would most likely preclude insights beyond the classical features of the CP model, such as the home market effect, demand-linked and cost-linked circular causality, catastrophic agglomeration, multiple equilibria, locational hysteresis and hump-shaped agglomeration rents (as a function of transport costs).

However, some (early) notable exceptions to the aforementioned are in order. One is the model proposed by Ottaviano et al. (2002), who consider a quasi-linear utility over preferences with a quadratic sub-utility over differentiated manufactures and additive transportation costs. Although most of the model's qualitative predictions are similar to Krugman's CP model, the model allows for firms' mark-ups to depend on the market size (they are constant under CES preferences), thus giving rise to competitive effects. This property, along with its analytical tractability, renders the model as one of the most widely used benchmark frameworks for several applications in NEG.

Another exception is the model proposed by Pflüger (2004), which also uses quasi-linear utility but retains the CES sub-utility for consumption of manufactured goods. By removing income effects for the demand of manufactured goods, agglomeration forces are mitigated, and agglomeration beyond the break point of the trade freeness becomes a smooth and gradual process (in other words, asymmetric spatial patterns may be stable long-run equilibria).

Further, NEG has been enriched to deal with multiple sectors other than the competitive agricultural nonskilled sector and the manufacturing skilled sector. For instance, a non-tradable goods sector was added to the other conventional two sectors by Pflüger and Südekum (2008). Others, like Pflüger and Tabuchi (2010), have considered the role of land as a production factor.

Beyond the multi-sectoral approach, a myriad of different works have also contributed to increase the dimensionality of NEG by extending it to the analysis of multiple regions. The advances on this matter allowed NEG researchers to explore several geometries, thus conferring more importance to the role of geography by considering different distance structures. Some have used Krugman's racetrack economy, such as Mossay (2003), Akamatsu et al. (2012) or Castro et al. (2012); others have studied agglomeration patterns on *two*-dimensional hexagonal lattices (e.g. Ikeda et al. 2014); others still focused on equally spaced regions along the real line (e.g. Ago et al. 2006); and a series of other contributions have considered many equidistant regions (e.g. Gaspar et al. 2018, 2019; Puga 1999; Tabuchi et al. 2005). The several multi-regional approaches (even beyond the aforementioned stylized settings) have contributed to render NEG susceptible to empirical testing and thus help guide regional policies.

The role of heterogeneity has also had a huge impact on NEG literature, well beyond that briefly discussed in Sect. 4.5.1. As Ottaviano (2010) put it, monopolistic competition has been enriched with a "finer micro-heterogeneity" that stresses the role of peoples' different skills and firms' productivity levels and the interaction between efficiency differences at the firm level and differences in production costs and market sizes, shedding light on industry dynamics and selection processes. Several works stress the role of firm heterogeneity as an additional dispersive force because less efficient firms have a higher incentive to relocate in the less advantageous location. On the other hand, Ehrlich and Seidel (2013) show that higher heterogeneity raises the number of exporting firms through a self-selection process, leading to agglomeration. Similarly, when workers have different skill sets, larger regions tend to improve the average matching between workers and jobs, which in turn strengthens the role of increasing returns (Fujita and Thisse 2013).

4.6 Concluding Remarks and the Way Forward

NEG, together with urban economics and location theory, is continuously paving the way towards an integrated framework that benefits from the cross-fertilization across the different fields that comprise spatial economics, allowing researchers to account for inter-regional spatial structures and the emergence and formation of urban city structures (Fujita and Thisse 2013). This synergy will allow to shed further light on the spatial selection, sorting and interaction of agents within regions. Although NEG is not without its issues, specially those stemming from its circumscription in a somewhat narrow framework, the sprawl of developments both within and outside the field is a testament to its relevance, both theoretical and empirical. As argued by Gaspar (2018), the promising path followed in the directions discussed here is evident when we look at the amount of contributions published in several reputed academic journals devoted to regional science, urban economics and economic geography. Today, we can say that NEG has come a long way in overcoming some of its earlier limitations.

The impact of NEG was so big that it far outreached the economics profession, in a way that it was met by geographers from the *Proper Economic Geography* (PEG) community with passionate critiques and reprehension. This was partly due to the NEG's abstraction from local specificity in the treatment of geographical places, that is, the lack of commitment to studying real places (Martin 1999). The critiques stem not only from both economic geographers and geographical economists alike but also from the more recent strand of *Evolutionary Economic Geography* (EEG). Such critiques were often rebutted on the grounds that NEG was initially devised to attract mainstream economists and that abstract models have more power and depth to answer "what if?" questions (Krugman 2011). In spite of this, several researchers in economics have been aware of the methodological limitations of NEG (see, e.g. Fujita and Krugman 2004). By way of disclaimer, it should be noted that the absence of attention devoted to discussing the differences and the (absence of) debate between economists and geographers, as well as some of the steps already being progressively undertaken to promote the interdisciplinarity between NEG, PEG and EEG does not reflect any lack of consideration towards these subjects; rather, this chapter attempts to provide an account of NEG and not on economic geography in the broadest sense possible.

Similarly, many excellent contributions from NEG have been left out due to space restrictions. However, a brief note is warranted regarding possible future avenues of research along which NEG should develop and improve. These include but are not limited to (1) the incorporation of heterogeneity in firm-level productivity and consumer preferences to account for the spatial sorting of agents across cities and regions; (2) the increasing rise in a body of empirical work to derive policy implications; (3) the devise of new models of monopolistic competition beyond the CES specification that allow for firms' mark-ups to vary with market size; (4) the recognition of the importance of different spatial topologies in allowing for the treatment of a more realistic geographical space; and (5) a better account of evolutionary processes of migration through the consideration of farsighted agents and forward-looking expectations.

For further reading and understanding on these and many more aspects regarding early and new developments in NEG, I refer the reader to reviews such as Fujita and Mori (2005), Fujita and Thisse (2009), Behrens and Robert-Nicoud (2011), Redding (2013), Gaigné and Thisse (2014) and Gaspar (2018) or the monographs by Fujita et al. (1999b), Baldwin et al. (2003), Combes et al. (2008) and Fujita and Thisse (2013).

Acknowledgments Funding from Fundação para a Ciência e Tecnologia (through projects UIDB/04105/2020, UIDB/00731/2020, PTDC/EGE-ECO/30080/2017 and CEECIND/02741/2017) is gratefully acknowledged.

References

Ago, T., Isono, I., & Tabuchi, T. (2006). Locational disadvantage of the hub. *The Annals of Regional Science, 40*(4), 819–848.

Akamatsu, T., Takayama, Y., & Ikeda, K. (2012). Spatial discounting, Fourier, and racetrack economy: A recipe for the analysis of spatial agglomeration models. *Journal of Economic Dynamics and Control, 36*(11), 1729–1759.

Alonso, W. (1964). *Location and land use.* Cambridge: Harvard University Press.
Baldwin, R., Forslid, R., Martin, P., Ottaviano, G., & Robert-Nicoud, F. (2003). *Economic geography and public policy.* Princeton: Princeton University Press.
Baldwin, R., & Martin, P. (2004). Agglomeration and regional growth. In J. V. Henderson & J.-F. Thisse (Eds.), *Handbook of regional and urban economics* (Vol. IV, pp. 2671–2711). Amsterdam: North-Holland.
Behrens, K., & Robert-Nicoud, F. (2011). Tempora mutantur: In search of a new testament for NEG. *Journal of Economic Geography, 11*(2), 215–230.
Blaug, M. (1997). *Economic theory in retrospect.* Cambridge: Cambridge University Press.
Castro, S. B. S. D., Correia-da-Silva, J., & Mossay, P. (2012). The core-periphery model with three regions and more. *Papers in Regional Science, 91*(2), 401–418.
Combes, P. P., Mayer, T., & Thisse, J. F. (2008). *Economic geography: The integration of regions and nations.* Princeton: Princeton University Press.
Christaller, W. (1933). *Die Zentralen Orte in Süddeutschland.* Jena: Gustav Fischer Verlag. English translation: *The central places of Southern Germany.* Englewood Cliffs: Prentice-Hall (1966).
Dixit, A. K., & Stiglitz, J. E. (1977). Monopolistic competition and optimum product diversity. *American Economic Review, 67*, 297–308.
Duranton, G. (2008). Spatial economics. In S. N. Durlauf & L. E. Blume (Eds.), *The new Palgrave dictionary of economics* (pp. 1–7). Basingstoke: Palgrave Macmillan.
Duranton, G., & Puga, D. (2001). Nursery cities: Urban diversity, process innovation, and the life cycle of products. *American Economic Review, 91*(5), 1454–1477.
Duranton, G., & Puga, D. (2004). Micro-foundations of urban increasing returns: Theory. In J. V. Henderson & J.-F. Thisse (Eds.), *Handbook of regional and urban economics* (Vol. 4, pp. 2063–2117). Amsterdam: North Holland.
Forslid, R., & Ottaviano, G. (2003). An analytically solvable core-periphery model. *Journal of Economic Geography, 3*, 229–240.
Fujita, M. (1988). A monopolistic competition model of spatial agglomeration: Differentiated product approach. *Regional Science and Urban Economics, 18*, 87–124.
Fujita, M. (2010). The evolution of spatial economics: From Thünen to the new economic geography. *The Japanese Economic Review, 61*(1), 1–32.
Fujita, M. (2012). Thünen and the new economic geography. *Regional Science and Urban Economics, 42*(6), 907–912.

Fujita, M., & Krugman, P. (1995). When is the economy monocentric? von Thünen and Chamberlin unified. *Regional Science and Urban Economics, 25*, 505–528.

Fujita, M., & Krugman, P. (2004). The new economic geography: Past, present and the future. *Papers in Regional Science, 83*, 139–164.

Fujita, M., Krugman, P., & Mori, T. (1999a). On the evolution of hierarchical urban systems. *European Economic Review, 43*, 209–251.

Fujita, M., Krugman, P., & Venables, A. J. (1999b). *The spatial economy. cities, regions and international trade*. Cambridge: The MIT Press.

Fujita, M., & Mori, T. (2005). Frontiers of the new economic geography. *Papers in Regional Science, 84*(3), 377–405.

Fujita, M., & Ogawa, H. (1982). Multiple equilibria and structural transformation of non-monocentric urban configurations. *Regional Science and Urban Economics, 12*, 161–196.

Fujita, M., & Thisse, J. F. (2003). Does geographical agglomeration foster economic growth? And who gains and loses from it?. *Japanese Economic Review, 54*(2), 121–145.

Fujita, M., & Thisse, J.-F. (2009). New economic geography: An appraisal on the occasion of Paul Krugman's 2008 Nobel Prize in Economic Sciences. *Regional Sciences and Urban Economics, 39*(2), 109–119.

Fujita, M., & Thisse, J.-F. (2013). *Economics of agglomeration: Cities, industrial location, and globalization* (2nd ed.). Cambridge: Cambridge University Press.

Gaigné, C., & Thisse, J. F. (2014). New economic geography: Past and future. In *Handbook of regional science* (pp. 539–568). Berlin: Springer.

Gaspar, J. M. (2018). A prospective review on New Economic Geography. *The Annals of Regional Science, 61*(2), 237–272.

Gaspar, J. M. (2020a). New Economic Geography: history and debate. *The European Journal of the History of Economic Thought*. https://doi.org/10.1080/09672567.2020.1767671.

Gaspar, J. M. (2020b). Paul Krugman: contributions to Geography and Trade. *Letters in Spatial and Resource Sciences*, 1-17. https://doi.org/10.1007/s12076-020-00247-0.

Gaspar, J. M, Castro, S. B. S. D., & Correia-da-Silva, J. (2018). Agglomeration patterns in a multi-regional economy without income effects. *Economic Theory, 66*(4), 863–899.

Gaspar, J. M., Castro, S. B. S. D., & Correia-da-Silva, J. (2019). The Footloose Entrepreneur model with a finite number of equidistant regions. *International Journal of Economic Theory*, 1–27. https://doi.org/10.1111/ijet.12215.

Guckenheimer, J., & Holmes, P. (2002). *Nonlinear oscillations, dynamical systems, and bifurcations of vector fields*. Berlin: Springer.

Helpman, E. (1998). The size of regions. In D. Pines, E. Sadka, & I. Zilcha (Eds.), *Topics in public economics: Theoretical and applied analysis* (pp. 33–54). Cambridge: Cambridge University Press.

Henderson, J. V. (1974). The sizes and types of cities. *American Economic Review, 64*(4), 640–656.

Henderson, J. V. (1991). *Urban development: Theory, fact, and illusion*. Oxford: Oxford University Press.

Hoover, E. M. (1937). Spatial price discrimination. *Review of Economic Studies, 4*, 182–191.

Hotelling, H. (1929). Stability in competition. *Economic Journal, 39*, 41–57.

Ikeda, K., Murota, K., Akamatsu, T., Kono, T., & Takayama, Y. (2014). Self-organization of hexagonal agglomeration patterns in new economic geography models. *Journal of Economic Behaviour & Organization, 99*, 32–52.

Isard, W. (1949). The general theory of location and space-economy. *Quarterly Journal of Economics, 63*, 476–506.

Isard, W. (1956). *Location and space-economy*. Cambridge: MIT Press.

Krugman, P. (1979). Increasing returns, monopolistic competition and international trade. *Journal of International Economics, 9*, 469–479.

Krugman, P. (1980). Scale economies, product differentiation and the pattern of trade. *American Economic Review, 70*, 950–959.

Krugman, P. (1991a). Increasing returns and economic geography. *Journal of Political Economy, 99*, 483–499.

Krugman, P. (1991b). *Geography and trade*. Cambridge: MIT Press.

Krugman, P. (1993). On the number and location of cities. *European Economic Review, 37*(2–3), 293–298.

Krugman, P. (1996). *The self organizing economy*. New York: Wiley-Blackwell.

Krugman, P. (2009). The increasing returns revolution in trade and geography. *American Economic Review, 99*(3), 561–571.

Krugman, P. (2011). The new economic geography, now middle aged. *Regional Studies, 45*(1), 1–7.

Krugman, P., & Elizondo, R. (1996). Trade policy and the third world metropolis. *Journal of Development Economics, 49*, 137–150.

Krugman, P., & Venables, A. J. (1995). Globalization and the inequality of nations. *Quarterly Journal of Economics, 110*, 857–880.

Launhardt, W. (1885). *Mathematische Begründung Der Volkswirtschaftslehre*. Leipzig: B.G. Teubner. Translated from German by Teubner, B. G. (1993) *Mathematical principles of economics*. Aldershot: Edward Elgar.
Lösch, A. (1940). *Die Räumliche Ordnung der Wirtschaft*. Jena: Gustav Fisher. English translation: *The economics of location*. New Haven: Yale University Press (1954).
Marshall, A. (1890). *Principles of economics*. London: Macmillan. 8th edition published in 1920.
Martin, P., & Rogers, C. (1995). Industrial location and public infrastructure. *Journal of International Economics, 39*(3), 335–351.
Martin, R. (1999). The new 'geographical turn' in economics: Some critical reflections. *Cambridge Journal of Economics, 23*, 63–91.
Mills, E. S. (1967). An aggregative model of resource allocation in a metropolitan area. *American Economic Review, 57*, 197–210.
Mossay, P. (2003). Increasing returns and heterogeneity in a spatial economy. *Regional Science and Urban Economics, 33*, 419–444.
Mossay, P., & Picard, P. (2011). On spatial equilibria in a social interaction model. *Journal of Economic Theory, 146*(6), 2455–2477.
Murata, Y. (2003). Product diversity, taste heterogeneity, and geographic distribution of economic activities: Market vs. non-market interactions. *Journal of Urban Economics, 53*(1), 126–144.
Murata, Y., & Thisse, J.-F. (2005). A simple model of economic geography à la Helpman-Tabuchi. *Journal of Urban Economics, 58*(1), 137–155.
Ogawa, H., & Fujita, M. (1980). Equilibrium land use patterns in a nonmonocentric city. *Journal of Regional Science, 20*(4), 455–475.
Ohlin, B. (1933). *Interregional and international trade*. Cambridge: Harvard University Press. Revised version published in 1968.
Ottaviano, G. (2001). Monopolistic competition, trade, and endogenous spatial fluctuations. *Regional Science and Urban Economics, 31*(1), 51–77.
Ottaviano, G. (2010). 'New' new economic geography: Firm heterogeneity and agglomeration economies. *Journal of Economic Geography, 11*(2), 231–240.
Ottaviano, G., Tabuchi, T., & Thisse, J.-F. (2002). Agglomeration and trade revisited. *International Economic Review, 43*, 409–436.
Pflüger, M. (2004). A simple, analytically solvable, Chamberlinian agglomeration model. *Regional Science and Urban Economics, 34*(5), 565–573.
Pflüger, M., & Südekum, J. (2008). Integration, agglomeration and welfare. *Journal of Urban Economics, 63*(2), 544–566.

Pflüger, M., & Tabuchi, T. (2010). The size of regions with land use for production. *Regional Science and Urban Economics, 40*(6), 481–489.
Puga, D. (1999). The rise and fall of regional inequalities. *European Economic Review, 43*(2), 303–334.
Redding, S. J. (2013). Economic geography: A review of the theoretical and empirical literature. In D. Bernhofen, R. Falvey, D. Greenaway, & U. Kreickemeier (Eds.), *Palgrave handbook of international trade*. London: Palgrave Macmillan.
Robert-Nicoud, F. (2005). The structure of simple "new economic geography" models (or, on identical twins). *Journal of Economic Geography, 5*(2), 201–234.
Starrett, D. (1978). Market allocations of location choice in a model with free mobility. *Journal of Economic Theory, 17*, 21–37.
Tabuchi, T., & Thisse, J.-F. (2002). Taste heterogeneity, labor mobility and economic geography. *Journal of Development Economics, 69*, 155–177.
Tabuchi, T., & Thisse, J.-F. (2011). A new economic geography model of central places. *Journal of Urban Economics, 69*(2), 240–252.
Tabuchi, T., Thisse, J.-F., & Zeng, D.-Z. (2005). On the number and size of cities. *Journal of Economic Geography, 5*(4), 423–448.
Venables, A. J. (1996). Equilibrium locations of vertically linked industries. *International Economic Review, 37*, 341–359.
Venables, A. J. (2010). Productivity in cities: Self-selection and sorting. *Journal of Economic Geography, 11*(2), 241–251.
von Ehrlich, M., & Seidel, T. (2013). More similar firms—More similar regions? On the role of firm heterogeneity for agglomeration. *Regional Science and Urban Economics, 43*(3), 539–548.
von Thünen, J. H. (1826). *Der Isolierte Staat in Beziehung auf Landwirtschaft und Nationalökonomie*. Hamburg: Perthes. English translation by Wartenberg, C. M. (1966) *von Thünen's Isolated State*. Oxford: Pergammon Press.
Weber, A. (1909). *Über den Standort der Industrien*. Tü bingen: J. C. B. Mohr. English translation: *The Theory of the Location of Industries*. Chicago: Chicago University Press (1929).

5

Location Games

Simon Loertscher

5.1 Introduction

Many problems of pertinent interest to economists, social scientists, political scientists, business strategists, and citizens with an interest in politics are suitably modeled as location games. Examples range from the provision of artwork including songs and movies; the production of articles; and, prior to that, the choice of research agendas to the programming choice of free-to-air radio and TV stations; drug development by pharmaceutical companies; the physical location of (chain) stores; the strategic choices of business managers regarding which territories and

I want to thank the editor, Stefano Colombo, for his patience and persistence, and Bing Liu and Laure Pavaday for their outstanding research assistance. Financial support from the Samuel and June Hordern Endowment is also gratefully acknowledged.

S. Loertscher (✉)
Department of Economics, University of Melbourne, Melbourne, VIC, Australia
e-mail: simonl@unimelb.edu.au

S. Colombo (ed.), *Spatial Economics Volume I*,
https://doi.org/10.1007/978-3-030-40098-9_5

business strands to be active in; and the choice of policy platforms by political parties or candidates.

In a location game, the set of actions available to strategic players is a point in a given space. For the purpose of this chapter, we take this space to be the unit interval, and we assume that there is a continuum of customers (buyers, voters) distributed continuously along that interval. This distribution of customers is captured by a cumulative distribution function F with density f. Customers have bliss point locations, and cater to the player whose location is closest to their bliss point. The payoff of a player is monotonically increasing in the mass of customers it attracts. Often, this payoff is assumed to be linear but, as we shall see, this assumption can typically be relaxed considerably by simply assuming that it is increasing. (Of course, the assumption of linearity is, for example, appropriate for broadcasters, newspapers, online portals, and YouTubers whose net profits are in proportion to the size of their audiences.)

To date, location games come in one of two forms. In a *simultaneous location game*, a given set of firms choose their locations simultaneously, and all firms enter. In contrast, in a *sequential location game*, a given (large) set of firms can enter and choose locations sequentially at some fixed cost. In any (subgame perfect) equilibrium, only a subset of these firms enter. Location games provide simple, parsimonious, and elegant frameworks that allow one to think about a host of interesting issues in a concise way. Last but not least, location games are fun to think about and great tools for teaching basic game theory.

(Un)fortunately, location games are surprisingly robust in some important aspects and terribly fragile in others. In this chapter, we review both robustness and fragility, and lack of tractability of simultaneous and sequential location games, and we discuss a new approach that may combine the pros of both approaches without any of their cons.

We identify as a main obstacle for tractability the *leapfrogging* motive that faces no countervailing incentives with simultaneous moves because of the absence of a need to deter entry and the *Stackelberg* problem. The Stackelberg problem arises, in general, in sequential location games because of the sequential nature of moves, and we review recent progress along both lines of research. Then we sketch possible ways to combine the pros of both approaches while avoiding their cons.

Specifically, we first discuss simultaneous location games, illustrating that they are both remarkably robust in the case of two players and remarkably fragile otherwise. With two players, the median location is the unique equilibrium for any distribution F, and it is a dominant strategy equilibrium with majority voting. In contrast, as is well known, with three players there is no pure strategy equilibrium, and, for all practical intents and purposes, the mixed strategy equilibrium is not tractable. The main issue of non-existence of a pure strategy equilibrium is the incentive for *business stealing*, which with simultaneous moves, has no countervailing incentive such as deterring entry. This leads to *leapfrogging*, which may render pure strategy equilibria non-existent (as in the case of three players) or fragile, which is the case for four players, as discussed next.

For F uniform and four players, as is also well known, the simultaneous location game has a pure strategy equilibrium in which two players locate at the one-quarter quantile and two at the three-quarter quantile. However, we show that this equilibrium itself is fragile because there is no pure strategy equilibrium with four players and any density f that is symmetric and single-peaked (as would be the case for the normal distribution, which is arguably the empirically most relevant one). This analysis will also bring to light the distinction between optimal locations within an interval and what, at this stage slightly loosely speaking, may be considered entry-deterring locations. This distinction is moot for the special case of uniform distributions but key otherwise. As an interesting aside, we also show that a pure strategy equilibrium with four players exists if f is symmetric trough-shaped (i.e. has a unique local minimum at its midpoint).

The non-existence of a pure strategy equilibrium with four players and a symmetric hump-shaped density arises because, in general, there is a subtle but important difference between how much market share a player can *grab* and how much he can *defend* in the sense of preventing others from stealing it. The uniform distribution is singular in that regard because it does not give rise to such a distinction. As all locations within a given interval give rise to the same share, it follows that a player can defend whatever share he can grab.

With this in mind, we then turn attention to *sequential location games*, which were introduced by Prescott and Visscher (1977, PV hereafter). In principle, sequential location games have a number of advantages. First, the equilibrium number of active players is determined endogenously. Second, because of the threat of subsequent entry, every player who enters faces a subtle trade-off between the ever-present motive of business stealing and the need to deter entry, thus giving hope for the existence of pure strategy equilibria. PV analyzed a sequential location game for the case where F is uniform, and Loertscher and Muehlheusser (2011, LM hereafter) extended the analysis beyond uniform distributions, including distributions with symmetric trough-shaped densities and monotone densities. We discuss both approaches and show that both PV and LM were lucky in their own ways by exploiting special properties of the models they studied.

The big downside to sequential location games is that they can be dauntingly complicated because subgame perfection in general requires that one solves the game backward. So, even if it were known that in equilibrium exactly, say, 5 players enter, there will be 124 different sequences in which the locations (ordered from, say, left- to rightmost) are occupied, with each different sequence being associated in principle with different locations. What gave traction to PV is the property, unique to the uniform distribution, that any entry-deterring location within an interval is always also an optimal (i.e. best-response) location within that interval absent the need to deter entry. This allowed them to determine equilibrium locations iteratively. LM discovered and exploited the property that for densities like the monotone ones or symmetric trough-shaped ones (which effectively consist of a combination of two monotone ones), the sequence in which equilibrium locations are occupied and the equilibrium locations themselves are independent, such that the equilibrium locations can be determined without even considering the order in which they are occupied. Needless to say, and notwithstanding footnote 5 in PV, these properties do not generalize. In particular, even though symmetric single-peaked densities are also combinations of two monotone densities, the sequence in which the equilibrium locations are occupied can no longer be disentangled from the equilibrium locations themselves. The key difference to trough-shaped densities is that the location underneath the peak may be attractive (and may be given by a first-order condition, giving rise to a "Stackelberg" problem), whereas the location at the minimum of a density is never occupied in equilibrium.

To paraphrase Vogel (2008), location games are simple games that do not necessarily have simple solutions. The purpose of this chapter is to demonstrate which features of existing location games make them tractable and which render them difficult to analyze and sketch promising paths for going forward.

The remainder of this chapter is organized as follows. The setups are introduced in Sect. 5.2. Sections 5.3 and 5.4 then analyze simultaneous and sequential location games, respectively. These sections are organized according to the nature of the distribution F—uniform and non-uniform—and in the case of simultaneous location games, according to the number of players choosing a location. Section 5.5 provides a discussion of promising avenues for future research and concludes the chapter.

5.2 Setups

In a location game, a continuum of *customers* is located along the [0,1] interval. Their mass normalized to 1. Each customer has a bliss point location y. These bliss points are distributed according to the commonly known distribution function $F(y)$, with density $f(y) > 0$ for all $y \in (0, 1)$. Every customer visits the player that is closest. So, if the locations of players i and j are x_i and x_j, the customer at y prefers i to j if and only if $|y - x_i| < |y - x_j|$. We assume *full market coverage*, that is, all customers participate.[1] Customers can be equivalently thought of as either consumers in a product market or voters in a political context. Each customer's bliss point is a given.

[1]A microfoundation for this assumption is that all customers have a gross utility v of participating (e.g. consuming the good if the application is product design). Let $t(z)$ denote the cost of traveling distance z, which increases in z, v, and $t(.)$ such that $v - t(1) > 0$, where 0 is the utility of not participating. Under these circumstances, a customer would travel the length of the whole line if that is required for participation.

Locations are chosen by *players*. A player who attracts a mass or share σ of customers obtains a variable profit of $g(\sigma)$, where $g(.)$ is an increasing function. (There may also be a fixed cost.) For most of the analysis, we will assume that $g(.)$ is the identified function, that is, we set $g(\sigma) = \sigma$. As we will see, this is without loss of generality for most intents and purposes. As mentioned previously, we distinguish between *simultaneous* and *sequential location games*.

Simultaneous location games. In a *simultaneous* location game, a given number $n \geq 1$ of players $i = 1, \ldots, n$ simultaneously choose locations $x_i \in [0, 1]$, to maximize $g(\sigma_i)$. There is no fixed cost of operation, and hence, the payoff of player i who obtains the share σ_i is simply $g(\sigma_i)$.

Sequential location games. In a *sequential* location game, in contrast, each player bears a fixed cost of entry $K > 0$, where 0 is the value of not entering. Players $i = 1, \ldots, n$ are given the move in the predetermined order according to their index, where n is a large number (say, larger than $[g(1)/K] + 1$). Upon given the move, player i chooses whether to enter, and if it enters, the location $x_i \in [0, 1]$ it occupies. These choices are irreversible, and all predecessors' choices are observed. There is no discounting. Of course, player i only enters if its expected variable profit $g(\sigma_i)$ exceeds K. (We assume that i does not enter if it is indifferent between entering and not).

The key "parameters" of a simultaneous location game are n and F, while in a sequential location game, they are K and F. In either variant, players are allowed to choose identical locations. If two or more players occupy the same location, they share the mass of customers this location attracts evenly.

Because the uniform distribution fares prominently in analyses of location games of either form, the following observation is useful. Let x_i, x_{i+1} and x_{i+2} be locations that are occupied by exactly one player such that $x_i < x_{i+1} < x_{i+2}$ and such that no player has located in between x_i and x_{i+1} and between x_{i+1} and x_{i+2}. Assume $g(\sigma) = \sigma$ and let $\sigma_y(a, b)$ denote the payoff to a player locating at $y \in (a, b)$ with a and b occupied and no other player having located inside (a, b). Then, if F is uniform, we have for all $y \in (x_i, x_{i+1})$:

$$\sigma y \left(x_i, x_{i+1}\right) = \left(x_{i+1} - x_i\right)/2.$$

Moreover, if $x_{i+2} - x_{i+1} = x_{i+1} - x_i \equiv \Delta$, then the market share of choosing any $y \in (x_i, x_{i+2})$, that is, including x_{i+1}, is $\Delta/2$. In words, these shares are independent of y.

5.3 Simultaneous Location Games

To analyze simultaneous location games, we begin with the case with $n = 2$ players. Assume for now that $g(\sigma) = \sigma$, and let $y_m = F^{-1}(1/2)$ be the location of the median customer. Then, the unique pure strategy equilibrium of this game is for both players $i = 1, 2$ to choose $x_i = y_m$. To see that this is an equilibrium, notice that each player's payoff is 1/2 in this equilibrium because they split the market evenly. Upon a deviation to some location $\hat{x}_i \neq y_m$, keeping the rival's strategy fixed, player i would obtain a payoff that is strictly less than 1/2. This is, of course, the well-known *median voter* result that has its origins in the work of Hotelling (1929) and Downs (1957). It is a robust result insofar as it holds regardless of F.[2]

To see that it is unique, stipulate to the contrary that there is an equilibrium with $x_i \neq y_m$ for at least one i. If the two players take the same location x in this conjectured equilibrium, either one would benefit from a small deviation to the side of x where there is more mass. If $x_1 \neq x_2$, a similar deviation to the long side of the opponent will pay off.

Unfortunately, the model is much less well behaved with $n = 3$ players. In this case, there is no pure strategy equilibrium, and the mixed strategy equilibrium is hopelessly complicated even when F is the uniform distribution. We confine ourselves here to showing that there is no pure strategy equilibrium. To that end, notice first that there cannot be a pure strategy equilibrium in which all three locations differ because if that were so, the payoffs of the players with the extreme locations increase by moving closer to the player in the middle, eventually driving that player's

[2]It also generalizes directly to problems with a discrete, odd number of individuals whose, say, social or political views can be ordered from left to right (or small to large) when there are two alternatives to be chosen (in or out, acquit or guilty, yes or not). In this case, the view of the individual with the median opinion will prevail in majority voting.

payoff to 0. However, this cannot be in equilibrium because then the player in the middle has an incentive to leapfrog to the outside, whereby he will make a positive payoff. Second, there is no equilibrium in which all players choose the same location since in this case each player's payoff would be 1/3, whereas by unilaterally deviating to the longer side, any player would get a payoff of at least 1/2. Finally, there cannot be an equilibrium in which two players choose the same location since the best response of the third player would be to locate adjacently on the long side, thereby getting at 1/2, which would give each of the two players who are supposed to choose the same location an incentive to leapfrog this third one as each of them obtains in the hypothesized equilibrium a payoff of less than 1/4.

Obviously, this non-tractability for $n = 3$ is bad news for location games as it prevents, for example, comparative statics with respect to n.

Interestingly, for $n = 4$ and F uniform, there exists a pure strategy equilibrium. In this equilibrium, two players choose the location 1/4 and two the location 3/4. In this configuration of locations, each player's payoff is 1/4. If player i deviates to a more extreme location, i will get a payoff that is weakly smaller, and if he deviates to some $x_i \in (1/4, 3/4)$, his payoff will be $(3/4 - 1/4)/2 = 1/4$ because of the observation made at the end of Sect. 5.2. Finally, if i who is supposed to locate at 1/4 deviates and chooses 3/4, his payoff will be 1/6, which makes him strictly worse off. Thus, the locations $x_i = 1/4$ for $i = 1, 2$ and $x_i = 3/4$ for $i = 3, 4$ are the equilibrium outcomes. It is not too hard to establish that, apart from relabeling players, there is no other pure strategy equilibrium.

This existence result is reasonably well known. However, it depends, in a sense that we will make precise shortly, critically on the fact that F is uniform. Away from the uniform distribution, some locations inside a given interval (a, b) with a and b occupied will be more profitable than others, and this can lead to the non-existence of a pure strategy Nash equilibrium for $n = 4$ even when f is symmetric.

To see this, consider two symmetric densities f that are either single-peaked, so that $f(1/2) = \max_{y \in [0,1]} f(y)$, to which we refer as *symmetric hump-shaped* densities, or minimized at 1/2, to which we refer as *symmetric trough-shaped densities*. For $y < 1/2$, the trough-shaped density is decreasing

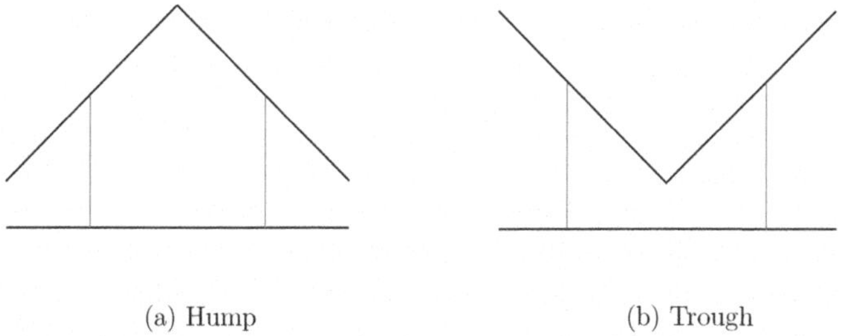

Fig. 5.1 Panel (a): Symmetric hump-shaped density. Panel (b): Symmetric trough-shaped density

and for $y > 1/2$ it is increasing. In contrast, the hump-shaped density is increasing for $y < 1/2$ and decreasing for $y > 1/2$. Figure 5.1 displays two examples. While single-peakedness is often a nice property and based on the normal distribution may often seem the empirically relevant case, we are now going to show that it is the symmetric hump-shaped case that leads to non-existence of a pure strategy equilibrium with $n = 4$. This result seems of interest in itself. The logic behind it is instructive in that it highlights peculiarities of the uniform distribution and foreshadows issues that arise in sequential location games.

It is intuitive and not too hard to establish rigorously that for there to be a pure strategy equilibrium with $n = 4$ players and symmetric densities, the equilibrium locations must be configured in the same way as for the uniform insofar as two players occupy the "left" location $x_L = F^{-1}(1/4)$ and two occupy the "right" locations $x_R = F^{-1}(3/4)$ so that, when occupying these locations all players obtain a share of 1/4. (We leave the proof of this auxiliary result to the reader.) The key difference between the hump-shaped and the trough-shaped cases comes from the optimal locations inside the (x_L, x_R) interval. For the trough-shaped, it is optimal to locate adjacently to either the right of x_L, denoted as x_L^+, or the left of x_R, denoted as x_R^-. At either location, the supremum of the payoff is 1/4, so deviations to the interior do not pay off in the trough-shaped case. Moreover, the optimal locations outside the (x_L, x_R) interval is x_L^- and x_R^+ for either density, generating a share of no more than 1/4. Hence, the symmetric trough-shaped density has a pure strategy equilibrium.

In any such equilibrium, two players choose x_L and two players choose x_R. In contrast, when f is hump-shaped, the uniquely optimal location inside (x_L, x_R) is 1/2. Notice that this is strictly larger than 1/4 because the density is largest around 1/2; this leads to a share that is strictly larger than 1/4. Hence, the deviation to the middle pays off. Thus, there is no pure strategy equilibrium for $n = 4$ when f is symmetric hump-shaped.

This analysis also highlights a peculiarity of the uniform distribution. For the purpose of this argument, let us consider a density f that is symmetric in the sense that for all $y \in [0, 1]$, $f(y) = f(1 - y)$, and let us assume that x_L and x_R are each occupied by exactly one player, with no one being located in between at the outset of the argument, with $x_L < 1/2 < x_R$ and $x_R = 1 - x_L$. Then the two players at x_L and x_R obtain the same share from within (x_L, x_R), namely, half of the mass of customers that is there. If f is the uniform density, then this is also the share that an additional player locating optimally inside (x_L, x_R) would obtain since such a player simply obtains half of the mass regardless of his location, as noted at the end of Sect. 5.2. The same is approximately true when f is trough-shaped because then the optimal locations inside (x_L, x_R) are x_L^+ and x_R^-, so that a player locating inside (x_L, x_R) obtains the same share as the players located at x_L and x_R obtain from the inside of that interval without the additional player. Hence, when f is uniform or symmetric trough-shaped, each player can grab as much as an additional player would obtain when locating inside (x_L, x_R). In this sense, for f is uniform or trough-shaped, a player grabs as much as he can defend. Interestingly, as already noted, this is *not* the case when f is symmetric hump-shaped: the players at x_L and x_R still obtain half of the mass inside (x_L, x_R) each, absent an additional player. However, if an additional player locates optimally inside (x_L, x_R), this additional player obtains strictly more. Thus, for f is symmetric hump-shaped, players cannot defend as much as they grab.

To summarize, simultaneous location games make the robust prediction that for $n = 2$, the median location y_m is the unique equilibrium location. For $n \geq 3$, the framework is much less robust in that either there is no pure strategy equilibrium or the existence of an equilibrium depends on the fine details of the model, such as the distribution. In particular, as we have seen, for $n = 4$ there is no pure strategy equilibrium for symmetric hump-shaped densities. As these are, among symmetric densities, arguably the empirically most relevant ones, this is bad news. At the source of the problem of non-existence is the incentive to leapfrog rivals' locations. In the case of $n = 3$ or $n = 4$ and symmetric hump-shaped densities, there is no countervailing incentive to prevent agents from such leapfrogging.

5.4 Sequential Location Games

This provides ample motivation to study sequential location games, in which, as we will see, the need to deter further entry is precisely such a countervailing incentive. However, as we will also see, sequential location games are not without problems of their own, and unfortunately, these are mostly pronounced in the case of hump-shaped densities, which, as mentioned, have empirical appeal. In a sequential location game, players still have incentives to steal business by, for example, moving closer to their neighbor if the distribution is uniform (or moving closer to areas where the density is larger if the distribution is non-uniform). However, the countervailing effect players have to account for in a sequential location game is that they cannot steal too much business without inducing additional entry. So, players need to balance their desire to steal business against their often vital need to deter additional entry.

5.4.1 Uniform Distribution

Assuming that F is uniform, $K < 1/2$, and, in our notation, $g(\sigma) = \sigma$, Prescott and Visscher (1977, PV) derived subgame perfect equilibria in which, when $1/K$ is not an even integer, the equilibrium locations are

$$\{K, 3K, \ldots, (m+1)K, \ldots, 1-3K, 1-K\}$$

if $(1 - 2(m+1)K)/2 \leq K$ and

$$\{K, 3K, \ldots, (m+1)K, 1/2, 1-(m+1)K, \ldots, 1-3K, 1-K\}$$

if $(1-2(m+1)K)/2 > K$, where $m \in \{0, 1, \ldots\}$ is determined by K. If $1/K$ is an even integer h, the equilibrium locations are

$$\{K, 3K, \ldots, (h/2+1)\,K, 1-K\},$$

where $(h/2+1)K = 1-3K$. Moreover, in the equilibria PV study, they assume that equilibrium locations are occupied from outside-in in the sense that K is occupied first, $1-K$ second, $3K$ third, and so on (or $1-K$ first, K second, and so on). All players, or all but two or three players, choose the locations closest to 1/2, including 1/2 if that is occupied in equilibrium, and obtain shares of $2K$.

The construction of these equilibria relies on the indifference property of the uniform distribution noted at the end of Sect. 5.2. Within a given interval (a, b), any entrant is indifferent between all locations. As long as $b \leq a + 2K$, additional entry will not occur in this interval. Implicitly, and with the benefit of hindsight, the tractability of the sequential location game with F uniform derives from a property that may be called the separation of *sequence of settlement* and *equilibrium locations*. By this, we mean that one can determine the locations that are occupied in equilibrium independently of the sequence in which these are occupied.[3] To see this, assume that K is occupied, and consider the player who in equilibrium is supposed to choose $3K$. This choice will be optimal if $5K$ is already occupied because it deters additional entry. It is also optimal if the right-hand "neighbor" of the player locating in equilibrium at $x = 3K$ is not there yet, but chooses to locate at $x + 2K$, where $x \leq 3K$ is the location the player who in equilibrium locates closest to K chooses.

5.4.2 Classes of Non-uniform Distributions

The separation of *sequence of settlement* and the *equilibrium locations* that obtains for certain classes of non-uniform distributions is also what gives the analysis of LM tractability. For the purpose of specificity, we first

[3]To be more precise, PV assume that a player who enters last inside in an interval (a, b) with a and b already occupied and satisfying $a + 2K < b \leq a + 4K$ locates at the midpoint $(a + b)/2$. This deters additional entry and, because of the indifference property of the uniform, the last entrant obtains the same share for all locations that deter subsequent entry, and so this choice is optimal.

assume $g(\sigma) = \sigma$. If $K \in [1/2, 1)$, the first player will enter and deter subsequent entry by choosing any location $y \in [F^{-1}(1-K), F^{-1}(K)]$. From now, let us therefore assume that $K < 1/2$, so that a single player cannot deter all subsequent entry (since $K < 1/2$ implies $F^{-1}(K) < F^{-1}(1-K)$).

Let us assume first that $f(y)$ is increasing in y. Generally, and very intuitively, in any outcome of a subgame perfect pure strategy equilibrium, the left- and rightmost locations that are occupied are $F^{-1}(K)$ and $F^{-1}(1-K)$. To see that these locations cannot be further to the middle, notice that then an additional player could profitably enter at $F^{-1}(K)$ and $F^{-1}(1-K)$, respectively. (The argument why these locations cannot be further away from the middle will be provided shortly.)

Consider an interval (a, b) with a and b occupied and no player having located anywhere in between. Because the density is increasing, it follows that the optimal locations inside (a, b) are as large as possible, that is, b^-. Of course, for a player to enter in this interval, it is necessary that the player who chooses b^- breaks even. That is, $F(b) - F((a+b)/2) > K$ has to hold. Moreover, because there are many players who could enter subsequently, any entrant needs to ensure that he breaks even by deterring subsequent entry. To derive the optimal entry-deterring location to the right of some occupied location a, let $\lambda(a)$ be the number such that

$$F(\lambda(a)) - F\left(\frac{\lambda(a) + a}{2}\right) = K.$$

Notice that $\lambda(a)$ is unique and increasing in a. By the preceding argument, a player entering inside $(a, \lambda(a))$ would optimally locate at $\lambda(a)^-$ and thereby net K (and hence not enter).

Assuming that $\lambda(a) < F^{-1}(1-K)$, it follows that if location a is occupied in equilibrium, the closest location occupied to its right is $\lambda(a)$. Notice that this means that we can determine the equilibrium location to the right of an equilibrium location a independently of what the locations further to the right of $\lambda(a)$ are. Moreover, it also does not matter whether they are already occupied or not. If the equilibrium locations are $\{a, \lambda(a), b\}$ and b is already occupied (or will be given by $F^{-1}(1-K)$), $\lambda(a)$ is the best response. If b is not occupied at the point where the player is supposed to locate at $\lambda(a)$, then a fortiori $\lambda(a)$ will be optimal because subsequently its right-hand "neighbor" will choose $\lambda(\lambda(a))$. Thus, while any smaller location than $\lambda(a)$ would also deter entry to its left, by choosing $\lambda(a)$ the player can induce its subsequently entering right-hand neighbor further to the right, which is profitable because f is increasing. As the same argument applies with a as the leftmost location, it follows that the leftmost equilibrium location will be as large as possible, which is $F^{-1}(K)$.

Moreover, none of the equilibrium locations to its left will depend on their right-hand neighbors. Hence, by analogous reasoning, the rightmost location will be as small as possible, that is, it will be $F^{-1}(1-K)$. Hence, the set of equilibrium locations will be

$$\left\{F^{-1}(K), \lambda\left(F^{-1}(K)\right), \lambda\left(\lambda\left(F^{-1}(K)\right)\right), \ldots, F^{-1}(1-K)\right\},$$

where all other locations are determined by iterative application of $\lambda(.)$ to their left-hand neighbors.

Observe that we have determined the equilibrium locations without saying anything about the sequence in which these locations are chosen. Under the assumption that f is concave, LM use a simple geometric argument to conclude that, quite generally, equilibrium locations with higher density are more profitable, with the exception applying to the comparison of the rightmost and second to rightmost locations, whose profitability cannot be ranked in general. Thus, for f is increasing and concave, one would expect the sequence of settlement to be, roughly from right to left (with the appropriate qualifications just mentioned).

Of course, symmetric results obtain when f is decreasing. In this case, the set of equilibrium locations is

$$\left\{F^{-1}(K), \ldots, \rho\left(\rho\left(F^{-1}(1-K)\right)\right), \rho\left(F^{-1}(1-K)\right), F^{-1}(1-K)\right\},$$

where $\rho(b)$ is such that

$$F\left(\left(\rho(b)+b\right)/2\right)-F\left(\rho(b)\right)=K.$$

Now that the case of monotone densities is understood, it seems natural to conjecture that one also has a hand on hump-shaped and trough-shaped densities as these are, after all, only piecewise combinations of monotone densities. As we are going to show now, this conjecture is correct in some ways and wrong in important others.

Consider first the case of trough-shaped densities, and assume for simplicity that these densities are symmetric.[4] The minimum will never be occupied, and hence because of symmetry, the two locations $F^{-1}(1/2 - K)$ and $F^{-1}(1/2 + K)$ will be mutually best responses to each other, in the sense that if they are occupied, no subsequent player enters in between. Moreover, these two locations cannot be further away from the minimum without inviting additional entry in between. Hence, there is an equilibrium in which these two locations are occupied. And in any such equilibrium, the equilibrium locations to the left of $F^{-1}(1/2 - K)$ will be given by iterative applications of $\rho(.)$, up to the point where one reaches $F^{-1}(K)$, and similarly to the right of $F^{-1}(1/2 + K)$, the equilibrium locations will be given by iterative applications of $\lambda(.)$ up to the point where one reaches $F^{-1}(1 - K)$.[5] Thus, again, one can separate the sequence of settlement from the equilibrium locations, and hence the model remains tractable.

So how about the hump-shaped case? Unfortunately, this problem is plagued by the following circumstance. Consider a symmetric hump-shaped density and assume (a, b) are occupied with no one in between and with $a < 1/2 < b$. Then, unless one of the constraints $x^* > a$ or $x^* < b$ is binding, the optimal location inside the (a, b) interval satisfies the first-order condition:

$$f\left(\left(a + x^*\right)/2\right) = f\left(\left(x^* + b\right)/2\right),$$

implying that x^* decreases in a and increases in b. In other words, x^* is of the wrong sort of monotonicity insofar as a player locating at a to the left of x^* may choose a smaller location if x^* has not be occupied yet than when the point "in the middle" is occupied. Put differently, with hump-shaped densities, the model loses, in general, its tractability. (To be sure,

---

[4]As will become clear from the argument, everything will go through under the weaker condition that the density is symmetric in a neighborhood around its minimum that contains a mass of K of customers.

[5]It is also not too hard to show that this is the unique equilibrium outcome.

LM derive parameter conditions such that the equilibrium locations can be determined, but this does not invalidate the point that, in general, the model is intractable.) For lack of a better term, we refer to the issues that arise from the first-order condition for the optimal location "underneath the hump" as *Stackelberg* problem.

We conclude this section with a short discussion of how the model generalizes to any $g(\sigma)$ that is increasing in σ and then provide a couple of problems that readers may find interesting to think about.

The assumption that the variable payoff to a player, $g(\sigma)$, is a linear function of its share is not universally appealing. For example, in a political economic context, whether a party obtains 1/3, 1/2 or 2/3 of parliamentary seats will make a noticeable difference. Fortunately, the assumption can easily be relaxed by defining $\hat{K} = g^{-1}(K)$ and then proceeding with the analysis as in the model where g is linear with K replaced by $\hat{K}$. At the end of the day, what matters for equilibrium locations is not how much payoff a player can get above and beyond K but whether he breaks even (and the extent to which he can deter others from breaking even).

As an exercise and illustration of how these games can be fun, consider the two symmetric densities in Fig. 5.2, where K is the same for both panels. The locations $F^{-1}(K)$ and $F^{-1}(1-K)$ are also both occupied in both panels, and no other location has been occupied. For each of the following statements, in which entry means entry inside the interval $(F^{-1}(K), F^{-1}(1-K))$, say whether it is true or not true:

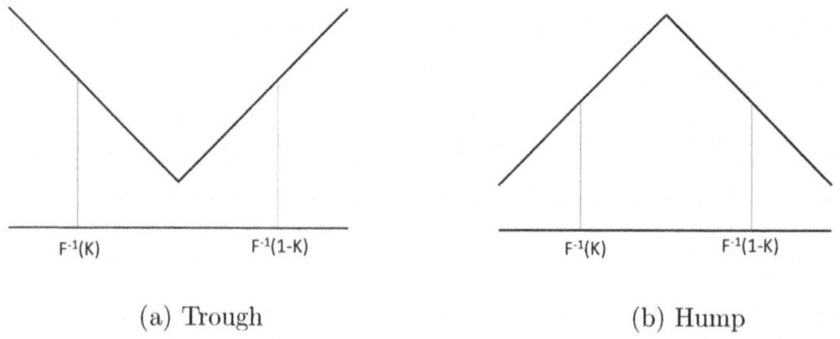

Fig. 5.2 Panel (a): Symmetric trough-shaped density. Panel (b): Symmetric hump-shaped density

1. If no additional entry occurs in (a), no additional entry occurs in (b).
2. If no additional entry occurs in (b), no additional entry occurs in (a).
3. If no additional entry occurs in (a), at most one player enters in (b).
4. If two additional players enter in (b), at least one player enters in (a).
5. If at least one player enters in (a), at least one player enters in (b).

The answers are provided in this footnote.[6]

5.5 Discussion

We conclude this chapter with a brief discussion of related literature and of promising avenues for going forward. From an empirical perspective, sequential location games have recently been used to gauge the value of standardization in retail chains (see Klopack (2019)). More research along these and similar lines would seem valuable.

We have abstracted away from price competition. Although in many situations of interest the first-order issue may indeed be location choice, extension of models such as Chen and Riordan (2007), D'Aspremont et al. (1979), Reggiani (2014), and the early work of Vickrey (1999, 1964) to account for non-uniform distributions would likewise add value.

Last but not least, there seems promise in the approach of Loertscher and Muehlheusser (2019), who study a dynamic model in which, on the equilibrium path, all locations are chosen simultaneously while at the same time being constrained by the need to deter additional entry. This is achieved by stipulating a model in which many players can enter in the first period. The need to deter subsequent entry arises because there is a second-period player who will enter as soon as he can net a share larger than K. This threat disciplines the first-period entrants and thereby gets rid of the leapfrogging problem. At the same time, because all locations are chosen simultaneously on the equilibrium path, there is no Stackelberg problem either. Thus, this "simultaneous location game with

[6]The answer to 1 is No. All other answers are Yes.

entry" combines the pros of both simultaneous and sequential location games without any of their cons.

References

Chen, Y., & Riordan, M. (2007). Price and Variety in the Spokes Model. *Economic Journal, 117*, 897–921.

D'Aspremont, C., Gabszewicz, J. J., & Thisse, J.-F. (1979). On Hotelling's 'Stability in Competition'. *Econometrica, 47*, 1145–1150.

Downs, A. (1957). *An Economic Theory of Democracy*. New York: Harper Collins.

Hotelling, H. (1929). Stability in Competition. *Economic Journal, 39*, 41–57.

Klopack, B. (2019). One Size Fits All? The Value of Standardized Retail Chains. *Job Market Paper*, Stanford.

Loertscher, S., & Muehlheusser, G. (2011). Sequential Location Games. *RAND – Journal of Economics, 42*, 639–663.

Loertscher, S., & Muehlheusser, G. (2019). *Multi-Party Competition: A Simultaneous Location Game with Entry*. Working Paper.

Prescott, E. C., & Visscher, M. (1977). Sequential Location Among Firms with Foresight. *Bell Journal of Economics, 8*, 378–393.

Reggiani, C. (2014). Spatial Price Discrimination in the Spokes Model. *Journal of Economics and Management Strategy, 23*, 628–649.

Vickrey, W. S. (1964). *Microstatics*. New York: Harcourt, Brace and World.

Vickrey, W. S. (1999). Spatial Competition, Monopolistic Competition, and Optimum Product Diversity. *International Journal of Industrial Organization, 17*, 953–963.

Vogel, J. (2008). Spatial Competition with Heterogenous Firms. *Journal of Political Economy, 116*, 423–466.

6

Non-localised Spatial Competition: The "Spokes Model"

Carlo Reggiani

6.1 Background

The spokes model is a model of *spatial non-localised* competition. The model was introduced almost at the same time by Chen and Riordan (2007a,b) and Caminal and Claici (2007). The model represents the market as a collection of spokes and it visually looks like the internal part of a bike's wheel. Consumers are located all over the spokes that compose the market. They have a preference for the good supplied by a firm on their own spoke. Firms, however, may or may not be present on all spokes. The model is represented graphically in Fig. 6.1.

In the example in Fig. 6.1, the market is constituted of $N = 5$ spokes and $n = 3$ firms. The firms are identified by the black dots. All firms are located at the extreme of their spoke, a location which we can denote by $y_i = 0$, with $i = 1, \ldots, N$. All the spokes join in the common centre, $x = 1/2$. Given that the firms are located at the extremes of their

C. Reggiani (✉)
Department of Economics, University of Manchester, Manchester, UK
e-mail: carlo.reggiani@manchester.ac.uk

S. Colombo (ed.), *Spatial Economics Volume I*,
https://doi.org/10.1007/978-3-030-40098-9_6

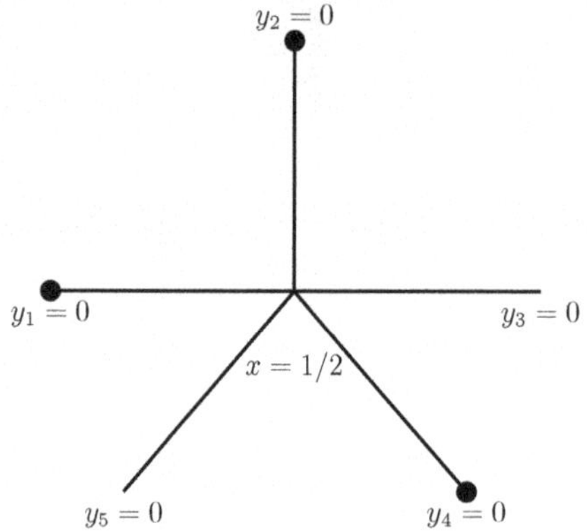

Fig. 6.1 A graphical illustration of the spokes model

respective spokes, a consumer located in the centre of the spokes structure is completely indifferent between any of the products supplied on the market. The absence of black dots on spokes 3 and 5 implies that no firm is located there.

The model is *spatial* as the preference for the good can be measured by the distance between a consumer and a firm. Such a distance can be interpreted in a geographical sense, as, for example, the meters separating a consumer from a shop, or in terms of product characteristics, as, for example, how different is a product from a consumer ideal specification. In the latter interpretation, the spokes model is suited to capture horizontal differentiation between firms or brands: whereas all products satisfy the same need or have the same quality, consumers have heterogeneous preferences for each. In this sense, it is an addition to the economist's toolkit, as a possible alternative to the Hotelling (1929) model, that represents the market as a linear city with sellers and consumer located over it, and the Salop (1979) model that extends the previous to a circle.

One distinguishing characteristic of the spokes model, also compared to the two recalled alternatives (Hotelling 1929; Salop 1979), is worth remarking. Each consumer has a favourite product in the one supplied by the firm or brand on its own spoke; however, there is no inner ranking between any of the other options available on the market. This is because the consumer would have to travel through the centre and then walk the exact same distance to reach any of the remaining firms, as they are all located at the extremes of their spoke. In this sense competition in the spokes model is *non-localised*, as it is not limited to a subset of neighbouring firms but it involves all the market actors.

The spokes model has been introduced relatively recently, but it has proved to be a valuable addition to an economist's toolkit. In the rest of the chapter, I will provide motivating examples and contexts where the model can be productively employed (Sect. 6.2). Then, I will describe the original version of the model in some more details (Sect. 6.3). The remaining sections will be dedicated to showcase some interesting research questions that have been posed in the context of the model. These include pricing (Sect. 6.4), location choices (Sect. 6.5), and market entry (Sect. 6.6). Section 6.7 briefly reviews further economic applications of the model. Section 6.8 concludes.

6.2 Motivating Examples

It is a familiar experience to many, unfortunately, that while driving in a different city or region a red led starts flashing on the dashboard. Depending on the intensity of the problem, you may find yourself browsing the internet for car repair garages in the vicinity.

This unpleasant situation is one for which the spokes model may well capture the choice set of the car driver. In fact, the driver's main need is to repair the car, and most likely all the available garages would be able to do a fair work. In terms of the model, the garages represent the firms on each spoke. For a number of reasons, though, one is likely to have a preference for a garage that specialises or that, at least, declares specialisation in the brand of one's car. Hence, the driver is located on a specific spoke and has a more or less strong preference for the specialised repair.

Such a specialised garage, however, may not be locally available. In that case, a generic repair shop may exist, corresponding to a firm locating in the centre of the spokes structure. Otherwise, the car's owner might be somewhat indifferent between all other available shops, specialising in the repair of different car brands.

This example is what motivates the study of competition and product service variety in the Dutch car repair market in Lijesen and Reggiani (2020). They employ the address dataset by BOVAG, the Dutch industry association for car repair firms. The association covers 86% of the car repair market in terms of firms and a much higher percentage in terms of turnover. The dataset provides information about the brand that a firm specialises in, if any. About half of all car repair firms in the sample are specialised in repairing one brand of car. The other half of the car repair shops is either generic or specialised in specific repair types (e.g., tyres).

The market has, indeed, characteristics that are in line with the spokes model. In fact, whereas there are on average 12 shops per local market, at the national level, there are specialised repairs for 16 brands. In line with the idea of "empty spokes", then, not all national brands are available in each local market. Moreover, the authors document how in most local markets, 60% of the total, both specialised and generic repair shops co-exist. However, 20% of the local markets feature only generic garages and 5% only specialised, whereas, in the remaining 15% mostly rural regions, no garage is available at all.

In this context, it is then worth asking what is the relation between the variety offered by the market, measured by the share of specialised garages, and the number of firms active locally. This is a question for which the spokes model is well suited, whereas other models in the traditional economist's toolkit fall short.

As shown in Fig. 6.2, Lijesen and Reggiani (2020) find that the probability of a repair being specialised increases with the number of competitors in a local market. The result is obtained controlling for a number of shifters as the number of households, the average household income, and the dummies for the level of urbanisation. The relation tends to flatten as the number of firms increases, but that happens for a high number of local competitors, even higher than the number of national level brands. This probably indicates that garages try to avoid local level competition with firms specialising in the same car brand.

Whereas the car repair example is particularly fitting, the model is also well suited to analyse most secondary and ancillary goods, as for instance appliances' parts, ink cartridges, phone covers, insurance policies, and

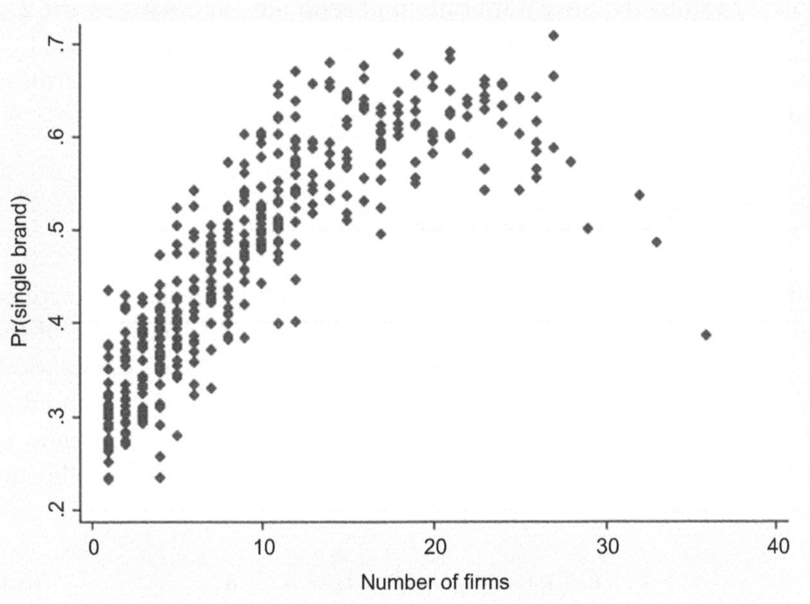

Fig. 6.2 Predicted probability of a garage being specialised in a local market. Source: Lijesen and Reggiani (2020)

so on. Moreover, the model can be employed to think productively of competition in situations with the following characteristics.

First, consumers may not have immediate neighbouring substitutes for the good in question. This can be the case of, say, sport shoes and equipment. A field hockey player, for example, needs very specific shoes. If those are not available, the player may need to settle for either generic trainers or indoor football boots; however, different players may differ in their ranking of the second best alternative. Similarly, whereas many when buying a soft drink may find Pepsi the obvious alternative to Coca-Cola, others may instead consider Fanta or Irn-Bru. A similar logic may apply for goods like whiskey, fashion brands, and so on. Second, national brands are not necessarily always present at the local level. Indeed, not all retailers or supermarkets stock all the available brands. Finally, some sellers may be more or less prominent than others and occupy a "central" position in the network of sellers. This point has been made by Firgo et al.

(2015) to study the price implications of centrality on pricing by the 273 gas stations of Vienna. Their results confirm that firms characterised by a more central position in a spatial network are more powerful in terms of having a stronger impact on their competitors' prices.

6.3 The Spokes Model

The spokes model, illustrated in the example of Fig. 6.1, can be described as follows. The market is constituted of N spokes. At most one of the $n \leq N$ firms can locate in each of the spokes. All spokes are identical: they have an origin ($x = 0$), a constant length normalised to $1/2$, and they all join at the centre of the market ($x = 1/2$). Consistently with most of the literature, the technology structure can be described by the following cost function:

$$C_i(q_i) = cq_i + f \quad \forall i = 1 \ldots n, \tag{6.1}$$

where the marginal cost c is constant and f is a fixed cost of entry. In the original version, which we follow closely, each firm charges a uniform price p_i (Chen and Riordan 2007a).

Consumers are assumed to be uniformly distributed on the N spokes, and each has a unit demand for the good supplied in the market. The uniform assumption is often analytically convenient, but, in many cases, the model works well even under a more general atomless distribution $f_s(x)$, as long as there is symmetry between the spokes. The valuation of the good v is identical for all consumers. Each of them also suffers a unit mismatch cost, t, if the exactly preferred variety is not available or, in the geographical interpretation, a unit transport cost. The overall mismatch is a function of the distance, $d(x_i, y_j)$, between a consumer located at x_i on spoke i and a firm located at y_j on spoke j.

A distinguishing feature of the model is that the distance between the consumer and the firm is *spoke dependent*: the distance between a consumer located at $x = 0.4$ and a firm in $y = 0.2$ depends on whether both are on the same spoke or on different ones. In the former case, the distance is $0.4 - 0.2 = 0.2$, in the latter $(0.5 - 0.4) + (0.5 - 0.2) = 0.4$, as the consumer needs to travel through the centre to reach the firm on a different spoke.

As a result of the previous assumptions, the utility function of a customer located in x_i considering to buy the product of the firm located at y_j is

$$U(x_i, y_j) = v - td(x_i, y_j) - p_i. \tag{6.2}$$

The utility function allows specifying the demand of each firm and closes the model. This last step is not straightforward, as it depends on the parameters of the model and an important assumption on consumer preferences. This is further discussed in Sect. 6.3.1. Given the stated framework, however, the game played by the n firms can be thought of being potentially constituted of at least the following three stages, which correspond to the broad categories of research questions to be addressed in the rest of this chapter:

1. *Entry decision*: firm i decides whether to enter the market or not, $i = 1, \ldots, n \leq N$;
2. *Location decision*: firm i chooses its location y_i on spokes i;
3. *Pricing decision*: firms simultaneously compete in prices and each chooses p_i.

6.3.1 Demand Specification

As recalled above, the definition of demand is crucial for the analysis of the model. In most spatial models, the key step to specify the demand and payoff functions is the identification of the set of indifferent consumers. To this end, there are two possibilities.

First, following Chen and Riordan (2007a) and Caminal and Claici (2007), we can assume that each consumer has preferences only for a *finite* number brands/spokes, for simplicity say two. No matter whether a brand is available on the market or not, the consumer likes it. The implication is that a consumer located, for example, on spoke 1 in Fig. 6.1 surely likes the product of firm 1. As a second favourite brand, he may like the product of firms 2 or 4, whose products are also available, or any of the other brands that are not supplied in the market, like 3 and 5. Hence, there are three types of consumers: (1) consumers with preference for two existing brands, (2) consumers for which only one of the favourite brands is available, and (3) consumers that like two brands that are not supplied. Firms compete for the first type of consumers, while the second type are *captive* to one of them. The third type of consumers is not served, so the market is not covered. Overall, this scenario can be identified as one of the *captive consumers* and we mostly focus on it in what follows.

The second scenario allows consumers to consider in their choice set *all* alternative suppliers that are available. As a result, consumers located on the empty spokes are not captive to any of the firms. We can refer to this scenario as *all-out competition* and we will mainly focus on it in Sect. 6.5.

Moving back to the *captive consumers* scenario, a consumer located on a given spoke, say 1, also has a second preferred brand, which is any of the remaining four brands in our example of Fig. 6.1, chosen randomly with probability $1/N-1$. More generally, for a consumer on spoke i, if the second brand j is available, then the indifferent consumer x^*_{ij} is found by solving:

$$\begin{aligned} U(x_i^*, y_i) &= v - td(x_i^*, y_i) - p_i \\ &= v - td(x_i^*, y_j) - p_j = U(x_i^*, y_j) \quad \forall j \neq i, j = 1, \ldots, n. \end{aligned} \tag{6.3}$$

The captive indifferent consumer x'_{ij}, instead, is identified by:

$$U(x_i', y_i) = v - td(x_i', y_i) - p_i = 0 \quad \forall j = n+1, \ldots, N \tag{6.4}$$

In trying to solve (6.3)–(6.4), there is a second issue to tackle. To simplify matters, we will start by assuming that the firms are all located at the extreme of their spoke, that is, $y_i = 0$, and the disutility $d(x_i, y_j)$ is just the distance (i.e., it is linear). Depending on the parameters of the model and the firms' prices, the indifferent consumers (x^*_{ij} and x'_{ij}), which represent a location on the spoke, can be any number. In other words, there can be corner solutions. For example, if the good valuation is low compared to the price, both types of consumers may not purchase at all (x_{ij}^*, $x_{ij}' \leq 0$); if, instead, the valuation is high, all captive may purchase ($x_{ij}' \geq 1$).

Solving (6.3)–(6.4) gives, respectively:

$$x_{ij}^* = \frac{1}{2} - \frac{p_i - p_j}{2t}, \quad x_{ij}' = \frac{v - p_i}{t}.$$

so that, assuming the prices are not too different and v is not extremely low, the demand function is derived by Chen and Riordan (2007a) as:

$$q_i = \begin{cases} \frac{2}{N}\frac{1}{N-1}\sum_{j=1...n}^{j\neq i}\left(\frac{1}{2} - \frac{p_i - p_j}{2t}\right) + \frac{2}{N}\frac{1}{N-1}\left(\frac{v-p_i}{t}\right) & \text{if } 0 < \frac{v-p_i}{t} \leq 1 \\ \frac{2}{N}\frac{1}{N-1}\sum_{j=1...n}^{j\neq i}\left(\frac{1}{2} - \frac{p_i - p_j}{2t}\right) + \frac{2}{N}\frac{1}{N-1} & \text{if} \frac{v-p_i}{t} > 1 \end{cases} \quad (6.5)$$

The first line of (6.5) corresponds to the case where some captive consumers with a bad match with firm i are not served, whereas the second line is when all captives purchase. In the equations, $2/N$ is the density of consumers on each spoke and, as recalled, $1/N-1$ represents the probability of each spokes to be a given consumer's second favourite brand.

Given the intricate procedure to define demand in the spokes model, it is worth noting the close relation with the workhorse of spatial competition, the Hotelling (1929) linear city model. The latter is, indeed, a special case of the spokes model when setting $n = N = 2$. Hence, the spokes model extends Hotelling (1929) competition to n firms and also allows addressing cases when not all brands are available to consumers ($n < N$).

6.4 Pricing

The properties of pricing in the spokes model can be analysed following Chen and Riordan (2007a). Before doing that, it is worth recalling some assumptions that ease the presentation of the results. First, we keep assuming that firms' location is fixed at the extreme of each spoke, $y_i = 0$. Second, for simplicity we normalise the marginal cost c to zero and the unit mismatch cost t to one. Finally, the mismatch disutility is linear in the distance, $d(x_i, y_j)$, separating the consumer from the firm. As a result, the firms' profit function is, simply, $\pi_i = p_i q_i$, and q_i is specified by (6.5).

The first-order condition for a symmetric equilibrium looks familiar:

$$\frac{\partial \pi_i}{\partial p_i} = D(p_i, p_{-i}) + p_i D_i'(p_i, p_{-i}) = 0,$$

and it highlights the usual trade-off between the marginal demand gains and the infra-marginal losses of lowering the price, p_i. Under the symmetry assumption, the demand function (6.5) simplifies to:

$$D_i(p_i, p^*) = \begin{cases} \frac{2}{N}\frac{n-1}{N-1}\left(\frac{1}{2} + \frac{p^*-p_i}{2}\right) + \frac{2}{N}\frac{N-n}{N-1}(v - p_i) \text{ if } \frac{1}{2} < (v - p_i) < 1 \\ \\ \frac{2}{N}\frac{n-1}{N-1}\left(\frac{1}{2} + \frac{p^*-p_i}{2}\right) + \frac{2}{N}\frac{N-n}{N-1} \quad \text{if} \quad (v - p_i) \geq 1 \end{cases},$$

from which it is also easy to compute $D_i'(p_i, p^*)$.

The pricing equilibrium of the spokes model can then be characterised as follows:[1]

Proposition 6.1 (Chen and Riordan 2007a) *The spokes model has a unique symmetric equilibrium. The equilibrium price is:*

$$p^* = \begin{cases} \frac{2N-n-1}{n-1} & if\ 2\frac{N-1}{n-1} < v \leq \overline{v}(n, N)\ Region\ I \\ v - 1 & if\quad 2 \leq v \leq 2\frac{N-1}{n-1}\ Region\ II \\ \frac{2(N-n)v+(n-1)}{4N-3n-1} & if\ \frac{1}{2} + \frac{N-1}{2N-n-1} < v < 2\ Region\ III \\ v - \frac{1}{2} & if\ 1 < v \leq \frac{1}{2} + \frac{N-1}{2N-n-1}\ Region\ IV \end{cases},$$

with $\overline{v}(n, N) = 2\frac{N-1}{n-1} + \frac{1}{2}\frac{2N-n-1}{N-n}$.

[1]The interested reader can find the proof in Chen and Riordan (2007a), pp. 917–919.

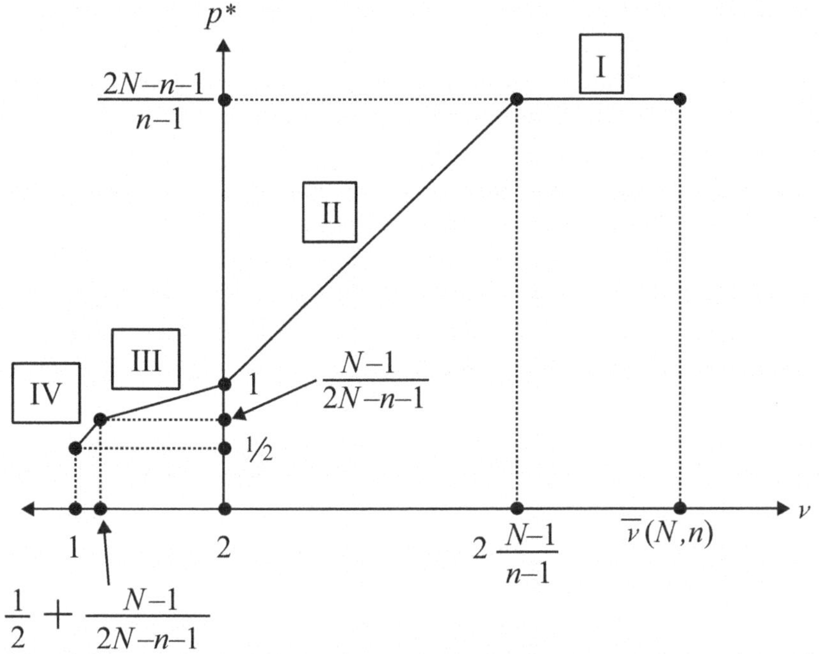

Fig. 6.3 Prices as a function of the value of the good. Source: Chen and Riordan (2007a)

Note first that the equilibrium price depends crucially on the consumers' intrinsic product valuation, v. This is also illustrated in Fig. 6.3. There are boundaries on the values of v for which a unique pure-strategy symmetric equilibrium exists. Indeed, if $v < 1$, then firms are effectively independent monopolists; if, instead, $v > \overline{v}(n, N)$, then a profitable deviation from the candidate equilibrium price exists. From a technical point of view, it is also worth remarking that the prices in Regions I and III are interior solutions, obtained from solving the first-order conditions; Regions II and IV are corner solutions, corresponding to kinks in the demand curve.

The intuition for the results is the following. Usual oligopoly competition takes place in Region I: all consumers whose both desired brands are available benefit from price competition between firms. Unlike other regions, the equilibrium price depends on the number of active firms, the total number of possible brands but not on the relatively high valuation for the good. In Region II, instead, firms exploit captive consumers, who only find one brand available on the market. The price is set such that the marginal consumer is indifferent between purchasing the least favourite brand and nothing at all. This is exactly where the kink in the demand takes place and price increases one to one with the good valuation.

In Region III, firms sell to both consumers who have a choice and captive ones. The marginal consumer in the competitive segment is indifferent between the two available brands, while the marginal captive consumer is indifferent between purchasing the second preferred variety and staying out of the market. The equilibrium price depends on all three parameters, v, n, and N. Region IV is characterised by a different kink in the demand, where only consumers whose first preferred brand is available do purchase the product, and the marginal consumer is indifferent between purchasing and not. Also for this kink, the equilibrium price only depends on the valuation.

Pricing in the spokes model has interesting comparative statics properties. Proposition 6.2 highlights the effect of an increase in the number of firms on the equilibrium prices.

Proposition 6.2 (Chen and Riordan 2007a)

$$\frac{dp^*}{dn} = \begin{cases} -\frac{2(N-1)}{(n-1)^2} < 0 & if \quad \textit{Region I} \\ 0 & if \quad \textit{Region II} \\ \frac{2(2-v)(N-1)}{(4N-3n-1)^2} > 0 & if \quad \textit{Region III} \\ 0 & if \quad \textit{Region IV} \end{cases}.$$

The equilibrium price does not respond to changes in the number of firms in the kinked demand equilibria of Regions II and IV. Dargaud and Reggiani (2015) relate this feature of the equilibria to ex-post evidence on the price effects of horizontal mergers. In fact, existing studies suggest that the undesirable effects on prices and consumer surplus, usually under the scrutiny of antitrust authorities, do not always take place and even relevant consolidations may end up having negligible price effects. A corollary of the above finding, in fact, is that mergers in the context of non-localised spatial competition may have zero price effects when firms target specific kinks of the demand function. In Region I, instead, the usual comparative statics is in place: prices decrease following an increase in the number of competitors in the market. The intuition relates to the higher relevance, *ceteris paribus*, of the duopoly competition segments *vis à vis* the captive ones.

More unusual, however, is the result for Region III: an increase in the number of competitors leads firms to increase their prices. Unlike other oligopoly models of price-increasing competition, Chen and Riordan (2007a) obtain such result under complete information and pure strategies. The region is characterised by a more elastic demand for the captive segment than for the competitive one. The property is due to the fact that, as the firm lowers its price, the marginal consumer in the monopoly segment always has zero surplus from its outside option (infinite elasticity), while the marginal consumer in the competitive segment becomes increasingly attracted by the alternative competing brand (finite). As the number of firms becomes higher, the captive segment shrinks and the competitive segment expands, reducing the overall average demand elasticity, ultimately leading to a higher equilibrium price. Chen and Riordan (2008) extend the latter result, by employing a more general discrete choice duopoly model of product differentiation, in which consumers' values for substitute products have an arbitrary symmetric joint distribution.

6.5 Location Choice

The original version of the spokes model assumes that firms are exogenously located at the end of their spoke. However, it is possible to allow firms to choose any location, either on the spokes or even outside of the area where consumers are located. In terms of the model notation, the location of firm i on that spoke, y_i, is not restricted to lie between 0 and $1/2$, but it can take negative values too. An example is provided in Fig. 6.4.

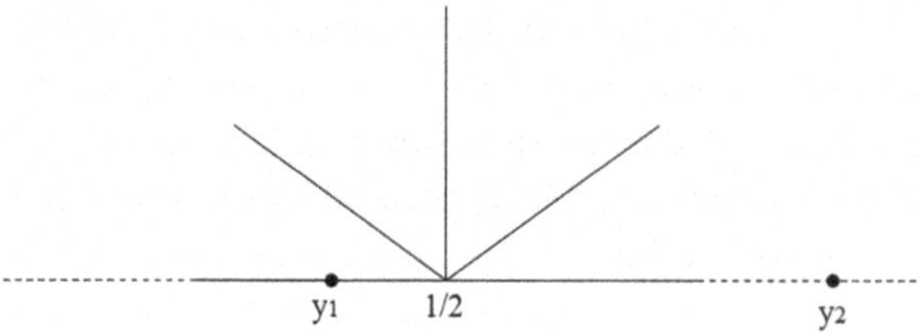

Fig. 6.4 A market with $n = 2$ firms and $N = 5$ spokes. Firm 1 is located within the spokes structure, $y_1 \in [0, 1/2]$, whereas firm 2 is located outside, $y_1 \in]-\infty, 0]$
Source: Lijesen and Reggiani (2019)

6.5.1 Location as Specialisation

Allowing for endogenous location, as by stage 2 of the timing presented in Sect. 6.3, enables to address further interesting research questions. For example, Lijesen and Reggiani (2019) observe that the choice of specialisation affects firms' brand perception by consumers and it is of crucial importance for their profitability in competitive markets. Specialisation is one of the keys to achieve strategic product differentiation and avoid fierce direct competition; a notion is present in economics models (e.g., Hotelling 1929) as well as in the strategy literature (Porter 1980).

The authors show that the spokes model, in its product characteristics interpretation, can be productively used to study the choice of specialisation. In the spokes model, in fact, only the *potential* level of variety, N, is exogenously fixed, and firms can choose freely where to locate in the product space, that is, specialise. In terms of the example in Fig. 6.4, one can say that firm 2 is more specialised than firm 1, as the latter supplies an almost generic product, appealing to a wider market. In that context, they ask the following. What drives a firm to choose a generic design *vis à vis* a specialised one? If a firm chooses to specialise, how much specialisation is optimal? Under which circumstances do specialised firms co-exist with generic ones? How does competition affect these choices?

It has to be noted that the traditional economics toolkit does not seem to provide a similarly suitable approach to address the previous questions. For example, most models of spatial competition (e.g., Hotelling 1929; Anderson et al. 1992) treat product differentiation as endogenous but predefine a constant product space. This clearly implies that, by construction, the level of specialisation decreases as the number of suppliers increases. On the other hand, in textbook approaches to monopolistic competition (e.g., Dixit and Stiglitz 1977), each firm is assumed to deliver one variety, and hence the market variety is positively related to the number of suppliers.

In order to tackle endogenous location, Lijesen and Reggiani (2019) need to assume that the transport costs $d(x_i, y_j)$ are proportional to the square of the distance separating consumers from the firm. It is well known, in fact, that a pure-strategy Nash equilibrium of the location subgame does not exist if transport costs are linear in distance. Sufficiently convex transport costs, instead, warrant pure-strategy existence (d'Aspremont et al. 1979; Economides 1986). This implies:

$$d(y_j, x_i) = \begin{cases} (y_j - x_i)^2 & j = i, \\ (1 - y_j + x_i)^2 & \forall j \neq i. \end{cases}$$

Finally but importantly, as discussed in Sect. 6.3.1, the analysis allows for firms to compete for all consumers (*all-out competition*), and the preferences of consumers are not restricted to only a subset of brands as in the benchmark version of the model.

Under these assumptions, the authors provide a general characterisation of the optimal pricing choices (stage 3 of the timing in Sect. 6.3) in the spokes model with endogenous location and all-out competition. The procedure is very similar to the benchmark case and relies on identifying indifferent consumers. Assuming that $y_i \geq y_j$, $j \neq i$, these are now identified by the two following expressions:

$$x_{ij}^j = \frac{1 - y_i + y_j}{2} + \frac{p_i + p_j}{2A_{ij}}, \quad i, j = 1, \ldots, n,$$

$$x_{ij}^k = \frac{1 - A_{ij}}{2} - \frac{p_i + p_j}{2(y_i - y_j)}, \quad i, j = 1, \ldots, n,$$

where $A_{ij} = 1 - y_i - y_j$ and k are the unoccupied spokes. The difference is that there are now no captive segments of demand and, hence, profits:

$$\pi_i = \frac{2}{N} p_i D_i(p_i, p_j), \quad \pi_j = \frac{2}{N} p_j D_j(p_i, p_j).$$

are characterised by different demand functions. These are given by:

$$D_i = \frac{2}{N}\left[\frac{1}{2} + \sum_{j=1,\dots,n}^{j \neq i} \left(\frac{1}{2} - x_{ij}^j\right)\right] + \frac{2}{N}(N-n)\max\left\{x_{ij}^k, \frac{1}{2}\right\}, \tag{6.6}$$

$$D_j = \frac{2}{N} x_{ij}^j + \frac{2}{N}(N-n)\min\left\{\frac{1}{2} - x_{ij}^k, 0\right\}, \tag{6.7}$$

The first terms in (6.6) and (6.7) represent the demand accruing from the occupied spokes, the second term is the demand (if any) from the empty ones. The latter assume values 1/2 and 0 in (6.6) and (6.7), respectively, when $n > 2$ if $N \leq \frac{5}{2}(n-1)$. This is an interesting property of the spokes model with quadratic transport cost and all-out competition. The convexity of the costs implies that firms may share even the empty spokes, contradicting the intuition by which the closer/less specialised firm must attract them all. However, as long as there are not too many empty segments of the market (i.e., if $n > 2$ and $N \leq \frac{5}{2}(n-1)$), it is optimal for the more specialised firms to focus on their own spokes. Note that such assumption always holds if there are no empty spokes ($n = N$). If empty segments are too important, then all firms would compete for them and the demand would be split.

Pricing in the spokes model with endogenous location and all-out competition can then be characterised in terms of the best response functions and, if symmetry between firms is assumed, even explicitly. As the number of spokes increases, the equilibrium price of all firms increases. Intuitively, the larger the number of empty segments in the market, the larger the proportion of consumers that the firm closer to the centre, firm i, serves: this leads to a higher equilibrium price, p_i. As prices are strategic complements, all other firms optimally raise their prices p_j too.

The main result, however, is about specialisation. Using the pricing results, it is in fact possible to address firms' choices in both a duopoly and a triopoly.

Proposition 6.3 (Lijesen and Reggiani 2019) *In the specialisation/location subgame of the spokes model with all-out competition:*

(i) if $n = 2 < N$ *firms, the subgame perfect Nash equilibria are:*

$$y_i^* = \frac{1}{2}, \quad y_j^* = \frac{N-5}{6(N-1)}, \qquad i, j = 1, 2. \tag{6.8}$$

(ii) if $n = N = 3$*, the game has two subgame perfect Nash equilibrium configurations. The equilibrium specialisations/locations are:*

$$(1)\ y_i^* = \frac{5}{16}, \qquad i = 1, 2, 3; \tag{6.9}$$

$$(2)\ y_i^* = \frac{1}{2},\ y_j^* = \frac{1}{8}\ \ i \neq j; \tag{6.10}$$

(iii) if $n = 3 < N = 4$*, one subgame perfect Nash equilibrium of the game is characterised by specialisation/location:*

$$y_i^* = \frac{1}{2},\ y_j^* = \frac{1}{8}\ \ i \neq j. \tag{6.11}$$

The results in Proposition 6.3 provide several insights. First and above all, market equilibria are characterised by the *co-existence* of specialised and generic firms. This is a theoretical prediction very much in line with our everyday experience. Local markets, in fact, feature specialised and generic firms and very often both of them. Restaurants catering a single cuisine (ethnic or regional, vegetarian, steak houses, and many more) can be found close to restaurants with a more generic menu. Stores for sports gear focused on a single brand or a single sport exist alongside firms that cater to many sports. General interest book stores partly serve the same markets as children's book stores and travel book stores. General hospitals can be found in the same local market as specialised hospitals and clinics.

This feature arises naturally in Lijesen and Reggiani (2019): as firms compete for all consumers in the market (all-out competition), one of them chooses a generic design to appeal to all market segments. Other firms, instead, specialise and focus on their own "niches". Despite all the real-life examples of markets that combine generic and specialised firms, the only model that does not predict either extreme specialisation or clustering is the sequential location choice version of the Hotelling's linear city model (Tabuchi and Thisse 1995). The spokes model delivers the result even in presence of simultaneous move and fully symmetric firms.

The above result applies to both duopoly and triopoly. The fact that the spokes model allows for an explicit solution with endogenous location for more than two players is noticeable in itself. In the related context of price and location choices in the Hotelling model, the only extension to a number of firms higher than two (Brenner 2005) relies on computational solutions rather than analytical ones.

Other noticeable features are the following. First, the specialisation of the non-generic firm j decreases in a duopoly, as the share of consumers on empty spokes increases. Intuitively, as N increases, the benefit of a more specialised design to soften competition is proportionally less relevant. Specialisation, instead, is unaffected by the unoccupied segments of the market when three firms compete in the market. Second, Lijesen and Reggiani (2019) also provide a version of the model with dichotomous specialisation. In that setting, the co-existence of generic and specialised firms holds more generally for any number of competitors, provided that the above restriction that empty spokes are not too relevant for firms holds. Third, in the triopoly case, it is also interesting to notice that both symmetric specialisation and the asymmetric generic-specialised co-existence are possible outcomes when there are no unoccupied segments of the market. Finally, the authors also solve the model under the usual assumption of captive consumers (Caminal and Claici 2007; Chen and

Riordan 2007a) and show that the results are not robust: in that case, the standard outcome of full specialisation, and no generic firms, is obtained.

6.5.2 Location and Product Line Design

Reggiani (2014) also studies endogenous location in the spokes model. In the model, however, firms are allowed to price discriminate using location-contingent pricing. The fact that firms know consumers' locations, and can adjust pricing accordingly, has a large influence on both pricing and optimal location. First, the analysis can be performed for both linear and quadratic transport costs. Second, once again the assumption of captive consumers does not need to be invoked, and all-out competition takes place. Third, firms bear transport costs and deliver the product to consumers' address, x_s.

In that context, as firms make personalised offers to consumers, they are basically engaging in Bertrand competition, with heterogeneous costs for serving each location. The cost heterogeneity reflects the distance from consumers, whose delivery cost is borne by the competing suppliers. There are, then, two segments of the demand faced by a firm i: the consumers for which it is the lowest cost provider, D_i, and those for which there is a tie in costs D_s. The latter segment is then divided between firms according to a sharing rule r: for example, each firm gets an equal proportion of these consumers. The profit function of a firm can then be written as:

$$\pi_i = \frac{2}{N}\left\{\int_{D_i} [p_i(x|y_i) - d(y_i, x)]\, dx \right.$$
$$\left. + \int_{D_S} [p_i(x|y_i) - d(y_i, x)]\, r(x) dx \right\}.$$

As in heterogeneous cost Bertrand competition, price competition under spatial price discrimination leads then the closest firm to get the consumer x_s and charge the price corresponding to the cost of delivery of the second most efficient firm. More formally, given the set of locations $y = (y_1, \ldots, y_i, \ldots, y_n)$, the unique equilibrium of the pricing stage is:

$$p_i^*(x|y) = \max\left\{d(y_i, x), \min_{j \neq i}\left\{d(y_j, x)\right\}\right\},$$

and the profit function simplifies to:

$$\pi_i = \frac{2}{N}\int_{D_i}\left[\min_{j \neq i}\{d(y_j, x)\} - d(y_i, x)\right]dx.$$

An established result in the literature on spatial price discrimination is that the equilibrium location pattern is consistent with social cost minimisation. This was proven under rather general conditions by Lederer and Hurter (1986). If there are no unoccupied segments of the market ($n = N$), the result also holds for the spokes model. This is quite easily seen. The socially optimal location configuration is defined as the one that minimises the total transport costs, that is, a vector of locations $y = (y_1, \ldots, y_n)$ that minimises over the spokes structure X:

$$SC(y) = \frac{2}{n}\int_X \min_{\forall i}\{d(y_i, x)\}dx$$

There is then a very close relation between the social cost function and the profits of a firm, as the following decomposition shows:

$$\begin{aligned}
\pi_i &= \frac{2}{n}\int_{D_i}\left[\min_{j \neq i}\{d(y_j, x)\} - d(y_i, x)\right]dx \\
&= \frac{2}{n}\int_X \min_{j \neq i}\{d(y_j, x)\}dx - \frac{2}{n}\int_X \min_{\forall j}\{d(y_j, x)\}dx \\
&= \frac{2}{n}\int_X \min_{j \neq i}\{d(y_j, x)\}dx - SC(y) \qquad (6.12)
\end{aligned}$$

It then follows immediately that the vector of locations $y^* = (y_1^*, \ldots, y_n^*)$ that maximises profits is also minimising the social cost.

The competitive pressure between firms drives prices down to cost; in case of a price tie, the most efficient firm "wins" the consumer as prescribed by the sharing rule. As the cost of the second most efficient firm is not affected by the firm's location, all that matters to the choice of location is to minimise cost over the firm's own turf; this implies that the incentives in choosing location are in line with minimising the social cost function.

The full characterisation of the equilibrium locations is also provided.

Proposition 6.4 (Reggiani 2014) *In the spokes model with $n = N$ firms and spatial price discrimination, the equilibrium locations are characterised by the following vectors:*

(i) $y_i^* = \frac{1}{4}, \forall i = 1, \ldots, n,$ *for* $n = 2, 3;$
(ii) $y_i^* = \frac{1}{4}, \forall i = 1, \ldots, n$ *and* $y_i^* = \frac{1}{2}, y_j^* = \frac{1}{6}\ \forall j \neq i,$ *for* $n = 4, 5;$
(iii) $y_i^* = \frac{1}{2}, y_j^* = \frac{1}{6}\ \forall j \neq i,$ *for* $n \geq 6.$

A highly asymmetric location pattern is one outcome if the number of firms is sufficiently high: in that case, one firm supplies a generally appealing product, whereas others focus on a specific niche.

The most important result, however, is that unlike in Lederer and Hurter (1986), social cost minimisation is not always achieved. For an intermediate number of competitors ($n = 3$ or $n = 4$), in fact, multiple equilibrium vectors are obtained: in this case, only asymmetric location configurations globally minimise the sum of transport costs.

Intuitively, such highly asymmetric location patterns are the only equilibrium in case some segment of the market is unoccupied by firms ($n < N$). In that case, in fact, the fierce competition for the consumers in the empty segments leads one firm to choose the centre of the spokes market; all other firms specialise on serving consumers on their own spoke. Such an outcome, with locations $y_i^* = \frac{1}{2}\ y_j^* = \frac{1}{6}$, is also social cost minimising.

Following MacLeod et al. (1988), Reggiani (2014) interprets spatial price discrimination in the characteristics space. In standard spatial models, transportation costs are a measure of consumers' disutility, and location is a product characteristic. In presence of spatial price discrimination, instead, firms personalise and adapt their product lines to the demand expressed by buyers. Despite in the last decade relationship marketing and one-to-one marketing have become established practices, firms are not yet offering a customised product to every buyer. The customised product interpretation also fits business-to-business contexts: software providers, for example, compete for customers with standardised products that can be adjusted at some cost to the specific needs of the customer. The results provided suggest that in these contexts some firms specialise in providing a range of products to a specific segment, while others may target several segments of the same market with even wider product ranges.

6.6 Entry and Variety Supply

After pricing and location, another natural question to ask in the context of the spokes model is how many firms do enter the market. In a different interpretation, if every brand supplied by the market is considered a variety, the model can provide further answers to the traditional issue of under or over provision of variety through market competition. Indeed, Chen and Riordan (2007a) themselves provide the first analysis of this issue in the context of the model.

6.6.1 Under or Over Provision of Variety?

Chen and Riordan (2007a) assume that there are many identical potential firms that can enter and supply a brand by incurring a fixed entry cost $f > 0$, as by Eq. (6.1). Unlike Sect. 6.5, the assumption of exogenous location, at the extreme of each spoke ($y_i = 0$), holds again. Entry takes place up to the point where the profits earned by firms are just sufficient to cover the fixed cost. In other words, n^* is found by ensuring that $\pi(n^*) - f > 0$ and $\pi(n^* + 1) - f < 0$. The equilibrium profits correspond to the equilibria obtained in Sect. 6.4, Proposition 6.1. Profit-based entry is then compared with the socially optimal level. The latter is defined as the number of firms needed on the market to maximise social welfare.

The relationship between the nature of competition and entry is not straightforward. In the spokes model of non-localised competition, both under and over provision of product varieties are possible and multiple equilibria can occur. Two polar cases are considered. First, if the valuation is sufficiently high, prices do not play a role and social surplus simply corresponds to the surplus generated by matching consumers to their favourite brand. In that case, for a given number of spokes, free entry can lead to either under or over provision of variety. In particular, free entry tends to be excessive when the fixed cost is relatively low. In fact, the entry of an additional firm has a negative externality on incumbent firms, as it reduces profits. However, there is also a positive impact, linked to both market expansion and improved matching effects. The first, negative, effect dominates if the fixed cost is low and makes entry excessive. The latter positive effects, instead, become more prominent if the fixed cost is large and entry becomes insufficient.

Second, the authors consider the case of relatively low valuation of the good. The analysis is further complicated by two elements: first, there can be multiple equilibria and, second, prices are not socially optimal. Hence, the authors consider both a regulator that also sets optimal prices and one that only affects variety supply for given prices to guarantee an optimal match. The results are qualitatively similar to the previous case but depend on one further effect, in addition to the ones previously discussed: the business-stealing effect associated with entry. The balance of these complicated effects is studied further by Caminal and Granero (2012) a series of follow-up articles that build on their methodology.

6.6.2 Variety Provision and Market Structure

Caminal and Granero (2012) focus their attention on the role of multi-product firms in the provision of product variety in the spokes model. In the presence of economies of scope, there may be a small number of multi-product firms that use their product range strategically in order to affect rivals' prices. Whereas, as in Chen and Riordan (2007a), variety can be both insufficient and excessive, the authors highlight that under some conditions, firms can drastically restrict their product range in order to soften price competition. This strategic effect leads to a substantial under provision of variety.

In doing so, a nice methodological innovation is introduced. The authors assume that the number of varieties is sufficiently large and formulate a continuous approximation by which the product range of a multi-product firm can be treated as a share, that is, a continuous variable. In particular, they consider the limiting case in which the number of possible varieties N tends to infinity, keeping the mass of consumers per variety equal to $1/2$. As a result, the fraction of active varieties can be denoted as $\gamma \in (0, 1)$ and consumers can be classified into three different groups. Fraction γ^2 has access to both desired varieties, fraction $2\gamma(1-\gamma)$ can purchase only one of them, and fraction $(1-\gamma)^2$ can access none and is therefore excluded from the market. There is also a fixed cost of entry per variety, such that the overall entry cost is γf.

Their formulation is so flexible that allows to address and compare provision of variety under many market forms: (1) the social optimal as chosen by a planner, γ^*, (2) a monopoly controlling all γ^M varieties, (3) monopolistic competition where each firm supplies one variety, γ^{MC}, and (4) multi-product oligopoly, where n firms hold a share of varieties and total provision is γ^O.

The presence of multi-product firms influences the overall provision of product variety through the following three main channels as described by Caminal and Granero (2012). (1) *Cannibalisation*: a multi-product firm internalises the impact of a new variety on the demand for the other varieties that it produces. This effect tends to reduce product diversity. (2) *Appropriability*: the presence of a small number of large multi-product firms is associated with prices that are higher than those set by single-product firms. This effect tends to expand product variety. (3) *Strategic price effect*: an oligopolistic firm anticipates that its product range influences the rivals' prices, and the sign of such effect is ambiguous. The way these effects play out in equilibrium is illustrated through an example in Fig. 6.5.

The neat methodology of Caminal and Granero (2012) has found other interesting applications around the themes of entry and variety supply. For example, Caminal (2010) focuses on content provision and

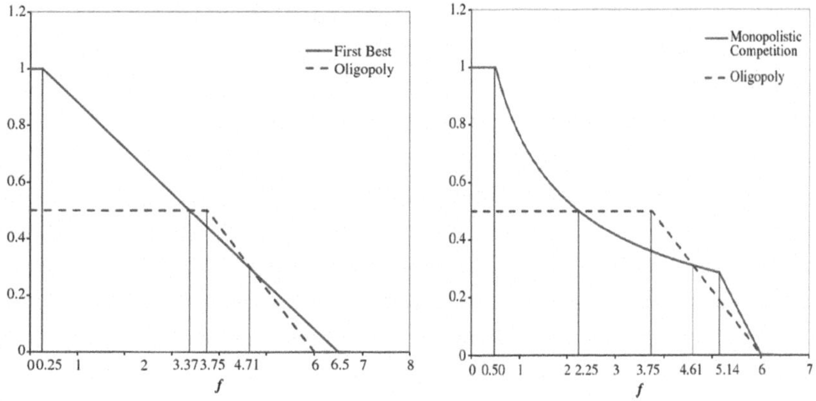

Fig. 6.5 Variety provision and entry cost: multi-product oligopoly compared with social planner (left) and monopolistic competition (right). Source: Caminal and Granero (2012)

language diversity. As cultural goods and media products can make content available to their audiences and readerships only through a particular language, the choice of language is a non-trivial decision in markets with bilingual or multilingual consumers. The article shows that the existence of bilingual consumers may seriously bias market outcomes against minority languages. In particular, the level of linguistic diversity determined by profit maximising firms tends to be inefficiently low, except when and where the cost of producing a second linguistic version becomes sufficiently low. The author concludes that the model provides an efficiency argument supporting government intervention to protect minority languages on the market.

Using a similar approach, Granero (2013) studies the price and variety effects of most-favoured-customer clauses in the case of a multi-product duopoly. As discussed, for example, in Cooper (1986), Baker (1995), Besanko and Lyon (1993), and Chen and Liu (2011), most-favoured-customer clauses are usually seen as anti-competitive coordination devices that firms adopt for the purpose of sustaining higher prices. The article examines the welfare impact of such clauses under endogenous product variety. Product variety is relevant because prospective higher prices from most-favoured-customer clauses can be anticipated by multi-product firms in designing product lines. Under such circumstances, it is not always the case that the clauses are harmful to consumers. In fact, most-favoured-customer clauses tend to be socially neutral for relatively large fixed costs of product line assortment, harmful for intermediate costs, and even beneficial for relatively small entry costs.

Finally, Granero (2019) adds to the analysis of variety supply the element of quality investment. Focusing on a multi-product duopoly, the article examines the linkages between strategic product assortment, quality choice, and pricing. The continuous approximation of the number of active varieties in the spokes model is adopted to derive the symmetric equilibria of a three-stage game. First, firms $i = 1, 2$ simultaneously choose the fraction of potential varieties they wish to supply, γ_i, and the resulting duopoly total fraction of active varieties is γ_D. Second, after observing such fractions, firms choose their product qualities, q_i. Third, firms compete in prices p_i. The model is solved and a symmetric equilibrium is studied under two configurations: first, social welfare maximisation and, second, the multi-variety duopoly profit maximisation.

The two configurations have in common that the equilibrium number of varieties weakly decreases and the quality supplied weakly increases, as the fixed cost of a variety increases. However, the duopoly quality supplied can be either too low or too high. Even in this case, the results depend on which of several effects dominates: (1) the impossibility to discriminate segments of consumers and price competition, both of which decrease the incentives to invest in quality; (2) business stealing from competitors, which encourages quality investment; and, finally, (3) a cannibalisation effect on a firm's own brands.

The balance of these effects, represented through an example in Fig. 6.6, is complicated but the author proposes the following interpretation. First, relatively high expected prices induce firms to expand their product range and, thus, to alter quality. On the other hand, however, a strategic multi-product firm anticipates that its product range affects price competition. This strategic price effect can also affect product variety and quality. In particular, when the strategic price effect dominates, for relatively high values of the fixed cost, the two firms have incentives to refrain from expanding their product range and relax price competition. In this case, product variety becomes insufficient and quality investment

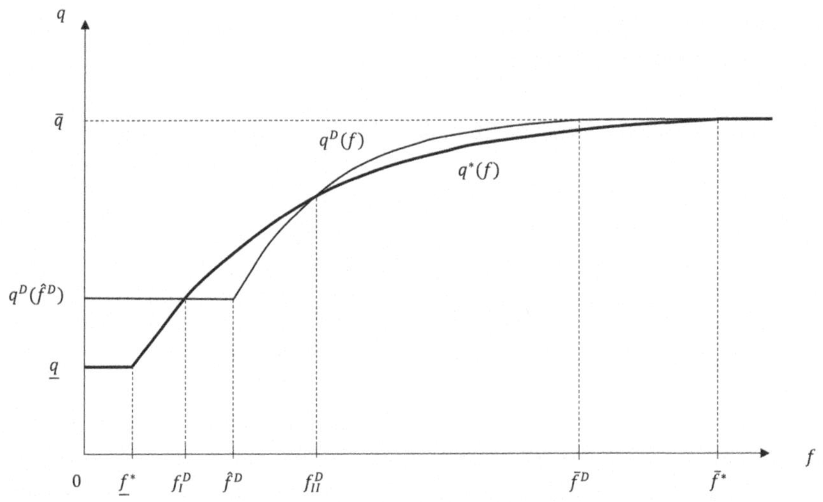

Fig. 6.6 Quality provision, entry, and fixed cost: over provision for low and relatively high levels of the fixed cost and under provision for relatively low and high levels. Source: Granero (2019)

excessive. In contrast, when business stealing dominates, for relatively low levels of the fixed cost, each multi-product firm produces an excessive number of brands and chooses an insufficient level of quality. Below those levels of the entry cost, firms restrict product assortment considerably in order to avoid fierce price competition, and this can lead to a sizable over provision of quality.

6.6.3 Limiting Properties of the Spokes Model

Last but not least, perhaps the most important result of Chen and Riordan (2007a)'s work is to show the limiting properties of the spokes model. In fact, they establish that as the number of firms grows to infinity, the spokes model tends to monopolistic competition *à la Chamberlin*. The "trick" is to observe that as n becomes large, also N must be large and assume further, following Hart (1985), that the relation between the number of firms and spokes is constant: $n = kN$ where $k \in]0, 1]$. In other words, as the number of possible varieties increases, the fixed cost declines appropriately to keep the number of entering firms constant. They then reach this important conclusion.

Proposition 6.5 (Chen and Riordan 2007a) *If $n = kN$ and $N \to \infty$, then:*

$$p^* \to \begin{cases} \frac{2-k}{k} & if \quad Region\ I \\ v - t & if \quad Region\ II \\ \frac{2(1-k)v+k}{4-3k} & if \quad Region\ III \\ v - \frac{t}{2} & if \quad Region\ IV \end{cases}$$

In the limit, as the market becomes less and less concentrated, price in the spokes model remains bound above the marginal cost. The spokes model provides a spatial representation of monopolistic competition, according to the general definition of Hart (1985), of which the model is a special case.

6.7 Further Applications of the Spokes Model

The previous discussion has illustrated how the spokes model, in its several variations, can be a useful modelling tool in situations where horizontal differentiation and competition between firms are important to understand the market outcomes. This observation helps explain why the spokes model, in spite of having barely reached teenage status, has already found several applications. These applications are particularly focused in industrial organisation, but the model can prove useful in several other fields, including marketing and management. A short review of the existing work based on the model is provided in what follows.

Caminal and Claici (2007), who introduced the model simultaneously to Chen and Riordan (2007a), use it to tackle the issue of loyalty rewards. Examples of these practices are frequent flyer programmes or supermarket point collection schemes. They observe that economists and policy analysts usually believe that such pricing schemes tend to reinforce firms' market power and, hence, are detrimental to consumers' welfare.

In order to study such schemes, they use a two-period model in which consumers are uncertain about their future preferences. In particular, following the captive consumers assumption, each consumer derives utility from the same pair of brands in both periods, but the location x_s is randomly and independently chosen in each period. In other words, the uncertainty refers to the future relative valuation of the two brands they are interested in. In the second period, firms are able to discriminate between first-time and repeat buyers, who can prove previous transaction with the same supplier and be rewarded.

The model generates loyalty rewarding schemes as, in equilibrium, the prices charged to repeat consumers are lower than those paid by switchers. However, in line with results from the customers' poaching literature (Fudenberg and Tirole 2000), the programmes are business-stealing devices that tend to enhance competition and lead to lower average transaction prices. The conclusion is robust to both full and partial price commitments.

Chen and Riordan (2007b), inspired by the cement and concrete market, focus on the connection between exclusive contracts and vertical organisation. A vertically integrated firm can use exclusive dealing to foreclose an equally efficient upstream competitor and to "cartelise" the downstream industry. Neither vertical integration nor exclusive dealing alone would lead to such anti-competitive effect. The extent of cartelisation depends, between other elements, on downstream market concentration and on the degree to which downstream competition is localised.

To illustrate the latter point, the authors use a version of the model with n downstream firms that incur transportation costs to deliver the intermediate good to a consumer at a particular location. As a result, as in Reggiani (2014), a firm located at the terminal node of a customer's spoke has a cost advantage over other competitors. Upstream firms use two-part prices. The main conclusion on the joint effect of exclusive dealing and integration is robust to this extension. Similar results do not apply if competition is localised (Salop 1979) and the number of downstream firms is sufficiently high.

Chen and Schwartz (2016) focus on an important question in the analysis of horizontal mergers. Policymakers are usually interested in what share of a firm's lost output from a unilateral price increase diverts to the merging partner. Such "diversion ratio" is often estimated using data on customer switching from a firm to its rivals, also known as "churn". The authors use a three-firm version of the spokes model to investigate the potential biases of such estimates.

Unlike what the often employed stylised models suggest, the conclusions crucially depend on what caused the churn. This can be either (1) shifts in quality or changes in the marginal cost of the firm or of a rival or (2) demand-side shifts due to changed circumstances or learning about product attributes. Perhaps less intuitively, churn can be greater between more distant competitors in the presence of demand-side shifts. Unfortunately, policymakers are often unable to observe what caused such shifts, and the identified biases can affect decisions. As a result, Chen and Schwartz (2016) conclude that when little is known about the reason for switching, raw churn data deserves less weight, especially when the patterns conflict with information from other sources about relative competitive closeness.

Chen and Hua (2017) study how a firm's incentive to invest in product safety is affected by both the market environment and product liability. They embed the spokes model into a simple two-period dynamic game with safety investment and product liability. Specifically, each firm's product may cause consumer harm with some probability. In Period 1, a firm can invest to produce a high-safety product in both periods at a positive marginal cost. Without investment, the product will have low safety and zero marginal cost. After purchasing a product, a consumer can take precaution effort. Without such effort, if a consumer is harmed, the damage is relatively small if the product is of high safety but large if the product is low safety. Then, if the fixed cost of safety investment is sufficiently small, it is efficient for firms to produce and sell the high-safety product. If a consumer is harmed, the firm is required to compensate the consumer a fraction of the damage according to its product liability: partial or full.

The results suggest that partial liability, together with reputation concerns, can motivate firms to invest in safety. Increased competition resulting from less product differentiation diminishes a firm's gain from maintaining reputation and raises the socially desired product liability. On the other hand, an increase in the number of competitors reduces the benefit of maintaining reputation, but the effect on the potential gain from cutting back safety investment is less clear. In particular, the optimal liability may vary non-monotonically with the number of firms. Therefore, the relationship between competition and product liability is subtle.

Rhodes (2011) observes the prevalence of search-related advertising in online markets. An implication is that consumer search is rarely random: sponsored links appear high up on a webpage, and consumers often click on them. Firms bid aggressively for these "prominent" positions at the top of the page. The question, then, is why prominence is valuable in those contexts, given that visiting an additional website is almost costless.

In the framework presented, consumers know their valuations for the products offered in the market, but do not know which retailer sells which product. The spokes model allows to capture the search results proposed by a gatekeeper, like Google or Bing, either in a random order or sorted to give prominence to a specific firm. The main contribution is to show that a prominent retailer earns significantly more profit than other firms, even when the cost of searching websites and comparing products is essentially zero.

The mechanism behind the result relies on consumers learning which retailer sells which product by visiting websites and stop searching once they believe they have found their best match. Consequently, a non-prominent retailer tends to attract consumers who already know that they value its product highly. Each non-prominent retailer exploits this by charging a high price, which deters consumers from searching at all. In equilibrium, the prominent retailer has a lower price, but a much wider market reach and higher equilibrium profits, even in presence of almost zero frictions.

Germano and Meier (2013) have analysed the incentive of media in reporting news. The article highlights the dependence of global newspaper publishing from advertising. In 2010 advertising counted for 80% of these firms' revenues in the US and 57% in OECD countries. This reliance has a bearing on the choice of news coverage and content. The spokes model is used to allow for an arbitrary number of media firms and outlets. Media content can be free to users, and they get utility from both quality and accuracy of sensitive information. The latter directly affects advertisers.

In this setting, the authors show that topics sensitive to advertisers can be under-reported by all outlets in the market. Under-reporting tends to increase with the concentration, that is, when there are not many news outlets on the market. Interestingly, ownership plays an important role. In fact, adding outlets while keeping the number of owners fixed can further increase the bias.

Amaldoss and He (2010) study firms' use of finely targeted advertising to inform consumers about their products in presence of horizontal differentiation. In that context, they use the spokes model to show how diversity in consumers tastes, informative advertising, and improvements in advertising technology influence prices.

The model shows that informative advertising can enhance competition if consumer valuations are high. However, for low consumer valuations, advertising is associated with higher prices. Moreover, when consumer valuations are high, price increases with greater diversity in tastes, whereas the opposite holds if consumer valuations are low. Finally, improvements in advertising technology lead to higher levels of advertising only if consumer valuation is sufficiently high.

Amaldoss and He (2013) note that some products are particularly salient, or prototypical, in their categories. When people think of colas, Coca-Cola comes to mind. Research in consumer psychology has long demonstrated that prototypicality influences memory, shapes the composition of the consideration set, and affects purchase decisions. The article studies how prototypicality affects competition between horizontally differentiated firms.

The authors use a variant of the spokes model in which prototypicality influences the probability of the product being included in consumers' consideration sets, without affecting its valuation. Their analysis shows that when consumer valuations are low, the prototypical product is priced lower than a non-prototypical product and, despite that, it earns more profits. However, when consumer valuations are high, it is the prototypical product to be priced higher but still more profitable. This is consistent with evidence by which some prototypical products are priced lower than other products in their category, whereas in certain other categories they are priced higher.

Mantovani and Ruiz-Aliseda (2016) provide a rationale for the burst in the amount of collaborative activities among firms selling complementary products. They also highlight factors that may result in a lower profitability for such firms overall. To this end, they use a version of the spokes model to capture the supply of two goods by two firms and two complements supplied by two different firms. Products are both horizontally and vertically differentiated, that is, both the consumer fit and objective quality are heterogeneous.

The companies can collaborate with producers of the complementary goods, to enhance the quality of the systems formed by their components. Collaboration makes it cheaper to enhance such quality: hence, building innovation ecosystems results in firms investing more if collaboration were impossible. In markets reaching saturation, however, firms are trapped in a prisoner's dilemma: the greater investment creates more value but not value capture, because the value created relative to competitors does not change.

Loginova (2019) studies price competition between online retailers when some operate their own branded websites and the others sell their products through an online platform, such as Amazon Marketplace. The spokes model is adopted because it can easily accommodate the two types of firms, owing to its non-localised nature. The firms face a trade-off. Selling through Amazon allows a firm to reach more customers: consumers are normally unaware of alternatives unless they use Amazon that greatly decreases search and comparison costs. On the other hand, starting one's own website can help the firm to increase the perceived value of its product and build brand reputation. In the long run each firm chooses between Amazon and its own website, whereas in the short run the chosen sale channel cannot be amended. The comparative statics of the resulting equilibria provides some interesting insights. For example, the number of firms that choose Amazon may decrease in response to increased competition. Moreover, a pure-strategy Nash equilibrium not always exists, which is interpreted as price dispersion. Firms are more likely to employ mixed strategies in less concentrated markets and when the increase in the perceived value of the product is relatively small.

Ganuza and Hauk (2006) develop a stylised model of horizontal and vertical competition in tournaments. The sponsor, a benefactor running the tournament to generate ideas, cares not only about the quality of the design but also about the design "location" in the characteristics space. A priori, not even the sponsor knows its preferred design location, which is only discovered once the actual proposals have been seen. The benchmark model with two competitors choosing one design each is then extended to allow for several competing designs using the spokes model.

The authors show that the more efficient competitor is more likely to be conservative when choosing the design location. Also, if some differentiation in design locations is desirable, the cost difference between contestants can be neither too small nor too big. Therefore, if the sponsor mainly cares about the variety of design locations proposed, participation in the tournament by the two lowest-cost contestants cannot be optimal.

Aydogan and Lyon (2004) take on the challenging task of modelling an intangible asset like tacit knowledge. In their framework, knowledge-trading coalitions can transfer tacit knowledge, but this is unverifiable and requires face-to-face contact. This makes spatial proximity important and the use of a simplified version of the spokes model suitable. Their work may help explain the structure and stability of multi-member technology-trading coalitions, of which the Silicon Valley is a prominent example.

The main result is that when there are sufficient "complementarities" in knowledge exchange, successful transfer is facilitated if firms can meet in a central location, thereby economising on travel costs. When complementarities are small, however, a central location may be undesirable because it is more vulnerable to knowledge withholding than a structure involving bilateral travel between firms.

Izmalkov and Sinyashin (2019) present an interesting "twist" in the spokes model, which they refer to as the "rake model", to study markets in which a general market-wide product co-exists with specific niche products, for example, local producers competing with a large online distributor. As Fig. 6.7 illustrates, the market-wide product is located at the top of the market structure, that is, above the centre where all

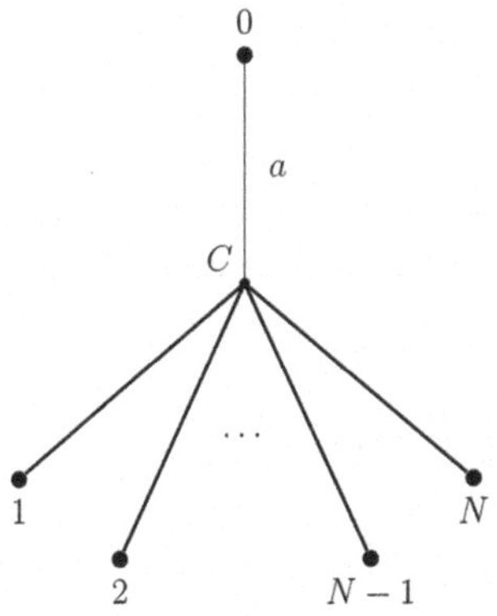

Fig. 6.7 The "rake model". Source: Izmalkov and Sinyashin (2019)

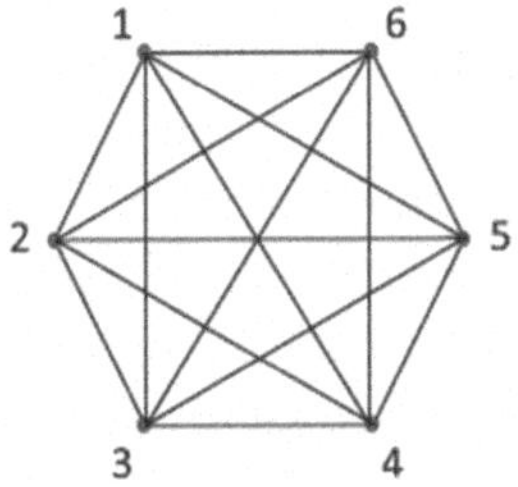

Fig. 6.8 The "network city" model. Source: Wang and Wang (2018)

spokes meet. In other words, there is an additional loss associated with demanding the generic product. Specific products are still located at the extremes of the spokes, which are all occupied. As a result, there are N spokes and $N + 1$ firms on the market.

The authors solve for both the monopoly and monopolistic competition equilibria. The results show that the general product can be sold even if it has a high additional cost associated and it is a poor substitute to the niche products. When the products are sufficiently valuable, the general product is overproduced by the monopolist and even more so under monopolistic competition.

Another interesting generalisation of the model is presented in Wang and Wang (2018). The authors analyse the "network-city model", in which firms compete simultaneously with all other firms setting prices. As Fig. 6.8 makes clear, the city network extends the spokes model by adding links between firms, still located at the extremes of their spokes. The model allows for heterogeneous product differentiation, marginal costs of production, and generic consumer densities, although requiring symmetry of densities between pair of firms. The article shows that the model has a unique and easily computable equilibrium.

6.8 Concluding Remarks

The spokes model is a relatively recently introduced model of non-localised spatial competition and it adds to the toolkit of economists when studying situations where product differentiation plays an important role.

The previous discussion has first motivated the use of the model, through real-world examples where its assumptions can fit particularly well. A benchmark version of the framework, broadly following Chen and Riordan (2007a), was then introduced. The analyses of non-localised competition in the spokes model were classified according to the focus on pricing decisions, location choices, or variety supply. Finally, other applications of the model to several relevant economic problems have been reviewed.

Whereas some empirical exercises based on the spokes model exist (Firgo et al. 2015; Lijesen and Reggiani 2020), the empirical literature is still rather scarce. Somaini and Einav (2013) analysis of partial lock-in of consumers to product is perhaps the only full-fledged attempt to a structural implementation of a dynamic model related to the spokes model. Empirical analyses based on the spokes model could be one of the frontiers to be further explored and developed in future research.

References

Amaldoss, W., & He, C. (2010). Product variety, informative advertising, and price competition. *Journal of Marketing Research, 47*(1), 146–156.

Amaldoss, W., & He, C. (2013). Pricing prototypical products. *Marketing Science, 32*(5), 733–752.

Anderson, S. P., De Palma, A., & Thisse, J. F. (1992). *Discrete choice theory of product differentiation*. Cambridge: MIT Press.

Aydogan, N., & Lyon, T. P. (2004). Spatial proximity and complementarities in the trading of tacit knowledge. *International Journal of Industrial Organization, 22*(8–9), 1115–1135.

Baker, J. B. (1995). Vertical restraints with horizontal consequences: Competitive effects of most-favored-customer clauses. *Antitrust LJ, 64*, 517.

Besanko, D., & Lyon, T. P. (1993). Equilibrium incentives for most-favored customer clauses in an oligopolistic industry. *International Journal of Industrial Organization, 11*(3), 347–367.

Brenner, S. (2005). Hotelling games with three, four, and more players. *Journal of Regional Science, 45*(4), 851–864.

Caminal, R. (2010). Markets and linguistic diversity. *Journal of Economic Behavior & Organization, 76*(3), 774–790.

Caminal, R., & Claici, A. (2007). Are loyalty-rewarding pricing schemes anticompetitive? *International Journal of Industrial Organization, 25*(4), 657–674.

Caminal, R., & Granero, L. M. (2012). Multi-product firms and product variety. *Economica, 79*(314), 303–328.

Chen, J., & Liu, Q. (2011). The effect of Most-Favored Customer clauses on prices. *Journal of Industrial Economics, 59*(3), 343–371.

Chen, Y., & Hua, X. (2017). Competition, product safety, and product liability. *Journal of Law, Economics, & Organization, 33*(2), 237–267.

Chen, Y., & Riordan, M. H. (2007a). Price and variety in the spokes model. *Economic Journal, 117*(522), 897–921.

Chen, Y., & Riordan, M. H. (2007b). Vertical integration, exclusive dealing, and expost cartelization. *RAND Journal of Economics, 38*(1), 1–21.

Chen, Y., & Riordan, M. H. (2008). Price-increasing competition. *RAND Journal of Economics, 39*(4), 1042–1058.

Chen, Y., & Schwartz, M. (2016). Churn versus diversion in antitrust: An illustrative model. *Economica, 83*(332), 564–583.

Cooper, T. E. (1986). Most-favored-customer pricing and tacit collusion. *RAND Journal of Economics, 17*, 377–388.

Dargaud, E., & Reggiani, C. (2015). On the price effects of horizontal mergers: A theoretical interpretation. *Bulletin of Economic Research, 67*(3), 236–255.

d'Aspremont, C., Gabszewicz, J. J., & Thisse, J. F. (1979). On Hotelling's "Stability in competition". *Econometrica, 47*(5), 1145–1150.

Dixit, A. K., & Stiglitz, J. E. (1977). Monopolistic competition and optimum product diversity. *American Economic Review, 67*(3), 297–308.

Economides, N. (1986). Minimal and maximal product differentiation in Hotelling's duopoly. *Economics Letters, 21*(1), 67–71.
Firgo, M., Pennerstorfer, D., & Weiss, C. R. (2015). Centrality and pricing in spatially differentiated markets: The case of gasoline. *International Journal of Industrial Organization, 40*, 81–90.
Fudenberg, D., & Tirole, J. (2000). Customer poaching and brand switching. *RAND Journal of Economics, 31*, 634–657.
Ganuza, J.-J., & Hauk, E. (2006). Allocating ideas: Horizontal competition in tournaments. *Journal of Economics & Management Strategy, 15*(3), 763–787.
Germano, F., & Meier, M. (2013). Concentration and self-censorship in commercial media. *Journal of Public Economics, 97*, 117–130.
Granero, L. M. (2013). Most-favored-customer pricing, product variety, and welfare. *Economics Letters, 120*(3), 579–582.
Granero, L. M. (2019). Strategic product variety and quality choice. *Economics Letters, 182*, 10–14.
Hart, O. D. (1985). Monopolistic competition in the spirit of chamberlin: A general model. *The Review of Economic Studies, 52*(4), 529–546.
Hotelling, H. (1929). Stability in competition. *Economic Journal, 39*, 41–57.
Izmalkov, S., & Sinyashin, A. (2019). *Davids and goliath: Spatial competition of niche and general products*. Mimeo.
Lederer, P. J., & Hurter, A. P. (1986). Competition of firms: Discriminatory pricing and location. *Econometrica, 54*, 623–640.
Lijesen, M. G., & Reggiani, C. (2019). *Specialization, generic firms and market competition*. Mimeo. https://papers.ssrn.com/sol3/papers.cfm?abstract_id=3246996
Lijesen, M. G., & Reggiani, C. (2020). *Product variety and market competition in the dutch car repair market*. Mimeo.
Loginova, O. (2019). *Price competition online: Platforms vs. branded websites*. Mimeo.
MacLeod, W. B., Norman, G., & Thisse, J.-F. (1988). Price discrimination and equilibrium in monopolistic competition. *International Journal of Industrial Organization, 6*(4), 429–446.
Mantovani, A., & Ruiz-Aliseda, F. (2016). Equilibrium innovation ecosystems: The dark side of collaborating with complementors. *Management Science, 62*(2), 534–549.
Porter, M. E. (1980). *Competitive strategy: Techniques for analyzing industries and competition* (Vol. 300, p. 28). New York: Simon and Schuster.

Reggiani, C. (2014). Spatial price discrimination in the spokes model. *Journal of Economics & Management Strategy, 23*(3), 628–649.
Rhodes, A. (2011). Can prominence matter even in an almost frictionless market? *Economic Journal, 121*(556), F297–F308.
Salop, S. C. (1979). Monopolistic competition with outside goods. *Bell Journal of Economics, 10*(1), 141–156.
Somaini, P., & Einav, L. (2013). A model of market power in customer markets. *Journal of Industrial Economics, 61*(4), 938–986.
Tabuchi, T., & Thisse, J.-F. (1995). Asymmetric equilibria in spatial competition. *International Journal of Industrial Organization, 13*(2), 213–227.
Wang, T., & Wang, R. (2018). A network-city model of spatial competition. *Economics Letters, 170*, 168–170.

7

Patent Licensing in Models of Spatial Competition: A Literature Review

Marcella Scrimitore

7.1 Introduction

Economic literature acknowledges that innovation is a major driver of productivity growth (Aghion et al. 2005) and allows firms to get a competitive advantage, augmenting their performance (Cellini and Lambertini 2008). Intellectual property rights' protection provides inventors with incentives to license their innovations and better appropriate the returns of their research and development (R&D) investments. Indeed, firms granting a patent can directly benefit from the exclusive right on an innovation or can transfer that right to other parties, which are then entitled to use it. Sharing or exclusively licensing inventions and discoveries stimulates further R&D, which favors technology and knowledge diffusion and brings long-term benefits to society.

Patent licensing is a fairly common practice in most industries (Rostoker 1984; Teece 1986; Macho-Stadler et al.1996). The analysis of private

M. Scrimitore (✉)
Università del Salento, Lecce, Italy
e-mail: marcella.scrimitore@unisalento.it

S. Colombo (ed.), *Spatial Economics Volume I*,
https://doi.org/10.1007/978-3-030-40098-9_7

and social incentives toward licensing carried out in game-theoretical setups has become central to R&D literature. A considerable body of oligopoly theory has focused on patent licensing as a means for either inside or outside innovators to get a strategic market advantage.[1] In the last decades, it has largely investigated the various methods used by a patent-holder to license either a process (cost-reducing) innovation or a product (creating a new good) innovation, questioning whether a licensing contract should be designed as an auction or to include a fixed or lump-sum fee, a royalty charged per unit of output, or a combination of a fixed fee and a variable royalty (i.e., a two-part contract). Research in this field starts from the seminal contributions of Kamien and Tauman (1984, 1986), Kamien et al. (1992), and Katz and Shapiro (1985, 1986), who have modeled oligopolistic competition to assess the private value of a patent for an outside innovator. The optimal behavior of an inside innovator deciding upon licensing a new technology to an actual or potential competitor has been investigated in an extensive body of subsequent literature (e.g., Wang 1998, 2002).[2] In both strands of literature, the optimal structure of a licensing contract and its welfare implications have been examined. The main findings reveal that the incentives to license may depend on the size of innovation (i.e., drastic or non-drastic),[3] on the industry structure (i.e., the number of potential licensees, the price elasticity of demand, the degree of product differentiation, the presence of vertical relationships), and on the mode of competition (Cournot or Bertrand).[4]

This chapter presents the results of a systematic review of literature on patent licensing in spatial competition models, namely in markets

[1]An innovating firm can be either a non-producer or a producer in the market. An outside innovator that discovers a new technology or develops a new product (a university or a research laboratory) licenses her innovation to firms producing within the market, thus reaping a reward from her R&D investment. By contrast, an inside innovator directly uses her patented invention for her production process, keeping the option to license it to current or potential competitors.

[2]Kamien and Tauman (2002) and Sen and Tauman (2007), among others, consider patent licensing by both an outside and an incumbent innovator.

[3]An innovation is drastic if it is large enough to create a monopoly, namely if the resulting equilibrium price is not affected by the threat of competition. It is non-drastic otherwise.

[4]Most of the above literature was reviewed in Kamien et al. (1992), but significant research has been done since then.

characterized by the presence of spatially differentiated firms and heterogeneity in consumers' preferences. The spatial dimension of competition is captured within two popular theoretical frameworks: the linear city of Hotelling (1929) and the circular city of Salop (1979). In these frameworks, one firm's location is interpreted as a product choice in the characteristics' space and each consumer's location denotes her most preferred attribute.[5] Modeling spatial competition using a framework à la Hotelling has become spread over the last decades in the theory of industrial organization, the results of which crucially depend on whether firms' locations are fixed or endogenous. While a number of studies have investigated the determinants of the firms' equilibrium locations in the characteristics' space, which define the optimal degree of product differentiation,[6] variants of the Hotelling model have been used to explain the dynamics of several types of firms' strategies including innovation strategies.[7]

Studying technology licensing in spatial models of competition has been acknowledged by a number of studies that constitute an established area of research in industrial organization. A spatial framework of competition succeeds in appropriately capturing the impact of technology transfer in markets that does not grow over time and where each consumer has her ideal brand. Two major types of location models represent the reference frameworks in the analysis carried out in the present work. First, we review the literature using either the linear or the circular shopping (or mill pricing) models à la Hotelling in which consumers pay the transport costs, the latter representing their disutility from buying a product. Second, we discuss the main literature based on the shipping models of spatial discrimination where firms bear transport costs (i.e., the cost of adapting products' characteristics to consumers tastes) and use

[5]While spatial economics is mainly concerned with the location of economic activities in a geographic space (Duranton 2008), the issue of firms' locations in the product characteristics' spaces of Hotelling or Salop is spread in industrial organization (Gabszewicz and Thisse 1986; Anderson et al. 1992) and is aimed to capture the degree of product differentiation endogenously chosen by firms.

[6]See Biscaia and Mota (2013) for a review of the literature on spatial competition.

[7]As regards innovation strategies, see Harter (1993) and Li and Zhang (2012) who introduce R&D into a Hotelling framework.

location-contingent (or delivered) pricing.[8] Referring to both approaches allows us to shed light on the key forces driving the licensing choices under both consumers' preference heterogeneity and firm's cost heterogeneity. Finally, the analysis of the two types of spatial models allows us to capture the implications of spatial competition under both Bertrand and Cournot.[9]

The present work suggests that the achievements in the literature of technology licensing modeling spatially differentiated competition may differ from those obtained using a representative consumer approach to product differentiation à la Singh and Vives (1984). The main results achieved in these conventional frameworks of price and quantity competition are presented in Sect. 7.2. By comparing the various licensing policies in the Hotelling shopping models, the present survey shows that the feature of inelastic demand characterizing a spatial framework plays an important role in determining the main differences with non-spatial literature. This issue is taken up in Sects. 7.3.1 and 7.3.2 that investigate literature assuming fixed locations and potential exogenous firms' cost asymmetries. Locations are conversely assumed to be strategically chosen by firms in Sect. 7.3.3, which provides insights on both equilibrium existence issues and the optimal patent licensing under endogenous cost asymmetries between the patentee and the licensee. Furthermore, Sect. 7.4 points out further issues regarding the optimal mode of licensing brought up in spatial discrimination literature under delivered pricing. Finally, Sect. 7.5 questions whether the choice of licensing is optimal with respect to either selling the property rights to third parties or outsourcing a technology, which has received some attention in literature and is a current debated issue of technology transfer. Some challenging questions for future research are offered in the last section that also concludes.

[8] Seminal contributions in the literature of spatial discrimination are Hamilton et al. (1989) and Anderson and Neven (1991).

[9] Each considered spatial model may deal with either Bertrand or Cournot competition. However, while the shopping models à la Hotelling are generally developed under Bertrand competition, Cournot-type models are considered within spatial discrimination literature. On this point, see Matsumura and Shimizu (2006, pp. 585–588).

7.2 The Main Achievements in Non-Spatial Literature

The landmark literature on technology licensing has been aimed to identify the market driving forces toward licensing and further assess the relative performance of the several licensing schemes. A large body of literature has focused on comparing the royalty, fixed-fee and two-part tariff licensing regimes, mostly dealing with the case of cost-reducing innovations.[10] There are two strands of the literature addressing this issue in a complete information framework. One strand considers the optimal licensing behavior of a patent-holder which is supposed to be outside the market. A major reference work in this field is Kamien and Tauman (1986) which proves the profit dominance of a fixed fee over a per unit royalty contract in a Cournot setting. This preference for the outsider innovator is due to the greater incentive to extract, through a fixed fee relative to a royalty, the additional rents caused by more intensive competition in the market. The same result is obtained by Kamien et al. (1992) who model competitive interactions à la Cournot and à la Bertrand to demonstrate that a royalty is inferior to both an auction and a fixed fee, this result holding for a wide class of demand functions. Furthermore, the competitive Bertrand scenario of Kamien et al. (1992) is revisited by Muto (1993) which allows for imperfect product substitutability. When the latter is not too low and the innovation size is small enough, the outside innovator is found to prefer a per unit royalty to a fixed fee.[11] A royalty contract, indeed, is optimal when a sufficiently low royalty rate, which equals the innovation size, limits the output contraction following the royalty payments and allows the patentee to extract higher rents by softening market competition than by letting firm compete under a fixed fee.

[10]Only a few cases of product innovations have been considered in literature. Some examples are given by Arya and Mittendorf (2006), Bagchi and Mukherjee (2014), and Chang (2017).

[11]The result that a royalty contract is more profitable than a fixed fee is also obtained in the Cournot oligopoly of Sen (2005) in which the number of licenses is subject to an integer constraint.

A more recent strand of literature considers technology licensing by a patentee who is also a producer in the market. The analysis carried out in this literature takes into consideration the competition effect which negatively affects the profits of the patentee sharing her innovation with one or more market rivals. By addressing the case of an insider innovator facing Cournot market competition by the licensee, Wang (1998) and Kamien and Tauman (2002), respectively in a duopoly and an oligopoly, demonstrate that licensing a non-drastic innovation by means of a royalty always generates larger returns to the patent-holder than fixed-fee licensing. More generally, the presence of an industry incumbent favors the emergence of royalty licensing as an optimal contract with respect to a fixed fee, since the royalty payment provides both sufficiently high licensing revenues and a competitive advantage in production. The extent to which the patentee's profits on her direct sales' channel are hurt by less intense market competition determines the conditions for a reversal result to hold, namely for a fixed fee to profit-dominate a royalty. This occurs in the differentiated Cournot model of Wang (2002) where larger competition induced by licensing reduces to a lesser extent the direct channel's profits of the patentee under high enough product differentiation, which leads competing on equal costs under a fixed fee to be better to the innovator than competing under cost asymmetries through a royalty. The same argument explains the fixed-fee dominance which occurs in the presence of a cost advantage by the licensee (Poddar and Sinha 2010; Wang et al. 2013).[12] By considering the insider innovator's licensing behavior in a Bertrand-type model, Wang and Yang (1999) show that royalty licensing is superior to fixed-fee licensing irrespective of the innovation size, which contrasts with Muto (1993) whose result holds only under certain conditions on the innovation size. The strategic role that a royalty contract plays in a price competition scenario, where it allows the patentee to commit to a higher price and soften market competition,

[12]Both Poddar and Sinha (2010) and Wang et al. (2013), in a Cournot setting with non-drastic innovation, study the impact of the cost differences between an insider patentee and a licensee on the choices of the optimal licensing contract. With respect to earlier literature, both works relax the assumption on licensee(s) with an inferior production technology. They show that, when the licensee has a production cost advantage relative to the licensor after licensing, a fixed fee turns out to be optimal and dominate both royalty and two-part tariff licensing.

makes the royalty dominance in Wang and Yang (1999) robust to any innovation size.[13]

Features of interest for patent licensing have been examined in further research. Works dealing with two-part tariffs have spread in literature starting from Kamien and Tauman (1984) and have extended to Faulí-Oller and Sandonis (2002), Eruktu and Richelle (2007), and Colombo and Filippini (2015), among others. All works within this literature generally share the result that the patentee's profit is higher under two-part tariff licensing than under either fixed-fee or royalty licensing. In recent years, renewed attention has been drawn to the analysis of licensing strategies in international markets (Kabiraj and Kabiraj 2017), in vertically differentiated industries (Li and Song 2010), under network externalities (Wang et al. 2012), and under costly technology transfer (Mukherjee and Tsai 2015). The role of licensing in affecting innovators' incentives for R&D investments has been finally considered by Colombo (2020).

7.3 Patent Licensing in the Shopping Hotelling Models

7.3.1 The Benchmark Model of Poddar and Sinha (2004)

Research on technology licensing in a spatial framework à la Hotelling has been carried out by assuming that two firms compete with respect to prices in a process innovation setting.[14] Our analysis of this literature starts from Poddar and Sinha (2004) who examine in a linear city the optimal licensing policy (i.e., auction, fixed fee, and royalty) of both an outside and an inside innovator. In this framework, transport costs are linear in

[13]This commitment effect of a royalty under Bertrand has been also highlighted by Faulí-Oller and Sandonis (2002), although they consider a two-part tariff. The authors also show how this strategic effect of a royalty on the one hand favors licensing a drastic innovation and on the other hand lets a social welfare detrimental result arise.

[14]The only work addressing the issue of licensing a product innovation in a spatial context is the article by Caballero-Sanz et al. (2005).

distance and the locations of cost-symmetric firms are taken fixed at the extreme ends of the bounded unit line. That is, product differentiation is given, that is, well-established in the product characteristics' space, and is maximal. By assuming that an outside patentee is enabled to grant either one or two licensees a cost-reducing innovation, royalty licensing turns out to be preferred to no licensing and to dominate both a fixed fee and an auction, irrespective of whether the innovation is drastic or non-drastic. Such a result can be explained as follows. While one license is offered in equilibrium under an auction or a fixed fee, which leads equilibrium prices to be lower than prior to licensing, the patentee finds optimal to license her innovation by means of a royalty to both firms. Indeed, in a context in which the demand is inelastic and there is no market expansion effect post licensing, a royalty contract does not alter the relative position of firms on the market and allows the patentee to extract a higher surplus than under a fixed fee/auction. This contrasts with the Bertrand differentiated model of Muto (1993) who shows that the superiority of a royalty contract over a fixed fee is conditioned to the existence of a sufficiently small size of innovation. Indeed, in his framework of product differentiation with elastic demand, a larger innovation size (i.e., a larger royalty rate) reduces market demand to a great extent, thus limiting the gains from royalty licensing relative to a fixed fee. Due to inelastic demand, this negative effect of royalty is not present in Poddar and Sinha (2004), where the profit dominance of a royalty scheme turns out to achieve greater robustness.

Poddar and Sinha (2004) also point out the peculiar features of a spatial market in affecting the optimal licensing policy when the patentee is a producer in the market. Despite the model assumes maximal differentiation, the fixed fee turns out to be never preferable to no licensing, regardless of whether the innovation is drastic or non-drastic.[15] A fixed-fee contract, indeed, enhances significantly price competition as the patentee and the licensee compete on equal footing under such a licensing scheme. Since market demand keeps constant with respect

[15]This contrasts with earlier literature in the non-spatial contexts showing that, under quantity competition, a fixed fee may be profitable when product differentiation is high enough (Wang 2002).

to no licensing in the considered scenario, the patentee chooses not to license her innovation, thus enjoying higher profits from more relaxed price competition, irrespective of any innovation size. In other words, in a standard framework with elastic demand, product differentiation reduces the negative effect of competition on the patentee's profit and can lead the positive market expansion effect due to greater product variety to dominate the former. By contrast, in a spatial context where the patentee cannot exploit a market expansion effect due to fixed locations and inelastic demand, the negative effect of competition associated with fixed-fee licensing is the only effect at work, which determines the decision of never granting the license.

Another interesting feature of Poddar and Sinha (2004) regards the insider patentee's decision to grant a royalty license under either drastic or non-drastic innovation. It is shown that royalty licensing always causes higher profits than under no licensing when innovation is non-drastic, since it lets the patentee gain from licensing revenues more than lose from sharing a cost advantage.[16] Conversely, in a drastic innovation scenario, no licensing is always optimal. In this case, indeed, the absence of a market expansion effect associated with bringing back the rival into the market leads the patentee not to engage in licensing to avoid the total surplus reduction associated with lower prices. This is in contrast with the result of Fauli-Oller and Sandonis (2002) that proves that licensing a drastic innovation under Bertrand competition occurs whenever the goods are not perfect substitutes, due to a positive market expansion/variety effect dominating the negative competition effect.[17]

---

[16]This is in line with the conventional literature proving that royalty licensing is always profitable with respect to no licensing in a Bertrand framework with an insider patentee (Wang 2002; Wang and Yang 1999).

[17]Notice that the superiority of a royalty contract offered by an outside patentee as compared to fixed fee/auction is also proved by Caballero-Sanz et al. (2002) who consider symmetric locations in a Salop circle, this result being robust to the possibility of licensing to a potential entrant. Conversely, Caballero-Sanz et al. (2005) demonstrate the dominance of a fixed fee under a product innovation.

7.3.2 The Role of Cost Asymmetries and Market Coverage

The role of firm cost asymmetries on the optimal licensing policy by an insider patentee is studied by Lu and Poddar (2014) which consider fixed locations in both a linear and a circular city. In these spatial frameworks of price competition, the authors compare a fixed fee, a royalty, and a two-part tariff contract potentially adopted by an insider patentee under the assumptions that transport costs are linear. Lu and Poddar (2014) basically relax the most common assumption that firms are cost symmetric prior to the innovation stage, which leads the innovator to be more efficient than the rival following cost-reducing licensing. This amounts to considering all possible pre-innovation and post-innovation cost asymmetries between the patentee and the licensee, which includes the case in which licensing occurs from a pre-innovation cost-inefficient firm to its efficient counterpart. When the patentee is the firm with an inferior technology and the size of innovation is low enough, fixed fee can be preferred to no licensing, regardless of whether the spatial market is linear or circular. The emergence of a fixed fee as superior to no licensing, which is not a likely result in the literature with an incumbent innovator, is due to the interplay between the following effects of licensing on the patentee's profits: a negative effect due to more intense price competition and a positive effect on the industry profits caused by a production costs' reduction. In the above circumstances, the latter effect dominates the former, leading industry profits to be higher under licensing and the patentee to be better off under a fixed fee than under no licensing. In both the considered spatial markets, however, a royalty is found to be more profitable than a fixed-fee contract, while a two-part tariff turns out to dominate any other strategy for all possible pre- and post-innovation firm cost asymmetries and irrespective of the size of the innovation.[18] The results achieved in Lu and Poddar (2014) validate the empirical findings in literature.[19]

The debate on the optimal licensing policy in spatial oligopolies has been growing steadily in the last decade and has been extended by Wang et al. (2017) to considering equity licensing. The latter consists in an agreement allowing the patentee to transfer her innovation in exchange of an equity share in the licensed firm. This type of license is compared with a royalty and a fixed-fee license in both a covered and an uncovered Hotelling linear market, with an insider patentee and a potential licensee located at the city endpoints. By dealing with a covered market, the authors show that equity licensing is preferred to royalty licensing when the transport rate is high relative to the innovation size. In the same circumstances, but in a framework with an uncovered market, equity and fixed-fee licensing are found to be indifferent to the patentee, both being superior to royalty licensing. These results point out some conditions under which a royalty contract is not the optimal licensing method, as conversely found by Poddar and Sinha (2004) using the same spatial framework. This occurs when a low transport rate relative to the innovation size reduces the degree of differentiation between the competing firms and makes price competition tougher. In this case, a royalty contract more effectively enables to the patentee to gain higher profits by softening overall market competition through the royalty payment imposed to the licensee. Equity licensing, conversely, allows firms to share the same and lower costs, thus yielding fiercer competition. It turns out that, when sufficiently high transport costs relative to the

[18]In this regard, it is worth mentioning that the superiority of a two-part tariff contract over a royalty contract is also found by Kabiraj and Lee (2011) in a Hotelling linear city with exogenous firms' locations, where the optimal licensing policy is discussed in relationship with the level of transportation costs and the endogenous outcome on market coverage. While a fixed-fee contract is shown to be never profitable, an equilibrium with royalty licensing is found to exist, provided that the transportation costs lie in a specific interval ensuring full market coverage.

[19]Rostoker (1984) finds that licensing by royalty is used in 39% of the cases, a fixed fee is used in 13%, and a two-part tariff is used in 46%. Some empirical evidence is also provided by Macho-Stadler et al. (1996) in a study based on a sample of licensing contracts between Spanish and foreign firms and showing that 59% of the contracts impose royalty payments and 28% include fixed-fee payments, while 13% consist of a two-part tariff.

innovation size make price competition less intensive, equity licensing is the optimal patentee's choice, even if it implies fiercer competition. This result is due to the collusive effect of equity sharing which enhances the patentees' profits more than it reduces them through cost sharing. Notice that the assumptions of a covered market and exogenous locations are crucial in delivering the main result. Wang et al. (2017), indeed, achieve a different conclusion when they assume that the spatial market is uncovered, that is, some consumers may choose not to purchase the product because the equilibrium prices are higher than their reservation utility. Due to this assumption, the two firms act as local monopolists of the linear city, which causes the patentee's licensing profits to be the same across fixed-fee and equity licensing (i.e., the extra profits gained by the patentee after licensing are the same). In such circumstances, royalty licensing turns out to be inferior to both equity and fixed-fee licensing to the positive effect of lower marginal costs on the monopoly firm profits under the latter with respect to the former.

7.3.3 The Literature Achievements Under Endogenous Locations

As suggested by Duranton (2008), the location choice of economic agents is the main focus of spatial economics. Since the Hotelling's acclaimed "principle of minimum differentiation," much attention in spatial competition literature has been devoted to the analysis of strategic interactions among firms competing in prices and deciding upon their optimal locations (i.e., the equilibrium degree of product differentiation) in the characteristics' space.[20] Within this framework, competition is modeled as a two-stage non-cooperative game: in the last stage firms choose their prices by taking locations as given, while in the first stage they decide upon locations (i.e., product characteristics). In what follows, we review some literature with an insider patentee showing how, on the

[20]Another well-known benchmark in this literature is D'Aspremont et al. (1979), which finds a principle of maximal differentiation with the two competing firms located at the opposite ends of the Hotelling line.

one hand, licensing can affect the equilibrium locations and, on the other hand, the demand and the cost effects caused by endogenous locations determine the optimality of the different licensing methods.[21]

A step forward in this line of research is given by Matsumura et al. (2010) who study the role of royalty licensing on the equilibrium locations in a linear city with quadratic transportation costs. In this duopoly market, price-then-location competition involves firms engaging in R&D to acquire the superior technology. Equilibrium locations are found to be the endpoints on the Hotelling line at equilibrium, which reveals that maximum differentiation arises as in a context without licensing (D'Aspremont et al. 1979).[22] The main contribution of this article is to show that royalty licensing solves the existence problem of equilibrium locations which conversely arises in the spatial contexts of Ziss (1993) and Matsumura and Matsushima (2009) under no licensing and exogenous firm cost asymmetries. In these works, indeed, the cost asymmetries between the two competitors lead the cost-efficient firm to locate as close as possible to the cost-inefficient rival with the aim of price-undercutting and stealing market shares, while the inefficient firm is willing to locate as far as possible from the rival. This clearly determines the absence of equilibrium. In the licensing scenario of Matsumura et al. (2010), however, both the (low cost) patentee and the (high cost) licensee choose to locate far apart from each other, which enables the patentee to gain from both softening price competition and extracting the licensee's rent through a royalty license.

The analysis carried out in the previous sections has demonstrated that price competition under symmetric fixed locations dramatically reduces the profitability of fixed-fee licensing. In what follows we show the different result obtained in literature under endogenous locations. To this aim, we examine Lin et al. (2013) who deal with the licensing decision by an incumbent patentee of a cost-reducing (drastic and non-drastic) innovation in a linear Hotelling market. In this setup, transportation costs

[21] Biscaia and Mota (2013) mainly focus on the strategic effects of location decisions in their critical review.

[22] As shown in D'Aspremont et al. (1979), transport costs must be quadratic in distance for the principle of maximum differentiation to hold.

are supposed to be linear and the locations' choices are sequential. The paper first demonstrates that, when the location leader is the patentee, she prefers not to adopt royalty licensing when the innovation size is sufficiently large, which contrasts with Poddar and Sinha (2004) in which royalty licensing is always profitable. This result is observed when both a sufficiently large degree of innovation and a licensees' location disadvantage reduce considerably the licensing revenues. Second, the paper proves that the patentee prefers fixed-fee licensing to no licensing only when the licensee is the location leader and the innovation size is low enough, which differs from Poddar and Sinha (2004) where fixed fee is never profitable with an insider patentee. In this case, indeed, the patentee can extract a significant licensee's rent through the fixed fee that overcomes her profit loss due to greater competition (the profit loss being lower, the lower is the innovation size). Third, the paper shows that the insider patentee decides upon licensing through a royalty rather than a fixed fee depending on the relative strength of the cost and location advantages, which yields a dominance of the royalty when the licensee is the leader.

7.4 Patent Licensing in Shipping Models of Spatial Discrimination

While the issue of technology licensing has received considerable attention in spatial economics literature using the shopping Hotelling models, it has been paid less attention in shipping models of spatial discrimination (Thisse and Vives 1988; Hamilton et al. 1989).[23] In what follows we highlight the different results achieved in spatial discrimination licensing literature with respect to the above-discussed findings obtained under both

[23]Spatial discrimination literature is mainly concerned with the determinants of equilibrium dispersion or agglomeration of firms in a spatial market. It has been shown that Cournot competition leads firms to agglomerate at the central point of a linear city (Hamilton et al. 1989; Anderson and Neven 1991) and to choose (dispersed) equidistant locations in a circular city (Shimizu 2002). Hamilton et al. (1989) also show that Bertrand competition promotes dispersion.

the conventional approach to product differentiation and the Hotelling approach.

Spatial discrimination implies that firms pay the transportation costs to ship the good to consumers, so that the consumers located at different points on a unit line segment are charged with discriminatory delivered prices for the same product. Using such a framework, existing literature has identified some circumstances in which a fixed fee is used by an internal innovator and may be preferred to a royalty. This comparison is performed by Heywood and Ye (2011) in a duopoly framework allowing for endogenous locations and a constrained demand, which implies that the consumer reservation price of each consumer is low relative to the sum of production and transport costs. It is moreover assumed that an internal patentee chooses whether to license her cost-reducing innovation to a rival by means of a fixed fee or to grant a royalty license. The two firms finally compete in this market by fixing a schedule of delivered prices. Both the profitability of a fixed fee compared to no licensing and the relative profitability of using a fixed fee vs. a royalty are found to be affected by the demand constraint under endogenous locations. In particular, the patentee finds optimal to license via a fixed fee when a sufficiently constrained demand reduces the monopoly profits to a higher extent than under fixed-fee licensing. As in the absence of a demand constraint, a royalty is always found to be profitable relative to no licensing. Moreover, a sufficiently low consumers' willingness to pay leads fixed fee to be more profitable to the innovator than royalty licensing. This is due to the more limited profit losses that the demand constraint causes under a fixed fee and symmetric locations relative to the losses under the asymmetric locations arising in the royalty case. This is in contrast with the unconstrained demand case in which a dominance of the royalty over the fixed fee always occurs, as the royalty lets the innovator benefit from both a cost advantage and a location advantage.

The same spatial discrimination framework with endogenous firms' locations as in Heywood and Ye (2011) has been adopted by Colombo (2014) to identify the optimal method to license a non-drastic innovation by an inside patentee. While Heywood and Ye (2011) assume that price-setting firms simultaneously choose their locations, Colombo (2014) addresses the quantity competition case under sequential firms' location choices. In the model, a requirement on the minimum distance between the two firms is imposed to refrain them from locating at the same central point, thus avoiding an equilibrium with firms' agglomeration which makes the spatial dimension immaterial for the analysis.[24] Minimization of total transportation costs leads the first mover at the location stage to choose the central point in the linear city, regardless of whether the patentee or the licensee moves first, while the second mover locates as close as possible to the rival, compatibly with the minimum distance requirement. This pattern of the equilibrium locations emerges irrespective of whether firms spatially discriminate (i.e., firms sell different quantities at the different consumers' locations) or they adopt a uniform delivered quantity strategy (i.e., firms deliver the same quantity in all points of the market). First, the analysis carried out in this framework provides a new rationale for fixed-fee licensing relative to no licensing, which is based on the endogenous spatial asymmetry between the patentee and her competitor. In particular, when the spatial distribution of the innovator with respect to the potential licensee determines a location advantage of the former over the latter, the fixed fee becomes less likely to be preferred to no licensing. In this case, indeed, the incentive compatible constraint of the licensee requires a low fixed fee to be set, since the no-licensing profits of the licensee are low. Since the patentee opts for licensing only when she can extract a sufficiently large fixed fee, a sufficiently large locational advantage of the licensee over the innovator is required for fixed-fee licensing to be profitable. Second, the paper confirms the result that Wang (1998) obtains in a non-spatial Cournot market that royalty is superior to both fixed fee and no licensing, as long as a discriminatory policy applies. This result is shown to hold even when the minimum distance requirement induces firms to locate very far apart from each other, but is conditioned to the assumption that firms spatially discriminate. In such circumstances, the innovator gains from the competitive advantage achieved through the cost asymmetry induced by a royalty to a higher extent than from a fixed fee. However, fixed-fee licensing may be preferred

[24] Agglomeration of firms toward the center of a linear city implies full symmetry of firms' behavior at all market addresses. See Hamilton et al. (1989) on this point.

to licensing by means of a royalty when firms adopt a uniform quantity delivered strategy. In this model, indeed, a more significant innovation size than under spatial discrimination leads both the locational and the efficiency positive effect of a fixed fee to be relatively high as compared to the cost advantages caused by a royalty.[25] This generates the conditions under which, as long as the patentee has a sufficiently high locational disadvantage, her profits by extracting the more relevant licensee's rent through a fixed fee are higher than those accruing from royalty payments.

We conclude that the spatial asymmetry in favor of the licensee plays a crucial role in defining the optimal choice of the licensing method in a spatial competition context. The standard result that a royalty always dominates a fixed-fee contract always applies in the Hotelling frameworks with exogenous spatial symmetry, as in the Poddar and Sinha (2004)'s linear city and the Caballero-Sanz et al. (2002)'s circular road. The result also holds in the model of Heywood and Ye (2011) as long as demand is unconstrained and the production cost advantage of the innovator determines a location advantage effect which reinforces the former, causing the dominance of the royalty over the fixed fee. In the same article, however, a sufficiently constrained demand under simultaneous location choices reduces the gains from the locational effect when a royalty is at work. This leads to the superiority of the fixed-fee contract even if the latter entails equal production costs due to symmetric locations. A preference of the innovator for the fixed-fee contract also arises in the uniform quantity delivered model of Colombo (2014) where it occurs when a relevant licensee's locational advantage leads the patentee's returns from a fixed fee to be higher than the returns from variable royalties.

Finally, the consideration that in a spatial discrimination framework transport costs play an important role in defining the optimal licensing behavior induces us to consider the work by Heywood and Wang (2015). This article deals with the payment structure used to license a transport cost-reducing innovation in a price-setting game. The authors compare a contract including a distance fee with the standard contracts based on

---

[25] We refer to the "efficiency effect" as the increase of the total quantity produced in the industry which positively affects the profits obtained by the licensee under a fixed fee.

a fixed fee, an ad valorem royalty, or a per unit royalty. Whether the innovator is inside or outside the market is shown to be crucial in defining the optimal licensing method. A unit distance fee turns out to provide an insider innovator with both sufficiently high licensing revenues and a better market position achieved through more competitive delivered prices. Conversely, in the circumstances in which the innovator is outside the market, lower transport costs achieved through innovation reduce the equilibrium prices and market profitability, which makes a distance fee never optimal.[26]

7.5 The Alternatives to Licensing and the Optimal Mode of Technology Transfer

In the above sections we have considered various licensing contracts potentially chosen by a patentee to transfer a new technology to the licensee(s).[27] In this section we discuss some works considering strategies used by a non-innovator in alternative to technology licensing, namely both the decision of outsourcing a crucial input and that of selling the property rights on a technology. A focus on the peculiarities that these phenomena assume in a spatial competition setting is given. Indeed, the choice between licensing and selling a technology has been modeled by Tauman and Weng (2012) in a conventional competitive environment, where the firm buying the property right on a new technology can also transfer it to potential licensees. Such a choice has been recently revisited by Banerjee and Poddar (2019) in a Hotelling market. This market is a unit line populated by two cost-asymmetric firms located at its extremes. An outside innovator can sell the property right on her innovation to

[26]In such circumstances, each market competitor chooses to acquire the innovation, thus lowering their transport costs, even if such a choice reduces overall market profitability and determines a prisoner-dilemma-type equilibrium.

[27]Technology transfer, as broadly defined by Maskus (2004), "refers to any process by which one party gains access to a second party's information and successfully learns and absorbs it into his production function."

one of two competing firms who can further license it to the rival.[28] In such a context, the authors find that the patent-holder unambiguously chooses to sell her innovation property right to one of the competing firms rather than directly licensing the technology to either one or two firms. This result is very general since it does not depend on the innovation size (drastic or non-drastic) and the degree of cost asymmetry between the licensees. In particular, selling the property rights to one firm, which further licenses to the other firm, is optimal as it allows the patentee to get the highest payoff by maximizing the value of the patent, no matter the buyer is the efficient or the inefficient firm. By selling to whatever firm between the two, the patentee directly exploits the willingness to pay of the purchasing firm and, through the latter, appropriates the rent extracted from the licensed firm. The resulting payoff will be higher than that gained in case of licensing to either one or two firms.[29] This contrasts with the market with cost-symmetric firms described by Tauman and Weng (2012) where both a sufficiently large number of licensees and a significant (but non-drastic) innovation size are required for the selling strategy to be superior to licensing. The result of Banerjee and Poddar (2019), moreover, contrasts with that obtained in an equivalent non-spatial Cournot setting by Sinha (2016). In the latter work, a patentee chooses to sell the innovation right only to the most efficient firm in order to take the advantage of a quantity expansion effect. Clearly, this effect disappears in the Banerjee and Poddar (2019)'s Hotelling model due to the presence of a fixed demand under given locations and full market coverage. Selling the property right on an innovation is finally proved to maximize its social value besides its private value, which implies a greater technology diffusion and higher social welfare compared to any other mode of technology licensing.

[28]The motivation for an outside innovator to sell her innovation property right is to avoid significant licensing costs and let an incumbent firm implement more efficiently a new technology. From a theoretical perspective, it is assumed that the auctioning innovator guarantees a higher payoff than an inside innovator (Tauman and Weng 2012).

[29]Banerjee and Poddar (2019) offer new insights to the analysis of licensing strategies under firm cost asymmetries showing that, when initial cost asymmetry is small enough, royalty licensing to both firms is optimal, while fixed-fee licensing to the efficient firm becomes optimal in the presence of a sufficiently large cost asymmetry.

Whether seeking a crucial input through either outsourcing or technology transfer is an issue addressed in the work of Pierce and Sen (2014). Indeed, both outsourcing and technology transfer enable one firm to use the more efficient technology of another firm.[30] By assuming that two firms locate at the two endpoints of a Hotelling line and compete with respect to prices, Pierce and Sen (2014) focus on the strategic reasons behind the adoption of either technology transfer or outsourcing relative to in-house production. They find that an outsourcing contract makes both firms and consumers better off, while technology transfer from one firm to another is never Pareto improving with respect to no contracting, since it benefits firms at the detriment of consumers.[31] Two features are relevant in determining such a result. First, a Stackelberg leadership effect arises through outsourcing, while it is absent under technology transfer. By allowing one firm to gain from a lower price, such a leadership effect yields benefits to consumers. Second, the incentive of the efficient firm to keep the demand of the input-seeking firm sufficiently high creates a distortive effect of technology transfer which raises the cost of the efficient firm and thus the equilibrium final prices. As a consequence, technology transfer contracts lead some consumers to be worse off. Such a distortion, however, is not observed under outsourcing, since orders are paid upfront in this case. The above effects always cause a conflict between firms' incentives and consumers' welfare when comparing outsourcing with technology transfer. This conflict is shown to be resolved, which implies that both firms prefer technology transfer while all consumers prefer outsourcing, when the input/technology supplier has a sufficiently high bargaining power in contracting with the input-seeking firm.

[30]The cost-inefficient firm might choose to outsource an input because of the significant costs associated with transferring labor-intensive technologies or a strict regulation of property rights. By contrast, technology transfer may be optimal since it can contribute to either enforcing tighter controls over product quality or limiting the hold-problem that may arise in the relationship with an external supplier.

[31]Both outsourcing and technology transfer are based on unit pricing policies.

7.6 Conclusions

Investigating patent licensing in a spatial framework of product differentiation brings new insights to the literature on technology transfer. The analysis carried out in the present work provides theoretical assessments for explaining the pattern of firms' strategic choices of technology licensing when a spatial dimension is introduced in modeling competition. We have identified the role of demand characteristics, as well as the role of spatial interactions in the shopping models vs. the shipping models, in defining the optimal licensing behavior. The latter has been shown to be also affected by market coverage assumptions and, moreover, by both firms' exogenous and endogenous (location-induced) cost heterogeneity. Such an analysis has allowed us to highlight the circumstances determining a reversal of the results popularized in non-spatial literature. By further discussing some alternatives to technology licensing, our work has contributed to a better understanding of the strategic reasons behind technology transfer in spatial markets. Two important aspects are not fully explored in spatial literature on technology licensing. First, there are no studies developed under incomplete information, to our knowledge. Second, in most cases the optimality of licensing contracts has been investigated under the assumption that consumers are uniformly distributed over the characteristics' space.[32] Therefore, extensions to incomplete information and to non-uniform distributions of consumers' preferences might be considered in future research.[33] The latter, finally, might be interestingly directed to explore the way in which firms' incentives to innovate interact with patent licensing decisions.

---

[32]Location equilibria with non-uniform consumer density are discussed by both Gupta et al. (1997) and Benassi (2014) in a spatial discrimination Cournot setting and by Neven (1986) in a location-price Hotelling game.

[33]The assumption of incomplete information may alter the existing results on technology licensing. As an example, the result that a fixed-fee contract is superior to a royalty contract for an outsider innovator does not hold in the non-spatial context of Gallini and Wright (1990) due to incomplete information.

References

Aghion, P., Bloom, N., Blundell, R., Griffith, R., & Howitt, P. (2005). Competition and Innovation: An Inverted-U Relationship. *Quarterly Journal of Economics, 120*, 701–728.

Anderson, S., & Neven, D. (1991). Cournot Competition Yield Spatial Agglomeration. *International Economic Review, 32*, 793–808.

Anderson, S. P., de Palma, A., & Thisse, J.-F. (1992). *Discrete Choice Theory of Product Differentiation*. Cambridge: MIT Press.

Arya, A., & Mittendorf, B. (2006). Enhancing Vertical Efficiency Through Horizontal Licensing. *Journal of Regulatory Economics, 29*, 333–342.

Bagchi, A., & Mukherjee, A. (2014). Technology Licensing in a Differentiated Oligopoly. *International Review of Economics and Finance, 29*, 455–465.

Banerjee, S., & Poddar, S. (2019). To Sell or Not to Sell: Licensing Versus Selling by An Outside Innovator. *Economic Modelling, 76*, 293–304.

Benassi, C. (2014). Dispersion Equilibria in Spatial Cournot Competition. *The Annals of Regional Science, 52*, 611–625.

Biscaia, R., & Mota, I. (2013). Models of Spatial Competition: A Critical Review. *Papers in Regional Science, 92*, 851–871.

Caballero-Sanz, F., Moner-Colonques, R., & Sempere-Monerris, J. J. (2002). Optimal Licensing in a Spatial Model. *Annales d'Economie et de Statistique, 66*, 258–279.

Caballero-Sanz, F., Moner-Colonques, R., & Sempere-Monerris, J. J. (2005). Licensing Policies for a New Product. *Economics of Innovation and New Technology, 14*, 697–713.

Cellini, R., & Lambertini, L. (2008). *The Economics of Innovation: Incentives, Cooperation and R&D Policy*. Bingley, UK: Emerald Publishing.

Chang, R.-Y., Hwang, H., & Peng, C.-H. (2017). Competition, Product Innovation and Licensing. *The B.E. Journal of Economic Analysis & Policy, 17*, 1–14.

Colombo, S. (2014). Fee Versus Royalty Licensing in Spatial Cournot Competition. *The Annals of Regional Science, 52*, 859–879.

Colombo, S. (2020). Does Licensing Promote Innovation? *Economics of Innovation and New Technology, 29*, 206–221.

Colombo, S., & Filippini, L. (2015). Patent Licensing with Bertrand Competitors. *The Manchester School, 83*, 1–16.

D'Aspremont, C., Gabszewicz, J. J., & Thisse, J.-F. (1979). On Hotelling's 'Stability in Competition. *Econometrica, 47*, 1145–1150.

Duranton, G. (2008). Spatial Economics. In S. N. Durlauf & J. E. Blume (Eds.), *The New Palgrave Dictionary of Economics* (2nd ed.). London: Palgrave Macmillan.

Eruktu, C., & Richelle, Y. (2007). Optimal Licensing Contracts and the Value of a Patent. *Journal of Economics and Management Strategy, 16*, 407–436.

Faulí-Oller, R., & Sandonis, J. (2002). Welfare Reducing Licensing. *Games and Economic Behavior, 41*, 192–205.

Gabszewicz, J. J., & Thisse, J.-F. (1986). Spatial Competition and the Location of Firms. In J. J. Gabszewicz, J.-F. Thisse, M. Fushita, & U. Schweizer (Eds.), *Location Theory*. Chur, Switzerland: Harwood Academic Publishers GmbH.

Gallini, N. T., & Wright, B. D. (1990). Technology Transfer Under Asymmetric Information. *Rand Journal of Economics, 21*, 147–160.

Gupta, B., Pal, D., & Sarkar, J. (1997). Spatial Cournot Competition and Agglomeration in a Model of Location Choice. *Regional Science and Urban Economics, 27*, 261–282.

Hamilton, J. H., Thisse, J.-F., & Weskamp, A. (1989). Spatial Discrimination: Bertrand Versus Cournot in a Model of Location Choice. *Regional Science and Urban Economics, 19*, 87–102.

Harter, J. F. R. (1993). Differentiated Products with R&D. *The Journal of Industrial Economics, 41*, 19–28.

Heywood, J. S., & Wang, Z. (2015). How to License a Transport Innovation. *Annals of Regional Science, 55*, 485–500.

Heywood, J. S., & Ye, G. (2011). Patent Licensing in a Model of Spatial Price Discrimination. *Papers in Regional Science, 90*, 589–603.

Hotelling, H. (1929). Stability in Competition. *Economic Journal, 39*, 41–57.

Kabiraj, A., & Kabiraj, T. (2017). Tariff Induced Licensing Contracts, Consumers' Surplus and Welfare. *Economic Modelling, 60*, 439–447.

Kabiraj, T., & Lee, C. (2011). Licensing Contract in Hotelling Structure. *Theoretical Economics Letters, 1*, 57–62.

Kamien, M., & Tauman, Y. (1984). The Private Value of a Patent: A Game Theoretic Analysis. *Journal of Economics, 4*(Supplement), 93–118.

Kamien, M., & Tauman, Y. (1986). Fees Versus Royalties and the Private Value of a Patent. *Quarterly Journal of Economics, 101*, 471–491.

Kamien, M., & Tauman, Y. (2002). Patent Licensing: The Inside Story. *The Manchester School, 70*, 7–15.

Kamien, M., Oren, S., & Tauman, Y. (1992). Optimal Licensing of Cost-Reducing Innovation. *Journal of Mathematical Economics, 21*, 483–508.

Katz, M., & Shapiro, C. (1985). On the Licensing of Innovation. *Rand Journal of Economics, 16*, 504–520.
Katz, M., & Shapiro, C. (1986). How to License Intangible Property. *Quarterly Journal of Economics, 101*, 567–590.
Li, C., & Song, J. (2010). Technology Licensing in a Vertically Differentiated Duopoly. *Japan and the World Economy, 21*, 183–190.
Li, C., & Zhang, J. (2012). R&D Competition in a Spatial Model with Technical Risk. *Papers in Regional Science, 92*, 667–682.
Lin, Y.-S., Hu, J.-L., & Xia, P.-C. (2013). Location Choice and Patent Licensing. *The Manchester School, 81*, 121–142.
Lu, Y., & Poddar, S. (2014). Patent Licensing in Spatial Models. *Economic Modelling, 42*, 250–256.
Macho-Stadler, I., Martínez-Giralt, X., & Pérez-Castrillo, J. D. (1996). The Role of Information in Licensing Contract Design. *Research Policy, 25*, 43–57.
Maskus, K. E. (2004). Encouraging International Technology Transfer, UNCTAD-ICTSD Issue Paper No. 7. https://unctad.org/en/PublicationsLibrary/ictsd2004ipd7_en.pdf.
Matsumura, T., & Matsushima, N. (2009). Cost Differentials and Mixed Strategy Equilibria in a Hotelling Model. *Annals of Regional Science, 43*, 215–234.
Matsumura, T., & Shimizu, D. (2006). Cournot and Bertrand in Shipping Models with Circular Markets. *Papers in Regional Science, 85*, 585–598.
Matsumura, T., Matsushima, N., & Stamatopoulos, G. (2010). Location Equilibrium with Asymmetric Firms: The Role of Licensing. *Journal of Economics, 99*, 267–276.
Mukherjee, A., & Tsai, Y. (2015). Does Two-part Tariff Licensing Agreement Enhance Both Welfare and Profit? *Journal of Economics, 116*, 63–76.
Muto, S. (1993). On Licensing Policies in Bertrand Competition. *Games and Economic Behavior, 5*, 257–267.
Neven, D. J. (1986). On Hotelling's Competition with Non-uniform Customer Distribution. *Economics Letters, 21*, 121–126.
Pierce, A., & Sen, D. (2014). Outsourcing Versus Technology Transfer: Hotelling Meets Stackelberg. *Journal of Economics, 111*, 263–287.
Poddar, S., & Sinha, U. B. (2004). On Patent Licensing in Spatial Competition. *The Economic Record, 80*, 208–218.
Poddar, S., & Sinha, U. B. (2010). Patent Licensing from a High-cost Firm to a Low-cost Firm. *The Economic Record, 86*, 384–395.

Rostoker, M. (1984). A Survey of Corporate Licensing. *Journal of Law and Technology, 24*, 59–92.

Salop, S. C. (1979). Monopolistic Competition with Outside Goods. *Bell Journal of Economics, 10*, 141–156.

Sen, D. (2005). Fee Versus Royalty Reconsidered. *Games and Economic Behavior, 53*, 141–147.

Sen, D., & Tauman, Y. (2007). General Licensing Schemes for a Cost-reducing Innovation. *Games and Economic Behavior, 59*, 163–186.

Shimizu, D. (2002). Product Differentiation in Spatial Cournot Markets. *Economics Letters, 76*, 317–322.

Singh, N., & Vives, X. (1984). Price and Quantity Competition in a Differentiated Duopoly. *RAND Journal of Economics, 15*, 546–554.

Sinha, U. B. (2016). Optimal Value of a Patent in an Asymmetric Cournot Duopoly Market. *Econonomic Modelling, 57*, 93–105.

Tauman, Y., & Weng, M.-H. (2012). Selling Patent Rights and the Incentive to Innovate. *Economics Letters, 114*, 241–244.

Teece, D. J. (1986). Profiting from Technological Innovation: Implications for Integration, Collaboration, Licensing, and Public Policy. *Research Policy, 15*, 285–305.

Thisse, J. F., & Vives, X. (1988). On the Strategic Choice of Spatial Price Policy. *American Economic Review, 78*, 122–137.

Wang, X. (1998). Fee Versus Royalty Licensing in a Cournot Duopoly Model. *Economics Letters, 60*, 55–62.

Wang, X. H. (2002). Fee Versus Royalty in a Differentiated Cournot Duopoly. *Journal of Economics and Business, 54*, 253–266.

Wang, X. H., & Yang, B. Z. (1999). On Licensing Under Bertrand Competition. *Australian Economic Papers, 38*, 106–119.

Wang, K.-C. A., Liang, W. J., & Lin, C. H. A. (2012). Licensing Under Network Externalities. *The Economic Record, 88*, 585–593.

Wang, K.-C. A., Liang, W.-J., & Chou, P.-S. (2013). Patent Licensing Under Cost Asymmetry Among Firms. *Economic Modelling, 31*, 297–307.

Wang, K.-C. A., Wang, Y.-J., Liang, W.-J., & Mai, C.-C. (2017). Optimal Licensing with Equity. *Papers in Regional Science, 96*, 207–220.

Ziss, S. (1993). Entry Deterrence, Cost Advantage and Horizontal Product Differentiation. *Regional Science and Urban Economics, 23*, 523–543.

Part III

Models of Spatial Economics

8

Zoning Regulations and Firms' Corporate Social Responsibility

Juan Carlos Bárcena-Ruiz and F. Javier Casado-Izaga

8.1 Introduction

The spatial location of firms in a linear city has been widely analyzed since the seminal paper by Hotelling (1929). He assumes that firms are free to locate along a linear city, but in modern cities it is common for firms not to be able to locate wherever they want. This is because municipal authorities regulate the different uses to which land may be

Financial support from Ministerio de Ciencia y Tecnología (ECO2015-66803-P) and the University of the Basque Country (GIU17/051) is gratefully acknowledged.

J. C. Bárcena-Ruiz (✉) · F. J. Casado-Izaga
Department of Fundamentals of Economic Analysis I, Faculty of Economic and Business Sciences, Universidad del País Vasco, UPV/EHU, Bilbao, Spain
e-mail: juancarlos.barcena@ehu.es; franciscojavier.casado@ehu.es

S. Colombo (ed.), *Spatial Economics Volume I*,
https://doi.org/10.1007/978-3-030-40098-9_8

put: residential, commercial, light and heavy industrial, agricultural, and recreational, among others. Zoning consists of dividing the land of a municipality into districts or zones and specifying the land uses allowed or prohibited for each one. Accordingly, firms may only use locations that meet the municipal zoning regulations. One branch of the literature on zoning studies the social welfare effects of legal restrictions on firms' locations in a linear city.

A common assumption in research on zoning is that private firms maximize their own profits. However, the objective function of private firms may also include socially responsible behavior. Empirical evidence shows a growing trend toward corporate social responsibility (hereafter CSR) among firms in many industries. This has led researchers to analyze this issue widely.[1] One approach to the study of this matter is to measure CSR concerns through the consumer surplus, so the objective function of a consumer-friendly firm is a convex combination of consumer surplus and profits. Following this approach, we analyze the spatial locations of two firms concerned about CSR and describe the optimal zoning constraints that a regulator must apply to achieve the locations of the firms that maximize social welfare.

One issue analyzed by the literature on zoning regulation is how it affects firms' locations and market competition, applying spatial models. The seminal paper in analyzing the location of competing firms in a linear city is "Stability in Competition" by Hotelling (1929). He assumes that two firms simultaneously locate within a linear city and then simultaneously decide their uniform prices. Consumers incur linear transportation costs to take their purchase home. He finds that both firms have incentives to locate in the center of the city: the so-called principle of minimum differentiation. Later, d'Aspremont et al. (1979) show that when transportation costs are linear there is no price equilibrium if firms are located very close together. This is because of the failure of the quasi-concavity of the profit function, which is a problem when the two firms locate close together. By removing the assumption of linear transportation

[1] See Porter and Kramer (2006), Bénabou and Tirole (2010), and Kitzmueller and Shimshack (2012) for a discussion on CSR. Empirical evidence can be found in a review of corporate responsibility and sustainability reporting from 4900 companies in 49 countries by KPMG (2017).

costs, d'Aspremont et al. (1979) avoid the problem of existence of price equilibrium. They show that under quadratic transportation costs, when firms must locate within the city, the game has one price equilibrium for all the locations of the firms. In that case firms locate at the endpoints of the city, according to the so-called principle of maximum differentiation.

Economides (1986) studies in depth the impact of different transportation cost functions on the locations adopted by firms. He analyzes a family of transportation cost functions between the linear and the quadratic. He finds that there is an equilibrium in locations when the curvature of the consumers' transportation cost function is sufficiently high. He concludes that when there is an equilibrium the locations of the firms are within the linear city if the curvature of the consumers' transportation cost function is low. Firms locate at the corners of the city for very convex transportation cost functions. Moreover, minimum product differentiation is never an equilibrium.

In the models cited above firms have to locate within a residential linear city. However, there may be non-residential areas in the surroundings. The case in which firms are free to locate outside the residential area is known as the unconstrained model. In that setting, Lambertini (1994, 1997a) and Tabuchi and Thisse (1995) show that under quadratic transportation costs firms locate outside the residential city boundaries in order to mitigate price competition.[2]

Another branch of this literature assumes that firms do not set a uniform price, but price discriminate between consumers (see Hurter and Lederer 1985; Lederer and Hurter 1986). In this setting, when firms price discriminate in a linear city they adopt the locations that maximize social welfare, defined as the sum of the consumer and producer surpluses.

It is common in towns for councils to regulate the use of their land, so firms cannot locate freely because they need a permit from the authorities. Zoning is intended to preserve the health, safety, harmonic development, and the welfare of the community. To that end, zoning ordinances and

[2]This unconstrained model has been used to analyze various issues such as the use of tax or subsidies to get firms to take up their optimal locations (Lambertini 1997b), the use of strategic reward contracts (Matsumura and Matsushima 2012), and the regulation of waste management (Bárcena-Ruiz and Casado-Izaga 2015).

regulations define the different uses of city land.[3] For example, municipal councils may reserve land exclusively for public amenities (such as sports centers, schools, or hospitals), or may design industrial parks where firms are allowed to locate. One reason why zoning laws are applied is that they can mitigate or eliminate the impact of negative externalities, for example by preventing the shared use of land for incompatible activities. To avoid negative externalities heavy industrial activities are kept far enough from the areas reserved for residential use, but light industry may be located closer to residential areas. Some commercial activities that generate negative externalities, such as discotheques or clubs, may be located far from residential or educational areas, while others with no negative externalities may be allowed within those areas. Moreover, restrictive residential zoning may be used as a means of excluding low-income residents from suburban communities. This last objective can be attained, for example, by reducing the number of apartments that may be built (Bates and Santerre 1994).[4]

Most papers that analyze spatial competition assume that firms maximize their own profits, but the objective function of these firms may include other goals in addition to profits.[5] In this regard, a growing trend in many industries in recent decades is for some private firms to be concerned about CSR. As pointed out by Lambertini and Tampieri (2015), a firm concerned about CSR cares not only about the interests of shareholders (i.e., profits) but also about how its decisions affect workers, consumers, and the environment. Kitzmueller and Shimshack (2012, p. 53) argue that "CSR is corporate social or environmental behavior that

[3]One feature of spatial competition models is that the linear city can also be used to analyze product differentiation. As a consequence, zoning regulation can also be interpreted as the regulator constraining the range of characteristics that products may have, or banning certain types of product. For example, in many countries the selling of alcohol is forbidden in residential areas to safeguard residents against negative externalities such as noise and delinquency.

[4]Zoning design is also concerned with so-called fiscal zoning, which means that local authorities may try to keep out relatively low-income residents when they consume more in public services than they pay in property taxes.

[5]For example, firms may be run by managers who maximize the weighted sum of profits and sale revenues (Bárcena-Ruiz and Casado-Izaga 2005; Heywood and Wang 2016). In mixed markets, private firms compete with public firms and the objective function of the latter includes the consumer surplus (Bárcena-Ruiz and Casado-Izaga 2018b; Matsumura and Tomaru 2015).

goes beyond the legal or regulatory requirements of the relevant market(s) and/or economy(s)." In fact, CSR has become an important business strategy, so this issue is receiving increasing attention from researchers. A large proportion of that research measures CSR concerns through the consumer surplus, so the objective function of a consumer-friendly firm is a convex combination of the consumer surplus and the firm's profits (see, e.g., Kopel and Brand 2012; Lambertini and Tampieri 2015; Kim et al. 2019).[6]

In this chapter we analyze how CSR concerns affect the spatial locations of two firms. We find that when concern for CSR is low (high) both firms locate further from (closer to) the rival than with social welfare maximizing locations. Moreover, an increase in CSR concern brings firms near to social welfare maximizing locations in two cases: when concern for CSR is low enough and when it is high enough. For intermediate values of this concern an increase moves firms further from social welfare maximizing locations. Thus, zoning constraints may enable the regulator to get firms to take up those locations that maximize social welfare. The guideline is to permit them to locate only outside the open interval between the two social welfare maximizing locations when their concern for CSR is high and allow only locations between (and including) the two social welfare maximizing locations when their concern for CSR is low.

Next we describe the rest of this chapter. Section 8.2 surveys the main theoretical results of the literature on zoning in a linear city. Section 8.3 sets the main characteristics of the CSR model. Section 8.4 studies firms' locations when they can locate freely. Section 8.5 analyzes the design of zoning by the regulator, and Sect. 8.6 presents the main conclusions.

[6]The fact that firms take into account goals other than profits in their objective functions may affect their profits negatively, so shareholders might oppose the inclusion of CSR in their objective functions (Baron 2007). However, there are positive factors associated with concerns about CSR. For example, Porter and Kramer (2006) argue that many organizations rank firms on their CSR performance, which attracts favorable publicity, so CSR is a priority for business leaders. Lambertini and Tampieri (2015) argue that a firm may strategically commit to CSR to gain market share and profits at the expense of rival profit-maximizing firms.

8.2 Review of the Literature on Zoning in Linear Cities

The literature that studies restrictions on the location of firms has focused mainly on zoning regulations assuming that firms are privately owned and may only locate inside the linear city limits.[7] That literature considers various scenarios that limit zoning design by imposing symmetric or asymmetric zoning restrictions. Lai and Tsai (2004) study one-sided asymmetric zoning that prohibits the two firms from locating in an exclusively residential area around the left border of the linear city. They show that under zoning regulations firms locate at the borders of the non-residential area, so the maximum differentiation principle is valid. Zoning regulations limit firms' profits and transfer them to consumers. The optimal policy sets an exclusively residential area of about 29.5 percent of the city to correct the distortion in transportation costs optimally.[8]

City land regulation when symmetric zoning is imposed has also been analyzed. Tsai et al. (2006) consider a linear city with a symmetric zoning constraint that forces firms to locate only in a central area of the city. Consumers can choose to live in the high-density internal area or outside in the low-density residential areas. Assuming that prices are constant, they focus on firms' locations and consumers' location patterns. They show that the equilibrium location region is smaller with the zoning constraint than without it.

A different symmetric central zoning is analyzed by Chen and Lai (2008). They consider that production activities are not allowed in the middle region of the city in a Cournot duopoly spatial location model. They find that zoning may improve welfare when firms compete with discriminatory quantities under central symmetric zoning. Colombo (2011) shows that when quantity-setting firms choose whether to discriminate or not and then set quantities, the unique equilibrium involves all firms

[7] Other papers in this literature analyze zoning restrictions assuming non-linear cities. For example, Hamoudi and Risueño (2012) consider a circular city, and Datta and Sudhir (2013) assume a square city.

[8] They also study an amenity effect for consumers who live in the exclusively residential area and land rent patterns. The aforementioned result is valid without the amenity effect.

selling a uniform quantity to all consumers. For this reason, Colombo (2012) studies a non-discriminating Cournot duopoly and a potentially asymmetric central zoning area where firms cannot locate. He finds that this regulation affects firms' equilibrium location. Moreover, the consumer surplus and firms' profits decrease as the zoning area increases. As a result, the optimal size of the area where firms cannot locate is zero.

The papers cited above impose symmetric or asymmetric restrictions on zoning regulation. Next we discuss other papers that extend the above analysis to study different scenarios that impose no restrictions on zoning design on firms' location in a linear city. We begin with three papers that assume that the objective function of the regulator is the weighted sum of the consumer and producer surpluses, so it has different sensitivities toward consumers and producers.[9] The zoning mechanism defines the area where firms are allowed to locate.

First, Bárcena-Ruiz et al. (2016) study an unconstrained Hotelling model in which the regulator may decide to force firms to locate inside the city or outside the city boundaries where there are no consumers. It is shown that if the regulator is highly concerned about consumers both firms must locate in the middle of the market. As the regulator becomes less concerned about consumers the area where firms can locate spreads out symmetrically from the middle of the city. This area may be shared by consumers and firms, while the peripheral areas are for residential use only. A regulator still less concerned about consumers restricts firms to locate outside the city limits, where no consumers live. So there is a strip of land outside the city, but close to its boundaries, for uses other than residential areas and industrial estates.

Second, Bárcena-Ruiz and Casado-Izaga (2014) analyze optimal zoning assuming a duopoly in which firms can price discriminate between consumers.[10] They consider a linear city and linear transportation costs.

[9]White (2002, p. 489) argues that "while the standard, equally-weighted welfare function may be desirable for normative reasons, based on utilitarianism or fairness doctrines (as in Harsanyi 1995), it may be restrictive for purposes of predicting the behavior of actual public firms and the resulting market outcomes." White (2002) assumes a weighted welfare function to analyze mixed markets.

[10]See Hurter and Lederer (1985) and Lederer and Hurter (1986) for an analysis of this issue without zoning regulations.

In this context, when firms freely choose their locations simultaneously they locate in the first and third quartiles. These locations maximize social welfare if the regulator gives the same weight to firms' profits and the consumer surplus. When the regulator has a bias toward firms, locations around the central area are forbidden. When there is a bias in the direction of consumers, only locations around the central area are allowed; when this bias is high enough firms have to locate in the middle of the city. The optimal area in which firms can or cannot locate is always symmetric with respect to the middle of the market.

Thirdly, literature on zoning mainly considers competition between fully domestic-owned firms. However, in economic literature it is well known that the nationality of firms plays a crucial role.[11] Bárcena-Ruiz and Casado-Izaga (2016) analyze optimal zoning under spatial price discrimination when firms may be partially foreign-owned. When the percentage of shares of the firms that is domestic-owned increases their optimal locations are further from the middle of the market, so the distance between them increases.[12] For high enough values of the bias of the regulator toward firms, the size of the zone in which firms are allowed to locate is greater when firms are partially foreign-owned than when they are fully domestic-owned.

The literature on zoning and firms' locations has mainly focused on privately owned firms, neglecting the fact that public and private firms may compete in the product market. Bárcena-Ruiz et al. (2014) analyze zoning regulation in a mixed duopoly where one firm is publicly owned and the other is private.[13] Firms sell their product in a linear city and the objective function of the regulator is the weighted sum of social surplus and the profit of the public firm. They find that when the weight that the regulator attaches to the profit of the public firm is not zero and not

[11]See, for example, Heywood and Ye (2009) and Matsushima and Matsumura (2006). They study the spatial location of firms in a mixed oligopoly when there are foreign firms.

[12]Moreover, the value of the bias of the regulator toward firms such that the optimal locations are the middle of the market decreases when firms are more domestic-owned.

[13]This market structure is common in many sectors such as airlines, railways, postal services, education, and healthcare. The location of private and public firms that compete in a linear city has been extensively analyzed. See, for example, Cremer et al. (1991), Matsushima and Matsumura (2006), and Bárcena-Ruiz and Casado-Izaga (2012).

high enough, there is a need to zone the city. This is because the regulator prefers the public firm to be placed closer to the middle of the market and the private firm further away. By simply restricting the location of the private firm to within a zone around a border of the city both firms locate optimally. There is no need to limit the location of the public firm since it locates optimally given the restriction placed on the private firm. However, in the case of a private duopoly the regulator needs to restrict the location of both private firms to obtain optimal locations.

Although the papers cited above analyze the zoning design of a city they do not study zoning regulation in nearby towns. They consider zoning in a single town, so there is no strategic interaction between regulators.[14] There is broad empirical evidence to support the strategic use of zoning in neighboring towns (see, e.g., Heim 2012; Henninger 2015; and other examples described in Bárcena-Ruiz and Casado-Izaga 2017), so it is relevant to analyze this issue. Next we discuss papers that study zoning of a cross-border linear city composed of two bordering towns. Only one firm operates in each town, though it can sell its product in both markets. Each town has its own regulator, which attempts to maximize local welfare, considering only the surpluses of the consumers and the producer that reside in its town. Each regulator decides whether to zone its town or not. Moreover, towns are run by city councils that seek to maximize local welfare, so each local authority may use zoning to push domestic firms, which must observe urban planning regulations, to locate in specific zones of the town. This may help them to capture rents from neighboring consumers or avoid losing local consumers. Consequently, strategic use of zoning could be observed in bordering towns.

Bárcena-Ruiz and Casado-Izaga (2017) consider two adjacent towns that belong to different countries. Zoning regulation affects firms' locations, since some urban areas are for residential use only, and depends on the fixed costs associated with the study and implementation of those

[14] Inoue et al. (2009) study the location of a public firm and a private firm in a city with two symmetric districts, each of which is run by a local government. However, they do not study zoning decisions.

policies.[15] When the cost of zoning is low both regulators zone their towns to make the local firm locate close to the border between the two towns. When zoned towns are of different sizes, the regulator of the larger town makes its local firm locate very close to the other town to reduce the loss of local consumers. Thus, the areas near the frontier between the two towns share residential and commercial uses and the areas far from the frontier are reserved for residential use only. When zoning costs are significant new equilibria may emerge. First, both regulators may refuse to zone when it is very costly to do so. Second, one regulator may not zone while the other applies zoning in an effort to avoid the loss of local consumers.[16]

The use of zoning as a strategic device by the regulators of two adjacent municipal districts that belong to the same country is analyzed in Bárcena-Ruiz and Casado-Izaga (2018a). The residential areas of the municipal districts are connected and together form a linear city with spare land in its surroundings (an unconstrained Hotelling model). Zoning costs are considered as meaningful. Both regulators zone their municipal districts when the fixed zoning cost is low enough and decline to zone when it is very high. These two symmetric equilibria coexist when the zoning costs take intermediate values. This result does not arise when the municipal districts do not have surrounding areas available in which firms may locate. In such cases, for intermediate values of the fixed zoning cost only one regulator zones, so two asymmetric equilibria emerge. It is also obtained that there are more incentives to apply zoning regulations in the unconstrained model than in the constrained one. Finally, from the viewpoint of the joint welfare of the two towns there is an excess in local regulations.

The aforesaid papers on strategic interaction between regulators assume that firms are owned by domestic investors. However, some of the firms located in each country may be foreign-owned. This issue is analyzed by Bárcena-Ruiz and Casado-Izaga (2020), who consider a linear city composed of two adjacent towns. In each town a percentage of the local

[15] There are costs linked to studying regulation, such as designing the maps and paying the staff who inform about and watch for non-fulfillment of the norms, among others.

[16] When towns are of different sizes only the regulator of the larger town resorts to zoning to reduce the loss of revenue from local consumers.

firm is owned by local investors and the rest is owned by investors from the neighboring town. Zoning does not entail a fixed cost and each regulator decides whether to zone its town or not. It is shown that zoning constraints when applied depend crucially on what percentage of the local firm is owned by local investors. When it is high enough both regulators zone their towns, and zoning constraints compel the local firm to locate very close to its rival. For intermediate percentages of ownership of the local firm by local investors only one regulator resorts to zoning. Therefore, an asymmetric result emerges despite the symmetry of the model. Fixed zoning costs are not considered so the asymmetric result arises because foreign profits are significant. Finally, for a low enough weight of local profits the objectives of the regulator and the firms are not in conflict.

The rest of this chapter considers a novel linear city model that studies the location of firms with socially responsible behavior and the optimal zoning regulations in this setting.

8.3 The CSR Linear City Model

The assumptions of the location model that we study are standard in the literature except for the consideration of CSR concern, which affects the objective functions of firms. Accordingly, consumers are distributed uniformly and with a unitary density along a linear city that corresponds to the interval [0, 1]. Consumers must pay to carry their purchase home, which entails a quadratic cost td^2, where d is the distance traveled from the firm's location to the consumer's home and t is a positive constant. Each consumer buys only one unit of the good at the lowest delivered price, that is the mill price plus transportation cost. Each consumer derives a gross surplus from consumption s which is so large that each consumer buys one unit of the product.

There are two firms indexed by i ($i = 1, 2$), which compete in the product market. Firms first choose their locations, in a long-term decision that cannot be changed in the future. Let $x_i \in (-\infty, +\infty)$ denote the location of firm i. Under zoning constraints the firms must locate within the area set by the regulator. Thus, the city may have three different zones:

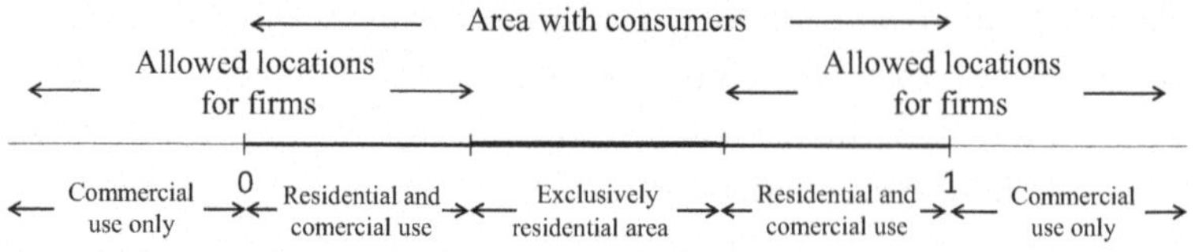

Fig. 8.1 Different uses of land

an exclusively residential area, an area that may be shared by consumers and firms, and finally the area surrounding the residential area, where firms may be allowed to locate. When firms are not allowed to locate outside the residential area this last area is just spare land. Figure 8.1 shows the different uses that land may have when firms are not allowed to locate in the middle of the residential area.

As usual, we assume that firm 1 locates to the left of or at the same point as firm 2, which means that $x_1 \leq x_2$. For the sake of simplicity, firms' production costs are normalized to zero.

Following Goering (2008a, b), Kopel and Brand (2012), and Lambertini and Tampieri (2015), we model CSR by introducing an objective function for firm i ($i = 1, 2$) that considers firm' profits, π_i, and the consumer surplus, CS.[17]

Specifically, under CSR the objective function of firm i, denoted by O_i, is given by:

$$O_i = \pi_i + z\,CS, i = 1, 2, \tag{8.1}$$

where $z \in [0,1]$ measures the weight that firms attach to the consumer surplus and is an indicator of CSR concerns.[18] Consumer surplus is defined as the difference between the gross surplus, s, and the sum of

[17] Lambertini and Tampieri (2015) study a Cournot oligopoly with pollution and one CSR firm operating in the market. We do not study environmental concerns in our model, so they are excluded from our objective function as in the case of Goering (2008a, b) and Kopel and Brand (2012).

[18] For the sake of simplicity we consider that both firms attach the same importance to CSR concerns.

the prices paid by the consumers (which equals the total profits of the firms, $\pi_1 + \pi_2$) plus total transportation costs.

To describe the regulator's objective function (W) we adopt the usual approach according to which social welfare is defined as the sum of the profits of the two firms and the consumer surplus: $W = \pi_1 + \pi_2 + CS$.

The timing of the game is the following: In the first stage of the game the regulator chooses the area where firms are allowed to locate. In the second stage the two firms simultaneously choose their locations observing the zoning constraints, if any. Finally, in the third stage the two firms choose their prices simultaneously. We solve the game by backward induction to obtain the subgame perfect Nash equilibria.

8.4 Firms' Locations Without Regulation

We first analyze the choice of locations by the two firms when they are not constrained by zoning regulations. Then we compare the locations that maximize social welfare with those freely chosen by the firms and describe the optimal zoning regulations.

Let p_i denote the price set by firm i ($i = 1, 2$). The location of the consumer who is indifferent as regards buying from either firm, $\overline{x}$, is obtained from the condition that shows that price plus transportation costs when buying from the firm on the left is the same as when buying from the firm on the right:

$$p_1 + t(\overline{x} - x_1)^2 = p_2 + t(\overline{x} - x_2)^2. \tag{8.2}$$

From expression (8.2) the following is obtained:

$$\overline{x} = \frac{p_2 - p_1}{2t\,(x_2 - x_1)} + \frac{x_2 + x_1}{2}. \tag{8.3}$$

Thus, the respective demands of firms 1 and 2 when they are not located at the same point are given by q_1 and q_2:

$$q_1 = \begin{cases} \overline{x} & if\ 0 \le \overline{x} \le 1 \\ 1 & if\ \overline{x} > 1 \\ 0 & if\ \overline{x} < 0 \end{cases}, \qquad q_2 = \begin{cases} 1-\overline{x} & if\ 0 \le 1-\overline{x} \le 1 \\ 1 & if\ 1-\overline{x} > 1 \\ 0 & if\ 1-\overline{x} < 0 \end{cases} \tag{8.4}$$

We first solve the third stage of the game to get equilibrium prices. In this stage firms simultaneously set their prices and their outputs are then determined via expression (8.4). The objective function of firm i is given by expression (8.1), which leads to the following:

$$O_1 = p_1\overline{x} + z\left[s - p_1\overline{x} - p_2\left(1-\overline{x}\right) - \int_0^{\overline{x}} t(x-x_1)^2dx - \int_{\overline{x}}^{1} t(x-x_2)^2dx\right], \tag{8.5}$$

$$O_2 = p_2\left(1-\overline{x}\right) + z\left[s - p_1\overline{x} - p_2\left(1-\overline{x}\right) - \int_0^{\overline{x}} t(x-x_1)^2dx - \int_{\overline{x}}^{1} t(x-x_2)^2dx\right]. \tag{8.6}$$

Substituting (8.3) into (8.1) and simplifying:

$$O_1 = \frac{1}{12t(x_2-x_1)}\left(3p_1^2\left(-2+z\right) - 6p_1\left(p_2 + t\left(-x_1^2+x_2^2\right)\right)\left(-1+z\right)\right. \\ + \left(3p_2^2 - 6p_2t\left(x_1-x_2\right)\left(-2+x_1+x_2\right) + t\left(x_1-x_2\right)\right. \\ \left.\left.\left(-12s + t\left(4+3x_1^3+3x_1^2x_2 - 3(-2+x_2)^2x_2 - 3x_1x_2^2\right)\right)\right)z\right), \tag{8.7}$$

$$O_2 = \frac{1}{12t(x_2-x_1)}\left(3p_2^2\left(-2+z\right) - 6p_2t\left(x_1-x_2\right)\left(-2+x_1+x_2\right)\left(-1+z\right)\right. \\ + 3p_1^2z + t\left(x_1-x_2\right)\left(-12s + t(4+3x_1^3+3x_1^2x_2 - 3(-2+x_2)^2x_2\right. \\ \left.\left. - 3x_1x_2^2\right)\right)z + 6p_1\left(p_2 - p_2z + t\left(x_1-x_2\right)\left(x_1+x_2\right)z\right)\Big). \tag{8.8}$$

Firm i sets the price that maximizes O_i ($i = 1, 2$). Solving these problems gives the reaction functions in prices:

$$\begin{aligned} p_1 &= \tfrac{(1-z)}{(2-z)} \left(p_2 + t\left(-x_1^2 + x_2^2\right)\right), \\ p_2 &= \tfrac{(1-z)}{(2-z)} \left(p_1 + t\left(x_1 - x_2\right)\left(-2 + x_1 + x_2\right)\right). \end{aligned} \tag{8.9}$$

The equilibrium prices when both firms sell the good are obtained from (8.9).[19]

$$\begin{aligned} p_1^* &= \tfrac{(1-z)}{(3-2z)} t\left(x_2 - x_1\right)\left(2 + x_1 + x_2 - 2z\right), \\ p_2^* &= \tfrac{(1-z)}{(3-2z)} t\left(x_2 - x_1\right)\left(4 - x_1 - x_2 - 2z\right). \end{aligned} \tag{8.10}$$

It can be shown from (8.10) that, given the location of the firms, equilibrium prices become lower as CSR concerns increase (i.e., as z increases). This is because firms are more concerned about the consumer surplus.

Now it is possible to analyze the second stage of the game and find the equilibrium locations. Firm i chooses the location that maximizes O_i ($i = 1, 2$). Substituting equilibrium prices (8.10) in (8.7) and (8.8) and taking the first-order condition of O_i with respect to the location for each firm x_i gives:

$$\begin{aligned} &3x_1^2\left(-2 + z\right) + 2x_1\left(-8 + \left(-2 + z\right)\left(x_2 - 8z^2\right)\right) \\ &- \left(-2 + z\right)\left(x_2^2 + 4\left(-1 + z\right)\left(1 + z\left(-7 + 4z\right)\right)\right)\Big) = 0, \end{aligned} \tag{8.11}$$

$$\begin{aligned} &-2\left(4 + x_1 - 3x_2\right)\left(-4 + x_1 + x_2\right) + \Big(8\left(-9 + x_2\right) + \left(x_1 - 3x_2\right) \\ &\left(x_1 + x_2\right)\Big)z + 8\left(11 + 4x_2\right)z^2 - 4\left(15 + 4x_2\right)z^3 + 16z^4 = 0. \end{aligned} \tag{8.12}$$

[19] The second-order conditions of the problems that we analyze are always satisfied.

Solving (8.11) and (8.12) gives firms' equilibrium locations. Proposition 1 shows the result.

Proposition 1 *The equilibrium locations of firms with CSR concerns are:*

$$x_1^* = \frac{(2-z)\left(1-10z+8z^2\right)}{4\left(-2-z+2z^2\right)} \text{ and } x_2^* = \frac{-10+17z-18z^2+8z^3}{4\left(-2-z+2z^2\right)}.$$

From Proposition 1 equilibrium locations are symmetric from the middle of the market: $x_2^* = 1 - x_1^*$. Once equilibrium locations are obtained it becomes possible to compute the prices set by the firms:

$$p_1^* = p_2^* = \frac{t\,(1-z)\,(3-2z)\,(2+z\,(-5+4z))}{2\left(2+z-2z^2\right)}. \tag{8.13}$$

Equilibrium prices decrease as z increases, but the reduction is greater when CSR concerns are initially very low than when they are high. It is useful to keep in mind the changes in equilibrium prices to understand the location results. CSR firms have an incentive to reduce their prices as z increases for given locations of the firms.

Figure 8.2 depicts equilibrium locations as a function of firms' CSR concerns.

When $z = 0$ firms are pure profit maximizers and their equilibrium locations are $x_1^* = -1/4$ and $x_2^* = 5/4$, so both firms locate outside the residential area. This is the result of the unconstrained Hotelling model as shown by Lambertini (1994, 1997a) and Tabuchi and Thisse (1995). In this case firms have no concerns about the consumer surplus, so the well-known demand and strategic effects drive them to the equilibrium locations. The demand effect pushes each firm toward its rival so as to gain more consumers. The strategic effect pushes each firm to locate far from its rival so as to mitigate price competition. When firms can locate outside the residential area, the two effects balance out if they locate outside the segment [0, 1] at $x_1^* = -1/4$ and $x_2^* = 5/4$.

When z is positive two new effects appear. To analyze them the objective function of firm i can be rewritten as $O_i = zs + (1-z)\pi_i - z\pi_j - z\,TTC$ $(i, j = 1, 2;\ i \neq j)$, where TTC stands for consumers' total

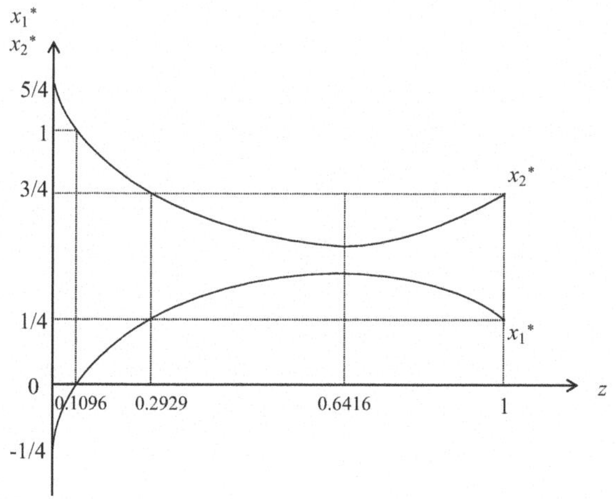

Fig. 8.2 Optimal locations

transportation costs. Taking the total derivative of O_i with regard to x_i, it is possible to find the previous demand and strategic effects weighted by $(1-z)$ and two additional effects (weighted by z) that depend on the profits of the rival and on consumers' transportation costs. An increase in x_i reduces the profits of the rival, and when firms are located far apart (e.g., when z is low) it also reduces consumers' transportation costs. As z increases CSR concerns become greater so these two new effects push firms to locate closer together so as to reduce both their rivals' profits and consumers' transportation costs. It increases the consumer surplus at the expense of firms' profits. Therefore, although firms locate outside the residential area, as z increases firms locate closer to that area when $z < 0.1096$. When $z = 0.1096$ firms locate at the boundaries of the residential area: $x_1^* = 0$ and $x_2^* = 1$.

A further increase in CSR concerns raises the relative intensity of these two new effects which pushes firms to locate still closer. When z reaches $z = 1 - \sqrt{1/2} \simeq 0.2929$ firms choose the locations $x_1^* = 1/4$ and $x_2^* = 3/4$. These locations minimize consumers' transportation costs and match those that maximize social welfare. This is because higher prices are only a transfer from consumers to firms and do not alter social welfare, given that consumers' demand is inelastic. Firms are pushed to locate closer as z

continues to rise, until it reaches $z = 0.6416$. For this critical value CSR firms locate at the minimum distance (0.2071).

A further increase in z changes the trend and pushes each firm to locate further from its rival and closer to the locations that minimize consumers' transportation costs. This is because prices are now very low and the reduction in prices is not so intense, so firms give priority to reducing consumers' transportation costs. Finally, when $z = 1$ firms choose the locations that maximize social welfare since equilibrium prices are null so firms choose the locations that minimize consumers' transportation costs.

Next, we analyze the zoning rules that enable the regulator to get firms to take up their optimal locations depending on the different weights (z) that firms attach to the consumer surplus. The zoning regulation sets the area where firms are allowed to locate.

8.5 The Design of Zoning by the Regulator

When the regulator implements the optimal zoning policy, the locations of the two firms are those that maximize social welfare: $x_1^* = 1/4$ and $x_2^* = 3/4$. We find that the optimal zoning policy depends on the degree of CSR concerns. When it is low (i.e., when z is low) firms are only allowed to locate in or between the social welfare maximizing locations, that is they must locate within the interval [1/4, 3/4]. When z is high enough firms are only allowed to locate outside the interval between the social welfare maximizing locations, that is they must locate in the interval $(-\infty, 1/4]$ and in the interval $[3/4, +\infty)$.

Proposition 2 *Under zoning regulations the locations that maximize social welfare can be obtained by imposing the following rules: (i) When* $z < 1 - \sqrt{1/2}$ *firms are only allowed to locate along the interval* [1/4, 3/4]; *(ii) when* $1 - \sqrt{1/2} < z < 1$ *firms are only allowed to locate outside the interval* (1/4, 3/4). *When* $z = 1 - \sqrt{1/2}$ *and when* $z = 1$, *firms adopt the locations that maximize social welfare with no need for zoning constraints.*

Proof. When $z = 1 - \sqrt{1/2} \simeq 0.2929$ and $z = 1$ firms locate at $x_1^* = 1/4$ and $x_2^* = 3/4$, the locations that maximize social welfare, as shown in Proposition 1. To complete the proof assume that firm 2 locates at $x_2^* = 3/4$. From (8.11) it can be seen that the best response of firm 1 is to choose $x_1^*(z) = \big(38 - 3z - 64z^2 + 32z^3 - 2\sqrt{196 + 1644z - 4903z^2 + 3968z^3 - 320z^4 - 832z^5 + 256z^6}\big) / (12(-2+z))$. The function $x_1^*(z)$ is strictly concave in z and meets the value $x_1^* = 1/4$ when $z = 1 - \sqrt{1/2}$ and when $z = 1$.

When $z < 1-\sqrt{1/2}$ it emerges that $x_1^*(z) < 1/4$, so firm 1 would choose to locate to the left of 1/4. This is not allowed by the zoning constraints, so firm 1 locates as close as possible to its optimal location, that is at $x_1^* = 1/4$ and the best response of its rival is to locate at $x_2^* = 3/4$. Because of the symmetry of the model we conclude that there is an equilibrium at which firms adopt the social welfare maximizing locations. Moreover, in this case this is the only equilibrium, because when firms can choose their locations freely they choose to locate outside the interval [1/4, 3/4], and this is forbidden by zoning rules.

When $1 - \sqrt{1/2} < z < 1$ and $x_2^* = 3/4$ it merges that $x_1^*(z) > 1/4$, so firm 1 would like to locate as close as allowed to 1/4. In this case the zoning design only allows firms to locate outside the interval (1/4, 3/4), so firm 1 locates at $x_1^* = 1/4$, and the best response of its rival is to locate at $x_2^* = 3/4$. This is the only equilibrium because if firms could freely choose their locations they would choose to locate inside the interval [1/4, 3/4], and this is forbidden by the zoning rules. ■

Zoning regulations forbid firms to locate very far apart when CSR concerns are low (i.e., when z is low). This is because firms seek to locate far from their rival because this increases equilibrium prices and firms' profits, and they have little interest in the consumer surplus.[20] By contrast, when CSR concerns are high firms sacrifice their profits and try to locate closer to their rival. Thus, the zoning constraints forbid firms to locate as close as they would like to.

[20]Consumers' transportation costs are very high when firms locate very far apart.

8.6 Conclusions

It is well known that the location of profit maximizing firms in a linear city depends on two issues: First, firms wish to locate near the middle of the city so as to be close to most consumers (the so-called demand effect or centripetal effect). Second, when a firm is close to its rival price competition is intense, and there is a strategic effect that pushes firms to locate far from their rival to mitigate price competition (the centrifugal effect). Profit maximizing firms take their location decisions taking these two effects into account. These locations usually do not match those that maximize social welfare. Under quadratic transportation costs firms that set uniform prices locate much further from their rival than if they occupied the locations that maximize social welfare. But local authorities have a powerful tool to get firms to adopt the desired locations: zoning regulations. When consumers are already distributed along the linear city, zoning regulations may set the areas of the city where firms can or cannot locate. This issue has been widely analyzed, as shown in the review of the literature.

Empirical evidence shows that many firms behave in a socially responsible manner, so it is relevant to analyze how zoning design is conditioned by these concerns. When firms have CSR concerns the balance between the standard centripetal and centrifugal effects is distorted because firms consider the consumer surplus, so consumers' transportation costs and the prices paid are also taken into account. As a result, the two firms locate closer together than profit maximizing firms. When CSR concerns are low firms still locate very far apart from a social welfare viewpoint because the profit of each firm is still a very important concern. When CSR concerns are high enough firms locate between the two locations that maximize social welfare, so they locate very close together. The zoning regulations required to obtain the optimal locations of the firms are the following: allowing firms to locate only outside the open interval between the two social welfare maximizing locations when their concern for CSR is high and allowing only locations in or between the two social welfare maximizing locations when concern for CSR is low. This means that local authorities have to take into account the intensity of socially responsible behavior by firms when designing optimal zoning regulations.

References

Bárcena-Ruiz, J. C., & Casado-Izaga, F. J. (2005). Should Shareholders Delegate Location Decisions? *Research in Economics, 59*(3), 209–222.

Bárcena-Ruiz, J. C., & Casado-Izaga, F. J. (2012). Location of Public and Private Firms Under Endogenous Timing of Choices. *Journal of Economics, 105*(2), 129–143.

Bárcena-Ruiz, J. C., & Casado-Izaga, F. J. (2014). Zoning Under Spatial Price Discrimination. *Economic Inquiry, 52*(2), 659–665.

Bárcena-Ruiz, J. C., & Casado-Izaga, F. J. (2015). Regulation of Waste Management Under Spatial Competition. *Journal of Cleaner Production, 92*(1), 216–222.

Bárcena-Ruiz, J. C., & Casado-Izaga, F. J. (2016). Foreign-owned Firms and Zoning Under Spatial Price Discrimination. *Letters in Spatial and Resource Sciences, 9*(2), 145–155.

Bárcena-Ruiz, J. C., & Casado-Izaga, F. J. (2017). Zoning a Cross-border City. *Journal of Regional Science, 57*(1), 173–189.

Bárcena-Ruiz, J. C., & Casado-Izaga, F. J. (2018a). Zoning a Metropolitan Area. *Papers in Regional Science, 97*(Supplement 1), S123–S137.

Bárcena-Ruiz, J. C., & Casado-Izaga, F. J. (2018b). Optimal Size of a Residential Area Within a Municipality. *Journal of Economics, 124*(1), 75–92.

Bárcena-Ruiz, J. C. & Casado-Izaga, F. J. (2020). Partial Ownership of Local Firms and Zoning of Neighboring Towns. *The Annals of Regional Science*, https://doi.org/10.1007/s00168-019-00972-5.

Bárcena-Ruiz, J. C., Casado-Izaga, F. J., & Hamoudi, H. (2014). Optimal Zoning of a Mixed Duopoly. *Annals of Regional Science, 52*(1), 141–153.

Bárcena-Ruiz, J. C., Casado-Izaga, F. J., Hamoudi, H., & Rodríguez, I. (2016). Optimal Zoning in the Unconstrained Hotelling Game. *Papers in Regional Science, 95*(2), 427–435.

Baron, D. (2007). Corporate Social Responsibility and Social Entrepreneurship. *Journal of Economics & Management Strategy, 16*(3), 683–717.

Bates, L. J., & Santerre, R. E. (1994). The Determinants of Restrictive Residential Zoning: Some Empirical Findings. *Journal of Regional Science, 34*(2), 253–263.

Bénabou, R., & Tirole, J. (2010). Individual and Corporate Social Responsibility. *Economica, 77*(305), 1–19.

Chen, C.-S., & Lai, F.-C. (2008). Location Choice and Optimal Zoning Under Cournot Competition. *Regional Science and Urban Economics, 38*(2), 119–126.

Colombo, S. (2011). On the Rationale of Spatial Discrimination with Quantity-setting Firms. *Research in Economics, 65*(3), 254–258.

Colombo, S. (2012). On Optimal Zoning in a Linear Town with Cournot Competitors. *Letters in Spatial and Resource Sciences, 5*(2), 113–118.

Cremer, H., Marchan, M., & Thisse, J.-F. (1991). Mixed Oligopoly with Differentiated Products. *International Journal of Industrial Organization, 9*(1), 43–53.

d'Aspremont, C., Gabszewicz, J. J., & Thisse, J.-F. (1979). On Hotelling's Stability in Competition. *Econometrica, 47*(5), 1145–1150.

Datta, S., & Sudhir, K. (2013). Does Reducing Spatial Differentiation Increase Product Differentiation? Effects of Zoning on Retail Entry and Format Variety. *Quantitative Marketing and Economics, 11*(1), 83–116.

Economides, N. (1986). Minimal and Maximal Product Differentiation in Hotelling's Duopoly. *Economics Letters, 21*(1), 67–71.

Goering, G. E. (2008a). Welfare Impacts of a Non-profit Firm in Mixed Commercial Markets. *Economic Systems, 32*(4), 326–334.

Goering, G. E. (2008b). Socially Concerned Firms and the Provision of Durable Goods. *Economic Modelling, 25*(3), 575–583.

Hamoudi, H., & Risueño, M. (2012). The Effects of Zoning in Spatial Competition. *Journal of Regional Science, 52*(2), 361–374.

Harsanyi, J. C. (1995). Cardinal Welfare, Individualistic Ethics, and Interpersonal Comparisons of Utility. *Journal of Political Economy, 63*(4), 309–321.

Heim, C. E. (2012). Border Wars: Tax Revenues, Annexation, and Urban Growth in Phoenix. *International Journal of Urban and Regional Research, 36*(4), 831–859.

Henninger, G. (2015). *How Municipal Finance Creates Regional Shopping Centers.* http://www.fromsuburbia.com/2015/01/how-municipal-finance-creates-regional-shopping-centers/.

Heywood, J. S., & Wang, Z. (2016). Strategic Delegation Under Spatial Price Discrimination. *Papers in Regional Science, 95*(Supplement 1), S193–S213.

Heywood, J. S., & Ye, G. (2009). Mixed Oligopoly and Spatial Price Discrimination with Foreign Firms. *Regional Science and Urban Economics, 39*(5), 592–601.

Hotelling, H. (1929). Stability in Competition. *Economic Journal, 39*(153), 41–57.

Hurter, A., & Lederer, P. (1985). Spatial Duopoly with Discriminatory Pricing. *Regional Science and Urban Economics, 15*(4), 541–553.

Inoue, T., Kamijo, Y., & Tomaru, Y. (2009). Interregional Mixed Duopoly. *Regional Science and Urban Economics, 39*(2), 233–242.

Kim, S.-L., Lee, S.-H., & Matsumura, T. (2019). Corporate Social Responsibility and Privatization Policy in a Mixed Oligopoly. *Journal of Economics, 128*(1), 67–89.

Kitzmueller, M., & Shimshack, J. (2012). Economic Perspectives on Corporate Social Responsibility. *Journal of Economic Literature, 50*(1), 51–84.

Kopel, M., & Brand, B. (2012). Socially Responsible Firms and Endogenous Choice of Strategic Incentives. *Economic Modelling, 29*(3), 982–989.

KPMG. (2017). *The Road Ahead. The KPMG Survey of Corporate Responsibility Reporting 2017*. KPMG International. https://assets.kpmg.com/content/dam/kpmg/xx/pdf/2017/10/kpmg-survey-of-corporate-responsibility-reporting-2017.pdf.

Lai, F.-C., & Tsai, J.-F. (2004). Duopoly Locations and Optimal Zoning in a Small Open City. *Journal of Urban Economics, 55*(3), 614–626.

Lambertini, L. (1994). Equilibrium Locations in the Unconstrained Hotelling Game. *Economic Notes, 23*, 438–446.

Lambertini, L. (1997a). Unicity of the Equilibrium in the Unconstrained Hotelling Model. *Regional Science and Urban Economics, 27*(6), 785–798.

Lambertini, L. (1997b). Optimal Fiscal Regime in a Spatial Duopoly. *Journal of Urban Economics, 41*(3), 407–420.

Lambertini, L., & Tampieri, A. (2015). Incentives, Performance and Desirability of Socially Responsible Firms in a Cournot Oligopoly. *Economic Modelling, 50*, 40–48.

Lederer, P., & Hurter, A. (1986). Competition of Firms: Discriminatory Pricing and Location. *Econometrica, 54*(3), 623–640.

Matsumura, T., & Matsushima, N. (2012). Locating Outside a Linear City Can Benefit Consumers. *Journal of Regional Science, 52*(3), 420–432.

Matsumura, T., & Tomaru, Y. (2015). Mixed Duopoly, Location Choice, and Shadow Cost of Public Funds. *Southern Economic Journal, 82*(2), 416–429.

Matsushima, N., & Matsumura, T. (2006). Mixed Oligopoly, Foreign Firms, and Location Choice. *Regional Science and Urban Economics, 36*(6), 753–772.

Porter, M. E., & Kramer, M. R. (2006). Strategy and Society: The Link Between Competitive Advantage and Corporate Social Responsibility. *Harvard Business Review, 84*(12), 78–92.

Tabuchi, T., & Thisse, J.-F. (1995). Asymmetric Equilibria in Spatial Competition. *International Journal of Industrial Organization, 13*(3), 213–227.

Tsai, J.-F., Peng, S.-K., & Lai, F.-C. (2006). Spatial Duopoly with Zoning. *Annals of Regional Science, 40*(3), 515–530.

White, M. D. (2002). Political Manipulation of a Public Firm's Objective Function. *Journal of Economic Behavior and Organization, 49*(4), 487–499.

9

Optimal Privatization in a Vertical Chain: A Delivered Pricing Model

John S. Heywood, Shiqiang Wang, and Guangliang Ye

9.1 Introduction

In an important earlier paper Gupta et al. (1994) examine the ability of downstream firms to strategically use location decisions to force an upstream monopoly to reduce its input price and transfer profit downstream. This transfer happens endogenously in equilibrium but generates large welfare loses. Additional research builds on this model to show that transport cost itself can also be set inefficiently high by downstream firms choosing a more costly transport mode. This forces the

J. S. Heywood
Department of Economics, University of Wisconsin-Milwaukee, Milwaukee, WI, USA

S. Wang
Institute of Economics, Chinese Academy of Social Sciences, Beijing, China

G. Ye (✉)
Institute of Economics, Hainan University, Haikou, Hainan, China
e-mail: gye@hainanu.edu.cn

S. Colombo (ed.), *Spatial Economics Volume I*,
https://doi.org/10.1007/978-3-030-40098-9_9

same accommodating behavior by the upstream monopoly (a lowering of the input price and a profit transfer downstream) and a similar loss of welfare (Gupta et al. 1995, 1997).

The fundamental insight of these showings is that downstream firms often face a spatial market that is largely irrelevant to an upstream firm. Thus, downstream firms make a product that has a high transport cost or for which horizontal differentiation is critical. Yet, the upstream firm produces a small critical input for which transportation costs are irrelevant. Indeed, it may provide intellectual property with no transport cost at all. Alternatively, while the downstream product faces consumers with horizontally differentiated preferences (proxied by distance in a spatial model), these simply need not apply to the input. Thus, consumers may care greatly about the characteristics of cell phones but these preferences may be largely irrelevant to the manufacturer of the basic chips. In such circumstances, the primary concern of the upstream firm is to avoid setting a price so high that it results in a dramatic loss of customers downstream. Given this concern, Gupta et al. (1994) show that the downstream firms can locate strategically to make such a dramatic loss of customers more likely for a given price increase. This, in turn, causes the upstream firm to lower its input price.

We return to these earlier models of vertical rivalry and incorporate the possibility that one of the downstream firms is a "mixed ownership firm." The enormous literature on public firms and mixed oligopolies has largely grown up since these early location models and has much to offer. The basic view is that a public firm regulates by participating in a private oligopolistic market. While the private firms maximize profit, the public firm sets quantity or some other choice variable to maximize social welfare. In a quantity game the public firm can increase consumer surplus by increasing total production. Yet, the assumption in this literature is that the government-owned firm produces at elevated costs.[1]

In a seminal article Matsumura (1998) recognizes that while a publically owned firm maximizing welfare can indeed improve welfare in an

[1]This is either because all firms have identical convex costs and the government-owned firm produces more than the private firms (De Fraja and Delbono 1989) or because political and bureaucratic constraints exogenously increase its per-unit costs (see, e.g., White 2002).

oligopoly, a mixed ownership firm can make an even larger improvement. The mixed ownership firm is presumed to maximize a combination of welfare, a public firm's objective, and own profit, a private firm's objective. As a consequence, it increases output to increase consumer surplus but not to the extent of the fully public firm saving on the total cost of production in the market and thereby increasing welfare.

Indeed, a large literature has followed this initial showing by determining the optimal private share in a mixed ownership firm in a wide variety of settings. Matsumura and Kanda (2005) imagine the optimal extent of privatization (the creation of a mixed ownership firm) in a free entry market. Fujiwara (2007) examines partial privatization in a differentiated product market. Heywood and Ye (2009b) examine optimal privatization in the context of an R&D rivalry while Heywood and Ye (2010) examine optimal privatization but assume a consistent conjecture equilibrium. Wang and Chen (2011) retain Cournot competition but include both foreign competition and multinational corporations. Heywood et al. (2017) imagine mixed ownership under asymmetric information in which only fully private firms directly know product demand. Tomaru and Wang (2017) and Lin and Matsumura (2018) each consider partial privatization in the face of state subsidy policies. Sato and Matsumura (2019) imagine a two-period model in which the government partially privatizes a state-owned public firm over multiple periods and includes the shadow cost of public funding. While far from an exhaustive review, this makes clear the strong ongoing interest in partial privatization policy.

For the first time in the literature, we imagine a mixed ownership firm that competes downstream with a private firm in a delivered pricing model and faces a monopoly upstream. We examine the ability of a public firm to locate in such a way so as to limit the private firm's inefficient attempt to gain an upstream price accommodation. We recognize that this may come with the increased production costs associated with the public firm and, following the literature, assume these costs can be reduced by partial privatization. As the extent of partial privatization increases, production costs fall but so does the incentive of the mixed ownership firm to locate efficiently. Thus, we identify the optimal extent of partial privatization in the original context of the Gupta et al. (1994) vertical rivalry.

The assumption of an inefficient public firm is critical. This assumption fits well with the literature on mixed oligopolies (see among others Pal and White 1998; Wang and Mukherjee 2012 and Gelves and Heywood 2013). Moreover, Matsumura and Matsushima (2004) provide theoretical support for such a cost disadvantage while Megginson and Netter (2001) provide supporting empirical evidence. The related idea that partial privatization can serve to lower those costs is also well supported. Indeed, private ownership well short of majority control increases efficiency by bringing the improved incentives and information about managerial performance associated with a stock price. A theoretical treatment of the power of such minority ownership and "yard stick competition" is provided by Laffont and Tirole (1993) while Gupta (2005) and Bhaskar et al. (2006) provide confirming empirical evidence.

In the classic spatial price discrimination model that we expand upon, the firm delivers the product to the consumer, and the delivered price is the sum of the marginal production cost and the transport cost of the rival firm. Thisse and Vives (1988) demonstrate that such pricing will be endogenously adopted if available and Greenhut (1981) identifies spatial price discrimination as "nearly ubiquitous" among actual markets in which the products have substantial freight costs. More generally, Behrens et al. (2018) confirm the continuing importance of transportation cost as a determinant of plant location. Finally, as emphasized, in addition to cases where transport cost is important, the model describes circumstances with differences among consumers in a horizontal product dimension and where firms must locate along that dimension. These circumstances include, but are not limited to, political orientation of a newspaper, times of airline flights, and the sweetness of breakfast cereals.

9.2 Model Setup and Solution

An upstream private firm, with 0 production cost, sells an input to two downstream firms. Firm 1 is a mixed ownership firm, with a private share of λ, while Firm 2 is a fully private firm. The two firms engage in delivered price competition along the market of a unit line segment. Following Gupta et al. (1994), consumers are uniformly distributed along the market and each has a one unit demand for the product with reservation price r. The per-unit transportation cost is normalized to be 1. While this setting of inelastic demand is classic for delivered pricing, it eliminates a second dimension of price discrimination that has been examined. Thus, either with or without delivered pricing, there could be downward sloping demand at each location and the price set (or alternatively quantity) at each location can differ to reflect that demand (see, among others, Anderson et al. 1989; Colombo 2011 and Heywood et al. 2018).

Per-unit production cost of the private firm is 0. The per-unit production cost of the mixed firm is $(1 - \lambda)c$ with $c > 0$. The presumption is that privatization decreases production cost and this is a simple way to capture that reality. Thus, when $\lambda = 1$, the mixed ownership firm becomes fully private and its per-unit cost is 0 matching the rival. Downstream production is characterized by fixed proportion such that each downstream product requires one unit of the upstream product. This can be particularly relevant when the upstream firm provides an essential input that cannot be substituted away from or when the downstream firms are viewed largely as retailers that add services and delivery for a wholesale product (Heywood et al. 2018).

The timing of the game begins with a welfare maximizing government adopting the optimal degree of privatization for the mixed ownership firm. Once this is known, the remainder of the time line follows Gupta et al. (1994) with the least reversible choice being first: the two downstream firms simultaneously choose locations $\{L_1, L_2\}$ assuming for convenience that $L_1 \leq L_2$ (for an example of sequential location see Heywood and Ye 2009a). In the third stage the upstream firm chooses an upstream price of w and in the final stage the two downstream firms determine the optimal delivered pricing schedule.

9.2.1 Equilibrium

We solve for the subgame perfect Nash equilibrium by backward induction.

In stage four the delivered pricing schedule emerges as the standard for spatial price discrimination and is the outer envelope of the rival's marginal costs. The private firm has an incentive to raise price to the delivered cost of the private firm. The public firm or partially public firm generates no welfare loss from pricing this way as the profit gain is exactly offset by the consumer surplus loss for a given location. Thus, the public firm is indifferent to the classic delivered pricing equilibrium and charging its own transport cost and a firm with any private share strictly prefers the classic delivered pricing scheme. Thus, the delivered pricing is unchanged by the presence of a mixed firm (for more on this see Heywood and Ye 2009b).

The equilibrium downstream price for the public mixed firm is then

$$p_1(x) = \begin{cases} r, 0 \leq x \leq -r + w + L_2 \\ w + L_2 - x, -r + w + L_2 \leq x \leq \frac{L_1 + L_2 - (1-\lambda)c}{2} \end{cases}$$

The equilibrium price for the private firm is

$$p_2(x) = \begin{cases} w + x - L_1 + (1-\lambda)\,c, \frac{L_1 + L_2 - (1-\lambda)c}{2} \leq x \leq r + L_1 - w - (1-\lambda)\,c \\ r, r + L_1 - w - (1-\lambda)\,c \leq x \leq 1 \end{cases}$$

The equilibrium price schedule given the upstream price and downstream locations is depicted as the bold line in Fig. 9.1.

The solution to the third stage is built from Gupta et al. (1994). The upstream firm must decide given the locations of the two downstream firms whether to push the upstream price just to the point where one of the delivered cost schedules intersects in the corner of the willingness to pay (as for Firm 1 in Fig. 9.1a) or to push further and allow the market to be cut and customers go unserved. Obviously, the lowest upstream price will be that which just pushes the delivered cost to the corner as anything lower forgoes upstream profit. A higher price becomes justified only when the gain in increase profit from the higher price is larger than the loss in profit from cutting the market and losing customers.

This higher price is more likely when r is small relative to c and transport cost, set equal to 1 in our model. Indeed, it can be shown that the requirement for the upstream firm not to cut the market is $r \geq \frac{3}{2} + (1-\lambda)\,c$. We impose this condition so as to focus on the

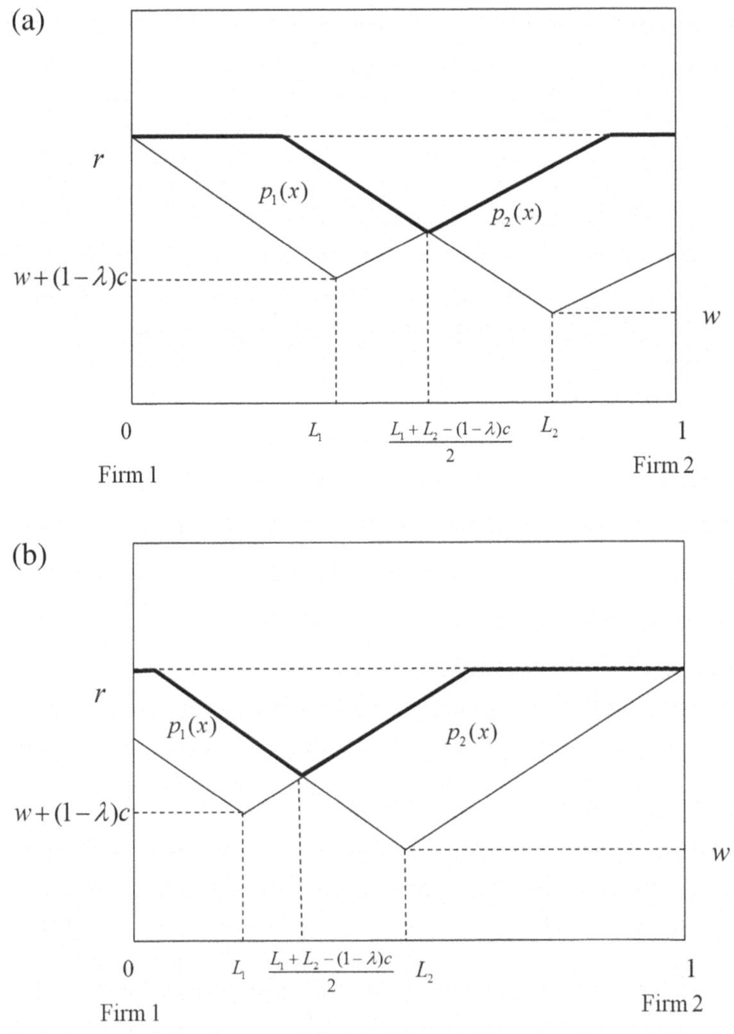

Fig. 9.1 (**a**) The delivered pricing equilibrium when the public firm is critical. (**b**) The delivered pricing equilibrium when the private firm is critical. Note: the solid thick line represents the equilibrium price schedule given the share of privatization, the costs, and locations

interesting case where the upstream firm accommodates strategic location and does not respond by cutting the market.[2]

The result of this logic is that the optimal wholesale price given downstream locations is $w = r - \max\left\{L_1 + (1-\lambda)c, L_2 - \frac{L_1+L_2-(1-\lambda)c}{2}, 1 - L_2\right\}$. These represent respectively the cases in which the mixed firm or both firms or the private firm is "critical." The full proof is in Appendix 1. Again, this is under the assumption that r is sufficiently large that it is not in the interest of the upstream firm to set a price that cuts the market.

In the second stage of the game the downstream firms locate so as to maximize their objective functions. The profit functions for the two firms are

$\pi_1 = \int_0^{\frac{L_1+L_2-(1-\lambda)c}{2}} (p_1(x) - |x - L_1|)\,dx, \pi_2 = \int_{\frac{L_1+L_2-(1-\lambda)c}{2}}^1 (p_2(x) - |x - L_2|)\,dx$

The total cost is the sum of transportation cost T and production cost C, where $T = \int_0^{\frac{L_1+L_2-(1-\lambda)c}{2}} |x - L_1|\,dx + \int_{\frac{L_1+L_2-(1-\lambda)c}{2}}^1 |x - L_2|\,dx, C = (1-\lambda)c\left(\frac{L_1+L_2-(1-\lambda)c}{2}\right)$

The social welfare function is $W = r - (T + C)$.

While the private firm maximizes its own profit, π_2, the mixed ownership firm follows Matsumura (1998) and maximizes $G = \lambda\pi_1 + (1-\lambda)W$. This generates two best response functions in the two locations that when solved simultaneously generate the locations.

We prove in Appendix 2 that the locations that make both firms critical cannot be an equilibrium and so the upstream price will take the form of $w = r - (L_1 + (1-\lambda)c)$ or $w = r - (1 - L_2)$. When $w = r - (L_1 + (1-\lambda)c)$, the public firm is critical (see Fig. 9.1a) but when $w = r - (1 - L_2)$, the private firm is critical (see Fig. 9.1b). As in Gupta et al. (1994), the critical firm is that which interacts directly with the input monopoly and can use location to generate accommodating pricing.

[2]The proof for this condition is available upon request and applies regardless of which firm is presumed to be critical.

When the public firm is critical, the equilibrium downstream locations are

$$L_1^* = L_1^a = \frac{4c\lambda^2 - 2c\lambda - 2c + 2\lambda + 1}{2(2+\lambda)}, \; L_2^* = L_2^a = \frac{2c\lambda^2 - 2c + 2\lambda + 3}{2(2+\lambda)} \quad (9.1)$$

When the private firm is critical, the equilibrium downstream locations are

$$L_1^* = L_1^b = \frac{1}{6} - \frac{(1-\lambda)\,c}{3}, \; L_2^* = L_2^b = \frac{1}{2} \quad (9.2)$$

The details are in Appendix 2. Note that this represents a generalization of Gupta et al. (1994) and that when $\lambda = 1$ (and so $c = 0$), our model collapses to theirs. The optimal downstream locations mimic their work, $\left\{\frac{1}{2}, \frac{5}{6}\right\}$ when the now privatized firm on the left is critical or $\left\{\frac{1}{6}, \frac{1}{2}\right\}$ when the always assumed private firm on the right is critical. These two sets of locations deviate substantially from the transport cost minimizing first best of $\left\{\frac{1}{4}, \frac{3}{4}\right\}$ and they result in an upstream price of $w = r - ½$.

Note that when the private firm is critical, it continues to behave strategically against the upstream firm. The public firm cannot change this behavior as its best response function merely has it locating in a socially optimal manner *given that of the private firm*. Thus, if one imagined a public firm without an elevated cost of production, it could do no better than a private firm and the locations would remain$\left\{\frac{1}{6}, \frac{1}{2}\right\}$. This reflect the well-known result that the profit maximizing and transport cost minimizing best responses are identical with delivered pricing (Lederer and Hurter 1986).

With an elevated cost of production, the mixed or public firm moves left to minimize the sum of production and transport cost, $L_1^b \le \frac{1}{6}$. Indeed, as the public share λ increases the mixed firm moves increasingly into the corner (see eq. 9.2). This may seem somewhat counterintuitive but reflects that only the critical private firm is able to alter the behavior of the upstream firm and that the mixed firm takes the resulting location as given. For a given c, it can be easily shown $L_1 = \frac{1}{6}$ yields the lowest total transportation cost T and $L_1 = 0$ yields the lowest total production cost. This follows as $L_2^b = \frac{1}{2}$ and implies that the equilibrium location L_1^b is between 0 and $\frac{1}{6}$ depending upon λ.

When the mixed firm is critical, it now directly interacts with the upstream firm. Its object in doing so dramatically differs from that of the private firm. This can again be illustrated by imagining a *fully public* firm without an elevated cost of production. If $c = 0$, the fully public firm locates at ¼ and the private firm maximizes profit at ¾. (see eq. 9.1). Here the public firm is able to completely eliminate the strategic behavior that Gupta et al. isolate and return to the first best. The public firm, in essence, allows the upstream price to increase to $w = r - ¼$ but improves welfare by doing so.

With an elevated cost of production, a *fully public* firm faces competing influences. The desire to reduce transport cost encourages it to retain a location close to ¼. Yet, the elevated production cost mutes this influence and encourages it to remain moving to the left of ¼. Specifically, the fully public firm would locate increasingly toward the left corner as c increases: $L_1^a\,(\lambda = 0) = \frac{1}{4} - \frac{c}{2}$.

Given the elevated cost, the optimal location of the *mixed* firm depends both on the size of c and on the extent of privatization. Specifically, as the extent of privatization increases that location varies between $L_1^a\,(\lambda = 0) = \frac{1}{4} - \frac{c}{2}$ and $L_1^a\,(\lambda = 1) = \frac{1}{2}$. The latter again corresponds to Gupta et al. (1994) when the left-hand-side firm is fully private.[3]

Finally, the equilibrium locations in (9.1) and (9.2) are returned to the welfare function to allow the government to determine the optimal share of the privatization parameter λ^*.

Proposition 1 When the private firm is critical, the optimal privatization is $\lambda^* = 1$. There is nothing to be gained by a mixed ownership firm.

Proof: Substituting L_1^b and L_2^b into W yields the associated equilibrium social welfare of the whole industry as W^{b*}. It satisfies $\frac{\partial W^{b*}}{\partial \lambda} = \frac{c}{3}\,(1 - 2\,(1 - \lambda)\,c) > 0$; therefore, the optimal privatization is 1 when the private firm is critical.

[3]In order to guarantee interior solutions for all $\lambda \in [0, 1]$, we assume that $0 < c \leq 1/2$ in our article, which is yielded via $L_1^a\,(\lambda = 0) \geq 0$ and $L_1^b\,(\lambda = 0) \geq 0$.

Full privatization follows naturally as mixed ownership increases the cost of production and causes the mixed ownership firm to move further toward the left corner increasing transportation costs. Both of these reduce social welfare.

This changes when the mixed ownership firm is critical.

Proposition 2 When the mixed ownership firm is critical and $c < \frac{1}{6}$ the optimal privatization share is $0 < \lambda^*(c) < 1$. When c is large $\frac{1}{6} < c < \frac{1}{2}$, $\lambda^*(c) = 1$.

Proof: See proof in Appendix 3.

This broadly follows intuition as when the cost differential between the mixed and private firm is large enough, it dominates the privatization decision. The government recognizes that any cost savings in transportation are dominated by increases in production cost. At lower cost differentials, the trade-off becomes relevant and determines an interior optimal extent of privatization.

9.3 Implications of Proposition 2

In this section we draw out a series of implications of the equilibrium identified in the previous section and isolate the specific consequence of the cost differential. We limit our attention to when the mixed firm is critical and discuss locations, optimal privatization, and welfare.

When the public firm is critical, it can be directly verified from (9.1) that the $\frac{\partial L_1^a}{\partial \lambda} > 0$ and $\frac{\partial L_2^a}{\partial \lambda} > 0$, indicating that both firms move right with λ, the extent of privatization. Moreover, $L_2^a - L_1^a = \frac{1+c\lambda-c\lambda^2}{2+\lambda}$ and this decreases with λ showing that privatization moves the firms closer together. This reflects the mixed firm placing greater emphasis on profit and so wishing to occupy a larger share of the market.

The object for the government in Proposition 2 is to use the public share to curtail this movement right without incurring an overly large increase in production cost. The optimal privatization share of λ^* is less than 1 when the costs are small ($c < 1/6$) and we can calculate the specific

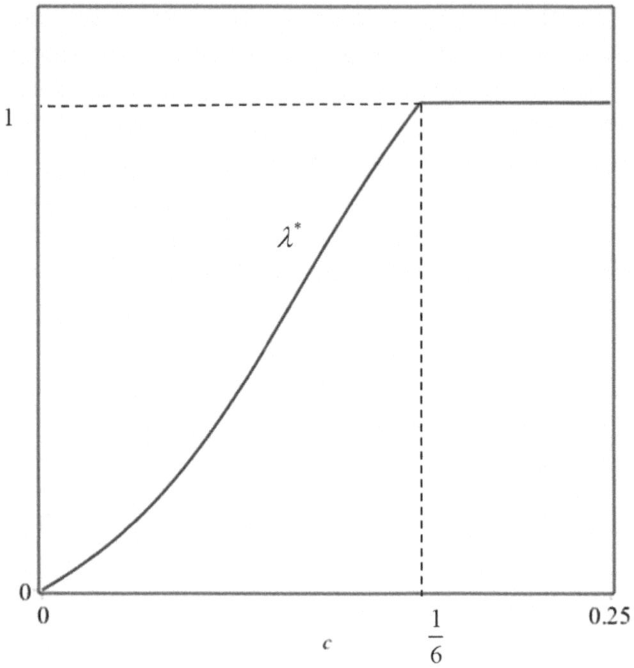

Fig. 9.2 Optimal privatization when the public firm is critical

value resulting using Cardano's formula. The resulting relevant root from that formula isolates the relationship between the optimal private share and the production cost differential of the public firm, c. This is shown in Fig. 9.2.

When c is small, the effect on production cost is modest for any given λ. Thus, higher levels of privatization generate equilibrium locations close to $\{L_1^a, L_2^a\} = \{\frac{1}{2}, \frac{5}{6}\}$ that yield much higher transportation cost than the symmetric locations of $\{\frac{1}{4}, \frac{3}{4}\}$. Thus, the government avoids privatization and starts with an almost completely public firm when the cost penalty is small so as to retain the more symmetric locations. As the cost differential increases, the government accepts great asymmetry in an effort to balance increasing production costs. As Fig. 9.2 shows, this relationship is continuous with the optimal privatization share starting at zero when $c = 0$ and increasing to one when $c = 1/6$.

Table 9.1 Isolating equilibrium values as the cost differential increases

c	λ_*	L_1^*	L_2^*	W	$W - W(\lambda = 1)$
0.02	0.0604	0.2618	0.7477	$r - 0.1345$	0.0321
0.04	0.1382	0.2779	0.7478	$r - 0.1430$	0.0237
0.06	0.2385	0.2998	0.7514	$r - 0.1503$	0.0164
0.08	0.3644	0.3284	0.7592	$r - 0.1563$	0.0103
0.10	0.5127	0.3638	0.7717	$r - 0.1609$	0.0058
0.12	0.6708	0.4038	0.7881	$r - 0.1640$	0.0026
0.14	0.8230	0.4454	0.8069	$r - 0.1659$	0.0008
0.16	0.9589	0.4866	0.8267	$r - 0.1666$	0.0001

Notes: The exogenous variable is the cost differential c that generates the equilibrium values of optimal privatization, λ_*; the locations, L_1^* and L_2^*; and welfare, W

We now illustrate various cost differentials that generate interior solutions and a mixed ownership firm. We use this to trace out the pattern of locations that result in equilibrium. These are shown in Table 9.1.

Starting with a very small differential of 0.02, the optimal extent of privatization is only around 6 percent. This largely public firm locates just to the right of the transport cost minimizing quartile. The location of the fully private firm and the resulting welfare are shown in the next two columns.[4] Finally the gain in welfare relative to a two fully private firm is shown in the final column. As the sum of all transport and production cost is 0.1345, the welfare savings of 0.0321 is meaningfully large.

As the cost differential grows, the optimal extent of privatization grows and the mixed firm moves increasingly to the right. This pushes the private firm also increasingly to the right. The combination of increased production cost and more asymmetric locations means that welfare falls monotonically with the cost differential. The savings relative to two fully private firms shrinks and eventually vanishes as the optimal extent of privatization becomes 100 percent when the elevated cost of the public firm simply dominates the government's decision.

[4]The fully private firm initially moves slightly to the left of ¾ because of the role of the cost differential but this is eventually overcome by the large movement to the right by the increasingly privatized mixed firm.

9.4 An Extension: Examining When the Market Would Be Cut

In this section we recognize the point by Gupta et al. (1994) that when the reservation willingness to pay r is small enough relative to the transport cost, the upstream firm will not accommodate strategic downstream location. Instead, it becomes profitable for the upstream firm to retain a higher input price and simply allow a portion of the critical firm's market not to be served. We previously ruled out such a circumstance by assuming that $r \geq \frac{3}{2} + (1-\lambda)\,c$. We note that this implies a new dimension, the possibility of simply fewer customers, to the welfare calculations associated with the mixed ownership firm. In this section, we explore when an optimally set private share less than one may forestall the welfare loss associated with the market being cut.

We consider three cases: (a) the private firm is critical and some portion of its market is cut; (b) the public firm is critical and some portion of its market will be cut and; and (c) the value of r is sufficiently low that the two firms have exclusive territories and both firms have their markets cut.

9.4.1 When the Private Firm Is Critical

When imagining that the upstream firm will optimally allow market to be cut, the price of the public firm in the SPD equilibrium above doesn't change, while the price of the private firm becomes:

$$p_2(x) = \begin{cases} w + x - L_1 + (1-\lambda)\,c, & \frac{L_1+L_2-(1-\lambda)c}{2} \leq x \leq r + L_1 - w - (1-\lambda)\,c \\ r, & r + L_1 - w - (1-\lambda)\,c \leq x \leq x_1 \end{cases}$$

where $x_1 = \{x : r = x - L_2 + w\}$. The demand in zone of $[x_1, 1]$ isn't covered.

Similarly we can deduce the optimal location as $L_{1c}^{*} = L_{1c}^{b} = \frac{r-5(1-\lambda)c}{7}$, $L_{2c}^{*} = L_{2c}^{b} = \frac{3r-8(1-\lambda)c}{7}$

Notice that the market cut as a result of these locations is $x_c^b = 1 - x_1\left(L_{1c}^b, L_{2c}^b\right) = 1 - \frac{5r}{7} + \frac{4c}{7} - \frac{4c\lambda}{7}$. As $x_c^b > 0$, we have $r < r_R^u$, where $r_R^u = \frac{7+4(1-\lambda)c}{5}$. As a consequence, it can be easily shown that the size of the cut market, x_c^b, decreases as privatization increases. Reversed, a larger public share causes the private firm to optimally move left resulting in a larger cut share of the market. This allows us to summarize.

Proposition 3 When the reservation price is sufficiently small that interaction between the upstream firm and the critical private firm results in a cut market, the optimal privatization is $\lambda^{*}= 1$. There is nothing to be gained by a mixed ownership firm.

Proof: Substituting L_{1c}^b and L_{2c}^b into W yields the associated equilibrium social welfare of the whole industry as W_c^{b*}. It satisfies $\frac{\partial W_c^{b*}}{\partial \lambda} = \frac{2c}{7}\left(3r - 5\left(1-\lambda\right)c\right) > 0$ given that L_{1c}^b and L_{2c}^b are interior solutions; therefore, the optimal privatization is 1 when the private firm is critical.

This carries over from the earlier presentation and argues that whenever the private firm is critical, the mixed firm should be completely privatized. The size of the reservation wage and whether the market is cut are irrelevant for this conclusion.

9.4.2 When the Mixed Ownership Firm Is Critical

Now the price of the private firm in the SPD equilibrium above doesn't change from the earlier examination, while the price of the mixed firm becomes

$$p_1(x) = \begin{cases} r, x_0 \leq x \leq -r + w + L_2 \\ w + L_2 - x, -r + w + L_2 \leq x \leq \frac{L_1+L_2-(1-\lambda)c}{2} \end{cases}$$

where $x_0 = \{x : r = L_1 - x + (1-\lambda)c + w\}$. The portion of the market not covered or cut is $[0, x_0]$.

In this case, the profit of the upstream firm is $\pi = (1 - x_0)w$, and the FOC of π with respect to w yields the optimal wholesale price as $w_1 = \frac{1}{2}(r + 1 - L_1 - (1 - \lambda)c)$.

The profit functions for the two downstream firms are $\pi_1 = \int_{x_0}^{\frac{L_1+L_2-(1-\lambda)c}{2}} (p_1(x) - |x - L_1|)\, dx, \pi_2 = \int_{\frac{L_1+L_2-(1-\lambda)c}{2}}^{1} (p_2(x) - |x - L_2|)\, dx$

The total transportation cost is $T = \int_{x_0}^{\frac{L_1+L_2-(1-\lambda)c}{2}} |x - L_1|\, dx + \int_{\frac{L_1+L_2-(1-\lambda)c}{2}}^{1} |x - L_2|\, dx$ and the total production cost is $C = (1 - \lambda)c\left(\frac{L_1+L_2-(1-\lambda)c}{2} - x_0\right)$. The social welfare becomes\break $W = (1 - x_0)r - (C + T)$. Finally, the objective of the mixed ownership firm is $G = \lambda\pi_1 + (1 - \lambda)W$.

Maximizing each firm's objective function with respect to location generates two best response functions that when solved simultaneously yield the optimal equilibrium locations:

$$L_{1c}^{*} = L_{1c}^{a} = \frac{11c\lambda^2 - 12c\lambda + 3\lambda r + c + 7\lambda - 9r + 7}{7(\lambda + 1)}$$

$$L_{2c}^{*} = L_{2c}^{b} = \frac{6c\lambda^2 - 4c\lambda + \lambda r - 2c + 7\lambda - 3r + 7}{7(\lambda + 1)}$$

Note that the lost market, the market that is cut, becomes $x_c^a = \frac{2c\lambda^2 - 6c\lambda - 2\lambda r + 4c + 7\lambda - 8r + 7}{7(1+\lambda)}$, where $x_c^a > 0$ requires that $r < r_L^u$, where $r_L^u = \frac{2c\lambda^2 - 6c\lambda + 4c + 7\lambda + 7}{2(4+\lambda)}$. Therefore, we have $\frac{\partial x_c^a}{\partial \lambda} = \frac{2(3r - (5 - \lambda^2 - 2\lambda)c)}{7(1+\lambda)^2}$. This can be signed. Specifically, $\frac{\partial x_c^a}{\partial \lambda} > 0$ when $\frac{c(5-\lambda^2-2\lambda)}{3} < r < r_L^u$, while $\frac{\partial x_c^a}{\partial \lambda} < 0$ when $r < \frac{c(5-\lambda^2-2\lambda)}{3}$. Thus, when the reservation price is relatively large, the sale zone that is cut increases as privatization increases. This is the opposite of what we derived when the private firm was critical and allows us to summarize.

Proposition 4 When the reservation price is sufficiently small that interaction between the upstream firm and the critical mixed ownership firm results in a cut market, the optimal privatization can be less than one when r is relatively large.

Proof: Substituting L_{1c}^{a} and L_{2c}^{a} into W yields the associated equilibrium social welfare of the whole industry as W_{c}^{a*}. It satisfies $\left.\frac{\partial W_{c}^{a*}}{\partial \lambda}\right|_{\lambda=1} = \frac{3r}{14}(2c - r)$. When$r > 2c$, $\left.\frac{\partial W_{c}^{a*}}{\partial \lambda}\right|_{\lambda=1} < 0$; therefore, the optimal privatization is less than 1 when r is large.

To illustrate Proposition 4 we imagine a specific value of $c = 0.3$ as shown in Fig. 9.3. While the exact range of r for the cut case is a little difficult to identify as lambda enters into the indifference condition of Gupta et al. (1994, p. 13). We have guaranteed an interior privatization ratio with a cut market as illustrated. We recognize that the range may be even larger and extend to an even smaller r.

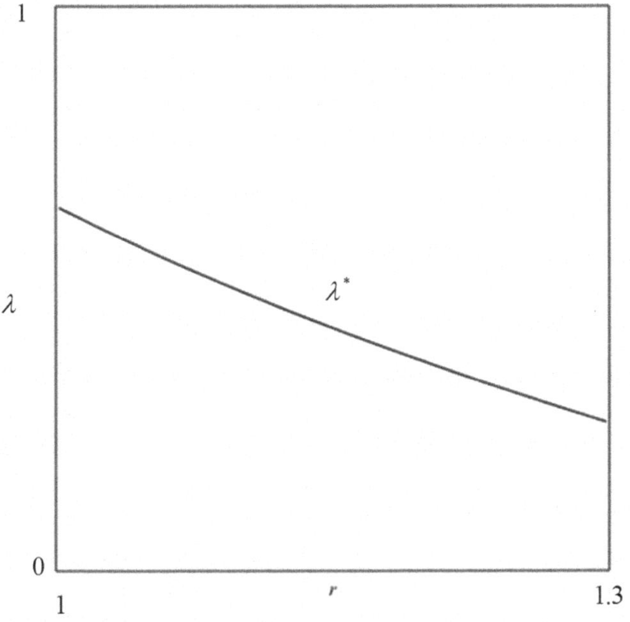

Fig. 9.3 Optimal privatization with a cut market when $c = 0.3$

To be more specific take the illustrated case of $c = 0.3$ and imagine that $r = 1.1$, the optimal private share is then $\lambda^* = 0.71$. This generates a lost market share of $x_c^{a*} = 0.154$ as a result of the upstream firm allowing the market to be cut. This can be compared with the fully private firm in which the lost market share will be $x_c^a\big|_{\lambda=1} = 0.214$. The welfare with the optimal degree of privatization is $W_c^{a*} = 0.8084$ and this exceeds that with the fully private firm of $W_c^a\big|_{\lambda=1} = 0.7779$.

The critical point is that within the region where the market will be cut, a trade-off exists. A larger public share can decrease the market cut because of the mixed firm's less strategic location. That less strategic location also plays a valuable role in reducing transport cost. On the other hand, the larger public share increases production cost.

This trade-off is evident in examining the locations. In our illustration with the mixed ownership firm ($c = 0.3$, $r = 1.1$, and so $\lambda^* = 0.71$), the market that is served starts at location 0.154 and goes to 1.0. The mixed ownership firm locates at 0.323 and the private rival at 0.746. This can be contrasted with a fully private where r remains 1.1 but where c=0 because of privatization. In this case the market runs from 0.214 to 1.0. The first private firm locates at 0.529 and the second at 0.843. The market for the mixed ownership firm is both larger and the two firms are more symmetrically located within it.

As the discussion above indicates, when r is relatively large, increasing privatization generates the more asymmetric locations we associate with private ownership for the earlier propositions and, in addition, the lost market increases $\left(\frac{\partial x_c^a}{\partial \lambda} > 0\right)$. Both tend to decrease social welfare. Meanwhile, the increase of privatization is associated with the decrease of production cost, which tends to increase social welfare. Eventually, when r is relatively small, that is, c is relatively large, the benefit of lower production cost dominates, and being fully privatized is optimal. This happens directly because of the increased production cost of the mixed firm and indirectly because when that increased production cost is large enough, the cut market will actually be larger with a mixed firm.

9.4.3 When Both Firms Are Critical (Exclusive Territories)

Notice that when r is extremely small, exclusive territories may arise. In this case r intersects with two firms' costs on both sides of L_1 and L_2, namely $L_1 - x + (1-\lambda)c + w$, $x - L_1 + (1-\lambda)c + w$,$L_2 - x + w$, $x - L_2 + w$. Let the four intersection points be x_2, x_3, x_4, and x_5. The upstream profit is $\pi^e = w(x_3 - x_2 + x_5 - x_4)$. The FOC yields the optimal wholesale price as $w^e = \frac{1}{2}r - \frac{1}{4}(1-\lambda)c$. When exclusive territories are about to emerge, we have that$x_2(w^e) = 0$, $x_3(w^e) = x_4(w^e)$, $x_5(w^e) = 1$, and this indicates that $r = r^e = \frac{1+(1-\lambda)c}{2}$. This is the threshold value for r such that exclusive territories exist. Therefore when r becomes small, that is, when $r < r^e$, exclusive territories can emerge. Notice that it can be easily proven that $r^e < r_L^u$, $r^e < r_R^u$.

The profit functions for the two firms under exclusive territories are $\pi_1^e = \int_{x_1}^{x_2}(r - |x - L_1|)\,dx$, $\pi_2^e = \int_{x_3}^{x_4}(r - |x - L_2|)\,dx$. As downstream price is r everywhere, the associated consumer surplus is 0. Thus the social welfare is $W^e = \pi_1^e + \pi_2^e + \pi^e$, and the equilibrium social welfare is $W^{e*} = W^e(w^e)$, and it satisfies $\frac{\partial W^{e*}}{\partial \lambda} = \frac{c(6r-7(1-\lambda)c)}{4}$. Notice that there is a lower bound for r such that exclusive territories can exist, and this threshold value is reached when $x_2(w^e) = x_1(w^e)$ or $x_4(w^e) = x_3(w^e)$, then it must satisfy that $r \geq \underline{r}^e = \frac{3(1-\lambda)c}{2}$ to ensure the existence of exclusive territories for both firms. Then we have $\frac{\partial W^{e*}}{\partial \lambda} > 0$, and full privatization is optimal, and then a proposition can be drawn as follows.

Proposition 5 When r is sufficiently small such that exclusive territories emerge, the optimal privatization is $\lambda^* = 1$. There is nothing to be gained by a mixed ownership firm.

Proposition 5 follows naturally as when exclusive territories arise, the downstream firms simply do not compete. One firm's location does not influence that of the other. This insures that there is no room for mixed ownership to increase the level of social welfare as it simply increases production costs.

9.5 Conclusions

We have imagined a mixed ownership firm in a downstream spatial market. The issue is the extent to which the firm can regulate by participation. This regulation comes from its willingness to locate in such a way as to reduce wasteful strategic location downstream. We have assumed that the firm maximizes an objective function which is a convex combination of welfare (as weighted by the public ownership share) and profit (as weighted by the private ownership share). The greater the public ownership is, the greater is the production cost. As in the classic paper by Matsumura (1998), this increased cost can give rise to an optimal degree of privatization.

The first insight is that when the mixed ownership firm is not critical and so does not directly interact with the upstream firm, it cannot influence downstream locations and so simply produces at a higher cost. This means that there is no scope for a mixed ownership firm that is not critical. This applies both when the reservation price is large enough that the full market is served and when it is small enough that some of the market is left unserved and cut.

The interesting case in which a mixed ownership can regulate by participation is when it is the critical firm. Here it becomes less interested in strategic location as the share of public ownership increases. The result is more symmetric locations and lower transport costs. Yet, this advantage comes with increased production cost.

Specifically, when the reservation price is large, the entire market is served. Given this, the government optimizes by retaining a public share when the production cost differential, c, is below 1/6 (recalling this is all relative to the unit transport cost normalized to 1). The optimal private share can be completely zero if the mixed ownership firm has no cost disadvantage. The optimal private share increases monotonically as that cost disadvantage increases. At $c \geq 1/6$, the production cost disadvantage completely outweighs the locational advantage and the fully private firm is optimal.

When the reservation price is small, the upstream engages in less accommodating pricing and the downstream market is cut with customers not being served. There remains a role for the mixed ownership firm when the reservation price is relatively larger within this case where the market will be cut. The critical comparison is now the size of the reservation price compared to the cost disadvantage. The logic now involves two advantages for having a public share. Within the market that is not cut, the mixed ownership firm locates more symmetrically saving transport cost. Moreover, the more symmetric location means that as the public share is larger, less market is cut increasing welfare. Yet, these advantages are completely outweighed by the increased production cost as the size of c grows relative to r.

Following the original work by Gupta et al. (1994) we assumed that either firm could be critical. Yet, the potential advantage of the mixed ownership firm arises only when it is the critical firm. Left undiscussed in that original work and in what we have presented is how the critical firm might be determined. The critical firm is that which interacts with the upstream monopoly by being located such that its most extreme delivered cost exceeds that of its rival.

Introducing timing might provide structure. Thus, if the government could locate first, it would choose to be critical. At the same time, if the private firm could locate first, it also would likely choose to be critical. This suggests that such timing would need to arise exogenously and could not be easily endogenized (Hamilton and Slutsky 1990).

Our interest has been in the role played by government ownership in regulating strategic behavior that hurts welfare. The government has a variety of policy tools and might undertake alternative actions short of simply dictating location. They might, for example, tax total transport cost. Designed appropriately such a tax might discourage the asymmetric locations that simultaneously waste resources but generate a lower input price. We leave such alternatives to future work.

A.1 Appendix 1

The possible highest costs in the spatial market for firms are reached when x takes the values of 0, 1, or $\frac{L_1+L_2-(1-\lambda)c}{2}$, which is the sale bound between firms 1 and 2. See Fig. 9.1. When the two firms' cost at any x exceeds r, there is no sale existing; therefore, the following conditions must hold:

$$x = 0 : w + (1 - \lambda)\, c + L_1 \leq r$$

$$x = \frac{L_1 + L_2 - (1 - \lambda)\, c}{2} : w + L_2 - \frac{L_1 + L_2 - (1 - \lambda)\, c}{2} \leq r$$

$$x = 1 : w + 1 - L_2 \leq r$$

Thus the wholesale price must satisfy

$$w \leq r - \max\left\{L_1 + (1 - \lambda)\, c,\, L_2 - \frac{L_1 + L_2 - (1 - \lambda)\, c}{2}, 1 - L_2\right\}$$

As the upstream firm wants to maximize his profit, namely, the wholesale price, we have that

$$w = r - \max\left\{L_1 + (1 - \lambda)\, c,\, L_2 - \frac{L_1 + L_2 - (1 - \lambda)\, c}{2}, 1 - L_2\right\}$$

B.1 Appendix 2

As $w = r - \max\left\{L_1 + (1 - \lambda)\, c,\, L_2 - \frac{L_1+L_2-(1-\lambda)c}{2}, 1 - L_2\right\}$, the wholesale price in stage 2 can take three forms:$w = r - (L_1 + (1 - \lambda)c)$, or $w = r - \left(L_2 - \frac{L_1+L_2-(1-\lambda)c}{2}\right)$, or$w = r - (1 - L_2)$.

First we will prove that $w = r - \left(L_2 - \frac{L_1+L_2-(1-\lambda)c}{2}\right)$ is not equilibrium. When $w = r - \left(L_2 - \frac{L_1+L_2-(1-\lambda)c}{2}\right)$, we denote the public firm's objective function as G_1. FOC of G_1 with respect to L_1 yields public firm's optimal location of $L_1(L_2)$ as the function of L_2. Then we obtain $G_1(L_2)$ as the function of L_2 and the associated wholesale price as $w_1 = r - \left(L_2 - \frac{L_1(L_2)+L_2-(1-\lambda)c}{2}\right)$.

If the public firm chooses a large location of $L_1^{'}$ that satisfies $L_1^{'} = \left\{L_1 : L_1 + (1-\lambda)\,c = L_2 - \frac{L_1(L_2)+L_2-(1-\lambda)c}{2}\right\}$ and meanwhile keep the wholesale price remain at the same level as w_1 (so that the upstream firm is indifferent), we can obtain the public firm's associated objective as the function of L_2, and we denote it as $G_2\,(L_2) = G\left(L_1^{'}\right)$.

We find that $G_2\,(L_2) - G_1\,(L_2) = \frac{\lambda^2(c\lambda+L_2-c)^2}{(6+\lambda)^2} \geq 0$, and the equality holds only when $\lambda = 0$. Therefore we have that the wholesale price of $w = r - \left(L_2 - \frac{L_1+L_2-(1-\lambda)c}{2}\right)$ is not equilibrium.

Now we derive downstream locations associated with the other two expressions.

Take $w = r - (L_1 + (1-\lambda)c)$ as an example. The FOCs of $\left\{\frac{\partial G}{\partial L_1} = 0, \frac{\partial \pi_2}{\partial L_2} = 0\right\}$ yield the optimal downstream location as

$L_1^a = \frac{4c\lambda^2-2c\lambda-2c+2\lambda+1}{2(2+\lambda)}, L_2^a = \frac{2c\lambda^2-2c+2\lambda+3}{2(2+\lambda)}$

Then the associated wholesale price is $w^a = r - \left(L_1^a + (1-\lambda)\,c\right)$.

When the private firm is critical, FOCs yield the downstream locations of other forms as $\overline{L}_1^b = \frac{1}{6} - \frac{2(1-\lambda)c}{3}$, $\overline{L}_2^b = \frac{1}{2} - (1-\lambda)\,c \leq \frac{1}{2}$, we will prove that this is not equilibrium.

When the private firm chooses $\overline{L}_2^b$ and the mixed firm chooses to jump to the right of the private competitor, then mixed firm is on the right side while the private firm is in the left side, and the equilibrium price of mixed firm becomes

$$p_1(x) = \begin{cases} w + x - L_2^b, & \frac{L_1+\overline{L}_2^b+(1-\lambda)c}{2} \leq x \leq r + \overline{L}_2^b - w \\ r, & r + \overline{L}_2^b - w \leq x \leq 1 \end{cases}$$

The equilibrium price of private firm becomes

$$p_2(x) = \begin{cases} r, & 0 \leq x \leq L_1 + w + (1-\lambda)\,c - r \\ w + L_1 - x + (1-\lambda)\,c, & L_1 + w + (1-\lambda)\,c - r \leq x \leq \frac{L_1+\overline{L}_2^b+(1-\lambda)c}{2} \end{cases}$$

Denote the new profit functions and social welfare as $\pi_1^{'}$, $\pi_2^{'}$, and $W^{'}$. The objective of the mixed firm is $G^{'} = \lambda\pi_1^{'} + (1-\lambda)\,W^{'}$.

The wholesale price may take three forms: $w = r - \overline{L}_2^b$, or $w = r - \left(\frac{L_1+\overline{L}_2^b+(1-\lambda)c}{2} - \overline{L}_2^b\right)$, or $w = r - (1 - L_1 + (1-\lambda)c)$.

Take $w = r - \overline{L}_2^b$ as an example. The FOC of $\pi_1^{'}$ with respect to L_1 yields the optimal location of mixed firm as $L_1^{'} = \frac{5}{6}$. Denote the associated maximized objective of mixed firm as $G^{'*}$ and the one under the original location of $\left\{\overline{L}_1^b, \overline{L}_2^b\right\}$ asG^*. Then we have

$$G^* - G^{'*} = \frac{2c}{3}(\lambda-1)\left((3\lambda+2)(\lambda-1)\,c+1\right) \le 0$$

" = " holds only when $\lambda = 1$. (Notice that in this case $\overline{L}_2^b$ is the largest among $\left\{\overline{L}_2^b, \frac{L_1+\overline{L}_2^b+(1-\lambda)c}{2} - \overline{L}_2^b, 1 - L_1 + (1-\lambda)\,c\right\}$, which indicates that $(1-\lambda)c \le 1/6$.)

The above condition indicates that the mixed firm can achieve higher value of its objective function if he jumps to the right side of the private firm who chooses $\overline{L}_2^b$.

The cases of $w = r - \left(\frac{L_1+\overline{L}_2^b+(1-\lambda)c}{2} - \overline{L}_2^b\right)$ and $w = r - (1 - L_1 + (1-\lambda)c)$ are similar; therefore, the mixed firm would jump to the right side when the private firm chooses $\overline{L}_2^b$.

Therefore, the private firm cannot locate anywhere left of $\frac{1}{2}$. The optimal location for the private firm becomes $L_2^b = \frac{1}{2}$. In this case, FOC yields the mixed firm's optimal location as $L_1^b = \frac{1}{6} - \frac{(1-\lambda)c}{3}$, which is right to $\overline{L}_1^b = \frac{1}{6} - \frac{2(1-\lambda)c}{3}$.

Notice that when $\lambda = 1$, $\left\{L_1^a, L_2^a\right\} = \left\{\frac{1}{2}, \frac{5}{6}\right\}$ and $\left\{L_1^b, L_2^b\right\} = \left\{\frac{1}{6}, \frac{1}{2}\right\}$. This is precisely as in Gupta et al. (1994).

C.1 Appendix 3

When the mixed firm is critical, the derivative of the associated social welfare W^* with respect to λ is $\frac{\partial W^*}{\partial \lambda} = -AS$, where $A = \frac{1-2c+2\lambda c}{(2+\lambda)^2} > 0$ and $S = 2c\lambda^3 + 6c\lambda^2 - 18c\lambda - 8c + 3\lambda$.

When $0 < c < \frac{1}{6}$, $\frac{\partial S}{\partial \lambda} = 6c\lambda^2 + 12c\lambda + 3(1 - 6c) > 0$; therefore, S increases as λincreases. As $S(\lambda = 0) = -8c < 0$, $S(\lambda = 1) = 3(1 - 6c) > 0$, there exists only a threshold value of $\overline{\lambda}$ so that $S\left(\overline{\lambda}\right) = 0$ and $0 < \overline{\lambda} < 1$. Then we have that for $0 \le \lambda < \overline{\lambda}$, $S(\lambda) < 0$, $\frac{\partial W^*}{\partial \lambda}(\lambda) = -A \cdot S(\lambda) > 0$, for $\overline{\lambda} < \lambda \le 1$, $S(\lambda) > 0$, $\frac{\partial W^*}{\partial \lambda}(\lambda) = -A \cdot S(\lambda) < 0$, and $\frac{\partial W^*}{\partial \lambda}\left(\lambda = \overline{\lambda}\right) = 0$. Thus, it can be concluded that an interior solution of $\overline{\lambda}$ for optimal privatization is reached when $0 < c < \frac{1}{6}$.

When $\frac{1}{6} < c < \frac{1}{2}$, let the two solutions of equation $\left\{\lambda : \frac{\partial S}{\partial \lambda} = 0\right\}$ be λ_1 and λ_2. As $\lambda_1 + \lambda_2 = -\frac{12c}{2 \cdot 6c} = -1 < 0$ and $\lambda_1 \cdot \lambda_2 = \frac{3(1-6c)}{6c} = \frac{1-6c}{2c} < 0$, only one of λ_1 and λ_2 can be in $\lambda \in [0, 1]$. As $\left.\frac{\partial S}{\partial \lambda}\right|_{\lambda=0} = 3(1 - 6c) < 0$, $\left.\frac{\partial S}{\partial \lambda}\right|_{\lambda=1} = 3 > 0$; there is one threshold value satisfying $\left\{\lambda : \frac{\partial S}{\partial \lambda} = 0\right\}$, so S first decreases and then increases with $\lambda \in [0, 1]$, and then $S \le \max\{S(\lambda = 0), S(\lambda = 1)\} = \max\{-8c, 3(1 - 6c)\} < 0$; therefore, $\frac{\partial W^*}{\partial \lambda} = -A \cdot S > 0$, and it can be concluded that the optimal privatization is $\lambda = 1$ when $\frac{1}{6} < c < \frac{1}{2}$.

Acknowledgements Ye would like to add the following for his participation: "Financial support is gratefully acknowledged from the National Natural Science Foundation of China (No. 71773129) and National Social Science Foundation of China (No. 19ZDA110)."

References

Anderson, S.P., de Palma, A., & Thisse, J.F. (1989). Spatial Price Policies Reconsidered. *Journal of Industrial Economics, 38*, 1–18.

Behrens, K., Brown, W. M., & Bougna, T. (2018). The World Is Not Yet Flat: Transport Costs Matter! *The Review of Economics and Statistics, 100*, 712–724.

Bhaskar, V., Gupta, B., & Khan, M. (2006). Partial Privatization and Yardstick Competition: Evidence from the Employment Dynamics in Bangladesh. *Economics of Transition, 14*, 459–477.
Colombo, S. (2011). On the Rationale of Spatial Discrimination with Quantity -Setting Firms. *Research in Economics, 65*, 254–258.
De Fraja, G., & Delbono, F. (1989). Alternative Strategies of a Public Enterprise in Oligopoly. *Oxford Economic Papers, 41*(2), 302–311.
Fujiwara, K. (2007). Partial Privatization in a Differentiated Mixed Oligopoly. *Journal of Economics, 92*, 51–65.
Gelves, J. A., & Heywood, J. S. (2013). Privatizing by Merger: The Case of an Inefficient Public Leader. *International Review of Economics and Finance, 27*, 69–79.
Greenhut, M. L. (1981). Spatial Pricing in the United States, West Germany and Japan. *Economica, 48*, 79–86.
Gupta, B., Katz, A., & Pal, D. (1994). Upstream Monopoly, Downstream Competition and Spatial Price Discrimination. *Regional Science and Urban Economics, 24*(5), 529–542.
Gupta, B., Heywood, J. S., & Pal, D. (1995). Strategic Behavior Downstream and the Incentive to Integrate: A Spatial Model with Delivered Pricing. *International Journal of Industrial Organization, 13*(3), 327–337.
Gupta, B., Heywood, J. S., & Pal, D. (1997). The Strategic Choice of Location and Transport Mode in a Successive Monopoly Model. *Journal of Regional Science, 39*(3), 525–539.
Gupta, N. (2005). Partial privatization and firm performance. *Journal of Finance, 60* (2), 987–1015.
Hamilton, J. H., & Slutsky, S. M. (1990). Endogenous Timing in Duopoly Games: Stackelberg or Cournot Equilibria. *Games and Economic Behavior, 2*, 29–46.
Heywood, J. S., & Ye, G. (2009a). Mixed Oligopoly, Sequential Entry and Spatial Price Discrimination. *Economic Inquiry, 47*, 589–597.
Heywood, J. S., & Ye, G. (2009b). Partial Privatization in a Mixed Duopoly with an R&D Rivalry. *Bulletin of Economic Research, 61*, 165–178.
Heywood, J. S., & Ye, G. (2010). Optimal Privatization in a Mixed Duopoly with Consistent Conjectures. *Journal of Economics, 101*, 231–246.
Heywood, J. S., Hu, X., & Ye, G. (2017). Optimal Partial Privatization with Asymmetric Demand Information. *Journal of Institutional and Theoretical Economics, 173*, 347–375.

Heywood, J. S., Wang, S., & Ye, G. (2018). Resale Price Maintenance and Spatial Price Discrimination. *International Journal of Industrial Organization, 57*, 147–174.

Laffont, J., & Tirole, J. (1993). *A Theory of Incentives in Procurement and Regulation*. Cambridge, MA: MIT Press.

Lederer, P., & Hurter, A. (1986). Competition of Firms: Discriminatory Pricing and Location. *Econometrica, 54*, 623–640.

Lin, M. H., & Matsumura, T. (2018). Optimal Privatization and Uniform Subsidy Policies: A Note. *Journal of Public Economic Theory, 20*, 416–423.

Matsumura, T. (1998). Partial Privatization in Mixed Duopoly. *Journal of Public Economics, 70*(3), 473–483.

Matsumura, T., & Kanda, O. (2005). Mixed Oligopoly at Free Entry Markets. *Journal of Economics, 84*, 27–48.

Matsumura, T., & Matsushima, N. (2004). Endogenous Cost Differentials Between Public and Private Enterprises: A Mixed Duopoly Approach. *Economica, 71*, 671–688.

Megginson, W. L., & Netter, J. M. (2001). From State to Market: A Survey of Empirical Studies of Privatization. *Journal of Economic Literature, 39*, 321–389.

Pal, D., & White, M. (1998). Mixed Oligopoly, Privatization and Strategic Trade Policy. *Southern Economic Journal, 65*, 264–282.

Sato, S., & Matsumura, T. (2019). Shadow Cost of Public Funds and Privatization Policies. *The North American Journal of Economics and Finance, 50*, 101026.

Thisse, J. F., & Vives, X. (1988). On the Strategic Choice of Spatial Price Policy. *American Economic Review, 78*, 122–137.

Tomaru, Y., & Wang, L.F.S. (2017). Optimal Privatization and Subsidization Policies in a Mixed Duopoly: Relevance of a Cost Gap. *Journal of Institutional and Theoretical Economics, 174*, 689–706.

Wang, L. F. S., & Chen, T. L. (2011). Mixed Oligopoly, Optimal Privatization and Foreign Penetration. *Economic Modeling, 28*, 1465–1470.

Wang, L. F., & Mukherjee, A. (2012). Undesirable Competition. *Economic Letters, 114*, 175–177.

White, M. D. (2002). Political Manipulation of a Public Firm's Objective Function. *Journal of Economic Behavior & Organization, 49*(4), 487–499.

10

Informative Versus Persuasive Advertising in a Dynamic Hotelling Monopoly

Luca Lambertini

10.1 Introduction

The analysis of the optimal behaviour of a monopolist in a dynamic model dates back to the pioneering contributions of Evans (1924), Tintner (1937), Eisner and Strotz (1963) and Gould (1968), which mostly focussed on pricing and investment decisions.[1] The building blocks (if not the earliest contributions) of the static approach to monopoly in discrete choice models are Mussa and Rosen (1978) for vertical differentiation and Bonanno (1987) for horizontal differentiation. Both deal with optimal product proliferation, and while Mussa and Rosen (1978) illustrate the well-known problem of downward quality distortion due to the firm's

[1]For an overview of optimal control or dynamic programming approaches to dynamic monopoly, see Lambertini (2018, ch. 2). For more on technical details, see Chiang (1992).

L. Lambertini (✉)
Department of Economics, University of Bologna, Bologna, Italy
e-mail: luca.lambertini@unibo.it

S. Colombo (ed.), *Spatial Economics Volume I*,
https://doi.org/10.1007/978-3-030-40098-9_10

intention to preserve its profit margin in the highest quality niche, Bonanno (1987) outlines the mechanism of symmetric product proliferation aiming at segmenting the market, as a form of spatial price discrimination.

The relatively scant literature on the dynamic analysis of a monopolistic industry *à la* Hotelling (1929) has investigated the issues of network externalities (Artle and Averous 1973; Dhebar and Oren 1985; Lambertini and Orsini 2004; Rohlfs 1974, *inter alia*), advertising (Lambertini 2005), product development (Lambertini 2007) and productive capacity accumulation (Lambertini 2009).

My aim in the present paper is to offer a view of different types of advertising campaigns in a dynamic Hotelling monopoly, in which neither one can be directly traced back to the classical approaches of Vidale and Wolfe (1957) and Nerlove and Arrow (1962), in particular as far as the formalisation of advertising campaigns is concerned. Here, the modelling approach will alternatively focus on informative versus persuasive advertising efforts, where by informative advertising it is meant that the monopolist aims at increasing the density of consumers at every point along the linear city, while by persuasive advertising it is meant that the advertising effort is devoted to increasing their reservation price. In both cases, partial market coverage is assumed and the magnitude not being targeted is a constant parameter.

The first problem can be solved via the method of dynamic programming, while the second must necessarily be coped with as an optimal control one, since its form does not suggest any plausible shape for the value function. In both cases, however, the existence of a single saddle-point equilibrium is analytically characterised. Then, the steady-state performances of the firm are comparatively evaluated, to find out that the monopolist's preferences about the nature of the advertising campaign crucially depend on the set of initial conditions.

The remainder of the chapter is organised as follows. The features of the two models are laid out in Sect. 10.2. Sections 10.3 and 10.4 illustrate the analysis of the two cases, which are then compared in Sect. 10.5. Concluding remarks are in Sect. 10.6.

10.2 The Setup

We model the optimal dynamic behaviour of a dynamic monopolist operating over continuous time $t \in [0, \infty)$ in a Hotelling (1929) linear city under partial market coverage, in which the firm, in addition to the price-quantity pair, may choose between informative and persuasive advertising to expand its demand basin or enhance consumers' willingness to pay for its product. For the time being, the explicit indication of the time argument will be omitted—for a reason that will become evident very soon.

Each consumer at $x \in [0, 1]$ is characterised by a linear-quadratic preference structure

$$U = s - p - (x - 1/2)^2 \tag{10.1}$$

where $s > 0$ is gross surplus (or the reservation price), p is the mill price and $(x - 1/2)^2$ is the disutility of transportation associated with reaching the firm optimally located in the middle of the linear city, along which there are d consumer at each point, so that d measures also the total mass of the population of consumers.

On the basis of the assumption of partial market coverage, the utility of the two marginal consumers symmetrically located to the left and right of 1/2 must be nil, and therefore monopoly price must be equal to

$$p_M = s - (x - 1/2)^2 = s - (2x - 1)^2 /4 \tag{10.2}$$

while demand (or the extent of market coverage) is $q_M = d (2x - 1)$, admissible for all $x \in (1/2, 1]$. This amounts to saying that the monopolist chooses the optimal demand to maximise its appropriate objective function by identifying two marginal consumers enjoying zero surplus, that is, by choosing x optimally.

The first scenario deals with informative advertising and relies on the idea that consumer density $d (t)$ be treated as a state variable obeying

$$\dot{d} = k (t) - \eta d (t) \tag{10.3}$$

where $k(t)$ is the firm's instantaneous advertising intensity aimed at attracting more costumers into the market. The presence of a constant decay rate $\eta > 0$ tells that, in the absence of advertising, the population of consumers shrinks as consumers are 'forgetful'.

The second scenario is a slightly modified version of Lambertini (2005). Here, persuasive advertising must convince customers to pay higher prices for the good being supplied, so that the relevant state variable is $s(t)$, obeying

$$\dot{s} = k(t) - \delta s(t) \tag{10.4}$$

in which the decay rate is δ, again time-invariant and positive, but not necessarily equal to η. In both scenarios, the instantaneous cost of advertising investment is $\Gamma(t) = bk^2(t)$, where b is a positive constant. Marginal cost is constant and, without further loss of generality, is posed equal to zero, in such a way that $\Gamma(t)$ is also the total instantaneous cost function.

In both settings, the firm has two controls and faces a single state. Quite interestingly, we are about to see that the first version of the dynamic problem, based upon (10.3), can be solved using the dynamic programming approach, that is, through the Hamilton-Jacobi-Bellman (HJB) equation by guessing a linear-quadratic value function, while the second version, based upon (10.4), cannot be treated in the same way (because its structure—in particular, the value function—does not lend itself to an intuitive guess, being not linear quadratic) and therefore must be solved as an optimal control problem on the basis of the Hamiltonian function (as in Lambertini 2005).

After the characterisation of the saddle-point equilibria of both models, the resulting steady-state magnitudes (prices, outputs, profits and advertising efforts) are compared in the space of states (d, s) to show that the firm's preferences concerning the nature of the advertising campaign are not univocally defined, as the choice essentially depends upon the initial conditions of both states.

10.3 Informative Advertising

Here the monopolist uses advertising to attract additional consumers by increasing density $d\left(t\right)$ along the linear city, while the reservation price s of the generic consumer remains constant. Accordingly, the relevant state equation is (10.3), and the firm's instantaneous profit function is

$$\pi\left(t\right)=p_{M}\left(t\right)q_{M}\left(t\right)-\Gamma\left(t\right)=\frac{s-\left[2x\left(t\right)-1\right]^{2}}{4}\cdot d\left(t\right)\left[2x\left(t\right)-1\right]-bk^{2}\left(t\right) \tag{10.5}$$

The firm has to solve the following problem:

$$\max_{x(t),k(t)}\ \Pi=\int_{0}^{\infty}\pi\left(t\right)e^{-\rho t}dt \tag{10.6}$$

s.t. (10.3), and the initial condition $d_0 = d\left(0\right) > 0$. Parameter $\rho > 0$ measures the constant discount rate. The Hamilton-Jacobi-Bellman (HJB) equation is the following:

$$\rho V\left(d\left(t\right)\right)=\max_{x(t),k(t)}\left\{\pi\left(t\right)+V'\left(d\left(t\right)\right)\cdot\dot{d}\right\} \tag{10.7}$$

where $V\left(d\left(t\right)\right)$ is the value function and $V'\left(d\left(t\right)\right)\equiv\partial V\left(d\left(t\right)\right)/\partial d\left(t\right)$ is its partial derivative w.r.t. the state variable.

From (10.7) we obtain the following first-order conditions (FOCs):

$$\begin{aligned} V'\left(d\left(t\right)\right)-2bk\left(t\right)&=0\\ d\left(t\right)\left[2s-\frac{3\left[2x\left(t\right)-1\right]^{2}}{2}\right]&=0 \end{aligned} \tag{10.8}$$

yielding[2]

$$k^* = \frac{V'(d(t))}{2b}\,;\; x^* = \frac{1}{2} + \sqrt{\frac{s}{3}} \tag{10.9}$$

It is worth noting that the solution determining the extent of market coverage, x^*, is indeed static and replicates unmodified forever, while the optimal advertising effort is endogenously determined by the state at all times, through the partial derivative of the value function. Moreover, since $x^* \in (1/2, 1]$, in order to respect the initial assumption of partial market coverage, we have to restrain s to the interval $(0, 3/4]$, outside which all consumers along the linear city would be able to buy the good supplied by the monopolist, irrespective of the level of consumer density.

Now we may stipulate $V(d(t)) = \varepsilon_1 d^2(t) + \varepsilon_2 d(t) + \varepsilon_3$, so that $V'(d(t)) = 2\varepsilon_1 d(t) + \varepsilon_2$. Plugging these and (10.9) into (10.7), the HJB equation can be simplified as follows:[3]

$$\frac{36\varepsilon_1\left[\varepsilon_1 - b(2\eta+\rho)\right]d^2 + 4\left[9\varepsilon_1\varepsilon_2 + b\left(4s\sqrt{3s} - 9\varepsilon_2(\eta+\rho)\right)\right]d + 9\left(\varepsilon_2^2 - 4b\rho\varepsilon_3\right)}{36b} = 0 \tag{10.10}$$

which gives rise to the system of Riccati equations:

$$\begin{aligned} 36\varepsilon_1\left[\varepsilon_1 - b(2\eta+\rho)\right] &= 0 \\ 9\varepsilon_1\varepsilon_2 + b\left(4s\sqrt{3s} - 9\varepsilon_2(\eta+\rho)\right) &= 0 \\ \varepsilon_2^2 - 4b\rho\varepsilon_3 &= 0 \end{aligned} \tag{10.11}$$

The above system has to be solved w.r.t. the triple of undetermined parameters $\{\varepsilon_1, \varepsilon_2, \varepsilon_3\}$, to obtain

$$\varepsilon_3 = \frac{\varepsilon_2^2}{4b\rho}\,;\; \varepsilon_2 = -\frac{4bs\sqrt{s}}{3\sqrt{3}\left[\varepsilon_1 - b(\eta+\rho)\right]} \tag{10.12}$$

$$\varepsilon_{11} = 0\,;\; \varepsilon_{12} = b(2\eta+\rho)$$

---

[2]The remaining solution of the second FOC, $x = 1/2 - \sqrt{s/3}$, can be disregarded in view of the definition of q_M.

[3]Henceforth, the time argument will be omitted throughout the analysis of this case, for the sake of brevity.

Of course, given the linear-quadratic form of the model at hand, we have two solutions for ε_1, which can be alternatively substituted into the expression of the optimal investment effort

$$k^* = \frac{d\varepsilon_1}{b} - \frac{2s\sqrt{s}}{3\sqrt{3}\left[\varepsilon_1 - b\left(\eta + \rho\right)\right]} \tag{10.13}$$

to deliver the pair of linear feedback strategies:

$$k_1^* = \frac{2s\sqrt{s}}{3\sqrt{3}b\left(\eta + \rho\right)}$$

$$k_2^* = d\left(2\eta + \rho\right) - \frac{2s\sqrt{s}}{3\sqrt{3}b\eta} \tag{10.14}$$

The first, k_1^*, is the open-loop control which would obtain from the solution of the corresponding optimal control problem based upon the Hamiltonian function (and, as such, it is independent of the state at any time t), while the second, k_2^*, is a proper feedback strategy defined as a function of the state at all times. Either one can be inserted into (10.3) to impose stationarity and obtain the single steady-state level of the state variable:

$$d^{ss} = \frac{2s\sqrt{s}}{3b\eta\sqrt{3}\left(\eta + \rho\right)} \tag{10.15}$$

where the meaning of superscript ss is intuitive.

The phase diagram drawn in Fig. 10.1 illustrates the stability properties of the state-control system (recall that the market variable has a quasi-static nature) and, given the sign of $\dot{d}$ above and below the steady-state advertising effort $k^{ss} = \eta d$, allows us to deduce that the state-independent open-loop control k_1^* is indeed the stable one.

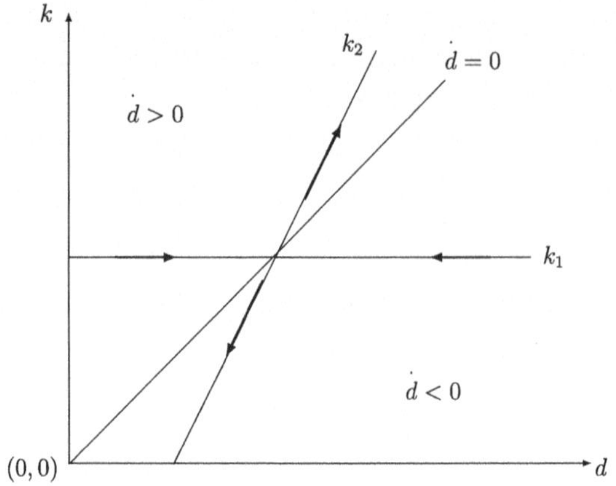

Fig. 10.1 The phase diagram under informative advertising

The foregoing discussion boils down to the following:

Proposition 10.1 *Assume* $s \in (0, 3/4]$. *If so, then there exists a unique saddle- point equilibrium at*

$$d^{ss} = \frac{2s\sqrt{s}}{3b\eta\sqrt{3}\,(\eta+\rho)}\,;\; k^{ss} = \eta d^{ss}\,;\; x^{ss} = \frac{1}{2} + \sqrt{\frac{s^{ss}}{3}}.$$

For later reference, we may also simplify the firm's profit function (10.5) in correspondence of the above steady-state coordinates, to obtain the level of steady-state profits:

$$\pi^{ss}(d) = \frac{4s^3(\eta+2\rho)}{27b\eta(\eta+\rho)^2} \tag{10.16}$$

10.4 Persuasive Advertising

In this case, the state variable is the reservation price $s(t)$; consequently, the relevant state equation is (10.4). The monopolist's instantaneous profit function looks much the same as in the previous section, except that d is an exogenous parameter:

$$\pi\left(t\right)=p_M\left(t\right)q_M\left(t\right)-\Gamma\left(t\right)=\frac{s\left(t\right)-\left[2x\left(t\right)-1\right]^2}{4}\cdot d\left[2x\left(t\right)-1\right]-bk^2\left(t\right) \tag{10.17}$$

The firm has to maximise the discounted profit flow

$$\max_{x(t),k(t)}\Pi=\int_0^{\infty}\pi\left(t\right)e^{-\rho t}dt \tag{10.18}$$

s.t. (10.4) and the initial condition $s_0=s\left(0\right)>0$.

It is easily ascertained that this problem cannot be treated via the dynamic programming approach, as the model is not defined in a linear-quadratic form and there is no intuitive guess about the shape of the value function appearing in the relevant HJB equation:

$$\rho V\left(s\left(t\right)\right)=\max_{x(t),k(t)}\left\{\pi\left(t\right)+V'\left(s\left(t\right)\right)\cdot\dot{s}\right\} \tag{10.19}$$

The FOCs deliver the same expression for the optimal choice of the marginal consumer x^* as in (10.9), except of course for the fact that the reservation price is the relevant state, and $k^*=V'\left(s\left(t\right)\right)/\left(2b\right)$. However, conjecturing a linear-quadratic value function $V\left(d\left(t\right)\right)=\zeta_1 s^2\left(t\right)+\zeta_2 s\left(t\right)+\zeta_3$ is not appropriate, as the simplified HJB equation reveals:

$$\frac{36\zeta_1\left[\zeta_1-b\left(2\delta+\rho\right)\right]s^2+16\sqrt{3}bds\sqrt{s}+36\zeta_2\left[\zeta_1-b\left(\delta+\rho\right)\right]s+9\left(\varepsilon_2^2-4b\rho\varepsilon_3\right)}{36b}=0 \tag{10.20}$$

The reason is the presence of $s\left(t\right)\sqrt{s\left(t\right)}$, as we already know from (10.10). Consequently, one has to solve the optimal control problem relying on the Hamiltonian function:

$$\mathcal{H}\left(t\right)=e^{-\rho t}\left\{\pi\left(t\right)+\lambda\left(t\right)\cdot\dot{s}\right\} \tag{10.21}$$

in this case written in current value, $\lambda(t) = \mu(t)e^{\rho t}$ being the 'capitalised' costate variable associated with the state dynamics, while $\mu(t)$ is the costate variable.

The resulting FOCs on controls are (the discount factor is omitted)

$$\frac{\partial \mathcal{H}(t)}{\partial x(t)} = \frac{d\left[4s(t) - 3(2x(t) - 1)^2\right]}{2} = 0 \tag{10.22}$$

$$\frac{\partial \mathcal{H}(t)}{\partial k(t)} = \lambda(t) - 2bk(t) = 0 \tag{10.23}$$

while the costate equation is

$$-\frac{\partial \mathcal{H}(t)}{\partial s(t)} = \dot{\lambda}(t) - \rho\lambda(t) \Rightarrow \tag{10.24}$$

$$\dot{\lambda}(t) = (\delta + \rho)\lambda(t) - d[2x(t) - 1]$$

Intuitively, $x^* = 1/2 + \sqrt{s/3}$ solves (10.22) once again. From (10.23), we obtain $\lambda^* = 2bk$ as well as the advertising control kinematics $\dot{k} = \dot{\lambda}/(2b)$ which, on the basis of (10.24) and λ^*, can be written in its final form as follows:

$$\dot{k} = k(\delta + \rho) - \frac{d}{b} \cdot \sqrt{\frac{s}{3}} \tag{10.25}$$

This, together with (10.4), constitutes the state-control system of the present optimal control problem. Its only solution identifies the steady-state point:

$$s^{SS} = \frac{d^2}{3b^2\delta^2(\delta + \rho)^2};\ k^{SS} = \delta s^{SS} \tag{10.26}$$

and the associated position of the marginal consumer to the r.h.s. of the firm is $x^{ss} = 1/2 + \sqrt{s^{ss}/3}$.

In order to evaluate the stability properties of the steady-state point (s^{ss}, k^{ss}), we have to examine the trace and determinant of the 2×2 Jacobian matrix associated with the state-control system:

$$J = \begin{bmatrix} \dfrac{\partial \dot{s}}{\partial s} = -\delta & \dfrac{\partial \dot{s}}{\partial k} = 1 \\ \dfrac{\partial \dot{k}}{\partial s} = -\dfrac{d}{2b\sqrt{3s}} & \dfrac{\partial \dot{k}}{\partial k} = \delta + \rho \end{bmatrix} \tag{10.27}$$

The trace is

$$\mathcal{T}(J) = \frac{\partial \dot{s}}{\partial s} + \frac{\partial \dot{k}}{\partial k} = \rho > 0 \tag{10.28}$$

and the determinant is

$$\Delta\left(J\right) = \frac{\partial \dot{s}}{\partial s} \cdot \frac{\partial \dot{k}}{\partial k} - \frac{\partial \dot{s}}{\partial k} \cdot \frac{\partial \dot{k}}{\partial s} = \frac{d}{2b\sqrt{3s}} - \delta\left(\delta + \rho\right) \tag{10.29}$$

which, posing $s = s^{ss}$, simplifies as $\Delta\left(J^{ss}\right) = -\delta\left(\delta + \rho\right)/2$. Consequently, we may formulate:

Proposition 10.2 *Assume $s \in (0, 3/4]$. If so, then the unique steady-state equilibrium at*

$$s^{ss} = \frac{d^2}{3b^2\delta^2\left(\delta + \rho\right)^2}\,;\; k^{ss} = \delta s^{ss}\,;\; x^{ss} = \frac{1}{2} + \sqrt{\frac{s^{ss}}{3}}.$$

is a saddle point.

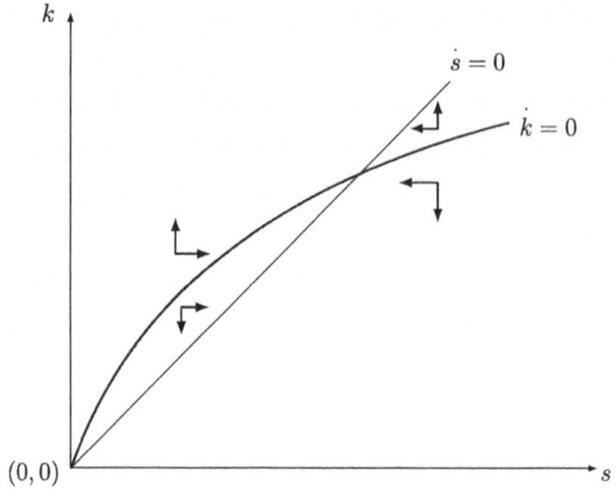

Fig. 10.2 The phase diagram under persuasive advertising

The saddle-point stability property is illustrated by the arrows appearing in the phase diagram drawn in Fig. 10.2, where the concavity of the locus $\dot{k} = 0$ is also intuitively suggesting the impossibility of using the HJB equation to solve this case. Moreover, the phase diagram also implies that the origin at which $s = k = 0$ is unstable and may therefore be disregarded (in addition to be inadmissible, as $s = 0$ implies that the market does not exist).

The level of steady-state profits at (s^{ss}, k^{ss}) amounts to

$$\pi^{ss}(s) = \frac{d^4(\delta + 4\rho)}{27b^3\delta^3(\delta + \rho)^4} \tag{10.30}$$

10.5 Comparing Equilibria

Now we are in a position to comparatively assess the equilibrium performance of the firm in the two settings. To begin with, we may take a look at steady-state profits. As it appears from (10.16) and (10.30), $\pi^{ss}(d)$ contains s as a parameter, while $\pi^{ss}(s)$ contains d. Hence, one might draw the conclusion that the profit comparison is problematic—to say the least—as the two problems considered in the foregoing analysis take either the consumer reservation price or density as given and endogenise the other magnitude as a state variable.

Yet, there is a sensible way out of this seemingly tricky conundrum which can be envisaged as follows. Since both cases require an exogenously given initial condition on the state, we may suppose that such initial level be also the relevant level of the same magnitude in the alternative scenario where either d or s is taken to be time-invariant, that is, a parameter. Once this standpoint is adopted, the issue of assessing the relative size of profit levels at the steady state becomes relatively easy to tackle.

The difference between profits (10.16) and (10.30) has the following feature:

$$
\begin{aligned}
& sign\left\{\pi^{ss}(d) - \pi^{ss}(s)\right\} \\
&\quad = sign\left\{4b^2 s^3 \delta^3 (\delta+\rho)^4 (\eta+2\rho) - d^4 \eta (\delta+4\rho)(\eta+\rho)^2\right\}
\end{aligned}
\tag{10.31}
$$

which involve a quartic polynomial in d. However, this can be treated (and easily solved) by posing $D = d^2$, whereby, since

$$
\Psi \equiv 4b^2 s^3 \delta^3 (\delta+\rho)^4 (\eta+2\rho) - D^2 \eta (\delta+4\rho)(\eta+\rho)^2 \tag{10.32}
$$

is concave in D, the sign of $\pi^{ss}(d) - \pi^{ss}(s)$ is positive for all D inside the interval identified by the roots of $\Psi = 0$, that is,

$$
D_{\pm} = \pm \frac{2bs\delta (\delta+\rho)^2 \sqrt{s\delta (\eta+2\rho)}}{(\eta+\rho)\sqrt{(\delta+4\rho)\eta}} \tag{10.33}
$$

and since the smaller root is negative, $\pi^{ss}(d) > \pi^{ss}(s)$ for all $D \in (0, D_+)$ or, equivalently, for all $d \in \left(0, \sqrt{D_+}\right)$. To complement this result, one may also note that D_+ increases monotonically in s.

There remains to check whether $\sqrt{D_+}$ is larger or smaller than d^{ss}. It turns out that the sign of $\sqrt{D_+} - d^{ss}$ is independent of s, the reason being that both are defined as a multiple of $s\sqrt{s}$, in such a way that

$$sign\left\{\sqrt{D_+}-d^{ss}\right\}$$
$$=sign\left\{9b^2\delta\eta\left(\delta+\rho\right)\sqrt{\delta\left(\eta+2\rho\right)}-\sqrt{3\eta\left(\delta+4\rho\right)}\right\} \quad (10.34)$$

so that $\sqrt{D_+}>d^{ss}$ for all

$$b>\frac{\sqrt{3\eta\left(\delta+4\rho\right)}}{9b^2\delta\eta\left(\delta+\rho\right)\sqrt{\delta\left(\eta+2\rho\right)}}\equiv\overline{b} \quad (10.35)$$

and conversely. Hence, keeping in mind that a parameter in one setting is taken to coincide with the initial condition in the other setting, we may formulate the following:

Corollary 10.3 *The relative size of steady-state profits* $\pi^{ss}(d)$ *and* $\pi^{ss}(s)$ *depends on the levels of initial conditions,* d_0 *and* s_0*, as well as the steepness of the instantaneous cost of advertising, measured by parameter* b*:*

- *if* $b>\overline{b}$*, then* $\pi^{ss}(d)>\pi^{ss}(s)$ *for all* $d_0\in(0,d^{ss})$*;*
- *if instead* $b\in\left(0,\overline{b}\right)$*, then* $\pi^{ss}(d)>\pi^{ss}(s)$ *for all* $d_0\in\left(0,\sqrt{D_+(s_0)}\right)$ *and conversely for all* $d_0\in\left(\sqrt{D_+(s_0)},d^{ss}\right)$*.*
- *Moreover, the threshold below which* $\pi^{ss}(d)>\pi^{ss}(s)$ *increases as* s_0 *increases, irrespective of its relative position w.r.t.* d^{ss}*.*

The above corollary can be spelt out more intuitively by saying that the richer is the generic consumer along the linear city, the more likely it becomes for the firm to find it preferable to invest in informative rather than persuasive advertising. Additionally, it appears that it is certainly so if the marginal cost of advertising is high enough. A plausible interpretation of this result may be found in a *quantity effect*, because monopoly output $q_M=d(2x-1)$ is linearly increasing in d and x, but the equilibrium level of x is concave in s, and this fact suggests that, all else equal (in particular, for any given b), informative advertising may turn out to be more profitable than persuasive advertising in a larger portion of the parameter constellation.

10.6 Concluding Remarks

The foregoing analysis has delved into the details of two alternative forms of advertising (informative or persuasive) in a Hotelling monopoly existing over an infinite horizon, under the assumption of partial market coverage. The stability analysis has analytically proved the existence of a single steady-state equilibrium enjoying the property of saddle-point stability in each of the two settings.

The exercise carried out on comparative profit evaluation at the steady state has shown that the relative performance of the two types of advertising is determined by the relative size of initial conditions on density and reservation price, respectively, with the former resulting relatively more effective than the latter, at least under the specific modelling strategy adopted here.

References

Artle, R., & Averous, C. (1973). The telephone systems as a public good: static and dynamic aspects. *Bell Journal of Economics, 4*, 89–100.

Bonanno, G. (1987). Location choice, product proliferation and entry deterrence. *Review of Economic Studies, 54*, 37–46.

Chiang, A. (1992). *Elements of dynamic optimization*. New York: McGraw-Hill.

Dhebar, A., & Oren, S. (1985). Optimal dynamic pricing for expanding networks. *Marketing Science, 4*, 336–351.

Eisner, R., & Strotz, R.H. (1963). Deteminants of business investment. In *Impacts of monetary policy, research studies prepared for the commission on money and credit*. Englewood Cliffs: Prentice-Hall.

Evans, G. C. (1924). The dynamics of monopoly. *American Mathematical Monthly, 31*, 75–83.

Gould, J. P. (1968). Adjustment costs in the theory of investment of the firm. *Review of Economic Studies, 35*, 47–55.

Hotelling, H. (1929). Stability in Competition. *Economic Journal, 39*, 41–57.

Lambertini, L. (2005). Advertising in a dynamic spatial monopoly. *European Journal of Operational Research, 166*, 547–556.
Lambertini, L. (2007). Dynamic spatial monopoly with product development. *Spatial Economic Analysis, 2*, 157–166.
Lambertini, L. (2009). Capital accumulation for production in a dynamic spatial monopoly. *Journal of Mathematical Sciences, 161*, 226–234.
Lambertini, L. (2018). *Differential games in industrial economics*. Cambridge: Cambridge University Press.
Lambertini, L., & Orsini, R. (2004). Network externality and the coordination problem. *Journal of Economics, 82*, 123–36.
Mussa, M., & Rosen, S. (1978). Monopoly and product quality. *Journal of Economic Theory, 18*, 301–317.
Nerlove, M., & Arrow, K. J. (1962). Optimal advertising policy under dynamic conditions. *Economica, 29*, 129–142.
Rohlfs, J. (1974). A theory of interdependent demand for a communications service. *Bell Journal of Economics, 5*, 16–37.
Tintner, G. (1937). Monopoly over time. *Econometrica, 5*, 160–170.
Vidale, M., & Wolfe, H. (1957). An operations research study of sales response to advertising. *Operations Research, 5*, 370–381.

11

Quality Preference, Congestion, and Differentiation Strategy

Zemin Hou and Yong Qi

11.1 Introduction and Background

In consumer theory, one essential component is preference relation. That is, the consumer is assumed to have preferences and could compare and rank various goods available in the economy. Given this preference assumption, we generally believe that the consumer strictly prefers high quality products; thus, quality is an important competitive strategy (Ishibashi 2001). Brekke et al. (2012), Laine and Ma (2017) say that quality is a major concern in general education, health care service, and transportation. Cellini et al. (2018) state further that quality in turn affects the way providers compete. The high quality preference attracts agglomeration of consumers, but, yet, it also yields some negative effects. And one of the most common effects is congestion.

Congestion is a widespread phenomenon in many markets (Matsumura and Matsushima 2007). For example, in China, patients with

Z. Hou (✉) · Y. Qi
Northeastern University, Shenyang, Liaoning Province, China
e-mail: yqi@mail.neu.edu.cn

S. Colombo (ed.), *Spatial Economics Volume I*,
https://doi.org/10.1007/978-3-030-40098-9_11

extremely serious diseases, such as cancer and leukemia, prefer to go to the hospitals in Beijing or Shanghai rather than go to the provincial hospitals. The hospitals in super cities possess high quality medical condition, but, yet, patients have to queue and wait for hospital assay, operation, and hospitalization. Congestion not only occurs in the healthcare system; it is especially common in tourism, retail trade, education, child care, and other service industries. Here, we take tourism and education as two examples. Visitors prefer to play in Disneyland instead of Fantawild, although they usually experience a quite long time queuing in Disneyland, especially in the legal holidays. Parents invest much in choosing an apartment located near key schools to fight for a quota in enrolling in a key school, since these key schools have high qualities in China. However, not every family has the opportunity to choose an apartment, as the housing resources are limited.

Therefore, it is critical to understand how consumers evaluate the positive effect of high quality and the negative effect of congestion. Moreover, the consumers' evaluation in turn affects firms' strategy, such as product quality, product differentiation, and price. In this paper, we aim at contributing to the understanding of the impact of congestion on firms' behavior. In addition, our research goal is also to determine the impact of the congestion cost and quality preference on the equilibrium outcomes.

We conceptualize two very vital aspects in a D'Aspremont et al. (1979)-type model—quality and congestion. There are many related literatures on quality competition. Brekke et al. (2010) emphasize the relationship between competition and quality within a spatial framework, and they find that lower transport costs always lead to high quality. Based on this paper, Pennerstorfer (2017) investigates the influence of competition on price and product quality following Salop (1979) model, he finds that intense competition has a positive impact on product quality and a negative effect on price. Siciliani and Straume (2019) consider a market for healthcare treatment in Hotelling (1929)-style model, and a key finding is that the competition may increase quality differences across hospitals. Li and Chen (2018) develop a model to study price and quality competition in a brand-differentiated supply chain, and they provide new insights on firms' choice of quality. The main insight of these papers is that quality choice affects price competition. However, they ignore the negative effect of quality competition.

The extant literature shows that congestion clearly represents a negative externality (Laussel et al. 2004; Fernández et al. 2005; Palma and Proost 2006; Brinkman 2016; Wadud and Chen 2018; Kim 2019). Palma and Proost (2006) present a model to study the effect of congestion on the urban structure, and it shows at most one sub-center in the city. Brinkman (2016) suggests that congestion may have ambiguous consequences for economic welfare when positive agglomeration externalities exist. Sweet (2014) examines that whether existing firms flee congested areas, the result shows that local congestion appears to function as an amenity while regional congestion appears to be a drag. In order to reduce the negative externality of congestion, Shao et al. (2016) and Niu et al. (2019) point out that O2O results in traffic congestion reduction. However, these literatures discuss the congestion effect from the perspective of traffic. In fact, congestion exists everywhere. Matsumura and Matsushima (2007) consider congestion from a queuing perspective. They propose an example wherein patients often wait for three hours to get medical treatment that only takes three minutes in Japan. Laussel et al. (2004) claim that congestion softens the price competition since it yields negative consumption externalities. Here, we use the concept of the congestion in Laussel et al. (2004) and Matsumura and Matsushima (2007).

In this paper, we introduce the consumers' quality preference and congestion cost in D'Aspremont et al. (1979) to investigate the firms' differentiation strategies. Different from the well-known tradition in D'Aspremont et al. (1979), our results show that both *Principle of Maximum Differentiation* and *Principle of Limited Differentiation* exist, depending on three key factors related to the characteristic of consumers, namely (i) the congestion cost, (ii) the quality preference, and (iii) the innovation cost. Specifically, the *Principle of Maximum Differentiation* only exists when the quality preference (the congestion cost and the innovation cost) is sufficiently low or high. There also is the *Principle of Limited Differentiation*, when the quality preference is not so high or low. Actually, in traditional spatial competition model, such as Hotelling

(1929) and D'Aspremont et al. (1979), the *demand effect* prompts the firms' agglomeration while the *competition effect* urges dispersion. However, neither the *competition effect* nor the *demand effect* dominates market when the consumers have quality preference and congestion cost. Actually, the quality preference enlarges the *demand effect* of high quality product, which would weaken the *Principle of Maximum Differentiation* in some conditions. However, an additional negative externality exists, that is, the *congestion effect.* The consumers would wait for a long time to get service and be worse off as the number of consumers patronizing the same firm rises. Therefore, the *congestion effect* obstructs the expansion of the *demand effect,* and the two firms would not agglomerate at the market center, and yields the *Principle of Limited Differentiation.* Additionally, we also study the impact of congestion costs and the quality preference on the equilibrium outcomes, which depends on the differentiation strategies.

The rest of this paper proceeds as follows. In Sect. 11.2 we introduce the model. In Sect. 11.3, we derive the equilibrium outcomes. In Sect. 11.4, we provide an analysis of social welfare. Section 11.5 concludes. At last, the proofs of the propositions are in the Appendix.

11.2 The Model

We set up a scenario in which two firms, A and B, locate at x_A and x_B of a unit interval [0,1] respectively and $x_A \leq x_B$. These two firms sell products to a continuum of consumers who are uniformly distributed along the unit interval with density $f(x) = 1$. Each consumer $x \in [0, 1]$ is willing to purchase at most one product from any one of the two firms. In order to purchase, consumers have to pay extra transportation cost following the widely used tradition in Hotelling model. Consumers' transportation cost is quadratic in distance; thus, the transportation cost to firm i ($i = A, B$) is $t(x - x_i)^2$. Without loss of generality, we set the unit transportation cost to unity so that $t = 1$. Note that the location of a consumer x represents his relative preference for firm B over A while t measures how much a consumer dislikes buying a less preferred brand (Esteves and Reggiani 2014). Therefore, the location of the two firms denotes the product differentiation. Different from standard Hotelling-style model, we introduce a negative externality with respect to the consumption of products following the assumption in Matsumura and Matsushima (2007). This negative externality corresponds to congestion[1]. In addition, we consider the consumers' preference on quality of the goods. Following the assumption in Brekke et al. (2012), the utility of consumer x is given by

$$U(x, x_i) = kq_i - (x - x_i)^2 - p_i - \theta s_i \tag{11.1}$$

where q_i is the quality offered by firm i, $k > 0$ is a parameter measuring the marginal willingness of consumer x to pay for quality, $(x_i - x)^2$ is the total transportation cost of consumer x who purchase from firm i, p_i denotes the price charged by firm i, θ expresses the degree of the negative externality, and s_i is the market share of firm i in the unit line market.

In this paper, the market is complete information, that is, consumers could predict the market share for each firm accurately. Therefore, the position of indifferent consumer $\hat{x}$ would divide the market share of firm A and firm B. That is, the consumers with $x < \hat{x}$ would choose to buy from firm A and $s_A \equiv \hat{x}$. The consumers with $x > \hat{x}$ would buy from firm B and $s_B \equiv 1 - \hat{x}$. Following the utility function in (11.1), the consumer who is indifferent between firm A and firm B is located at $\hat{x}$. Therefore, the indifferent consumer is implicitly given by

$$kq_A - \left(\hat{x} - x_A\right)^2 - p_A - \theta\hat{x} = kq_B - \left(\hat{x} - x_B\right)^2 - p_B - \theta\left(1 - \hat{x}\right) \tag{11.2}$$

Solving (11.2), we have the indifferent point on the line between the two firms as follows:

$$\hat{x} = \frac{p_A - p_B - kq_A + kq_B + {x_A}^2 - {x_B}^2 - \theta}{2\left(x_A - x_B - \theta\right)} \tag{11.3}$$

[1]Grilo et al. (2001) name the negative externality as vanity in consumer behavior since consumers are always worse off as the number of consumers patronizing the same store rises.

The two firms' profits are respectively:

$$\pi_A = p_A\hat{x} - \frac{\beta {q_A}^2}{2}, \pi_B = p_B\left(1-\hat{x}\right) - \frac{\beta {q_B}^2}{2} \tag{11.4}$$

where $(\beta {q_i}^2)/2$ is total cost for firm i to carry out the quality innovation, which, in general, depends on product quality. This cost function is convex with respect to q_i, which is often used in product innovation (see, e.g., Ishida et al. 2011; Reimann et al. 2019).

The game is played in three stages. In Stage 1, the two firms decide simultaneously their spatial locations. In Stage 2, the two firms set their respective quality levels. In Stage 3, the two firms compete in prices. We solve the game by using backward induction. In this paper, we focus on the characterization of symmetric equilibria in pure strategies.

11.3 Equilibrium Outcomes

In this section, we consider the equilibrium outcomes. Given the profits function of the two firms in (11.4), in Stage 3, both the two firms choose price p_i to maximize their own profits. Hence, the equilibrium prices in the third stage are given by

$$\begin{aligned} p_A &= \frac{k\left(q_A - q_B\right) - \left(x_A - x_B\right)\left(2 + x_A + x_B\right) + 3\theta}{3}, \\ p_B &= \frac{k\left(q_B - q_A\right) - \left(x_A - x_B\right)\left(4 - x_A - x_B\right) + 3\theta}{3} \end{aligned} \tag{11.5}$$

The second-order derivative is $\partial^2\pi_A/\partial {p_A}^2 = \partial^2\pi_B/\partial {p_B}^2 \equiv 1/(x_A - x_B - \theta) < 0$. Therefore, the equilibrium prices in (11.5) maximize the profits of the two firms. In Stage 2, both firm A and firm B decide their quality. The first-order derivatives of the profits with respect to the quality are

$$\begin{aligned} \frac{\partial\pi_A}{\partial q_A} &= \frac{k^2(q_B-q_A)+k[x_A(2+x_A)-x_B(2+x_B)-3\theta]+9q_A\beta(x_B-x_A+\theta)}{9(x_A-x_B-\theta)} \\ \frac{\partial\pi_B}{\partial q_B} &= \frac{k^2(q_B-q_A)+k[(x_A-x_B)(-4+x_A+x_B)+3\theta]-9q_B\beta(x_B-x_A+\theta)}{9(x_B+\theta-x_A)} \end{aligned} \tag{11.6}$$

Two sufficient conditions for a maximization problem are $\partial^2\pi_A/\partial q_A{}^2 = \partial^2\pi_B/\partial q_B{}^2 = -\beta + k^2/[9(x_B + \theta - x_A)] < 0$. Hence, we have a constraint on parameters, that is, $k^2 < 9\beta(x_B + \theta - x_A)$. The equilibrium qualities of two firms are

$$\begin{aligned} q_A &= \frac{1}{3}k\left[\frac{1}{\beta} + \frac{3(x_A - x_B)(-1 + x_A + x_B)}{2k^2 + 9\beta(x_A - x_B - \theta)}\right], \\ q_B &= \frac{1}{3}k\left[\frac{1}{\beta} + \frac{3(x_B - x_A)(-1 + x_A + x_B)}{2k^2 + 9\beta(x_A - x_B - \theta)}\right] \end{aligned} \tag{11.7}$$

In Stage 1, the two firms decide their location simultaneously. The following proposition characterizes the firms' optimal location.

Proposition 1 The equilibrium locations of the two firms are as follows[2]:

$$\begin{cases} x_A{}^* = 0, x_B{}^* = 1 & if\ \ k^2 \in (0, 9\beta(1+\theta)/4)\ \ or \\ & k^2 \in (9\beta(1+\theta)/2, 9\beta(1+\theta)) \\ x_A{}^* = x_{A1}, x_B{}^* = x_{B1} \equiv 1 - x_A{}^*\ if & k^2 \in \left(9\beta(1+\theta)/4, k_1{}^2\right) \\ x_A{}^* = x_{A3}, x_B{}^* = x_{B3} \equiv 1 - x_A{}^*\ if & k^2 \in \left(k_1{}^2, 9\beta(1+\theta)/2\right) \end{cases}$$

Proof. See the Appendix.

Hotelling (1929) proposes the *Principle of Minimum Differentiation.* He claims that the gravitation of one firm toward the competitor increases profits as it could occupy a more extensive section of the market. He names it as the *demand effect.* However, D'Aspremont et al. (1979) assert that the *Principle of Minimum Differentiation* is invalid when the transport costs are quadratic with respect to the distance. They suggest that "the *oligopolies should gain an advantage by dividing the market into submarkets in each of which some degree of monopoly would reappear,*" which is well-known as the *competition effect.* In their model, the *competition effect* exceeds the *demand effect,* and the two firms perform the *Principle of Maximum Differentiation.*

In this paper, we find that the *Principle of Maximum Differentiation* is possible if and only if the quality preference of consumers is sufficiently

[2]The parameter values x_{A1}, x_{A3}, and $k_1{}^2$ can be found in the Appendix.

low or high. When the quality preference is low, the two firms' vertical differentiation plays no role in affecting competition, which is similar to D'Aspremont et al. (1979). Thus, the two firms locate at the endpoint of the linear market. When the quality preference of consumers is high, the *demand effect* fades as the firm with high quality product always attracts a majority of consumers. In this case, the two firms also locate at the endpoint of the linear market.

In addition, Proposition 1 also shows that firm A and firm B may move toward the market center, but would not agglomerate. That is, neither the *competition effect* nor the *demand effect* dominates the market. Intuitively, a third power emerges which affects the firms' location behavior. With the increase of the quality preferences, the quality and the total innovation costs increase ($q_i = k/(3\beta)$).[3] In order to offset the cost loss, the firms enlarge their market share. Consequently, firm A will seek to make x_A as large as possible. This means that firm A will come just as close to firm B. However, an additional negative externality exists when *the demand effect* increases; we named it as the *congestion effect*. That is, the consumers may have to wait for a long time to get service and be worse off as the number of consumers patronizing the same firm rises. Therefore, the *congestion effect* obstructs the expansion of the *demand effect*, and the two firms would not agglomerate at the market center.

Given the location of the two firms, the equilibrium prices are

$$\begin{cases} p_A{}^*|_{\substack{x_A{}^*=0 \\ x_{B^*}=1}} = p_B{}^*|_{\substack{x_A{}^*=0 \\ x_{B^*}=1}} = 1-\theta \\ p_A{}^*|_{\substack{x_A{}^*=x_{A1} \\ x_B{}^*=x_{B1}}} = p_B{}^*|_{\substack{x_A{}^*=x_{A1} \\ x_B{}^*=x_{B1}}} \\ \quad = \frac{2k^2+9\beta(3+2\theta)+\sqrt{4k^4+81\beta^2(3+2\theta)^2-36k^2\beta(9+2\theta)}}{36\beta} \\ p_A{}^*|_{\substack{x_A{}^*=x_{A3} \\ x_B{}^*=x_{B3}}} = p_B{}^*|_{\substack{x_A{}^*=x_{A3} \\ x_B{}^*=x_{B3}}} = \frac{2k^2}{9\beta} \end{cases} \tag{11.8}$$

[3]The total innovation costs for firm i are $\beta q_i{}^2/2$.

In deriving insights regarding the role of the quality preference (k), the innovation cost (β), and the congestion cost (θ), we begin by considering the prices impacts. Given the equilibrium prices in (11.8), we have

Proposition 2 The quality preference k, the innovation cost β, and the congestion cost θ yield different price strategies when the two firms use different location strategies.

(1) The optimal prices $p_A{}^*$ and $p_B{}^*$ are only related to θ, and the prices decrease in θ for firms' maximization differentiation locations.

(2) The optimal prices $p_A{}^*$ and $p_B{}^*$ decrease in θ and k while increase in β for the location strategy $(x_A{}^* = x_{A1}, x_B{}^* = x_{B1})$;

(3) The optimal prices $p_A{}^*$ and $p_B{}^*$ increase in k while decrease in β for the location strategy $(x_A{}^* = x_{A3}, x_B{}^* = x_{B3})$.

Proof. See the Appendix.

It is a very interesting conclusion as Proposition 2(2) and Proposition 2(3) are opponents. Intuitively, the prices decrease in θ and k while increase in β, in other words, Proposition 2(1) and Proposition 2(2) explain economic intuition. When the consumers' quality preference (k) and congestion cost (θ) increase, the firms will set a low price to attract consumers. When the innovation cost (β) increases, the firms will increase prices to offset cost loss. However, we also find that the equilibrium prices increase in k and decrease in β. With the increases of the consumers' quality preference (k), the firms produce higher quality goods ($\partial q_A{}^*/\partial k = \partial q_B{}^*/\partial k = 1/(3\beta)$). [4]Thus, the equilibrium prices increase. Moreover, with the increases of the innovation cost (β), the firms produce lower quality goods ($\partial q_A{}^*/\partial \beta = \partial q_B{}^*/\partial \beta = -k/(3\beta^2)$), and the equilibrium prices decrease.

Given the location of the two firms, the equilibrium qualities are

$$q_A{}^* = q_B{}^* = \frac{k}{3\beta} \tag{11.9}$$

Proposition 3 The equilibrium qualities $q_A{}^*$ and $q_B{}^*$ increase (decrease) in k (β).

[4]See formula (11.9).

Proof. Given the equilibrium qualities in (11.9), we have $\partial q_A{}^*/\partial k = \partial q_B{}^*/\partial k = 1/(3\beta)$ and $\partial q_A{}^*/\partial \beta = \partial q_B{}^*/\partial \beta = -k/(3\beta^2)$.

Proposition 3 shows a very intuitive principle on the firms' quality decisions. When the consumers' quality preferences are high, the firms prefer to produce a high quality product to satisfy the market demands. However, if the innovation cost is high, the firms prefer to produce a low-quality good to reduce costs.

11.4 Social Welfare

In this section, we consider social welfare effects of the consumers' quality preferences and congestion costs. We use the social costs to reflect the social welfare. Therefore, the social cost, which accounts for the innovation costs, the congestion costs, and the transportation costs is,

$$\begin{aligned} sc = &\left[\int_0^{s_A} (x - x_A)^2 dx + \int_{s_A}^1 (x - x_B)^2 dx\right] \\ &+ \left[\int_0^{s_A} \theta s_A dx + \int_{s_A}^1 \theta s_B dx\right] + \left[\frac{\beta q_A{}^2}{2} + \frac{\beta q_B{}^2}{2}\right] \end{aligned} \tag{11.10}$$

In (11.10), the first term denotes the transportation costs, the second term is the congestion costs, and the third term is the innovation costs. Given the equilibrium locations of the two firms in Proposition 1, we have the social costs:

$$\begin{cases} sc^*\Big|_{\substack{x_A{}^* = 0 \\ x_{B^*} = 1}} = \frac{1}{36}\left(3 + \frac{4k^2}{\beta} + 18\theta\right),\ sc^*\Big|_{\substack{x_A{}^* = x_{A3} \\ x_B{}^* = x_{B3}}} \\ = \frac{4k^4 + 18k^2\beta(1-2\theta) + 27\beta^2[1+3\theta(3+\theta)]}{324\beta^2} \\ sc^*\Big|_{\substack{x_A{}^* = x_{A1} \\ x_B{}^* = x_{B1}}} \\ = \frac{\left[\begin{array}{l} 4k^4 + 144k^2\beta + 459\beta^2 - 72k^2\beta\theta + 1620\beta^2\theta + 324\beta^2\theta^2 \\ + (2k^2 + 9\beta - 19\beta\theta)\sqrt{4k^4 + 81\beta^2(3+2\theta)^2 - 36k^2\beta(9+2\theta)} \end{array}\right]}{2592\beta^2} \end{cases} \tag{11.11}$$

Given the equilibrium costs in (11.11), we have

Proposition 4 (1) The total costs increases (decrease) in k and θ (β) for $(x_A{}^* = 0, x_B{}^* = 1)$ and $(x_A{}^* = x_{A3}, x_B{}^* = x_{B3})$.

(2) The total costs increases in k (β) if $\theta \in (1/3, 1)$ and $k^2 \in (9\beta(1+\theta)/4, k^{2*})$; the total costs decrease in θ if $\theta \in \left(\left(2\sqrt{2}-1\right)/3, 1\right)$ and $k^2 \in \left({k_1}^{2*}, 9\beta\left(5+2\theta-\sqrt{2\left(11+6\theta\right)}\right)/2\right)$ when two firms locate at $(x_A{}^* = x_{A1}, x_B{}^* = x_{B1})$.

Proof. See the Appendix. k^{2*} and ${k_1}^{2*}$ are two critical values.

Proposition 4 shows that when the consumers' quality preferences and the congestion cost are high, the total costs increase. That is, when the consumers' quality preferences increase, firm A and firm B would improve the products' quality to attract more consumers, which yields higher total costs. With the increase of β, firm A and firm B may decrease their motivation in quality innovation and the total costs decrease. It is easy to understand that the total costs increase in θ as the congestion cost yields a negative effect on consumers' purchasing. However, in case (2), in which firm A and firm B locate at $(x_A{}^* = x_{A1}, x_B{}^* = x_{B1})$, we also find that in some special conditions, the economic intuition of the quality preference (k), the innovation cost (β), and the congestion cost (θ) are in contrast with case (1). Actually, when we consider the consumers' quality preference and congestion cost, it changes the market configuration which also changes the social total costs. When $\theta \in (0, 1/3)$, consumers' congestion cost is low, and the quality preference is also low. (Since we consider the location set $(x_A{}^* = x_{A1}, x_B{}^* = x_{B1})$, the parameter range is $k^2 \in (9\beta(1+\theta)/4, {k_1}^2)$. In this case, we have $\partial[9\beta(1+\theta)/4]/\partial\theta > 0$ and $\partial {k_1}^2/\partial\theta > 0$). With the increase of k, the high quality products mean a higher cost. As consumers' quality preference is low, the demand expansion through improving quality cannot offset the high cost, and the firms have less motivation to produce high quality goods. In this case, the total costs decrease in k (β) (since k and β play a different role in affecting firms' product behavior and the Appendix also proves that $\partial tc^*/\partial k^2 = -\partial tc^*/\partial\beta \times (k^2/\beta)$). When $\theta \in (1/3, 1)$ and $k^2 \in (k^{2*}, {k_1}^2)$, that is, both the congestion cost and the quality preference are high. In this case, consumers' quality requirement is very high, which brings a new challenge for the firms to produce high quality goods. As the two firms are symmetric, they may not improve the quality as high quality generates high costs. The total costs decrease in θ if $\theta \in \left(\left(2\sqrt{2}-1\right)/3, 1\right)$ and $k^2 \in \left({k_1}^{2*}, 9\beta\left(5+2\theta-\sqrt{2\left(11+6\theta\right)}\right)/2\right)$. In this case, the congestion cost is very high and consumers would transfer their negative utility caused by the congestion to their positive utility of the high quality. Therefore, the total costs decrease in θ.

11.5 Concluding Remarks

Congestion is a common phenomenon nowadays. Not only the consumers but also firms focus on the congestion gradually, since congestion causes resources waste. In this study, we introduce consumers' evaluation on the congestion and quality, investigating how the firms conduct quality strategy, differentiation strategy, and price strategy. Our results show that, firstly, the firms conduct the *Principle of Maximum Differentiation* if and only if the quality preference is sufficiently high or low. Secondly, the *Principle of Limited Differentiation* is also possible when the quality preference is not so high and low. We claim that, apart from the competition effect and the demand effect, the congestion effect plays a role in deciding the differentiation strategies of the two firms. Additionally, we also find that the quality preferences, the innovation cost, and the congestion cost affect the two firms' price strategies and the total social costs under different location strategies. However, the firms' qualities increase (decrease) in the quality preference (the cost coefficient), and it is irrelevant to the congestion cost.

Our results have several implications for practitioners. Firstly, the *Principle of Maximum Differentiation* is conditional. Intuitively, majority of firms maximize products' differentiation to satisfy the differentiated demands of consumers. However, the differentiation strategy may also increase congestion, which weakens the utility of consumers. Secondly, firms' quality strategies and differentiation strategies are affected by the consumers' quality preference. Actually, consumers have different quality preferences for different products or services. In relatively high preference industries, such as education and healthcare, the firms should provide high quality products. This conclusion explains the reason why congestion is usually common in these industries.

Our model can be extended to the future. First, the setup ignores the role of e-commerce. In reality, e-commerce plays a vital role in changing consumers' lifestyle which may also induce congestion as consumers would only click the mouse to reserve. However, as the online world is a virtual world, consumers could not enjoy the products online immediately. In this case, the differentiation strategies of firms may change, which would also change the relationship between quality, price, and differentiation. Secondly, the congestion introduces resources waste, but, yet, we could not consider the negative externality from the perspective of resource-based theory.

Appendix

Proof of Proposition 1. Before we solve the location decision of two firms in Stage 1, we make some restrictions on the parameters. Firstly, given the symmetry of firm A and firm B in Hotelling (1929) style model, a location pair that could be candidates for the equilibrium of Stage 1 must be symmetric around 1/2 (see Cremer and Thisse 1991, 1994; Lambertini and Orsini 2005). Using the standard axioms of symmetry, the location decisions of firm A and firm B satisfy $x_A + x_B = 1$. In addition, the symmetry requires $0 \leq x_A \leq 1/2$ as we assume that $0 \leq x_A \leq x_B \leq 1$. Thus, we could confine our attention to firm A's location. Secondly, since $k^2 < 9\beta(x_B + \theta - x_A)$ and $x_B = 1 - x_A$, it is easy for us to have that $x_A < [9\beta(1+\theta) - k^2]/(18\beta)$. Moreover, as we assume the two firms locate at the interior of the market, we have $[9\beta(1+\theta) - k^2]/(18\beta) > 0$, and it is easy to see that $k^2 < 9\beta(1+\theta)$. In summary, we obtain two important conditions; they are $0 \leq x_A < x_{A\max} \equiv \min\{[9\beta(1+\theta) - k^2]/(18\beta), 1/2\}$ and $k^2 < 9\beta(1+\theta)$. Therefore, we could write these two conditions as follows:

$$\begin{cases} x_A \in \left[0, \frac{1}{2}\right] & if\ \ k^2 \in (0, 9\beta\theta] \\ x_A \in \left[0, \frac{9\beta(1+\theta)-k^2}{18\beta}\right) & if\ \ k^2 \in (9\beta\theta, 9\beta\theta + 9\beta) \end{cases} \tag{11.12}$$

In Stage 1, both firm A and firm B decide their locations simultaneously. Substituting the equilibrium prices in (11.5) and the equilibrium qualities in (11.7) into profits function of firm A in (11.4), and then differentiating π_A with x_A given $x_B = 1 - x_A$, the first-order derivative is

$$\frac{\partial \pi_A}{\partial x_A} = \frac{-4k^2(1 + x_A) + 9\beta(1 + 4x_A)(1 - 2x_A + \theta)}{6\left[2k^2 - 9\beta(1 - 2x_A + \theta)\right]} \tag{11.13}$$

It is easy to see that the optimal location strategy of firm A depends on the characteristic of the numerator and denominator in (11.13). We use two parameters N and D to denote the numerator and the denominator separately, that is, $N = -4k^2(1 + x_A) + 9\beta(1 + 4x_A)(1 - 2x_A + \theta)$ and $D = 6[2k^2 - 9\beta(1 - 2x_A + \theta)]$. Consider numerator N firstly, which is a concave parabola with respect to x_A. Therefore, it is easy to see that (i) N is less than 0 if and only if ${k_1}^2 < k^2 < 9\beta(1 + \theta)$and (ii) there are two real roots for $N = 0$ if and only if $0 < k^2 < {k_1}^2$, denoted by x_{A1} and x_{A2}, where [1]

$$\begin{aligned} x_{A1} &= \frac{-2k^2+9\beta(1+2\theta)-\sqrt{4k^4+81\beta^2(3+2\theta)^2-36k^2\beta(9+2\theta)}}{72\beta} \\ x_{A2} &= \frac{-2k^2+9\beta(1+2\theta)+\sqrt{4k^4+81\beta^2(3+2\theta)^2-36k^2\beta(9+2\theta)}}{72\beta} \end{aligned} \tag{11.14}$$

Thus, we now focus on the sign of N under $0 < k^2 < {k_1}^2$. Before we analyze the sign of N, it is a must for us to focus on the relationship

[1]From (A-3), it is easy to see that there are two real roots if and only if $4k^4 + 81\beta^2(3 + 2\theta)^2 - 36k^2\beta(9 + 2\theta) > 0$, which is a convex parabola with respect to k^2. There are two solutions for $4k^4 + 81\beta^2(3 + 2\theta)^2 - 36k^2\beta(9 + 2\theta) = 0$, denoted by ${k_1}^2$ and ${k_2}^2$, where $0 < {k_1}^2 \equiv \frac{9\beta\left(9+2\theta-2\sqrt{6}\sqrt{3+\theta}\right)}{2} < 9\beta(1+\theta)$ and ${k_2}^2 \equiv \frac{9\beta\left(9+2\theta+2\sqrt{6}\sqrt{3+\theta}\right)}{2} > 9\beta(1+\theta)$. Therefore, we always have $4k^4 + 81\beta^2(3 + 2\theta)^2 - 36k^2\beta(9 + 2\theta) < 0$ if ${k_1}^2 < k^2 < 9\beta(1 + \theta)$; otherwise, $4k^4 + 81\beta^2(3 + 2\theta)^2 - 36k^2\beta(9 + 2\theta) > 0$ if $0 < k^2 < {k_1}^2$. In addition, we also have ${k_1}^2 > 9\beta\theta$ if and only if $\theta \in (0, 3/8)$.

among x_{A1}, x_{A2} and the critical conditions of x_A (0 and $x_{A\max}$). It is easy to see that[2]

$$x_{A1}\begin{cases} > 0 \ if\ k^2 \in \left(\frac{9\beta(1+\theta)}{4}, {k_1}^2\right) \\ < 0 \ if\ k^2 \in \left(0, \frac{9\beta(1+\theta)}{4}\right) \end{cases}, \ x_{A1} - \frac{1}{2} < 0, \ x_{A1} - \frac{9\beta(1+\theta)-k^2}{18\beta} < 0$$
$$x_{A2} > 0, x_{A2} - \frac{1}{2}\begin{cases} > 0 \ if\ k^2 \in \left(0, \frac{9\beta\theta}{2}\right) \\ < 0 \ if\ k^2 \in \left(\frac{9\beta\theta}{2}, \min\left({k_1}^2, 9\beta\theta\right)\right) \end{cases}, x_{A2} - \frac{9\beta(1+\theta)-k^2}{18\beta} < 0 \tag{11.15}$$

Therefore, we have the following five cases of the numerator N[3]:

Case 1): Case 1 is effective if and only if $k^2 \in (0, 9\beta\theta/2)$; in this case, we always have $N > 0$.

[2]Consider the sign of x_{A1}, which depends on the numerator $-2k^2 + 9\beta(1+2\theta) - \sqrt{4k^4 + 81\beta^2(3+2\theta)^2 - 36k^2\beta(9+2\theta)}$, as the denominator is positive. The first two terms $-2k^2 + 9\beta(1+2\theta)$ are positive as $0 < -2{k_1}^2 + 9\beta(1+2\theta) < -2k^2 + 9\beta(1+2\theta)$. Thus, we have $(-2k^2 + 9\beta(1+2\theta))^2 - (4k^4 + 81\beta^2(3+2\theta)^2 - 36k^2\beta(9+2\theta)) = 72\beta[4k^2 - 9\beta(1+\theta)]$. Thus, x_{A1} is large than 0 if and only if $k^2 \in (9\beta(1+\theta)/4, {k_1}^2)$. Similarly, we have$x_{A1} - \frac{1}{2} = \frac{\left(2k^2+9\beta(3-2\theta)+\sqrt{4k^4+81\beta^2(3+2\theta)^2-36k^2\beta(9+2\theta)}\right)}{-72\beta}$; it is easy to see that the numerator is positive while the denominator is negative; thus, $x_{A1} < 1/2$.We could also focus on x_{A1} and $\frac{9\beta(1+\theta)-k^2}{18\beta}$; we have $x_{A1} - \frac{9\beta(1+\theta)-k^2}{18\beta} = \frac{2k^2-9\beta(3+2\theta)-\sqrt{4k^4+81\beta^2(3+2\theta)^2-36k^2\beta(9+2\theta)}}{72\beta}$, which is meaningful if and only if $k^2 < {k_1}^2$. Since $2{k_1}^2 - 9\beta(3+2\theta) < 0$, we always have $x_{A1} < \frac{9\beta(1+\theta)-k^2}{18\beta}$. x_{A2} is always larger than zero since we have $0 < -2{k_1}^2 + 9\beta(1+2\theta) < -2k^2 + 9\beta(1+2\theta)$. Comparing x_{A2} and 1/2, we have $x_{A2} - \frac{1}{2} = \frac{-2k^2+9\beta(-3+2\theta)+\sqrt{4k^4+81\beta^2(3+2\theta)^2-36k^2\beta(9+2\theta)}}{72\beta}$; it is easy to see that the sign of $x_{A2} - \frac{1}{2}$ depends on the numerator. And $[4k^4 + 81\beta^2(3+2\theta)^2 - 36k^2\beta(9+2\theta)] - [-2k^2 + 9\beta(-3+2\theta)]^2 = 216\beta(-2k^2 + 9\beta\theta)$; thus, the numerator is positive if and only if $k^2 \in (0, 9\beta\theta/2)$, yielding $x_{A2} > \frac{1}{2}$; otherwise, $x_{A2} < \frac{1}{2}$. Comparing x_{A2} and $\frac{9\beta(1+\theta)-k^2}{18\beta}$, we have $x_{A2} - \frac{9\beta(1+\theta)-k^2}{18\beta} = \frac{2k^2-9\beta(3+2\theta)+\sqrt{4k^4+81\beta^2(3+2\theta)^2-36k^2\beta(9+2\theta)}}{72\beta}$. Since $2k^2 - 9\beta(3+2\theta) < 2{k_1}^2 - 9\beta(3+2\theta) < 0$, we have $[4k^4 + 81\beta^2(3+2\theta)^2 - 36k^2\beta(9+2\theta)] - [2k^2 - 9\beta(3+2\theta)]^2 = -216\beta k^2 < 0$, yielding $x_{A2} < \frac{9\beta(1+\theta)-k^2}{18\beta}$.

[3]We omit a case in which $0 < x_{A1} < x_{A\max} < x_{A2}$, as we always have $x_{A2} < x_{A\max}$ when $x_{A1} > 0$. Moreover, we have the axis of symmetry of N that is equal to $\frac{-2k^2+9\beta(1+2\theta)}{72\beta}$, which can be negative or positive when $k^2 > {k_1}^2$ as $\frac{9\beta(1+2\theta)}{2} > {k_1}^2$.

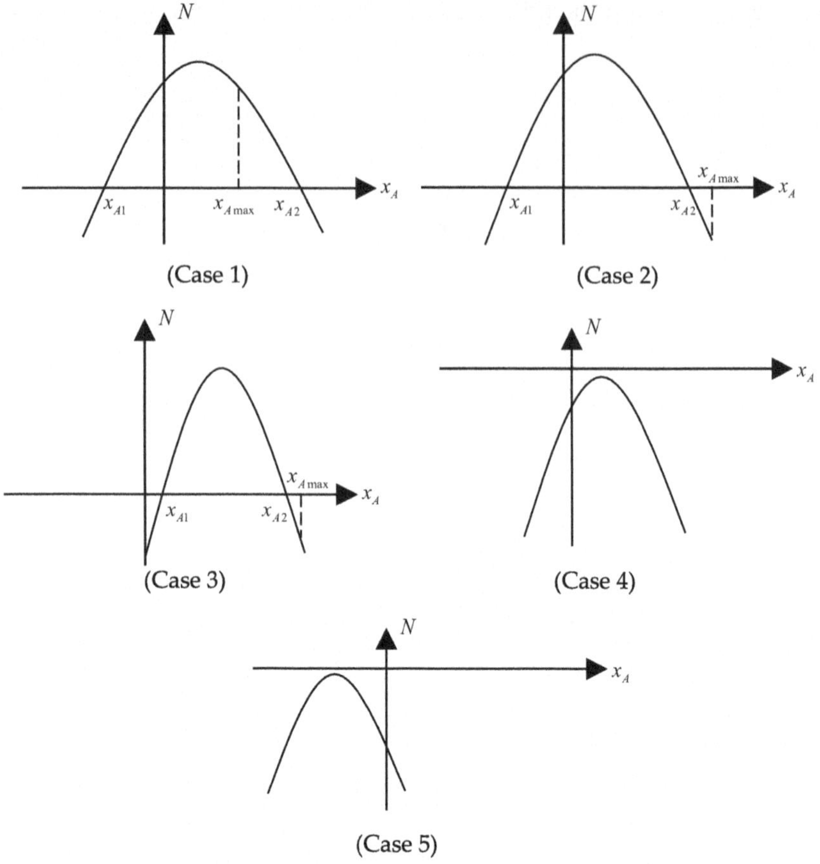

Fig. A.1 The possible cases of the numerator of $\partial\pi_A/\partial x_A$Therefore, we could calculate the interval of the parameters of prior five cases and give the sign of N

Case 2): Case 2 is effective if $k^2 \in (9\beta\theta/2, 9\beta(1+\theta)/4)$. In this case, we have $N > 0$ if and only if $x_A \in (0, x_{A2})$, while $N < 0$ if $x_A \in (x_{A2}, x_{A\max})$.

Case 3): Case 3 is effective if $k^2 \in (9\beta(1+\theta)/4, k_1{}^2)$. In this case, we have $N > 0$ if and only if $x_A \in (x_{A1}, x_{A2})$; while $N < 0$ if $x_A \in (0, x_{A1})$ or $x_A \in (x_{A2}, x_{A\max})$;

Case 4) and Case 5): Case 4 and Case 5 are effective if $k^2 \in (k_1{}^2, 9\beta(1+\theta))$. In this case, we have $N < 0$.

Consider the denominator D secondly, which is a linear function of x_A. Solving $D = 0$, we have that $x_{A3} = [-2k^2 + 9\beta(1+\theta)]/18\beta$. Considering the sign of D now, we have the following three cases:

Case I): When $k^2 \in (0, 9\beta\theta/2)$, we have $D < 0$ as $x_{A3} > 1/2$;
Case II): When $k^2 \in (9\beta\theta/2, 9\beta(1+\theta)/2)$, we have $D < 0$ if and only if $x_A \in (0, x_{A3})$ while $D > 0$ if $x_A \in (x_{A3}, x_{A\max})$
Case III): When $k^2 \in (9\beta(1+\theta)/2, 9\beta(1+\theta))$, we have $D > 0$.

Therefore, we could analyze the sign of $\partial\pi_A/\partial x_A$ and get the optimal location of firm A based on profits maximization given the characteristic of N and D. Therefore, we have the following cases[4]:

Case A): Given $k^2 \in (0, 9\beta\theta/2)$, it is easy to see that $\partial\pi_A/\partial x_A < 0$ as $N > 0$ and $D < 0$. Thus, the optimal location of firm A is $x_A{}^* = 0$.
Case B): Given $k^2 \in (9\beta\theta/2, 9\beta(1+\theta)/4)$, it is easy to see that $\partial\pi_A/\partial x_A < 0$ as $N > 0$ and $D < 0$ when $x_A \in (0, x_{A2})$; $\partial\pi_A/\partial x_A > 0$ as $N < 0$ and $D < 0$ when $x_A \in (x_{A2}, x_{A3})$; and$\partial\pi_A/\partial x_A < 0$ as $N < 0$ and $D > 0$ when $x_A \in (x_{A3}, x_{A\max})$. The graphic of π_A is illustrated in Fig. A.2.

That is, firm A may get the highest profits at 0 or x_{A3}; comparing the profits of firm A under these two locations, we have

$$\pi_A|_{x_A=0} - \pi_A|_{x_A=x_{A3}} = \frac{9\beta(1+\theta) - 2k^2}{18\beta} > 0 \tag{11.16}$$

Thus, the optimal location of firm A is $x_A{}^* = 0$ when $k^2 \in (9\beta\theta/2, 9\beta(1+\theta)/4)$.

Case C): Given $k^2 \in (9\beta(1+\theta)/4, k_1{}^2)$, it is easy to see that $\partial\pi_A/\partial x_A > 0$ as $N < 0$ and $D < 0$ when $x_A \in (0, x_{A1})$; $\partial\pi_A/\partial x_A < 0$ as $N > 0$ and $D < 0$ when $x_A \in (x_{A1}, x_{A2})$; $\partial\pi_A/\partial x_A > 0$ as $N < 0$ and $D < 0$

[4]Comparing $x_{A2} - x_{A3} = \frac{6k^2 - 9\beta(3+2\theta) + \sqrt{4k^4 + 81\beta^2(3+2\theta)^2 - 36k^2\beta(9+2\theta)}}{72\beta}$ and $6k^2 - 9\beta(3 + 2\theta) < 6k_1{}^2 - 9\beta(3 + 2\theta) < 0$, thus, $4k^4 + 81\beta^2(3 + 2\theta)^2 - 36k^2\beta(9 + 2\theta) - [6k^2 - 9\beta(3 + 2\theta)]^2 = 16k^2(9\beta\theta - 2k^2)$, and $x_{A2} > x_{A3}$ if $k^2 \in (0, 9\beta\theta/2)$.

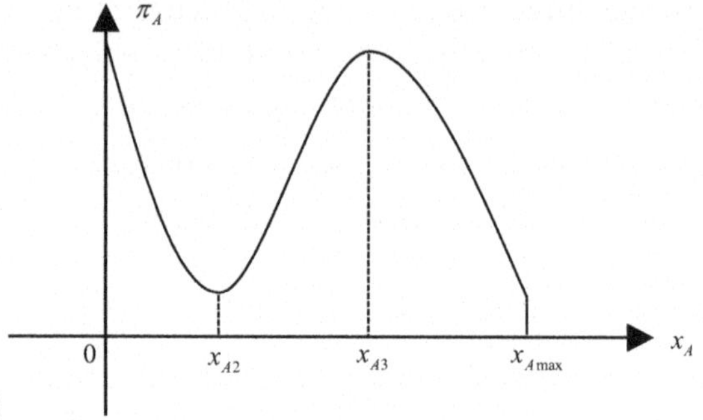

[h]

Fig. A.2 The profits of firm A with respect to the location, given $k^2 \in (9\beta\theta/2, 9\beta(1+\theta)/4)$

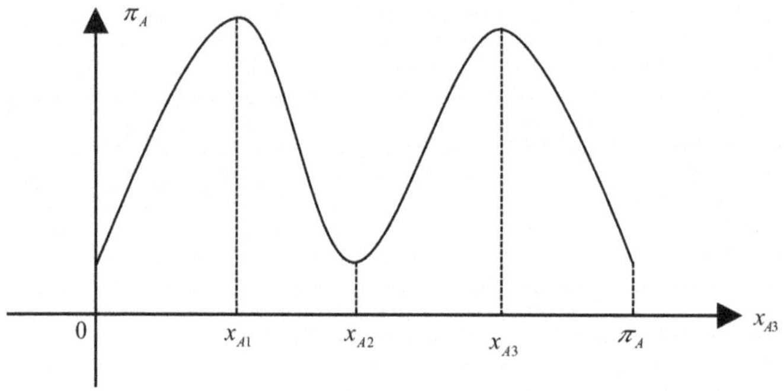

[h]

Fig. A.3 The profits of firm A with respect to the location, given $k^2 \in (9\beta(1+\theta)/4, k_1{}^2)$

when $x_A \in (x_{A2}, x_{A3})$; and $\partial\pi_A/\partial x_A < 0$ as $N < 0$ and $D > 0$ when $x_A \in (x_{A3}, x_{A\max})$. The graphic of π_A is illustrated in Fig. A.3.

That is, firm A may get the highest profits at x_{A1} or x_{A3}; comparing the profits of firm A under these two locations, we have

$$\pi_A|_{x_A=x_{A1}} - \pi_A|_{x_A=x_{A3}} = \frac{-6k^2+9\beta(3+2\theta)+\sqrt{4k^4+81\beta^2(3+2\theta)^2-36k^2\beta(9+2\theta)}}{72\beta} > 0 \tag{11.17}$$

Thus, the optimal location of firm A is $x_A{}^* = x_{A1}$ when $k^2 \in (9\beta(1+\theta)/4, k_1{}^2)$.

Case D): Given $k^2 \in (k_1{}^2, 9\beta(1+\theta)/2)$, it is easy to see that $\partial\pi_A/\partial x_A > 0$ as $N < 0$ and $D < 0$ when $x_A \in (0, x_{A3})$ and $\partial\pi_A/\partial x_A < 0$ as $N < 0$ and $D > 0$ when $x_A \in (x_{A3}, x_{A\max})$. Thus, the optimal location of firm A is $x_A{}^* = x_{A3}$.

Case E): Given $k^2 \in (9\beta(1+\theta)/2, 9\beta(1+\theta))$, it is easy to see that $\partial\pi_A/\partial x_A < 0$ as $N < 0$ and $D > 0$. Thus, the optimal locations of firm A is $x_A{}^* = 0$.

Hence, we can conclude:

- Firm A's optimal location is $x_A{}^* = 0$ if $k^2 \in (0, 9\beta(1+\theta)/4)$ or $k^2 \in (9\beta(1+\theta)/2, 9\beta(1+\theta))$;
- Firm A's optimal location is $x_A{}^* = x_{A1}$ if $k^2 \in (9\beta(1+\theta)/4, k_1{}^2)$;
- Firm A's optimal location is $x_A{}^* = x_{A3}$ if $k^2 \in (k_1{}^2, 9\beta(1+\theta)/2)$.

Proof of (11.8). It is easy to get the equilibrium price and qualities when firm A and firm B's optimal location are $(x_A{}^* = 0, x_B{}^* = 1)$ and $(x_A{}^* = x_{A1}, x_B{}^* = x_{B1})$. Substituting the equilibrium locations of firm A and firm B into (11.5) and (11.7), we have the equilibrium prices and equilibrium qualities

$$\begin{aligned} &p_A{}^*|_{x_A{}^*=0} = p_B{}^*|_{x_B{}^*=1} = 1-\theta,\ q_A{}^*|_{x_A{}^*=0} = q_B{}^*|_{x_B{}^*=1} = \frac{k}{3\beta} \\ &p_A{}^*|_{x_A{}^*=x_{A1}} = p_B{}^*|_{x_B{}^*=x_{B1}} = \frac{2k^2+9\beta(3+2\theta)+\sqrt{4k^4+81\beta^2(3+2\theta)^2-36k^2\beta(9+2\theta)}}{36\beta}, \\ &q_A{}^*|_{x_A{}^*=x_{A1}} = q_B{}^*|_{x_B{}^*=x_{B1}} = \frac{k}{3\beta} \end{aligned} \tag{11.18}$$

It is difficult to get the equilibrium prices and qualities directly when the optimal locations are $(x_A{}^* = x_{A3}, x_B{}^* = x_{B3})$. We use the L'Hopital theory to get the equilibrium prices and qualities. Given the quality functions in (11.7) and the equilibrium locations ($x_{A^*} = x_{A3}, x_{B^*} = x_{B3}$), we first solve the equilibrium qualities of firm A:

$$\begin{aligned} q_A^*|_{x_A^*=x_{A3}} &= \lim_{\substack{x_A^* \to x_{A3} \\ x_B^* \to x_{B3}}} \left[\frac{k}{3\beta} + \frac{k(x_A-x_B)(-1+x_A+x_B)}{2k^2+9\beta(x_A-x_B-\theta)} \right] \\ &= \frac{k}{3\beta} + \lim_{x_A^* \to x_{A3}} \frac{k[x_A-(1-x_A)](-1+x_A+1-x_A)}{2k^2+9\beta[x_A-(1-x_A)-\theta]} \\ &= \frac{k}{3\beta} + \lim_{x_A^* \to x_{A3}} \frac{0}{18\beta} = \frac{k}{3\beta} \end{aligned} \tag{11.19}$$

Since firm A and firm B are symmetric, we also have

$$q_B^*\big|_{x_B^*=x_{B3}} = \frac{k}{3\beta} \tag{11.20}$$

Similarly, given the prices functions in (11.5), the qualities functions in (11.7), and the equilibrium locations ($x_{A^*} = x_{A3}, x_{B^*} = x_{B3}$), we now solve the equilibrium prices of firm A:

$$\begin{aligned} p_A^*|_{x_A^*=x_{A3}} &= -\lim_{\substack{x_A^* \to x_{A3} \\ x_B^* \to x_{B3}}} \frac{\{2k^2+3\beta[x_A(2+x_A)-x_B(2+x_B)-3\theta]\}(x_A-x_B-\theta)}{2k^2+9\beta(x_A-x_B-\theta)} \\ &= -\lim_{x_A^* \to x_{A3}} \frac{\{2k^2+3\beta[x_A(2+x_A)-(1-x_A)(2+1-x_A)-3\theta]\}[x_A-(1-x_A)-\theta]}{2k^2+9\beta[x_A-(1-x_A)-\theta]} \\ &= -\lim_{x_A^* \to x_{A3}} \frac{4[k^2+9\beta(-1+2x_A-\theta)]}{18\beta} = \frac{4k^2}{18\beta} = \frac{2k^2}{9\beta} \end{aligned} \tag{11.21}$$

Similarly, firm B's equilibrium prices are

$$p_B^*\big|_{x_B^*=x_{B3}} = \frac{2k^2}{9\beta} \tag{11.22}$$

Proof of Proposition 2. When the two firms locate at the endpoint of the linear market, the optimal prices of firm A and firm B are $1-\theta$; thus, $\partial p_{A^*}/\partial\theta = \partial p_{B^*}/\partial\theta \equiv -1$. When the spatial location strategy of the two firms is $(x_A{}^* = x_{A3}, x_B{}^* = x_{B3})$, we have $\partial p_A{}^*/\partial k^2 = \partial p_B{}^*/\partial k^2 \equiv 2/(9\beta)$ and $\partial p_A{}^*/\partial \beta = \partial p_B{}^*/\partial \beta \equiv -2k^2/(9\beta^2)$. When the location strategy is$(x_A{}^* = x_{A1}, x_B{}^* = x_{B1})$, we have

$$\begin{aligned} \frac{\partial p_A{}^*}{\partial k^2} &= \frac{\partial p_B{}^*}{\partial k^2} \equiv \frac{1}{18\beta} + \frac{2k^2-9\beta(9+2\theta)}{18\beta\sqrt{4k^4+81\beta^2(3+2\theta)^2-36k^2\beta(9+2\theta)}} < 0 \\ \frac{\partial p_A{}^*}{\partial \beta} &= \frac{\partial p_B{}^*}{\partial \beta} \equiv -\frac{k^2}{18\beta^2} - \frac{k^2\left[2k^2-9\beta(9+2\theta)\right]}{18\beta^2\sqrt{4k^4+81\beta^2(3+2\theta)^2-36k^2\beta(9+2\theta)}} > 0 \\ \frac{\partial p_A{}^*}{\partial \theta} &= \frac{\partial p_B{}^*}{\partial \theta} \equiv \frac{1}{2} + \frac{-2k^2+9\beta(3+2\theta)}{2\sqrt{4k^4+81\beta^2(3+2\theta)^2-36k^2\beta(9+2\theta)}} < 0 \end{aligned} \quad (11.23)$$

Proof of (11.11). It is easy to get the social costs when firm A and firm B's optimal location are $(x_A{}^* = 0, x_B{}^* = 1)$ and $(x_A{}^* = x_{A1}, x_B{}^* = x_{B1})$. Substituting the equilibrium locations of firm A and firm B into (11.10), we have the social costs which have been shown in (11.11). It is difficult to get the social costs directly when the equilibrium spatial locations are $(x_A{}^* = x_{A3}, x_B{}^* = x_{B3})$. We also use the L'Hopital theory to solve this problem. Given the equilibrium locations of firm A and firm B $(x_A{}^* = x_{A3}, x_B{}^* = x_{B3})$, the transportation costs are,

$$\begin{aligned} tc = \frac{1}{12}\Bigg\{ & 4 - 3x_A^* + 6x_A^{*2} - 9x_B^* + 6x_B^{*2} \\ & - \frac{27\left(x_A^*-x_B^*\right)^3\left(-1+x_A^*+x_B^*\right)^2\beta^2}{\left[2k^2+9\beta\left(x_A^*-x_B^*-\theta\right)\right]^2} + \frac{18\left(x_A^*-x_B^*\right)^2\left(-1+x_A^*+x_B^*\right)^2\beta}{2k^2+9\beta\left(x_A^*-x_B^*-\theta\right)} \Bigg\} \end{aligned} \quad (11.24)$$

We could split the transportation costs into three parts; therefore, the first term is

$$\begin{aligned} & \lim_{\substack{x_A{}^* \to x_{A3} \\ x_B{}^* \to x_{B3}}} \frac{4-3x_A^*+6x_A^{*2}-9x_B^*+6x_B^{*2}}{12} \\ & = \frac{4k^4-18k^2(\beta+2\beta\theta)+27\beta^2[1+3\theta(1+\theta)]}{324\beta^2} \end{aligned} \quad (11.25)$$

The second term is

$$\begin{aligned}
&\lim_{\substack{x_A{}^* \to x_{A3} \\ x_B{}^* \to x_{B3}}} -\frac{1}{12}\left\{\frac{27\left(x_A^*-x_B^*\right)^3\left(-1+x_A^*+x_B^*\right)^2\beta^2}{\left[2k^2+9\beta\left(x_A^*-x_B^*-\theta\right)\right]^2}\right\} \\
&= \lim_{x_A{}^*\to x_{A3}} -\frac{1}{12}\left\{\frac{27\left[x_A^*-\left(1-x_A^*\right)\right]^3\left[-1+x_A^*+\left(1-x_A^*\right)\right]^2\beta^2}{\left\{2k^2+9\beta\left[\left(x_A^*-\left(1-x_A^*\right)-\theta\right)\right]\right\}^2}\right\} \\
&= \lim_{x_A{}^*\to x_{A3}} -\frac{1}{12}\left\{\frac{0}{36\beta\left\{2k^2+9\beta\left[\left(x_A^*-\left(1-x_A^*\right)-\theta\right)\right]\right\}}\right\} \\
&= \lim_{x_A{}^*\to x_{A3}} -\frac{1}{12}\left\{\frac{0}{648\beta^2}\right\} = 0
\end{aligned} \tag{11.26}$$

The third term is

$$\begin{aligned}
&\lim_{\substack{x_A{}^* \to x_{A3} \\ x_B{}^* \to x_{B3}}} \frac{1}{12}\left\{\frac{18\left(x_A^*-x_B^*\right)^2\left(-1+x_A^*+x_B^*\right)^2\beta}{2k^2+9\beta\left(x_A^*-x_B^*-\theta\right)}\right\} \\
&= \lim_{x_A{}^*\to x_{A3}} \frac{1}{12}\left\{\frac{18\left[x_A^*-\left(1-x_A^*\right)\right]^2\left[-1+x_A^*+\left(1-x_A^*\right)\right]^2\beta}{2k^2+9\beta\left[x_A^*-\left(1-x_A^*\right)-\theta\right]}\right\} = \lim_{x_A{}^*\to x_{A3}} \frac{1}{12}\left\{\frac{0}{18\beta}\right\} = 0
\end{aligned} \tag{11.27}$$

Similarly, we could calculate the congestion cost:

$$cc = \frac{\theta\left(4k^4+36k^2\beta(x_A^*-x_B^*-\theta)+9\beta^2\left\{(x_A^*-x_B^*)^2\left[10+x_A^{*\,2}+2x_A^*(x_B^*-1)+(x_B^*-2)x_B^*\right]+18(x_B^*-x_A^*)\theta+9\theta^2\right\}\right)}{2\left[2k^2+9\beta(x_A^*-x_B^*-\theta)\right]^2} \tag{11.28}$$

Hence, we have

$$\begin{aligned}
&\lim_{\substack{x_A{}^* \to x_{A3} \\ x_B{}^* \to x_{B3}}} \frac{\theta\left(4k^4+36k^2\beta(x_A^*-x_B^*-\theta)+9\beta^2\left\{(x_A^*-x_B^*)^2\left[10+x_A^{*\,2}+2x_A^*(x_B^*-1)+(x_B^*-2)x_B^*\right]+18(x_B^*-x_A^*)\theta+9\theta^2\right\}\right)}{2\left[2k^2+9\beta(x_A^*-x_B^*-\theta)\right]^2} \\
&= \lim_{x_A{}^*\to x_{A3}} \left\{\frac{36\beta\theta\{2k^2+9\beta[x_A^*-(1-x_A^*)-\theta]\}}{72\beta\{2k^2+9\beta[x_A^*-(1-x_A^*)-\theta]\}}\right\} = \frac{\theta}{2}
\end{aligned} \tag{11.29}$$

Similarly, we could calculate the innovation cost:

$$ic = \frac{k^2}{9\beta} + \frac{k^2\left(x_A^* - x_B^*\right)^2\left(-1 + x_A^* + x_B^*\right)^2\beta}{\left[2k^2 + 9\beta\left(x_A^* - x_B^* - \theta\right)\right]^2} \tag{11.30}$$

Hence, we have

$$\begin{aligned} &\lim_{\substack{x_A{}^* \to x_{A3} \\ x_B{}^* \to x_{B3}}} \frac{k^2}{9\beta} + \frac{k^2\left(x_A^*-x_B^*\right)^2\left(-1+x_A^*+x_B^*\right)^2\beta}{\left[2k^2+9\beta\left(x_A^*-x_B^*-\theta\right)\right]^2} \\ &= \frac{k^2}{9\beta} + \lim_{x_A{}^* \to x_{A3}} \frac{k^2\left(x_A^*-x_B^*\right)^2\left[-1+x_A^*+x_B^*\left(1-x_A^*\right)\right]^2\beta}{\left\{2k^2+9\beta\left[x_A^*-\left(1-x_A^*\right)-\theta\right]\right\}^2} \\ &= \frac{k^2}{9\beta} + \lim_{x_A{}^* \to x_{A3}} \frac{0}{648\beta^2} = \frac{k^2}{9\beta} \end{aligned} \tag{11.31}$$

Therefore, when the two firms locate at $(x_A{}^* = x_{A3}, x_B{}^* = x_{B3})$, the social costs are

$$sc = tc + cc + ic = \frac{4k^4 + 18k^2\beta\,(1 - 2\theta) + 27\beta^2\,[1 + 3\theta\,(3 + \theta)]}{324\beta^2} \tag{11.32}$$

Proof of Proposition 4. When the two firms locate at $(x_A{}^* = 0, x_B{}^* = 1)$, the total costs have been illustrated in (11.11), solving the first-order derivative with respect to k^2, β, and θ, we have

$$\frac{\partial tc^*}{\partial k^2} = \frac{1}{9\beta} > 0, \quad \frac{\partial tc^*}{\partial \beta} = -\frac{k^2}{9\beta^2} < 0, \quad \frac{\partial tc^*}{\partial \theta} = \frac{1}{2} > 0 \tag{11.33}$$

When the two firms locate at $(x_A{}^* = x_{A1}, x_B{}^* = x_{B1})$, the total costs have been illustrated in (11.11), solving the first-order derivative with respect to k^2, we have

$$\frac{\partial tc^*}{\partial k^2} = \frac{2k^4-9\beta k^2(13+4\theta)+81\beta^2\theta(7+2\theta)+\left[k^2+9\beta(2-\theta)\right]\sqrt{4k^4+81\beta^2(3+2\theta)^2-36k^2\beta(9+2\theta)}}{324\beta^2\sqrt{4k^4+81\beta^2(3+2\theta)^2-36k^2\beta(9+2\theta)}} \tag{11.34}$$

We also split the numerator into two items; the first item is $P_1 = 2k^4 - 9\beta k^2(13 + 4\theta) + 81\beta^2\theta(7 + 2\theta)$ and the second item is $P_2 = \left[k^2 + 9\beta(2-\theta)\right]\sqrt{4k^4 + 81\beta^2(3+2\theta)^2 - 36k^2\beta(9+2\theta)}$. It is easy to see that $P_2 > 0$ and,

$$P_1 \begin{cases} < 0 \; if \; \theta \in \left(0, \frac{\sqrt{41}-4}{3}\right) \; or \; \theta \in \left(\frac{\sqrt{41}-4}{3}, 1\right) \; and \; k^2 \in \left(\frac{9\beta\left(13+4\theta-\sqrt{169+48\theta}\right)}{4}, {k_1}^2\right) \\ > 0 \; if \; \theta \in \left(\frac{\sqrt{41}-4}{3}, 1\right) \; and \; k^2 \in \left(\frac{9\beta(1+\theta)}{4}, \frac{9\beta\left(13+4\theta-\sqrt{169+48\theta}\right)}{4}\right) \end{cases} \tag{11.35}$$

When $P_1 < 0$, considering the first term and the second term, we have

$$\begin{aligned} P_3 &= \left[2k^4 - 9\beta k^2(13+4\theta) + 81\beta^2\theta(7+2\theta)\right]^2 \\ &\quad -\left[k^2 + 9\beta(2-\theta)\right]^2\left[4k^4 + 81\beta^2(3+2\theta)^2 - 36k^2\beta(9+2\theta)\right] \\ &= 36\beta\left\{-8k^6 + 216k^4\beta(3+\theta) + 729\beta^3(3+4\theta)\right. \\ &\quad \left.[-3+\theta(3+2\theta)] - 243k^2\beta^2[-9+\theta(27+8\theta)]\right\} \end{aligned} \tag{11.36}$$

Thus, we have

$$\frac{\partial P_3}{\partial k^2} = 36\beta\left\{-24k^4 + 432k^2\beta(3+\theta) - 243\beta^2[\theta(27+8\theta)-9]\right\} \tag{11.37}$$

Solving $\partial P_3/\partial k^2 = 0$, we have

$$\begin{aligned} {k_2}^2 &= \tfrac{9\beta}{4}\left(12 + 4\theta - \sqrt{6}\sqrt{27+7\theta}\right), \\ {k_3}^2 &= \tfrac{9\beta}{4}\left(12 + 4\theta + \sqrt{6}\sqrt{27+7\theta}\right) \end{aligned} \tag{11.38}$$

And it is easy to see that ${k_2}^2 < 9\beta(1+\theta)/4 < {k_1}^2 < {k_3}^2$; thus, $\partial P_3/\partial k^2 > 0$. P_3 is increasing in k^2. Hence, we have

$$\begin{aligned} P_3|_{k^2=\frac{9\beta(1+\theta)}{4}} &= \tfrac{6561}{2}\beta^4(-1+3\theta)\left(-17+9\theta^2\right), \\ P_3|_{k^2={k_1}^2} &= -39366\beta^4(3+\theta)\left(-43 - 6\theta + 10\sqrt{6}\sqrt{3+\theta}\right) > 0 \end{aligned} \tag{11.39}$$

[h]

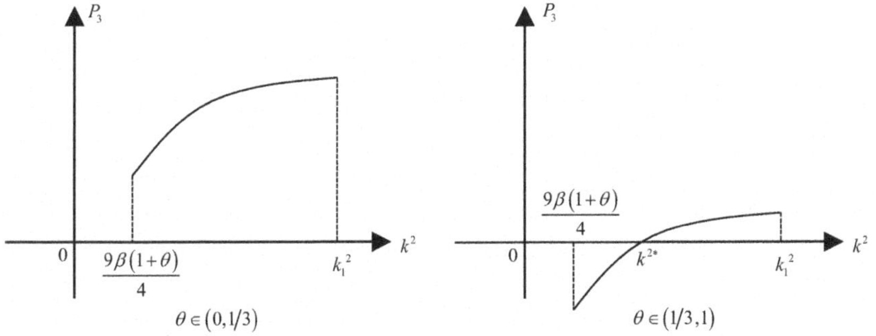

Fig. A.4 The graph of P_3 with respect to k^2

From (11.39), it is easy to see that $P_3 > 0$ if $\theta < 1/3$ while P_3 is negative if $\theta > 1/3$ and k^2 is low. Solving $P_3 = 0$, we could obtain a critical value k^{2*}. That is

Summarizing all the above cases, we have the following conclusions:

1) If $\theta \in (0, 1/3)$, we have $P_3 > 0$. Hence, the result shows that $P_1 + P_2 < 0$ and $\partial tc^* / \partial k^2 < 0$.
2) If $\theta \in \left(1/3, \left(\sqrt{41} - 4\right)/3\right)$ and $k^2 \in (9\beta(1 + \theta)/4, k^{2*})$, we have $P_3 < 0$. The result shows that $P_1 + P_2 > 0$ and $\partial tc^* / \partial k^2 > 0$.
3) If $\theta \in \left(1/3, \left(\sqrt{41} - 4\right)/3\right)$ and $k^2 \in (k^{2*}, k_1{}^2)$, we have $P_3 > 0$. The result shows that $P_1 + P_2 < 0$ and $\partial tc^* / \partial k^2 < 0$.
4) If $\theta \in \left(\left(\sqrt{41} - 4\right)/3, 1\right)$ and $k^2 \in \left(9\beta\left(1+\theta\right)/4, 9\beta\left(13 + 4\theta - \sqrt{169 + 48\theta}\right)/4\right)$, we have $P_1 + P_2 > 0$ and $\partial tc^* / \partial k^2 > 0$.
5) If $\theta \in \left(\left(\sqrt{41} - 4\right)/3, 1\right)$ and $k^2 \in \left(9\beta\left(13 + 4\theta - \sqrt{169 + 48\theta}\right)/4, k^{2*}\right)$, we have $P_3 < 0$. The result shows $P_1 + P_2 > 0$ and $\partial tc^* / \partial k^2 > 0$;
6) If $\theta \in \left(\left(\sqrt{41} - 4\right)/3, 1\right)$ and $k^2 \in (k^{2*}, k_1{}^2)$, we have $P_3 > 0$. The result shows that $P_1 + P_2 < 0$ and $\partial tc^* / \partial k^2 < 0$.

Therefore,

$$\frac{\partial tc^*}{\partial k^2}\begin{cases} < 0 \ if \ \theta \in (0, 1/3) \ \ or \ \ \theta \in (1/3, 1) \ \ and \ \ k^2 \in \left(k^{2*}, k_1{}^2\right) \\ > 0 \ if \ \theta \in (1/3, 1) \ \ and \ \ k^2 \in \left(9\beta\,(1+\theta)\,/4, k^{2*}\right) \end{cases} \tag{11.40}$$

When the two firms locate at ($x_A{}^* = x_{A1}, x_B{}^* = x_{B1}$), solving the first-order derivative of the total costs with respect to β, we have

$$\frac{\partial tc^*}{\partial \beta} = -\frac{k^2\left\{2k^4-9\beta k^2(13+4\theta)+81\beta^2\theta(7+2\theta)+\left[k^2+9\beta(2-\theta)\right]\sqrt{4k^4+81\beta^2(3+2\theta)^2-36k^2\beta(9+2\theta)}\right\}}{324\beta^3\sqrt{4k^4+81\beta^2(3+2\theta)^2-36k^2\beta(9+2\theta)}} \tag{11.41}$$

The first-order derivative is $\partial tc^* / \partial k^2$; therefore,

$$\frac{\partial tc^*}{\partial \beta}\begin{cases} > 0 \ if \ \theta \in (0, 1/3) \ \ or \ \ \theta \in (1/3, 1) \ \ and \ \ k^2 \in \left(k^{2*}, k_1{}^2\right) \\ < 0 \ if \ \theta \in (1/3, 1) \ \ and \ \ k^2 \in \left(9\beta\,(1+\theta)\,/4, k^{2*}\right) \end{cases} \tag{11.42}$$

When the two firms locate at ($x_A{}^* = x_{A1}, x_B{}^* = x_{B1}$), solving the first-order derivative of the total costs with respect to θ, we have

$$\frac{\partial tc^*}{\partial \theta} = \frac{\left\{-4k^4+36\beta k^2(5+2\theta)-81\beta^2(3+8\theta+4\theta^2)+\left[-2k^2+9\beta(5+2\theta)\right]\sqrt{4k^4+81\beta^2(3+2\theta)^2-36k^2\beta(9+2\theta)}\right\}}{72\beta\sqrt{4k^4+81\beta^2(3+2\theta)^2-36k^2\beta(9+2\theta)}} \tag{11.43}$$

Using the same analysis method in $\partial tc^* / \partial k^2$, it is easy to see that the denominator is positive. We split the numerator into two items; the first item is $P_4 = -4k^4 + 36\beta k^2(5+2\theta) - 81\beta^2(3+8\theta+4\theta^2)$, and the second item is $P_5 = \left[-2k^2 + 9\beta\,(5+2\theta)\right]\sqrt{4k^4 + 81\beta^2(3+2\theta)^2 - 36k^2\beta\,(9+2\theta)}$. It is easy to see that $P_5 > 0$ and,

$$P_4\begin{cases} < 0 \ if \ \theta \in \left(\frac{2\sqrt{2}-1}{3}, 1\right) \ \ and \ \ k^2 \in \left(\frac{9\beta(1+\theta)}{4}, \frac{9\beta(5+2\theta-\sqrt{2}\beta\sqrt{11+6\theta})}{2}\right) \\ > 0 \ if \ \theta \in \left(0, \frac{2\sqrt{2}-1}{3}\right) \ \ or \ \ \theta \in \left(\frac{2\sqrt{2}-1}{3}, 1\right) \ \ and \ \ k^2 \in \left(\frac{9\beta(5+2\theta-\sqrt{2}\beta\sqrt{11+6\theta})}{2}, k_1{}^2\right) \end{cases} \tag{11.44}$$

When $P_4 < 0$, considering the first term and the second term, we have

$$\begin{aligned} P_6 &= \left[-4k^4 + 36\beta k^2 (5 + 2\theta) - 81\beta^2 \left(3 + 8\theta + 4\theta^2\right)\right]^2 \\ &\quad -\left[-2k^2 + 9\beta (5 + 2\theta)\right]^2 \left[4k^4 + 81\beta^2(3 + 2\theta)^2 - 36k^2\beta (9 + 2\theta)\right] \\ &= 72\beta \left\{8k^6 - 54k^4\beta (9 + 4\theta) - 729\beta^3(3 + 2\theta)^3 + 972k^2\beta^2 (2 + \theta) (5 + 2\theta)\right\} \end{aligned} \tag{11.45}$$

Thus, we have

$$\frac{\partial P_6}{\partial k^2} = 864\beta \left[k^2 - 9\beta (2 + \theta)\right] \left[2k^2 - 9\beta (5 + 2\theta)\right] > 0 \tag{11.46}$$

P_3 is increasing in k^2. Hence, we have

$$\begin{aligned} P_6\big|_{k^2=\frac{9\beta(1+\theta)}{4}} &= -\frac{729}{8}\beta^3 (2 + 3\theta) [1 + 9\theta (2 + \theta)] < 0, \\ P_6\big|_{k^2=k_1{}^2} &= -\frac{2187}{2}\beta^3 \left[-747 + 176\sqrt{6}\sqrt{3+\theta} - 4\theta \left(65 + 3\theta - 8\sqrt{6}\sqrt{3+\theta}\right)\right] > 0 \end{aligned} \tag{11.47}$$

From (11.47), it is easy to see that there is a critical value $k_1{}^{2*}$ which satisfies $P_6 = 0$, that is,

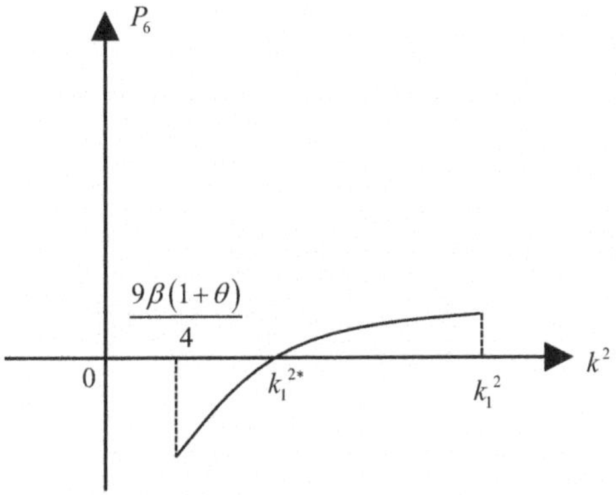

Fig. A.5 The graph of P_6 if $P_4 < 0$

Summarizing all the above cases, we have the following conclusions:

1) If $\theta \in \left(0, \left(2\sqrt{2}-1\right)/3\right)$, we have $P_4 > 0$ and $\partial tc^*/\partial\theta > 0$.
2) If $\theta \in \left(\left(\sqrt{41}-4\right)/3, 1\right)$ and $k^2 \in (9\beta(1+\theta)/4, {k_1}^{2*})$, we have $P_6 < 0$. The result shows that $P_4 + P_5 > 0$ and $\partial tc^*/\partial\theta > 0$.
3) If $\theta \in \left(\left(\sqrt{41}-4\right)/3, 1\right)$ and $k^2 \in \left({k_1}^{2*}, 9\beta\left(5+2\theta - \sqrt{2}\beta\sqrt{11+6\theta}\right)/2\right)$, we have $P_6 > 0$. The result shows that $P_4 + P_5 < 0$ and $\partial tc^*/\partial\theta < 0$.
4) If $\theta \in \left(\left(\sqrt{41}-4\right)/3, 1\right)$ and $k^2 \in \left(9\beta\left(5+2\theta-\sqrt{2}\beta\sqrt{11+6\theta}\right)/2, k^{2*}\right)$, we have $\partial tc^*/\partial\theta > 0$.

Therefore,

$$\frac{\partial tc^*}{\partial\theta}\begin{cases} < 0 \ if\ \theta \in \left(\left(2\sqrt{2}-1\right)/3, 1\right) \ and\ k^2 \in \left({k_1}^{2*}, 9\beta\left(5+2\theta-\sqrt{2}\beta\sqrt{11+6\theta}\right)/2\right) or \\ \theta \in (1/3, 1) \ and\ k^2 \in \left(k^{2*}, {k_1}^2\right) \\ > 0 \ if\ \theta \in \left(0, \left(2\sqrt{2}-1\right)/3\right) \ or\ \theta \in \left(\left(2\sqrt{2}-1\right)/3, 1\right) and \\ k^2 \in \left(9\beta(1+\theta)/4, {k_1}^{2*}\right) \\ \quad or\ \theta \in \left(\left(2\sqrt{2}-1\right)/3, 1\right) and\ k^2 \in \left(9\beta\left(5+2\theta-\sqrt{2}\beta\sqrt{11+6\theta}\right)/2, {k_1}^{2*}\right) \end{cases} \tag{11.48}$$

When the two firms locate at $(x_{A^*} = x_{A3}, x_{B^*} = x_{B3})$, the total costs have been illustrated in (11.11), solving the first-order derivative with respect to k^2, β, and θ, we have

$$\begin{aligned} \frac{\partial tc^*}{\partial k^2} &= \frac{4k^2 + 9\beta - 18\beta\theta}{162\beta^2} > 0, \\ \frac{\partial tc^*}{\partial \beta} &= -\frac{k^2\left[4k^2 + 9\beta(1-2\theta)\right]}{162\beta^3} < 0, \\ \frac{\partial tc^*}{\partial \theta} &= \frac{27\beta - 4k^2 + 18\beta\theta}{36\beta} > 0 \end{aligned} \tag{11.49}$$

References

Brekke, R. K., Siciliani, L., & Straume, O. R. (2010). Price and Quality in Spatial Competition. *Regional Science and Urban Economics, 40*(6), 471–480.

Brekke, R. K., Siciliani, L., & Straume, O. R. (2012). Quality Competition with Profit Constraints. *Journal of Economic Behavior and Organization, 84*(6), 642–659.

Brinkman, J. C. (2016). Congestion, Agglomeration, and the Structure of Cities. *Journal of Urban Economics, 94*(1), 13–31.

Cellini, R., Siciliani, L., & Straume, O. R. (2018). A Dynamic Model of Quality Competition with Endogenous Prices. *Journal of Economic Dynamic and Control, 94*(9), 190–206.

Cremer, H., & Thisse, J.-F. (1991). Location Models of Horizontal Differentiation: A Special Case of Vertical Differentiation Models. *The Journal of Industrial Economics, 39*(4), 383–390.

Cremer, H., & Thisse, J.-F. (1994). Commodity Taxation in Differentiated Oligopoly. *International Economic Review, 35*(3), 613–633.

D'Aspremont, C., Gabszewicz, J. J., & Thisse, J.-F. (1979). On Hotelling's "Stability in Competition". *Econometrica, 47*(5), 1145–1150.

Esteves, R.-B., & Reggiani, C. (2014). Elasticity of Demand and Behaviour Based Price Discrimination. *International Journal of Industrial Organization, 32*(9), 46–56.

Fernández, L. J. E., de Cea Ch, J., & de Grange C, L. (2005). Production Costs, Congestion, Scope and Scale Economies in Urban Bus Transportation Corridors. *Transportation Research Part A, 39*(9), 383–403.

Grilo, I., Shy, O., & Thisse, J.-F. (2001). Price Competition When Consumer Behavior Is Characterized by Conformity or Vanity. *Journal of Public Economics, 80*(3), 385–408.

Hotelling, H. (1929). Stability in Competition. *Economic Journal, 39*(153), 41–57.

Ishibashi, K. (2001). Strategic Delegation under Quality Competition. *Journal of Economics, 73*(1), 25–56.

Ishida, J., Matsumura, T., & Matsushima, N. (2011). Market Competition, R&D and Firm Profits in Asymmetric Oligopoly. *The Journal of Industrial Economics, 59*(3), 484–505.

Kim, J. (2019). Estimating the Social Cost of Congestion Using the Bottleneck Model. *Economics of Transportation, 19*(1), 1–20.

Laine, T. L., & Ma, C.-t. A. (2017). Quality and Competition Between Public and Private Firms. *Journal of Economic Behavior and Organization, 140*(6), 336–353.

Lambertini, L., & Orsini, R. (2005). The Existence of Equilibrium in a Differentiated Duopoly with Network Externalities. *The Japanese Economic Review, 56*(1), 55–66.

Laussel, D., de Montmarin, M., & Van Long, N. (2004). Dynamic Duopoly with Congestion Effects. *International Journal of Industrial Organization, 22*(1), 655–677.

Li, W., & Chen, J. (2018). Pricing and Quality Competition in a Brand-Differentiated Supply Chain. *International Journal of Production Economics, 202*(1), 97–108.

Matsumura, T., & Matsushima, N. (2007). Congestion-Reducing Investments and Economic Welfare in a Hotelling Model. *Economic Letters, 96*(2), 161–167.

Niu, B., Mu, Z., & Li, B. (2019). O2O Results in Traffic Congestion Reduction and Sustainability Improvement: Analysis of "Online-to-Store" Channel and Uniform Pricing Strategy. *Transportation Research Part E, 122*(1), 481–505.

de Palma, A., & Proost, S. (2006). Imperfect Competition and Congestion in the City. *Journal of Urban Economics, 60*(1), 185–209.

Pennerstorfer, D. (2017). Can Competition Keep the Restrooms Clean? Price, Quality and Spatial Competition. *Regional Science and Urban Economics, 64*(5), 117–136.

Reimann, M., Yu, X., & Yu, Z. (2019). Managing a Closed-Loop Supply Chain with Process Innovation for Remanufacturing. *European Journal of Operation Research, 276*(2), 510–518.

Salop, C. S. (1979). Monopolistic Competition with Outside Goods. *The Bell Journal of Economics, 10*(1), 141–156.

Shao, J., Yang, H., Xing, X., & Yang, L. (2016). E-Commerce and Traffic Congestion: An Economic and Policy Analysis. *Transportation Research Part B, 83*(1), 91–103.

Siciliani, L., & Straume, O. R. (2019). Competition and Equity in Health Care Markets. *Journal of Health Economics, 64*(3), 1–14.

Sweet, M. N. (2014). Do Firms Flee Traffic Congestion? *Journal of Transport Geography, 35*(1), 40–49.

Wadud, Z., & Chen, D. (2018). Congestion Impacts of Shopping Using Vehicle Tracking Data. *Journal of Transport Geography, 70*(1), 123–130.

12

Quality and Price Competition in Spatial Markets

Kurt R. Brekke, Luigi Siciliani, and Odd Rune Straume

12.1 Introduction

In many spatial markets, firms do not compete only on price but also on the quality of the product or service they offer. In particular, quality is a key issue in markets such as health care, elderly care, child care and

K. R. Brekke
Department of Economics, Norwegian School of Economics (NHH), Bergen, Norway
e-mail: kurt.brekke@nhh.no

L. Siciliani
Department of Economics and Related Studies, University of York, York, UK
e-mail: luigi.siciliani@york.ac.uk

O. R. Straume (✉)
Department of Economics/NIPE, University of Minho, Braga, Portugal

Department of Economics, University of Bergen, Bergen, Norway
e-mail: o.r.straume@eeg.uminho.pt

S. Colombo (ed.), *Spatial Economics Volume I*,
https://doi.org/10.1007/978-3-030-40098-9_12

education. Although prices are sometimes regulated in these industries, this is far from a universal rule. In many OECD countries, providers (e.g., hospitals, nursing homes, nurseries, schools) compete on both quality and price.[1] In these markets, quality is not only a key factor for consumers but also an important concern for policy makers. In particular, the role of provider competition is often a hotly debated issue. In many countries, policy makers have introduced measures to enhance competition, such as public reporting of quality measures, but the perceived effects of competition on quality provision are far from unanimous, neither in the public debate nor in the academic literature.

In this chapter we provide a comprehensive theoretical analysis of the relationship between competition and quality provision in spatial markets where providers compete along two different dimensions: quality and price. We do so by synthesising the key insights from four different papers in the literature, Brekke et al. (2010, 2017, 2018) and Cellini et al. (2018), into a unified theoretical framework. This allows us to paint a very broad picture of the various mechanisms that potentially determine the effect of competition on quality provision in such markets, and it allows us to analyse and discuss the interrelationships among these mechanisms.

The richness of our analysis is exhibited along at least three different dimensions. First, we conduct our analysis both in a static and in a dynamic setting. The main part of our analysis, where we apply the most general set of assumptions, is based on a static framework in which providers choose price and quality in a one-shot game. However, a simplified version of this model is then extended to a dynamic differential-game setting, where providers interact strategically over an infinite time horizon. This allows us to identify additional relevant mechanisms, related to intertemporal strategic interaction, that are absent in a static framework.

Second, we analyse the relationship between competition and quality provision by using a wide range of competition measures: (1) as is common in the spatial competition literature, we use the marginal cost of travelling as an inverse measure of competition intensity; (2) we study

[1] See, e.g., Brekke et al. (2018) and Cellini et al. (2018) for a wide range of examples.

the effect of entry and exit, using the number of providers in the market as a measure of the degree of competition; (3) we analyse the effects of reduced competition in the form of a merger between incumbent providers; and, finally, (4) in the dynamic part of the analysis, we compare the outcomes under two dynamic solution concepts that differ in terms of the 'competitiveness' of the assumed strategic environment.

Third, we consider a set of assumptions regarding consumer and provider preferences that is much richer than in most of the existing spatial competition literature. On the consumer side, we allow for the possibility of *income effects in demand* by modelling utility as being concave in income. On the provider side, we allow for the possibility that providers are both *risk averse*, in the sense of having decreasing marginal utility of profits, and *motivated*, in the sense that the provision of high quality has an independent value for providers beyond the profits generated.

Although our modelling framework is in principle applicable to all types of spatial markets in which firms compete on price and quality, we believe that our analysis is particularly relevant for the kind of markets that we have previously mentioned: health care, long-term care, child care and education. There are several reasons for this. First, these are markets where the spatial dimension is very important and where consumer choices rely crucially on both quality and travel distance (in addition to price).[2] Second, these are also markets where the unit demand assumption of standard spatial competition models is particularly appropriate, since each consumer demands one medical treatment or one admission to a school or a nursing home, for example.

Third, we also believe that our 'non-standard' assumptions of income effects in demand and risk-averse and motivated providers are highly relevant in these markets. *Income effects in demand* are likely to be relevant because of the magnitude of the consumption expenditures involved in these markets. The considerable cost involved in paying for child care, for

[2]There are many empirical studies confirming that travelling distance and quality are key predictors for the choice of hospitals (Gutacker et al. 2016; Kessler and McClellan 2000; Tay 2003), nursing homes (Grabowski et al. 2013; Rahman and Foster 2015; Shugarman and Brown 2006; Zwanziger et al. 2002) and schools (Chumacero et al. 2011; Gibbons et al. 2008; Hastings et al. 2005).

example, implies that the price-elasticity of demand is likely to depend on the parents' level of income. *Provider motivation*, as in concern for quality provision beyond profit maximisation, is also arguably a relevant feature in these markets. In the theoretical health economics literature, the idea that providers (doctors, nurses, health-care managers) care about the quality offered to patients has long been recognised.[3] The same can reasonably be argued for teachers who care about the learning of their students, for example. Finally, a sizeable share of the providers in these kinds of markets is made up of relatively small organisations with sole or highly concentrated ownership.[4] This makes it reasonable to assume that providers might be *risk averse*, with decreasing marginal utility of profits.

Our analysis shows that the relationship between competition and quality provision is highly ambiguous and depends on a number of different factors, including income effects in demand, provider risk aversion and motivation, the nature of the cost dependence between output and quality, and the presence (or not) of dynamic strategic interaction. This relationship is also much more complex than what is suggested by the earlier (and very scarce) theoretical literature on price and quality competition in spatial markets, such as Economides (1993), Ma and Burgess (1993) and Gravelle (1999).[5]

The theoretical complexity and general ambiguity of the relationship between competition and quality is also reflected in the available (though still fairly limited) empirical evidence. Due to the availability of quality indicators, the largest body of evidence is found in hospital and nursing home markets. For both types of markets, the findings are mixed.[6] The

---

[3]See, e.g., Ellis and McGuire (1986), Chalkley and Malcomson (1998), Eggleston (2005), Choné and Ma (2011), Kaarboe and Siciliani (2011), Brekke et al. (2011, 2012).

[4]See Brekke et al. (2018) for a wide range of examples.

[5]Outside the spatial competition literature, there is also a small literature studying the relationship between competition and quality provision using a representative consumer framework and typically also finding this relationship to be ambiguous. Examples of this literature include Banker et al. (1998), Sutton (1996) and Symeonidis (2000).

[6]For the US hospital market, a positive effect of competition on quality is found by Gowrisankaran and Town (2003) and Escarce et al. (2006), while a negative effect is found by Mukamel et al. (2002). Similarly, regarding the effect of competition on quality in nursing home markets, Zhao (2016) finds a positive effect in the US, whereas Grabowski (2004) and Forder and Allan (2014) find negative effects in the US and in the UK, respectively.

main contribution of our comprehensive theoretical analysis is to uncover key mechanisms that can inform the interpretation of the mixed empirical evidence and that can help in determining under which circumstances a positive or negative relationship between competition and quality provision in spatial markets can be expected.

The rest of the chapter is organised as follows. The next section presents a spatial duopoly model of quality and price competition, which is first applied in a context of a static non-cooperative game and then subsequently applied (in a simplified form) to a dynamic differential-game setting. Section 12.3 extends the static version of the model from two to n providers, and we use this extended version of the model to analyse the effects of entry/exit and mergers. Finally, Sect. 12.4 concludes the chapter with a brief summary of our main findings.

12.2 A Spatial Duopoly Model of Quality and Price Competition

Consider a market for a good that is offered by two firms (which we will henceforth refer to as *providers*) located at each endpoint of the unit line $S = [0, 1]$. Consumers are uniformly distributed on S with a total mass normalised to 1. Each consumer has a gross income Y and demands one unit of the good from the most preferred provider. For a consumer located at $x \in S$, the utility of buying the good from Provider i, located at $z_i \in S$ and offering the good with quality q_i at price p_i, is assumed to be given by

$$U(x, z_i) = u(y(p_i)) + \beta q_i - \tau |x - z_i|, \qquad (12.1)$$

where $y(p_i) = Y - p_i$ is the net income of the consumer if buying the good from Provider i. The marginal utility of quality and the marginal disutility of travelling are given by $\beta > 0$ and $\tau > 0$, respectively.[7] As is

[7]For simplicity, the marginal utility of quality and the marginal disutility of travelling are both assumed to be constant. However, all our main results remain qualitatively unchanged under the

a standard convention in the spatial economics literature, we will use τ as an inverse measure of the degree of competition in the market. We also assume that $u'(y_i) > 0$ and $u''(y_i) \leq 0$. The case of strictly decreasing marginal utility of income, $u''(y_i) < 0$, implies that there are income effects in consumption of the good.[8]

Each consumer located on S decides which provider to attend by considering costs and benefits along three different dimensions: quality differences, price differences and differences in travelling costs. If each consumer in the market makes a utility-maximising choice of provider, the demand for Provider i is given by

$$D_i\left(p_i, p_j, q_i, q_j\right) = \frac{1}{2} + \frac{\beta\left(q_i - q_j\right) + u\left(y\left(p_i\right)\right) - u\left(y\left(p_j\right)\right)}{2\tau};$$
$$i, j = 1, 2; \; i \neq j. \tag{12.2}$$

Under the assumptions of unit demand and full market coverage, the demand for the competing Provider j is given by $D_j = 1 - D_i$.

Suppose that the total cost of providing x units of the good with quality q is given by a general cost function $c(x, q)$, where $\partial c/\partial x > 0$, $\partial c/\partial q > 0$, $\partial^2 c/\partial x^2 \geq 0$, $\partial^2 c/\partial q^2 < 0$ and $\partial^2 c/\partial q \partial x \gtrless 0$. Thus, we allow for the possibility that output and quality are either complements ($\partial^2 c/\partial q \partial x < 0$) or substitutes ($\partial^2 c/\partial q \partial x > 0$) in terms of production costs. In the latter case, a higher quality level increases the marginal cost of output, which would typically be the case if higher quality requires the use of better (and therefore more expensive) inputs. However, in the case of cost complementarity, a higher quality level reduces the marginal cost of output (or, equivalently, a higher level of output reduces the marginal

alternative assumptions of decreasing marginal utility of quality and increasing marginal cost of travelling.

[8]Our specific formulation of the utility function in (12.1), where the marginal utility of income is affected by a price change but not by a change in travelling costs, implies that we should interpret these costs as *non-monetary* costs (or, more generally, as the disutility of travelling). See Brekke et al. (2010) for a more general case in which travelling costs are partly monetary and partly non-monetary.

cost of quality provision), which could be the case if there are sufficiently strong 'learning-by-doing' effects in the provision of the good.

Given the above assumptions regarding demand and costs, the profits of Provider i are given by

$$\pi_i\left(p_i, p_j, q_i, q_j\right) = p_i D_i\left(p_i, p_j, q_i, q_j\right) - c\left(D_i\left(p_i, p_j, q_i, q_j\right), q_i\right); \quad i, j = 1, 2; \; i \neq j. \tag{12.3}$$

However, we allow for the possibility that the providers in this market are not necessarily pure profit maximisers. More specifically, we assume that the providers are partly *motivated* and therefore attach a *separate* value (i.e., independent of profits) to the quality of the good they offer. Furthermore, we also allow for the possibility that the providers are *risk averse*, in the sense that they derive decreasing marginal utility from profits. As argued in the introduction to this chapter, the assumption of partly motivated providers in markets like health care, elderly care, child care and education is widely accepted in the theoretical literature. Many markets of these kinds also exhibit a high prevalence of small providers with highly concentrated (or even sole) ownership, which makes the assumption of risk aversion more plausible (see Brekke et al. 2018, for examples and further discussion).

The above-described assumptions are incorporated by letting Provider i maximise the following objective function

$$\Omega_i\left(p_i, p_j, q_i, q_j\right) = v\left(\pi_i\left(p_i, p_j, q_i, q_j\right)\right) + b\left(q_i\right); \quad i, j = 1, 2; \quad i \neq j, \tag{12.4}$$

where $v'(\pi_i) > 0$, $v''(\pi_i) \leq 0$, $b'(q_i) \geq 0$ and $b''(q_i) \leq 0$. Provider risk aversion is captured by $v''(\pi_i) < 0$, whereas provider motivation is captured by $b'(q_i) > 0$. The standard case of risk-neutral profit-maximising providers is given by $v''(\pi_i) = 0$ and $b'(q_i) = 0$.

Finally, we assume that competition in this market takes the form of a static non-cooperative game in which each provider chooses quality and price simultaneously. The most plausible alternative to this game, as suggested by the literature, is a dynamic game in which quality and price decisions are made sequentially. However, our main results do not depend crucially on simultaneous versus sequential decision making (see Brekke et al. 2010, 2018, for further details). In this chapter we therefore maintain the assumption of simultaneous quality and price decisions, which greatly eases the analytical exposition.

12.2.1 Qualities and Prices in the Symmetric Nash Equilibrium

The first-order conditions for the optimal price and quality of Provider i are given by, respectively,[9]

$$\frac{\partial \Omega_i}{\partial p_i} = v'(\pi_i)\left[D_i - \left(p_i - \frac{\partial c(D_i, q_i)}{\partial D_i}\right)\frac{u'(y(p_i))}{2\tau}\right] = 0 \quad (12.5)$$

and

$$\frac{\partial \Omega_i}{\partial q_i} = v'(\pi_i)\left[\left(p_i - \frac{\partial c(D_i, q_i)}{\partial D_i}\right)\frac{\beta}{2\tau} - \frac{\partial c(D_i, q_i)}{\partial q_i}\right] + b'(q_i) = 0. \quad (12.6)$$

For a given quality level, the optimal price is given by the standard inverse elasticity rule, $(p_i - \partial c(D_i, q_i)/\partial D_i)/p_i = 1/[(\partial D_i/\partial p_i)\, p_i/D_i]$, whereby more price-elastic demand leads to a lower price, all else equal. Notice, however, that the price-elasticity of demand is affected by the potential presence of income effects in demand, through the marginal utility of income, $u'(y)$.

[9] The second-order conditions are provided in Appendix 1.

For a given price, the optimal quality is set at a level that balances profit concerns and motivational concerns for quality provision. The profitability of quality provision depends crucially on the magnitude of the *profit margin*, defined as $p_i - \partial c(D_i, q_i)/\partial D_i$, which determines how profitable it is to increase demand by offering higher quality. Notice also that, in the presence of motivated providers (i.e., $b'(q_i) > 0$), quality is set at a level where *marginal profits* (defined as $\partial \pi_i/\partial q_i$ and given by the expression in square brackets in (12.6)) are negative. At the optimal quality level, the marginal loss of profits is exactly offset by the marginal motivational benefit of quality provision.

In the symmetric Nash equilibrium, $p_i = p_j = p^*$ and $q_i = q_j = q^*$, implying $D_i = D_j = \frac{1}{2}$. The equilibrium price and quality in this equilibrium are implicitly given by the following pair of equations:[10]

$$F_p := \frac{1}{2} - \left(p^* - \frac{\partial c\left(\frac{1}{2}, q^*\right)}{\partial D_i}\right) \frac{u'\left(y\left(p^*\right)\right)}{2\tau} = 0, \tag{12.7}$$

$$F_q := v'\left(\pi\left(p^*, q^*\right)\right)\left[\left(p^* - \frac{\partial c\left(\frac{1}{2}, q^*\right)}{\partial D_i}\right)\frac{\beta}{2\tau} - \frac{\partial c\left(\frac{1}{2}, q^*\right)}{\partial q_i}\right] + b'\left(q^*\right) = 0, \tag{12.8}$$

where $\pi\left(p^*, q^*\right) = \frac{p^*}{2} - c\left(\frac{1}{2}, q^*\right)$.

12.2.2 Effects of Increased Competition

How do the providers respond, in terms of price and quality choices, to a situation where competition intensifies? As previously indicated, we are primarily interested in the relationship between competition intensity and equilibrium quality provision. In this version of our model, an increase in the degree of competition is measured by a reduction in the parameter τ. Using a standard comparative statics approach, the effect of increased

[10]Conditions for stability and uniqueness of this equilibrium are given in Appendix 1.

competition on the equilibrium *price* is given by (see Appendix 1)

$$\frac{\partial p^*}{\partial \tau} = -\frac{u'(y(p^*))\left(p^* - \frac{\partial c\left(\frac{1}{2},q^*\right)}{\partial D_i}\right)}{2\tau^2\Delta} \times \left[b''(q^*) - \frac{\partial^2 c\left(\frac{1}{2},q^*\right)}{\partial q_i^2}\left(v'(\pi(p^*,q^*)) + v''(\pi(p^*,q^*))\right)\right], \tag{12.9}$$

where $\Delta := \left(\partial F_p/\partial p^*\right)\left(\partial F_q/\partial q^*\right) - \left(\partial F_q/\partial p^*\right)\left(\partial F_p/\partial q^*\right) > 0$.

When providers compete along two dimensions (price and quality), prices do not necessarily fall as a result of intensified competition. It can be shown (see Appendix 1) that $\partial p^*/\partial \tau > 0$ (i.e., more competition leads to lower prices) if one of the following two conditions are met: (i) the degree of cost substitutability between output and quality is not too strong (i.e., $\partial^2 c/\partial q_i \partial D_i$ is non-positive or positive but sufficiently small), or (ii) the degree of provider risk aversion is not too strong (i.e., the value of $-v''(\pi_i)/v'(\pi_i)$ is not too large). We can also show (see again Appendix 1) that higher prices as a result of more competition is a possibility only if more competition also leads to higher quality in equilibrium. Thus, and not surprisingly, higher price and lower quality as a result of more competition is not a feasible outcome.

The effect of competition on equilibrium *quality* provision is even more ambiguous and analytically given by

$$\frac{\partial q^*}{\partial \tau} = \frac{\left(p^* - \frac{\partial c\left(\frac{1}{2},q^*\right)}{\partial D_i}\right)}{8\tau^3\Delta}\left[\begin{array}{c}\beta\left(p^* - \frac{\partial c\left(\frac{1}{2},q^*\right)}{\partial D_i}\right)\left[\begin{array}{c} u'(y(p^*))\,v''(\pi(p^*,q^*)) \\ +2u''(y(p^*))\,v'(\pi(p^*,q^*))\end{array}\right] \\ -2\tau\frac{\partial c\left(\frac{1}{2},q^*\right)}{\partial q_i}u'(y(p^*))\,v''(\pi(p^*,q^*))\end{array}\right]. \tag{12.10}$$

In order to isolate the different mechanisms at play, we will first consider three different special cases, before giving a more general condition characterising the sign of (12.10).

12.2.2.1 No Income Effects in Demand and Risk-Neutral Providers

This case is captured by $v''(\pi) = u''(y) = 0$. From (12.10) it is straightforward to see that, in this case, $\partial q^*/\partial \tau = 0$. In other words, increased competition has no effect on equilibrium quality provision. This is a result of two counteracting effects that exactly offset each other. On the one hand, a reduction in τ makes demand more quality-elastic, leading to an increase in quality provision for given prices. However, a reduction in τ also makes demand more price-elastic, leading to lower optimal prices. This price drop reduces each provider's profit margin and therefore reduces the incentives to attract more demand by increasing quality. When both demand and firm objectives are linear in prices, these two effects exactly cancel each other. This is the 'standard' case considered in the literature (e.g., Gravelle 1999; Ma and Burgess 1993). Notice that profit maximisation is not a necessary condition for this result. As long as $v''(\pi) = u''(y) = 0$, the relationship between competition intensity and equilibrium quality provision does not depend on whether the providers are motivated or not. In any case, $\partial q^*/\partial \tau = 0$.

12.2.2.2 Income Effects in Demand and Risk-Neutral Providers

This case is captured by $v''(\pi) = 0$ and is a somewhat simplified version of the case studied in Brekke et al. (2010). Setting $v''(\pi) = 0$, (12.10) reduces to

$$\frac{\partial q^*}{\partial \tau} = \frac{2\beta u''(y(p^*))\, v'(\pi(p^*, q^*)) \left(p^* - \frac{\partial c\left(\frac{1}{2}, q^*\right)}{\partial D_i}\right)^2}{8\tau^3 \Delta}. \tag{12.11}$$

It is straightforward to see that $\partial q^*/\partial \tau < 0$ if $u''(y(p^*)) < 0$. Thus, when we introduce income effects in demand, more competition leads to higher quality in equilibrium. The reason is that the presence of income effects makes the demand functions concave in prices in this model. Because of decreasing marginal utility of income, the marginal effect of a price reduction on demand gets smaller as the price drops. This implies that the price reduction following a reduction in τ is smaller in the presence of income effects, which in turn means that the indirect negative effect of increased competition on quality provision, through a lower profit margin, is smaller.[11] Consequently, the dominating effect of competition is the direct effect of more quality-elastic demand, leading to higher quality in equilibrium. Notice, once more, that provider motivation is irrelevant for the relationship between competition and quality in this case.

12.2.2.3 No Income Effects in Demand and Risk-Averse Providers

This case is captured by $u''(y) = 0$ and is similar to the scenario analysed in Brekke et al. (2018). Setting $u''(y) = 0$, (12.10) reduces to

$$\frac{\partial q^*}{\partial \tau} = \frac{\left(p^* - \frac{\partial c\left(\frac{1}{2}, q^*\right)}{\partial D_i}\right)\left[\beta\left(p^* - \frac{\partial c\left(\frac{1}{2}, q^*\right)}{\partial D_i}\right) - 2\tau \frac{\partial c\left(\frac{1}{2}, q^*\right)}{\partial q_i}\right] u'\left(y\left(p^*\right)\right) v''\left(\pi\left(p^*, q^*\right)\right)}{8\tau^3 \Delta}. \tag{12.12}$$

Notice that the expression in square brackets in (12.12) is negative if $b'(q^*) > 0$ and zero if $b'(q^*) = 0$. From this observation, we can immediately draw the following conclusion: $\partial q^*/\partial \tau > (=) 0$ if $b'(q^*) > (=) 0$. Thus, in the presence of provider risk aversion, increased competition yields *lower* quality provision, but only if the providers are *motivated*. In this case, each provider chooses quality at a level where

---

[11]Keeping the quality level constant, we can derive the effect of increased competition on the equilibrium price by total differentiation of (12.7), yielding

$$\left|\frac{\partial p^*}{\partial \tau}\right|_{q^* \text{ constant}} = -\frac{\partial F_p/\partial \tau}{\partial F_p/\partial p^*} > 0.$$

The presence of income effects in demand does not affect the numerator, but adds another negative term to the denominator, making it larger in absolute value (see Appendix 1). In turn, this reduces the magnitude of the price increase (for a given quality level).

marginal profits are negative (i.e., $\partial \pi_i / \partial q_i < 0$). In equilibrium, this marginal loss is optimally traded off against the marginal motivational gain of quality provision (i.e., $b'(q_i) > 0$). However, when providers are risk averse, the valuation of the marginal profit loss is not constant but depends on the size of the profits. More precisely, the lower (higher) the provider's profits, the larger (smaller) is the weight attached to a given loss associated with negative marginal profits. This mechanism has an impact on the indirect effect of competition on quality provision, via the price responses. As previously explained, increased competition leads to a price reduction, all else equal, because of more price-elastic demand. This has two relevant effects on a risk-averse provider's optimal choice of quality, both of which go in the same direction. As before, a lower price reduces the profit margin, which reduces the incentive for quality provision. In addition, a lower price also reduces the profit *level*, which amplifies the loss associated with negative marginal profits and therefore yields an incentive to reduce the quality level. The presence of this latter effect implies that the indirect effect of competition on quality (via the price responses) outweighs the direct effect.[12] As a result, increased competition leads to lower quality in equilibrium.

12.2.2.4 The General Case

Finally, in the general case, where we allow for both income effects in demand and risk-averse providers, we can derive from (12.10) an easily interpretable condition for the relationship between competition intensity and equilibrium quality provision. Define $\sigma_u := -u''(y(p^*))/u'(y(p^*))$ and $\sigma_v := -v''(\pi(p^*, q^*))/v'(\pi(p^*, q^*))$ as the Arrow-Pratt measures of absolute risk aversion for consumers and providers, respectively. The effect of competition on quality can then be

[12] The sign of $\partial q^*/\partial \tau$ is given by the sign of $(\partial F_q/\partial p^*)(\partial F_p/\partial \tau) - (\partial F_p/\partial p^*)(\partial F_q/\partial \tau)$. Provider risk aversion only affects $\partial F_q/\partial p^* > 0$, adding a positive term to this factor and thereby making it larger (see Appendix 1). Thus, the presence of provider risk aversion reinforces the strategic quality response to a change in prices.

characterised as follows:

$$\frac{\partial q^*}{\partial \tau} < (>)\, 0 \text{ if } \frac{\sigma_u}{\sigma_v} > (<) \frac{-\left[\left(p^* - \frac{\partial c\left(\frac{1}{2}, q^*\right)}{\partial D_i}\right)\beta - 2\tau \frac{\partial c\left(\frac{1}{2}, q^*\right)}{\partial q_i}\right]}{2\beta\left(p^* - \frac{\partial c\left(\frac{1}{2}, q^*\right)}{\partial D_i}\right)}. \tag{12.13}$$

Thus, increased competition leads to higher (lower) quality provision if the income effects in demand are sufficiently large relative to the degree of provider risk aversion. Furthermore, a necessary (but not sufficient) condition for lower quality in response to increased competition is that the providers are motivated (which implies that the numerator on the right-hand side of (12.13) is positive). The intuition for this condition follows from the discussion of each of the three special cases analysed above.

12.2.3 Dynamic Quality and Price Competition

The above analysis is conducted in a static setting where the providers choose price and quality once and for all. This approach ignores a potentially relevant dynamic aspect of quality competition, namely, that quality provision requires investments and that quality could be seen as a *stock* that can be increased over time only if the investment in quality is higher than its depreciation. Again, this approach is arguably particularly relevant for health care and education markets, in which key dimensions of quality require investments in machinery and/or staff. We will therefore extend the previous analysis by placing the duopoly model in a differential-game framework, in which each provider chooses price and quality investments repeatedly over an infinite time horizon. Due to the analytical complexity of the differential-game framework, we simplify the model by setting $v''(\pi) = u''(y) = b'(q) = 0$. Thus, the analysis in this section, which builds on the analysis in Cellini et al. (2018), can be seen as a dynamic version of the 'standard' spatial competition model analysed in Sect. 12.2.2.1.

Let $I_i(t)$ be the investment in quality by Provider i at time t, while $q_i(t)$ is reinterpreted as the stock of quality at time t. Assuming that the quality stock depreciates at a rate of $\delta > 0$, the law of motion of quality is given by

$$\frac{dq_i(t)}{dt} := \dot{q}_i(t) = I_i(t) - \delta q_i(t). \tag{12.14}$$

The separation of quality into an investment and a stock variable also necessitates a reformulation of the provider cost function, which we now parameterise as follows:

$$c(D_i, q_i, I_i) = wD_i + \frac{1}{2}\left(\gamma I_i^2 + \theta q_i^2\right), \tag{12.15}$$

where w, γ and θ are all positive constants. Thus, we assume cost independence between output and quality. Instantaneous profits for Provider i at time t are then given by

$$\pi_i(t) = (p_i(t) - w) D_i(t) - \frac{1}{2}\left(\gamma (I_i(t))^2 + \theta (q_i(t))^2\right), \tag{12.16}$$

where D_i is defined as previously.

We consider two different solution concepts: *open-loop* and *feedback closed-loop*. In the *open-loop* setting, each provider commits to a complete investment plan at the start of the game and sticks to it forever. An open-loop strategy is thus a time profile of quality investments, depending only on the initial state of the world (i.e., the quality stocks at $t = 0$) and time. In the *feedback closed-loop* setting, on the other hand, each provider is allowed to update the investment choice at each point in time, in response to the current values of the states (which summarise the past history of the game). Thus, a feedback closed-loop strategy for Provider i specifies the investment choice in period t as a function of own and rival's quality stocks in the same period, $q_i(t)$ and $q_j(t)$. Although the feedback closed-loop solution is arguably a more appealing solution concept, partly since it is strongly time consistent, the open-loop solution might nevertheless be appropriate in strongly regulated contexts, where the providers are required to commit to long-term investment plans.

12.2.3.1 Open-Loop Solution

Suppose that the providers use open-loop decision rules. Assuming a constant time preference discount rate ρ, the maximisation problem of Provider i is given by

$$\max_{I(t),p(t)} \int_0^{+\infty} \pi_i (t) e^{-\rho t} dt, \tag{12.17}$$

subject to (12.14) and an equivalent condition for Provider j and the initial conditions $q_i (0) = q_{i0} > 0$ and $q_j (0) = q_{j0} > 0$. The derivation of the equilibrium strategies is given in Appendix 2. Here we focus on the *steady-state* values of price and quality, which are given by

$$p^{OL} = w + \tau, \tag{12.18}$$

$$q^{OL} = \frac{\beta}{2 (\gamma\delta (\delta + \rho) + \theta)}. \tag{12.19}$$

In qualitative terms, this steady-state outcome is very similar to the Nash equilibrium of the static version of the game, which is not surprising, given the one-shot nature of the open-loop strategies. Thus, just as in the static case, increased competition (measured by a reduction in τ) has no effect on steady-state quality provision when providers are risk-neutral and when there are no income effects in demand.

12.2.3.2 Feedback Closed-Loop Solution

Suppose now that the providers use closed-loop strategies and therefore interact strategically over time. A unique and globally asymptotically stable feedback closed-loop solution exists if the cost parameters θ and/or τ are sufficiently large relative to the marginal willingness to pay for quality, β. In this case, the equilibrium dynamic strategies of Provider i are given by (see Appendix 2)

$$p_i(t) = w + \tau + \frac{\beta\left(q_i(t) - q_j(t)\right)}{3}, \tag{12.20}$$

$$I_i(t) = \frac{1}{\gamma}\left(\alpha_1 + \alpha_3 q_i(t) + \alpha_5 q_j(t)\right), \tag{12.21}$$

for $i, j = 1, 2$, $i \neq j$, where the coefficients $\alpha_1 > 0$, $\alpha_3 < 0$ and $\alpha_5 < 0$ are functions of the model's parameters. A key feature of these strategies is the negative sign of the coefficient α_5, which implies that quality investments are *intertemporal strategic substitutes*, meaning that Provider i responds to a higher quality stock of Provider j by reducing quality investments. The intuition is related to the strategic relationship between price and quality. A quality increase by Provider j implies, all else equal, a demand reduction for Provider i. This demand loss implies that the demand for Provider i becomes more price-elastic and Provider i therefore responds by reducing the price. But this price reduction lowers the profit margin and therefore also reduces the profitability of attracting more demand by offering higher quality. Consequently, Provider i will also respond by reducing quality investments.

In the symmetric *steady state*, price and quality are given by

$$p^{CL} = w + \tau, \tag{12.22}$$

$$q^{CL} = \frac{\beta\gamma}{3\left(\gamma(\delta + \rho) - \alpha_3\right)\left(\gamma\delta - (\alpha_3 + \alpha_5)\right)}. \tag{12.23}$$

Whereas the steady-state price is the same under the two solution concepts (open-loop and feedback closed-loop), and equal to the Nash equilibrium prices in the static version of the game, the steady-state provision of quality differs. There are two things worth noticing. First, it can be shown that $\partial q^{CL}/\partial\tau < 0$. Thus, in a dynamic setting with feedback closed-loop investment strategies, the direct effect of increased competition on quality provision outweighs the indirect effect via lower prices, implying that more intense competition yields higher steady-state quality provision, even in the absence of provider risk aversion and income effects in demand.

However, the two dynamic solution concepts also provide us with an alternative measure of the intensity of competition. One can reasonably argue that the feedback closed-loop solution implies a more competitive framework than the open-loop solution, since—in the former solution concept—each provider can respond strategically to its competitor's investment choices at each point in time. By comparing the steady-state quality provision under the two solution concepts, it is possible to show that $q^{CL} < q^{OL}$.[13] Thus, the introduction of dynamic competition (as represented by the feedback closed-loop solution) adds an additional strategic effect that leads to lower quality provision, all else equal. This dynamic strategic effect is related to how current quality investments affect future price competition. Suppose that Provider j increases its quality stock by investing more. From (12.20), the strategic response of Provider i is to reduce the price. Thus, higher quality today will induce stronger price competition in the future. This intertemporal strategic mechanism dampens the providers' incentives to invest in quality, thus yielding lower steady-state quality provision.

12.3 A Spatial n-Firm Model of Quality and Price Competition

Thus far, we have conducted our analysis (static or dynamic) in a duopoly framework with only two providers. In this section we extend the static analysis of Sect. 12.2 to the case of an n-firm oligopoly. This allows us to analyse other relevant dimensions of competition, such as entry/exit of providers and horizontal mergers, and their implications for equilibrium quality provision.

[13] See Cellini et al. (2018) for formal proofs of $\partial q^{CL}/\partial \tau < 0$ and $q^{CL} < q^{OL}$.

Suppose that n providers are equidistantly located a circle with circumference equal to 1 and that consumers (with total mass equal to 1) are uniformly distributed on the same circle. All other assumptions are identical to the ones of the duopoly model presented in Sect. 12.2.

We assume that n providers simultaneously choose price and quality. Since competition is localised, the demand of each provider depends, in addition to own price and quality, on the prices and qualities of the provider's two neighbours. In the symmetric equilibrium, though, all prices and all qualities are equal. For simplicity, we can therefore express the demand function of Provider i when $p_{i-1} = p_{i+1} = p_j$ and $q_{i-1} = q_{i+1} = q_j$. In this case, the demand of Provider i is given by

$$D_i\left(p_i, p_j, q_i, q_j\right) = \frac{1}{n} + \frac{\beta\left(q_i - q_j\right) + u\left(y\left(p_i\right)\right) - u\left(y\left(p_j\right)\right)}{\tau}. \tag{12.24}$$

The first-order conditions for optimal price and quality choices, respectively, are given by[14]

$$\frac{\partial \Omega_i}{\partial p_i} = v'\left(\pi_i\right)\left[D_i - \left(p_i - \frac{\partial c\left(D_i, q_i\right)}{\partial D_i}\right)\frac{u'\left(y_i\right)}{\tau}\right] = 0, \tag{12.25}$$

$$\frac{\partial \Omega_i}{\partial q_i} = v'\left(\pi_i\right)\left[\left(p_i - \frac{\partial c\left(D_i, q_i\right)}{\partial D_i}\right)\frac{\beta}{\tau} - \frac{\partial c\left(D_i, q_i\right)}{\partial q_i}\right] + b'\left(q_i\right) = 0. \tag{12.26}$$

In the symmetric Nash equilibrium, $p_i = p_j = p^*$ and $q_i = q_j = q^*$, implying $D_i = \frac{1}{n}$. The equilibrium price and quality in this equilibrium are implicitly given by the following pair of equations:[15]

[14]The second-order conditions are almost identical to the ones in the duopoly game and therefore not reported.

[15]Conditions for stability and uniqueness of this equilibrium are given in Appendix 3.

$$G_p := \frac{1}{n} - \left(p^* - \frac{\partial c\left(\frac{1}{n}, q^*\right)}{\partial D_i}\right)\frac{u'\left(y\left(p^*\right)\right)}{\tau} = 0, \qquad (12.27)$$

$$G_q := v'\left(\pi\left(p^*, q^*\right)\right)\left[\left(p^* - \frac{\partial c\left(\frac{1}{n}, q^*\right)}{\partial D_i}\right)\frac{\beta}{\tau} - \frac{\partial c\left(\frac{1}{n}, q^*\right)}{\partial q_i}\right] + b'\left(q^*\right) = 0, \qquad (12.28)$$

where $\pi\left(p^*, q^*\right) = \frac{p^*}{n} - c\left(\frac{1}{n}, q^*\right)$.

12.3.1 Entry

Suppose that there is entry of more providers to the industry, increasing the competition in the market. What are the effects on equilibrium prices and qualities? We answer this question by considering a marginal increase of n in the symmetric equilibrium, thus applying the standard (though admittedly unrealistic) assumption that entry leads to reallocation of all incumbent providers until symmetry is regained. An alternative and more plausible interpretation is that different levels of n correspond to different market configurations related to population density (e.g., with high levels of n related to urban areas and low levels of n related to rural ones).

The effect of entry on equilibrium *prices* is given by (see Appendix 3 for details)

$$\frac{\partial p^*}{\partial n} = \frac{\left[\begin{array}{c}\left(b''\left(q^*\right) - v'\left(\pi\left(p^*, q^*\right)\right)\frac{\partial^2 c\left(\frac{1}{n}, q^*\right)}{\partial D_i^2} - v''\left(\pi\left(p^*, q^*\right)\right)\frac{\partial^2 c\left(\frac{1}{n}, q^*\right)}{\partial q_i^2}\right)\\ \left(\tau + u'\left(y\left(p^*\right)\right)\frac{\partial^2 c\left(\frac{1}{n}, q^*\right)}{\partial D_i^2}\right) - v'\left(\pi\left(p^*, q^*\right)\right)\frac{\partial^2 c\left(\frac{1}{n}, q^*\right)}{\partial D_i \partial q_i}\\ \left(\beta - u'\left(y\left(p^*\right)\right)\frac{\partial^2 c\left(\frac{1}{n}, q^*\right)}{\partial D_i \partial q_i}\right)\end{array}\right]}{\Theta n^2 \tau}, \qquad (12.29)$$

where $\Theta := \left(\partial G_p / \partial p^*\right)\left(\partial G_q / \partial q^*\right) - \left(\partial G_q / \partial p^*\right)\left(\partial G_p / \partial q^*\right) > 0$. Although the effect is generally ambiguous, it follows from inspection of (12.29) that a sufficient condition for $\partial p^* / \partial n < 0$, implying that more entry reduces prices, is that both $v''(\pi)$ and $\partial^2 c/\partial D_i \partial q_i$ are sufficiently small in magnitude.

The effect of entry on equilibrium *quality* provision is given by

$$\frac{\partial q^*}{\partial n} = \frac{\left[\begin{array}{l} -n\tau v'(\pi(p^*, q^*))\left[\beta - \frac{\partial^2 c\left(\frac{1}{n}, q^*\right)}{\partial D_i \partial q_i} u'(y(p^*))\right] \\ -nu''(y(p^*))\, v'(\pi(p^*, q^*))\left(\beta \frac{\partial^2 c\left(\frac{1}{n}, q^*\right)}{\partial D_i^2} + \tau \frac{\partial^2 c\left(\frac{1}{n}, q^*\right)}{\partial D_i \partial q_i}\right) \\ \left(p^* - \frac{\partial c\left(\frac{1}{n}, q^*\right)}{\partial D_i}\right) - v''(\pi(p^*, q^*))\left(\tau + \frac{\partial^2 c\left(\frac{1}{n}, q^*\right)}{\partial D_i^2} u'(y(p^*))\right) \\ \left(\beta\left(p^* - \frac{\partial c\left(\frac{1}{n}, q^*\right)}{\partial D_i}\right) - \tau \frac{\partial c\left(\frac{1}{2}, q^*\right)}{\partial q_i}\right) \end{array}\right]}{\Theta n^3 \tau^2}. \tag{12.30}$$

The sign of this expression is determined by the sign of the numerator, which consists of three terms. It is once more useful to consider a few special cases. If there are no income effects and providers are risk-neutral, the second and third terms vanish, and the sign of $\partial q^*/\partial n$ is given by the sign of the first term in the numerator. We are then left with two effects that potentially counteract each other. First, higher n reduces demand for each provider, which makes demand more price-elastic and therefore leads to lower prices. This reduces in turn the profit margin and therefore also leads to lower quality, all else equal. This is the sole effect identified by Economides (1993), who reports a negative relationship between the number of firms and equilibrium quality provision in a similar type of Salop model. However, as long as output and quality are not cost-independent, lower demand (because of higher n) either increases (if $\partial^2 c/\partial D_i \partial q_i < 0$) or reduces (if $\partial^2 c/\partial D_i \partial q_i > 0$) the marginal cost of quality provision, thus reinforcing or counteracting the first effect. Provider entry therefore leads to lower quality provision as long as the degree of cost substitutability between output and quality is sufficiently low.

If we allow for *income effects in demand* but keep the assumption of risk-neutral providers, the sign of $\partial q^*/\partial n$ depends also on one additional term, namely, the second term in the numerator of (12.30). If

$\partial^2 c/\partial D_i \partial q_i$ is positive, or negative but small in magnitude, this extra term is positive, contributing towards higher quality as a result of firm entry. The intuition is similar to the equivalent mechanism caused by a reduction in τ, as discussed in Sect. 12.2.2.

Finally, if there are no income effects in demand but *providers are risk averse*, the sign of $\partial q^*/\partial n$ is determined by the sign of the sum of the first and the third term in the numerator of (12.30). The third term is unambiguously negative as long as providers are motivated (which makes the last factor in this term negative), thus contributing towards lower quality as a result of entry. Once more, the intuition is similar to the equivalent mechanism resulting from a reduction in τ.

Summing up, if we use an increase in n as our measure of competition, instead of a reduction in τ, the scope for a negative relationship between competition and quality provision is generally larger. In both cases, though, the presence of risk-averse and motivated providers enlarges the scope for such a negative relationship. On the other hand, the presence of income effects in demand generally contributes in the opposite direction.

12.3.2 Merger

The number of competing providers in a market can change not only through entry or exit of providers but also through mergers between incumbent providers in the market. In this final part of the analysis, which builds on Brekke et al. (2017), we will consider the effects of a merger between two providers, assuming that there is no plant closure after the merger, implying that post-merger competition takes the form of an asymmetric game between single-plant and multi-plant providers.[16] For analytical tractability, we set $n = 3$ in the pre-merger game and revert to the case of $v''(\pi) = u''(y) = b'(q) = 0$. We also parameterise the cost function as follows:

$$c(D_i, q_i) = wq_i D_i + \frac{1}{2}\theta q_i^2, \qquad (12.31)$$

[16] In this model there are no incentives for plant closure after a merger unless there are sufficiently large plant-fixed costs.

where $w > 0$ and $\theta > 0$. Thus, we assume that output and quality are cost substitutes. This is a likely scenario reflecting, for example, unit cost increasing in quality and total costs linear in output. With $n = 3$, the demand function for Provider i is

$$D_i\left(p_{i-1}, p_i, p_{i+1}, q_{i-1}, q_i, q_{i+1}\right) = \frac{1}{3} + \frac{\beta\left(2q_i - q_{i-1} - q_{i+1}\right) - \left(2p_i - p_{i-1} - p_{i+1}\right)}{2\tau}. \quad (12.32)$$

In the symmetric *pre-merger* game, the Nash equilibrium is given by

$$p^* = \frac{\tau\theta + w\left(\beta - w\right)}{3\theta}, \quad (12.33)$$

$$q^* = \frac{\beta - w}{3\theta}. \quad (12.34)$$

Existence, stability and uniqueness of this equilibrium require that θ and τ are sufficiently high. We also see from (12.34) that $\beta > w$ is required for an interior solution with positive quality levels.

Suppose now that two of the providers merge, implying a coordination of price and quality decisions at the two plants controlled by the merged entity. Let us denote the merged provider's price and quality choices by subscript m and the corresponding choices for the remaining provider by subscript o. In the asymmetric *post-merger* game, the Nash equilibrium is given by

$$p_m = \frac{\left(7\tau\theta - 12\left(\beta - w\right)^2\right)\left(\tau\theta + w\left(\beta - w\right)\right)}{9\theta\left(3\tau\theta - 4\left(\beta - w\right)^2\right)}, \quad (12.35)$$

$$p_o = \frac{\left(5\tau\theta - 4\left(\beta - w\right)^2\right)\left(\tau\theta + 3w\left(\beta - w\right)\right)}{9\theta\left(3\tau\theta - 4\left(\beta - w\right)^2\right)}, \quad (12.36)$$

$$q_m = \frac{\left(7\tau\theta - 12\left(\beta - w\right)^2\right)\left(\beta - w\right)}{9\theta\left(3\tau\theta - 4\left(\beta - w\right)^2\right)}, \tag{12.37}$$

$$q_o = \frac{\left(5\tau\theta - 4\left(\beta - w\right)^2\right)\left(\beta - w\right)}{3\theta\left(3\tau\theta - 4\left(\beta - w\right)^2\right)}. \tag{12.38}$$

What are the effects of the merger on prices and qualities? Comparing (12.33)–(12.34) with (12.35)–(12.38), it is fairly straightforward to verify that $p_m < p^*$, $p_o \gtrless p^*$, $q_m < q^*$ and $q_o > q^*$.[17] Thus, a merger leads to a reduction of both prices and qualities for the merger participants. These are the results of conflicting incentives for the merged provider. If we look at each of the two dimensions of competition (quality and price) in isolation, the merged provider has an incentive to reduce competition along each of these dimensions, which implies higher prices (for given quality levels) and lower qualities (for given price levels). However, higher prices give an incentive to increase quality (because of a higher profit margin), and lower qualities give an incentive to reduce prices (because of lower, and therefore more price-elastic, demand). It turns out that, in this particular model, the incentives to reduce competition along the quality dimension outweigh the incentives to reduce competition along the price dimension. Consequently, a merger leads to a reduction in quality provision, and the prices drop because of the quality reduction.

However, for the outside provider, which does not take part in the merger, the incentives are very different. This provider will respond to a merger by *increasing* quality provision. The reason is that qualities are what we choose to call *net strategic substitutes* in this model.[18] The dominating mechanism is one that goes through the price responses to a change in quality provision. Suppose that Provider j increases its quality level. This will shift demand towards the other providers, including Provider $i \neq j$. This lowers the price-elasticity of demand for Provider

[17] All results in this section are derived by straightforward algebra and the formal proofs are therefore omitted. We refer the interested reader to Brekke et al. (2017) for a more detailed analysis.

[18] See Brekke et al. (2017) for a more precise and comprehensive analysis.

i, who therefore responds by increasing the price. But a price increase implies a higher profit margin, so Provider i will therefore also increase the quality.

Interestingly, we can also show that the *average quality* in the market (i.e., average quality provision weighted by the market shares of the providers) *increases* as a result of the merger. A contributing factor to this result is that the merged providers lose market shares after the merger. Thus, the merger implies that some consumers switch to a higher quality provider. In terms of average quality, this effect is sufficiently strong to outweigh the quality reduction by the merged providers.

12.4 Conclusions

In this chapter we have presented a comprehensive theoretical analysis of two-dimensional competition in spatial markets, where providers compete on both quality and price. The main focus of our analysis is to provide a detailed characterisation of the relationship between competition and quality provision. The analysis is based on a unified theoretical framework that synthesises the key insights of several existing theoretical contributions to the spatial competition literature, more specifically, Brekke et al. (2010, 2017, 2018) and Cellini et al. (2018). Our unified framework also allows us to capture the insights of earlier contributions, such as Economides (1993), Ma and Burgess (1993) and Gravelle (1999), as special cases.

Our analysis shows that the relationship between competition and quality provision is complex and highly ambiguous and depends on several factors such as the presence (or not) of income effects in demand, provider risk aversion and motivation, cost dependence between output and quality, and dynamic strategic interaction. It also depends on how the degree of competition is measured. All else equal, the scope for a positive effect of competition on quality provision is smaller if increased competition is measured by an increase in the number of providers rather than a decrease in the marginal cost of travelling. Furthermore, the presence of income effects in demand contributes in the direction of a positive relationship between competition and quality provision, whereas the presence of risk-averse and motivated providers generally contributes in the opposite direction.

Although our analysis in principle applies to all spatial markets with price and quality competition, we think that it is particularly applicable to markets such as health care, long-term care, child care and education, which are all characterised by features that fit the key assumptions of our theoretical framework. Thus, we believe that our analysis can both guide the interpretation of empirical evidence and also serve to inform policy making directed towards such markets.

Appendix 1

In this appendix we provide existence conditions for the Nash equilibrium in the static duopoly game and underlying details of the comparative statics results.

The second-order conditions for Provider i's optimal choices of price and quality are given by

$$\frac{\partial^2 \Omega_i}{\partial p_i^2} = v'(\pi_i)\frac{1}{2\tau}\left[\left(p_i - \frac{\partial c(D_i, q_i)}{\partial D_i}\right)u''(y(p_i)) - \left(2 + \frac{\partial^2 c(D_i, q_i)}{\partial D_i^2}\frac{u'(y(p_i))}{2\tau}\right)u'(y(p_i))\right] < 0 \quad (12.39)$$

and

$$\frac{\partial^2 \Omega_i}{\partial q_i^2} = v''(\pi_i)\left[\left(p_i - \frac{\partial c(D_i, q_i)}{\partial D_i}\right)\frac{\beta}{2\tau} - \frac{\partial c(D_i, q_i)}{\partial q_i}\right]^2 - v'(\pi_i)\left[\left(\frac{\beta}{2\tau}\frac{\partial^2 c(D_i, q_i)}{\partial D_i^2} + \frac{\partial^2 c(D_i, q_i)}{\partial D_i \partial q_i}\right) + \frac{\partial^2 c(D_i, q_i)}{\partial q_i^2}\right] + b''(q_i) < 0. \quad (12.40)$$

Since the first-order condition for the optimal price implies $p_i > \partial c(D_i, q_i)/\partial D_i$, then (12.39) always holds, while (12.40) holds if output and quality are cost substitutes (i.e., $\partial^2 c(D_i, q_i)/\partial D_i \partial q_i > 0$) or, in case of cost complementarities, if the magnitude of $\left|\partial^2 c(D_i, q_i)/\partial D_i \partial q_i\right|$ is not too large.

From (12.7)–(12.8), which implicitly define the symmetric Nash equilibrium, we derive

$$\frac{\partial F_p}{\partial p^*} = -\frac{u'(y(p^*))}{2\tau} + \left(p^* - \frac{\partial c\left(\frac{1}{2}, q^*\right)}{\partial D_i}\right)\frac{u''(y(p^*))}{2\tau} < 0, \quad (12.41)$$

$$\begin{aligned}\frac{\partial F_q}{\partial q^*} &= -v''(\pi(p^*, q^*))\frac{\partial^2 c\left(\frac{1}{2}, q^*\right)}{\partial q_i^2} \\ &\quad - v'(\pi(p^*, q^*))\left[\frac{\partial^2 c\left(\frac{1}{2}, q^*\right)}{\partial D_i \partial q_i}\frac{\beta}{2\tau} + \frac{\partial^2 c\left(\frac{1}{2}, q^*\right)}{\partial q_i^2}\right] + b''(q^*) < 0,\end{aligned} \quad (12.42)$$

$$\frac{\partial F_p}{\partial q^*} = \frac{\partial^2 c\left(\frac{1}{2}, q^*\right)}{\partial D_i \partial q_i}\frac{u'(y(p^*))}{2\tau} > (<)\, 0 \text{ if } \frac{\partial^2 c\left(\frac{1}{2}, q^*\right)}{\partial D_i \partial q_i} > (<)\, 0, \quad (12.43)$$

$$\begin{aligned}\frac{\partial F_q}{\partial p^*} &= \frac{v''(\pi(p^*, q^*))}{2}\left[\left(p^* - \frac{\partial c\left(\frac{1}{2}, q^*\right)}{\partial D_i}\right)\frac{\beta}{2\tau} - \frac{\partial c\left(\frac{1}{2}, q^*\right)}{\partial q_i}\right] \\ &\quad + v'(\pi(p^*, q^*))\frac{\beta}{2\tau} > 0,\end{aligned} \quad (12.44)$$

$$\frac{\partial F_p}{\partial \tau} = \left(p^* - \frac{\partial c\left(\frac{1}{2}, q^*\right)}{\partial D_i}\right)\frac{u'(y(p^*))}{2\tau^2} > 0, \quad (12.45)$$

$$\frac{\partial F_q}{\partial \tau} = -v'(\pi(p^*, q^*))\left(p^* - \frac{\partial c\left(\frac{1}{2}, q^*\right)}{\partial D_i}\right)\frac{\beta}{2\tau^2} < 0. \quad (12.46)$$

Existence and stability of the Nash equilibrium require that $\partial F_p/\partial p^* < 0$, $\partial F_q/\partial q^* < 0$ and $(\partial F_p/\partial p^*)(\partial F_q/\partial q^*) - (\partial F_q/\partial p^*)(\partial F_p/\partial q^*) > 0$. Using (12.41)–(12.44), the latter condition is equivalent to the condition

$$
\begin{aligned}
&4\tau \left(\begin{array}{c} u'(y(p^*)) \\ -u''(y(p^*))\left(p^* - \frac{\partial c(\frac{1}{2},q^*)}{\partial D_i}\right) \end{array} \right) \\
&\times \left(\begin{array}{c} \frac{\partial^2 c(\frac{1}{2},q^*)}{\partial q_i^2}\left(v'(\pi(p^*,q^*)) + v''(\pi(p^*,q^*))\right) \\ -b''(q^*) \end{array} \right) \\
&+ \frac{\partial^2 c\left(\frac{1}{2},q^*\right)}{\partial D_i \partial q_i} \left(\begin{array}{c} 2\tau u'(y(p^*))\, v''(\pi(p^*,q^*)) \frac{\partial c(\frac{1}{2},q^*)}{\partial q_i} \\ -\beta \left[\begin{array}{c} u'(y(p^*))\, v''(\pi(p^*,q^*)) \\ +2u''(y(p^*))\, v'(\pi(p^*,q^*)) \end{array} \right] \left(p^* - \frac{\partial c(\frac{1}{2},q^*)}{\partial D_i}\right) \end{array} \right) \\
&> 0.
\end{aligned}
\tag{12.47}
$$

If output and quality are cost substitutes, this condition is satisfied if the degree of provider risk-aversion (measured by $-v''(\pi)/v'(\pi)$) is not too large. In case of cost complementarity, we need to impose the additional condition that the magnitude of $\left|\partial^2 c(D_i, q_i)/\partial D_i \partial q_i\right|$ is not too large.

Applying Cramer's Rule, the effects of a marginal reduction in τ on equilibrium prices and qualities are given by, respectively,

$$
\frac{\partial p^*}{\partial \tau} = \frac{\frac{\partial F_q}{\partial \tau}\frac{\partial F_p}{\partial q^*} - \frac{\partial F_p}{\partial \tau}\frac{\partial F_q}{\partial q^*}}{\frac{\partial F_p}{\partial p^*}\frac{\partial F_q}{\partial q^*} - \frac{\partial F_q}{\partial p^*}\frac{\partial F_p}{\partial q^*}} \tag{12.48}
$$

and

$$
\frac{\partial q^*}{\partial \tau} = \frac{\frac{\partial F_q}{\partial p^*}\frac{\partial F_p}{\partial \tau} - \frac{\partial F_p}{\partial p^*}\frac{\partial F_q}{\partial \tau}}{\frac{\partial F_p}{\partial p^*}\frac{\partial F_q}{\partial q^*} - \frac{\partial F_q}{\partial p^*}\frac{\partial F_p}{\partial q^*}}. \tag{12.49}
$$

A sufficient (but not necessary) condition for the numerator in (12.48) to be positive (and thus for $\partial p^*/\partial \tau$ to be positive) is $\partial F_p/\partial q^* \leq 0$, which requires $\partial^2 c\left(1/2, q^*\right)/\partial D_i \partial q_i \leq 0$. By applying the relevant expressions in (12.41)–(12.46), (12.48) can be expressed as (12.9) in Sect. 12.2. Using that expression, it is straightforward to show that $\partial p^*/\partial \tau > (<) \, 0$ if

$$\sigma_v := -\frac{v''\left(\pi\left(p^*, q^*\right)\right)}{v'\left(\pi\left(p^*, q^*\right)\right)} < (>) \, 1 - \frac{b''\left(q^*\right)}{v'\left(\pi\left(p^*, q^*\right)\right) \frac{\partial^2 c\left(\frac{1}{2}, q^*\right)}{\partial q_i^2}}. \quad (12.50)$$

What is the scope for a price increase as a result of more competition, that is, $\partial p^*/\partial \tau < 0$? Using again (12.48), $\partial p^*/\partial \tau < 0$ requires

$$\frac{\partial F_p}{\partial q^*} > \frac{\frac{\partial F_p}{\partial \tau}\frac{\partial F_q}{\partial q^*}}{\frac{\partial F_q}{\partial \tau}}. \quad (12.51)$$

On the other hand, equilibrium existence requires

$$\frac{\partial F_p}{\partial q^*} < \frac{\frac{\partial F_p}{\partial p^*}\frac{\partial F_q}{\partial q^*}}{\frac{\partial F_q}{\partial p^*}}. \quad (12.52)$$

Thus, a price increase as a result of more competition is possible only if

$$\frac{\frac{\partial F_p}{\partial p^*}\frac{\partial F_q}{\partial q^*}}{\frac{\partial F_q}{\partial p^*}} > \frac{\frac{\partial F_p}{\partial \tau}\frac{\partial F_q}{\partial q^*}}{\frac{\partial F_q}{\partial \tau}}. \quad (12.53)$$

Using (12.41)–(12.46), this condition is equivalent to the condition

$$\frac{\sigma_u}{\sigma_v} > \frac{-\left(\left(p^* - \frac{\partial c\left(\frac{1}{2}, q^*\right)}{\partial D_i}\right)\beta - 2\tau \frac{\partial c\left(\frac{1}{2}, q^*\right)}{\partial q_i}\right)}{2\beta\left(p^* - \frac{\partial c\left(\frac{1}{2}, q^*\right)}{\partial D_i}\right)}, \quad (12.54)$$

which is identical to the condition for $\partial q^*/\partial\tau < 0$, given by (12.13) in Sect. 12.2. Thus, higher prices as a result of more competition is only possible if quality also increases.

Appendix 2

In this appendix we provide a relatively brief and general overview of the solution procedures for deriving the open-loop and feedback closed-loop equilibria presented in Sect. 12.2.3. For further details, we refer to Cellini et al. (2018).

Open-Loop Solution

Given the optimisation problem of Provider i defined by (12.17), the current-value Hamiltonian is given by[19]

$$H_i = (p_i - c)\left(\frac{1}{2} + \frac{\beta\left(q_i - q_j\right)}{2\tau} - \frac{p_i - p_j}{2\tau}\right) - \frac{\gamma}{2}I_i^2 - \frac{\theta}{2}{q_i}^2 + \mu_i\left(I_i - \delta q_i\right) + \mu_j\left(I_j - \delta q_j\right), \qquad (12.55)$$

where μ_i and μ_j are the current-value co-state variables associated with the two state equations. The solution is a set of linear differential equations that satisfy the following conditions: (i) $\partial H_i/\partial I_i = 0$, (ii) $\partial H_i/\partial p_i = 0$, (iii) $\dot{\mu}_i = \rho\mu_i - \partial H_i/\partial q_i$, (iv) $\dot{q}_i = \partial H_i/\partial \mu_i$ and (v) $\dot{\mu}_j = \rho\mu_j - \partial H_i/\partial q_j$. In addition, the solution has to satisfy the transversality condition $\lim_{t\to+\infty} e^{-\rho t}\mu_i(t)q_i(t) = 0$. The second-order conditions are satisfied if the Hamiltonian is concave in the control and state variables (Léonard and van Long 1992), which requires $H_{I_iI_i} = -\gamma < 0$, $H_{p_ip_i} = -1/\tau < 0$, $H_{q_iq_i} = -\theta < 0$ and $H_{p_ip_i}H_{q_iq_i} - \left(H_{q_ip_i}\right)^2 = \left(4\tau\theta - \beta^2\right)/4\tau^2 > 0$. Thus, the solution

[19] To save notation, we henceforth drop the time indicator t.

exists if the cost parameters τ and/or θ are sufficiently large relative to the marginal willingness to pay for quality, β.

From conditions (i)–(v) we can derive

$$p_i = w + \tau + \frac{\beta(q_i - q_j)}{3}, \tag{12.56}$$

$$\dot{I}_i = (\delta + \rho) I_i + \frac{\theta}{\gamma} q_i - \frac{\beta(p_i - c)}{2\tau\gamma}, \tag{12.57}$$

which characterise the optimal prices set in each period and the optimal dynamic investment path. In the steady state, $\dot{q}_i = \dot{I}_i = 0$, $q_i = q_j = q^{OL}$ and $p_i = p_j = p^{OL}$. Using (12.56)–(12.57) and the dynamic constraint (12.14), the steady-state prices and qualities are given by (12.18)–(12.19) in Sect. 12.2.

Feedback Closed-Loop Solution

To solve for the feedback closed-loop solution, we restrict attention to stationary linear Markovian strategies, which we derive using the Hamilton-Jacobi-Bellman (HJB) equation. Since the instantaneous objective function and the linear dynamic constraint of Provider i constitute a linear-quadratic problem, we define the value function as

$$V^i(q_i, q_j) = \alpha_0 + \alpha_1 q_i + \alpha_2 q_j + (\alpha_3/2) q_i^2 + (\alpha_4/2) q_j^2 + \alpha_5 q_i q_j. \tag{12.58}$$

If we define the investment strategies as functions $I_i = \phi_i(q_i, q_j)$ and $I_j = \phi_j(q_i, q_j)$, the above-defined value must satisfy the HJB equation, given by

$$\rho V^i(q_i, q_j) = \max \left\{ \begin{array}{l} (p_i - c)\left(\frac{1}{2} + \frac{\beta(q_i - q_j)}{2\tau} - \frac{p_i - p_j}{2\tau}\right) - \frac{\gamma}{2} I_i^2 - \frac{\theta}{2} {q_i}^2 \\ + V^i_{q_i}(q_i, q_j)(I_i - \delta q_i) + V^i_{q_j}(q_i, q_j)\left(I_j - \delta q_j\right) \end{array} \right\}. \tag{12.59}$$

Maximisation of the right-hand side of (12.59) with respect to I_i yields $V^i_{q_i} = \gamma I_i$, which after substitution yields

$$I_i = \phi_i(q_i, q_j) = \frac{\alpha_1 + \alpha_3 q_i + \alpha_5 q_j}{\gamma}, \quad i, j = 1, 2; \quad i \neq j. \tag{12.60}$$

Maximisation of the right-hand side of (12.59) with respect to p_i yields

$$\frac{1}{2} + \frac{\beta(q_i - q_j)}{2\tau} - \frac{p_i - p_j}{2\tau} - (p_i - w)\frac{1}{2\tau} = 0, \quad i, j = 1, 2; \quad i \neq j. \tag{12.61}$$

Solving the two-equation system defined by (12.61) yields

$$p_i = w + \tau + \frac{\beta(q_i - q_j)}{3}, \quad i, j = 1, 2; \quad i \neq j. \tag{12.62}$$

By substituting $I_i = \phi_i(q_i, q_j)$, $I_j = \phi_j(q_i, q_j)$, $V^i_{q_i}(q_i, q_j) = \alpha_1 + \alpha_3 q_i + \alpha_5 q_j$, $V^i_{q_j} = \alpha_2 + \alpha_4 q_j + \alpha_5 q_i$ and V^i, as defined by (12.58), into the HJB equation, we obtain

$$\begin{aligned}
&\left(\rho\alpha_0 - \frac{1}{2}\tau - \frac{1}{2\gamma}\alpha_1^2 - \frac{1}{\gamma}\alpha_1\alpha_2\right) \\
&\quad + q_i\left(\alpha_1(\delta + \rho) - \frac{1}{3}\beta - \frac{1}{\gamma}\alpha_1\alpha_3 - \frac{1}{\gamma}\alpha_2\alpha_5 - \frac{1}{\gamma}\alpha_1\alpha_5\right) \\
&\quad + q_j\left(\alpha_2(\delta + \rho) + \frac{1}{3}\beta - \frac{1}{\gamma}\alpha_2\alpha_3 - \frac{1}{\gamma}\alpha_1\alpha_4 - \frac{1}{\gamma}\alpha_1\alpha_5\right) \\
&\quad + q_i^2\left(\alpha_3\left(\delta + \frac{1}{2}\rho\right) - \frac{1}{2\gamma}\alpha_3^2 - \frac{1}{\gamma}\alpha_5^2 + \frac{1}{2}\theta - \frac{1}{18}\frac{\beta^2}{\tau}\right) \\
&\quad + q_j^2\left(\alpha_4\left(\delta + \frac{1}{2}\rho\right) - \frac{1}{\gamma}\alpha_3\alpha_4 - \frac{1}{2\gamma}\alpha_5^2 - \frac{1}{18}\frac{\beta^2}{\tau}\right)
\end{aligned}$$

$$+ q_i q_j \left((2\delta + \rho)\,\alpha_5 + \frac{1}{9}\frac{\beta^2}{\tau} - \frac{2}{\gamma}\alpha_3\alpha_5 - \frac{1}{\gamma}\alpha_4\alpha_5 \right)$$
$$= 0 \tag{12.63}$$

There are six possible solutions. By imposing the (sufficient but not necessary) condition

$$\frac{9}{4}\tau \left(\left(\delta + \frac{1}{2}\rho \right)^2 \gamma + \theta \right) \geq \beta^2, \tag{12.64}$$

it can be shown that only one of these solutions satisfy the criteria for equilibrium existence.[20] In this unique solution, the coefficients of the equilibrium dynamic investment strategy, (12.21), are given by

$$\alpha_1 = \frac{\beta\gamma}{3\,(\gamma\,(\delta + \rho) - \alpha_3)} > 0, \tag{12.65}$$

$$\alpha_3 = \left(\delta + \frac{1}{2}\rho \right)\gamma - \left(\frac{36\tau \left(\left(\delta + \frac{1}{2}\rho\right)^2 \gamma + \theta \right) - 5\beta^2}{4\beta^2} - \frac{81\tau\psi}{16\beta^2\gamma} \right)\sqrt{\psi} < 0, \tag{12.66}$$

$$\alpha_5 = -\frac{1}{2}\sqrt{\psi} < 0, \tag{12.67}$$

where

$$\psi := \frac{4\gamma}{27}\left(6\left(\left(\delta + \frac{1}{2}\rho \right)^2 \gamma + \theta \right) - \frac{\beta^2}{\tau} - 2\sqrt{3\varphi} \right) > 0 \tag{12.68}$$

[20]Notice that the condition is satisfied if τ and/or θ are sufficiently large relative to β and is therefore qualitatively similar to the equilibrium existence condition for the open-loop solution.

and

$$\varphi := \left(3\left(\left(\delta + \frac{1}{2}\rho\right)^2 \gamma + \theta\right) - \frac{\beta^2}{\tau}\right)\left(\left(\delta + \frac{1}{2}\rho\right)^2 \gamma + \theta\right) > 0. \tag{12.69}$$

The steady-state solution, (12.22)–(12.23), is then derived by setting $q_i = q_j = I_i/\delta$, which implies $\dot{I}_i = 0$.

Appendix 3

In this appendix we provide the underlying details of the comparative statics results in the n-firm Salop model presented in Sect. 12.3.

From (12.27)–(12.28), which implicitly define the symmetric Nash equilibrium, we derive

$$\frac{\partial G_p}{\partial p^*} = -\frac{u'\left(y\left(p^*\right)\right)}{\tau} + \left(p^* - \frac{\partial c\left(\frac{1}{n}, q^*\right)}{\partial D_i}\right)\frac{u''\left(y\left(p^*\right)\right)}{\tau} < 0, \tag{12.70}$$

$$\begin{aligned}\frac{\partial G_q}{\partial q^*} &= -v''\left(\pi\left(p^*, q^*\right)\right)\frac{\partial^2 c\left(\frac{1}{n}, q^*\right)}{\partial q_i^2} \\ &\quad - v'\left(\pi\left(p^*, q^*\right)\right)\left[\frac{\partial^2 c\left(\frac{1}{n}, q^*\right)}{\partial D_i \partial q_i}\frac{\beta}{\tau} + \frac{\partial^2 c\left(\frac{1}{n}, q^*\right)}{\partial q_i^2}\right] + b''\left(q^*\right) < 0,\end{aligned} \tag{12.71}$$

$$\frac{\partial G_p}{\partial q^*} = \frac{\partial^2 c\left(\frac{1}{n}, q^*\right)}{\partial D_i \partial q_i}\frac{u'\left(y\left(p^*\right)\right)}{\tau} > (<)\, 0 \text{ if } \frac{\partial^2 c\left(\frac{1}{2}, q^*\right)}{\partial D_i \partial q_i} > (<)\, 0, \tag{12.72}$$

$$\frac{\partial G_q}{\partial p^*} = v''\left(\pi\left(p^*, q^*\right)\right)\frac{1}{n}\left[\left(p^* - \frac{\partial c\left(\frac{1}{n}, q^*\right)}{\partial D_i}\right)\frac{\beta}{\tau} - \frac{\partial c\left(\frac{1}{n}, q^*\right)}{\partial q_i}\right]$$
$$+ v'\left(\pi\left(p^*, q^*\right)\right)\frac{\beta}{\tau} > 0, \tag{12.73}$$

$$\frac{\partial G_p}{\partial n} = -\frac{1}{n^2}\left(1 + \frac{\partial^2 c\left(\frac{1}{n}, q^*\right)}{\partial D_i^2}\frac{u'\left(y\left(p^*\right)\right)}{\tau}\right) < 0, \tag{12.74}$$

$$\frac{\partial G_q}{\partial n} = \frac{v'\left(\pi\left(p^*, q^*\right)\right)}{n^2}\left[\frac{\partial^2 c\left(\frac{1}{n}, q^*\right)}{\partial D_i^2}\frac{\beta}{\tau} + \frac{\partial^2 c\left(\frac{1}{n}, q^*\right)}{\partial D_i \partial q_i}\right] \lesseqgtr 0. \tag{12.75}$$

Existence and stability of the Nash equilibrium require that $\partial G_p/\partial p^* < 0, \partial G_q/\partial q^* < 0$ and $\left(\partial G_p/\partial p^*\right)\left(\partial G_q/\partial q^*\right) - \left(\partial G_q/\partial p^*\right)\left(\partial G_p/\partial q^*\right) > 0$. In qualitative terms, these conditions are similar to the equivalent conditions in the duopoly version of the model.

Applying Cramer's Rule, the effects of a marginal increase in n on equilibrium prices and qualities are given by, respectively,

$$\frac{\partial p^*}{\partial n} = \frac{\frac{\partial G_q}{\partial n}\frac{\partial G_p}{\partial q^*} - \frac{\partial G_p}{\partial n}\frac{\partial G_q}{\partial q^*}}{\frac{\partial G_p}{\partial p^*}\frac{\partial G_q}{\partial q^*} - \frac{\partial G_q}{\partial p^*}\frac{\partial G_p}{\partial q^*}} \tag{12.76}$$

and

$$\frac{\partial q^*}{\partial n} = \frac{\frac{\partial G_q}{\partial p^*}\frac{\partial G_p}{\partial n} - \frac{\partial G_p}{\partial p^*}\frac{\partial G_q}{\partial n}}{\frac{\partial G_p}{\partial p^*}\frac{\partial G_q}{\partial q^*} - \frac{\partial G_q}{\partial p^*}\frac{\partial G_p}{\partial q^*}}. \tag{12.77}$$

References

Banker, R. D., Khosla, I., & Sinha, K. K. (1998). Quality and competition. *Management Science, 44*, 1179–1192.

Brekke, K. R., Siciliani, L., & Straume, O. R. (2010). Price and quality in spatial competition. *Regional Science and Urban Economics, 40*, 471–480.

Brekke, K. R., Siciliani, L., & Straume, O. R. (2011). Hospital competition and quality with regulated prices. *Scandinavian Journal of Economics, 113*, 444–469.

Brekke, K. R., Siciliani, L., & Straume, O. R. (2012). Quality competition with profit constraints. *Journal of Economic Behaviour & Organization, 84*, 642–659.

Brekke, K. R., Siciliani, L., & Straume, O. R. (2017). Horizontal mergers and product quality. *Canadian Journal of Economics, 50*, 1063–1103.

Brekke, K. R., Siciliani, L., & Straume, O. R. (2018). Can competition reduce quality? *Journal of Institutional and Theoretical Economics, 174*, 421–447.

Cellini, R., Siciliani, L., & Straume, O. R. (2018). A dynamic model of quality competition with endogenous prices. *Journal of Economic Dynamics & Control, 94*, 190–206.

Chalkley, M., & Malcomson, J. M. (1998). Contracting for health services when patient demand does not reflect quality. *Journal of Health Economics, 17*, 1–19.

Choné, P., & Ma, C. A. (2011). Optimal health care contracts under physician agency. *Annales d'Economie et de Statistique, 101/102*, 229–256.

Chumacero, R. A., Gomez, D., & Paredes, R. (2011). I would walk 500 miles (if it paid): Vouchers and school choice in Chile. *Economics Educaction Review, 30*, 1103–1114.

Economides, N. (1993). Quality variations in the circular model of variety-differentiated products. *Regional Science and Urban Economics, 23*, 235–257.

Eggleston, K. (2005). Multitasking and mixed systems for provider payment. *Journal of Health Economics, 24*, 211–223.

Ellis, R. P., & McGuire, T. (1986). Provider behavior under prospective reimbursement: Cost sharing and supply. *Journal of Health Economics, 5*, 129–151.

Escarce, J. J., Jain, A. K., & Rogowski, J. (2006). Hospital competition, managed care, and mortality after hospitalization for medical conditions: Evidence from three states. *Medical Care Research and Review, 63*, 112S–140S.

Forder, J., & Allan, S. (2014). The impact of competition on quality and prices in the English care homes market. *Journal of Health Economics, 34*, 73–83.

Gibbons, S., Machin, S., & Silva, O. (2008). Choice, competition, and pupil achievement. *Journal of the European Economic Association, 6*, 912–947.

Gowrisankaran, G., & Town, R. (2003). Competition, payers, and hospital quality. *Health Services Research, 38*, 1403–1422.

Grabowski, D. C. (2004). A longitudinal study of Medicaid payment, private-pay price and nursing home quality. *International Journal Health Care Finance and Economics, 4*, 5–26.

Grabowski, D. C., Feng, Z., Hirth, R., Rahman, M., & Mor, V. (2013). Effect of nursing home ownership on the quality of post-acute care: An instrumental variablesapproach. *Journal of Health Economics, 32*, 12–21.

Gravelle, H. (1999). Capitation contracts: access and quality. *Journal of Health Economics, 18*, 315–340.

Gutacker, N., Siciliani, L., Moscelli, G., & Gravelle, H. (2016). Choice of hospital: Which type of quality matters? *Journal of Health Economics, 50*, 230–246.

Hastings, J., Kane, T., & Staiger, D. O. (2005). *Parental Preferences and School Competition: Evidence from a Public School Choice Program*, National Bureau of Economic Research working paper #11805, November.

Kaarboe, O., & Siciliani, L. (2011). Quality, multitasking and pay for performance. *Health Economics, 2*, 225–238.

Kessler, D., & McClellan, M. (2000). Is hospital competition socially wasteful? *Quarterly Journal of Economics, 115*, 577–615.

Léonard, D., & van Long, N. (1992). *Optimal Control Theory and Static Optimization in Economics*. Cambridge: Cambridge University Press.

Ma, C. A., & Burgess, J. F. (1993). Quality competition, welfare and regulation. *Journal of Economics, 58*, 153–173.

Mukamel, D., Zwanziger, J. A., & Bamezai, A. (2002). Hospital competition, resource allocation and quality of care. *BMC Health Services Research, 2*, 10–18.

Rahman, M., & Foster, A. D. (2015). Racial segregation and quality of care disparity in US nursing homes. *Journal of Health Economics, 39*, 1–16.

Shugarman, L. R., & Brown, J. A. (2006). *Nursing Home Selection: How Do Consumers Choose? Volume I: Findings from Focus Groups of Consumers and Information Intermediaries*. Washington, DC. Prepared for Office of Disability, Aging and Long-Term Care Policy, Office of the Assistant Secretary for Planning and Evaluation, U.S. Department of Health and Human Services, Contract #HHS-100-03-0023.

Sutton, J. (1996). Technology and market structure. *European Economic Review, 40*, 511–530.

Symeonidis, G. (2000). Price and nonprice competition with endogenous market structure. *Journal of Economics & Management Strategy, 9*, 53–83.

Tay, A. (2003). Assessing competition in hospital care markets: The importance of accounting for quality differentiation. *RAND Journal of Economics, 34*, 786–814.

Zhao, X. (2016). Competition, information, and quality: Evidence from nursing homes. *Journal of Health Economics, 49*, 136–152.

Zwanziger, J., Mukamel, D.B., & Indridason, I. (2002). Use of resident-origin data to define nursing home market boundaries. *Inquiry, 39*, 56–66.

Index (Spatial Economics I: Theory)

Note: Page numbers followed by 'n' refer to notes.

S. Colombo (ed.), *Spatial Economics Volume I*,
https://doi.org/10.1007/978-3-030-40098-9

D

E

The manufacturer's authorised representative in the EU is Springer Nature Customer Service Centre GmbH, Europaplatz 3, 69115 Heidelberg, Germany. If you have any concerns regarding our products, please contact ProductSafety@springernature.com

Printed and bound by CPI Group (UK) Ltd, Croydon, CR0 4YY
30/09/2026
02225645-0011

Made in the USA
Monee, IL
04 November 2026

67381908R00125